Comparative Politics

The problem of establishing equivalence in order to compare the same concepts or phenomena in different settings is common for researchers in comparative politics. Despite the importance of the task there are few strategies to deal effectively with it.

Comparative Politics tackles the issues involved and explores strategies to deal with many of the problems of establishing equivalence. Each contribution focuses on a theoretically relevant theme, such as tolerance, political values, religious orientations, gender roles, voluntary associations, party organisations, party positions, democratic regimes, and the mass media. The chapters cover different topics, methods, data and countries, making use of previously unpublished empirical research to illustrate the difficulties in finding similar or identical indicators in realistic research settings.

This useful study reveals the potential for pragmatic solutions to the problems of establishing equivalence. Many of the strategies used show how the complicated search for equivalence can unearth substantial additional information which can enhance the quality and reliability of any research.

Jan W. van Deth is Professor of Political Science and International Comparative Social Research at the University of Mannheim, and Head of Research Department II of the Mannheim Centre for European Social Research.

Routledge Advances in International Relations and Politics

Comparative Politics

The problem of equivalence

Edited by Jan W. van Deth

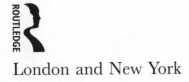

London and New York

First published 1998
by Routledge
11 New Fetter Lane, London EC4P 4EE

Simultaneously published in the USA and Canada
by Routledge
29 West 35th Street, New York, NY 10001

Typeset in Baskerville by J&L Composition Ltd, Filey, North Yorkshire
Printed and bound in Great Britain by
T.J. International Ltd, Padstow, Cornwall

British Library Cataloguing in Publication Data
A catalogue record for this book is available from the British Library

Library of Congress Cataloguing in Publication Data
Comparative politics: the problem of equivalence/edited by Jan W. van Deth.
  Includes bibliographical references and indexes.
  1. Comparative government.   I. Deth, Jan W. van.
  JF128.C66   1998
  320.3′01 – dc21   98–39197

ISBN 0–415–19245–5

Contents

Figures

Tables

Contributors

Michael Braun is Senior Project Director and was formerly Director of the German General Social Survey (ALLBUS) at the Centre for Survey Research and Methodology (ZUMA) in Mannheim. He received his doctorate from the University of Munich in 1985. He is mainly interested in rational choice theory and research methodology, and has worked especially on international comparative research in the fields of inequality, work orientations, and the family.

Martin Feldkircher is Researcher at the Mannheim Centre for European Social Research in a comparative project on the change of intermediary organisations and value orientations in political subcultures. He has published articles in *Blickpunkt Gesellschaft 3* (Westdeutscher Verlag 1994) and *Soziale Ungleichheit* (Leske + Budrich 1997). His main research focus is on social change, especially on value orientations and their change.

Ronald Inglehart is a Professor of Political Science and a Program Director in the Institute for Social Research at the University of Michigan. He helped found the Eurobarometer surveys, and is coordinator of the World Values Surveys. He is author of more than a hundred publications, including *Modernization and Postmodernization: Cultural, Economic, and Political Change in 43 Societies* (Princeton 1997).

André Kaiser is Assistant Professor at the Faculty of Social Sciences of the University of Mannheim. He is author of *Staatshandeln ohne Staatsverständnis, Die Entwicklung des Politikfeldes Arbeitsbeziehungen in Grossbritannien 1965–1990* (Brockmeyer 1995), and editor of *Regieren in Westminster-Demokratien* (Nomos, forthcoming). He has published widely on several aspects of British politics. His current research interest is institutional adaptation and reform in established democracies.

Frauke Kreuter was Researcher at the Mannheim Centre for European Social Research in a project on social participation and is now at the Faculty of Political and Administrative Science of the University of Konstanz.

Thomas Poguntke is Research Fellow at the Mannheim Centre for European Social Research of the University of Mannheim. He is author of *Alternative Politics: The German Green Party* (Edinburgh University Press 1993) and co-editor of *New Politics* (Dartmouth 1995) and 'The Politics of Anti-Party Sentiment' (special issue of the *European Journal of Political Research* 1996) and has published articles in *Political Studies, West European Politics, European Journal of Political Research, Zeitschrift für Parlamentsfragen, Environmental Politics* and *German Politics*. He has been part of the twelve-nation research group on organisational change and adaptation of political parties. His main research interests are 'new politics', party system change, and political parties.

Rüdiger Schmitt-Beck is an Assistant Professor at the Faculty of Social Sciences of the University of Mannheim. His main research interests are political communication, electoral behaviour, political value change, social movements, and political participation. He is author of *Die Friedensbewegung in der Bundesre-publik Deutschland* (Westdeutscher Verlag 1990), and has published articles in edited volumes and in national as well as international journals such as *European Journal of Political Research, German Politics, International Journal of Public Opinion Research*, and *European Journal of Communication*.

Gábor Tóka is an Assistant Professor at the Political Science Department of the Central European University, Budapest, Hungary. He is editor of *The 1990 Hungarian Elections to the National Assembly* (Sigma 1995), and has published articles in the *European Sociological Review*, the Czech *Sociologicky casopis* and *Politologická revue*, the Polish *Sisyphus*, and the Hungarian *Politikatudományi Szemle*. His works on electoral behaviour, political parties, and democratic consolidation appear mostly in edited volumes such as *Consolidating the Third Wave Democracies: Themes and Perspectives* (Johns Hopkins University Press 1997), *Stabilising Fragile Democracies* (Routledge 1996), and *Citizens and the State* (Oxford University Press 1995).

Jan W. van Deth is Professor of Political Science and International Comparative Social Research at the University of Mannheim, and Head of Research Department II of the Mannheim Centre for European Social Research. He is author of a number of articles and books, and recently editor of *Private Groups and Public Life* (Routledge 1997) and *The Impact of Values* (with Elinor Scarbrough, Oxford University Press 1995). His main research areas are political culture, social change, and comparative research methods. He is a Corresponding Member of the Royal Netherlands Academy of Arts and Sciences, and Book Series Editor of the *European Political Science Series* of the European Consortium for Political Research.

Bettina Westle is Associate Professor at the Faculty of Sociology at the University of Bielefeld. She is author of *Kollektive Identität der Deutschen* (Leske + Budrich 1998), and has published articles on political support and on attitude research. Her main research areas are political sociology and political culture.

Preface

For some problems the prospect of finding adequate solutions looks so onerous that neglect, avoidance, and underestimation appear to be the most reasonable strategies. The question of identity and equivalence in comparative politics belongs to this category. By implication, the nature of the problem precludes the finding of a solution, and even intelligent attempts are doomed to bog down into plausible interpretations only.

Confronted with this situation, researchers working in distinct areas of empirical comparative politics arranged a number of meetings at the Mannheim Centre for European Social Research (MZES) in 1996 and 1997. During these gatherings each participant presented specific problems he or she encountered in their own investigations. None of the investigations had been designed to deal explicitly with the problem of identity and equivalence; that is, in each study the problem is approached within the context of existing research and with the aim to find pragmatic solutions to it. Moreover, each participant was fully aware of the provisional and disputable character of such approaches.

This collection of essays is the result of the activities of many people. First, Katja Ahlstich, Michael Braun, Gunther Braun, Martin Feldkircher, Ronald Inglehart, André Kaiser, Frauke Kreuter, Karin Lasthuizen, Thomas Poguntke, Hermann Schmitt, Rüdiger Schmitt-Beck, Gábor Tóka, and Bettina Westle attended one or more of our meetings and contributed to the lively discussions. Second, Birgit Blum again showed her competence and patience by taking care of all organisational aspects of the project. She managed the delicate process of turning a pile of papers of self-assured researchers into a single manuscript, and she produced many revised versions of each contribution in a very short period of time without losing the general outlook (or her sense of humour and relativity). Third, James Antonich did much more than simply fix language errors. He corrected the whole manuscript thoroughly, rewrote many sentences, and offered a number of helpful suggestions for improving the presentation of the arguments. Fourth, Daniela Mix worked many days patiently and conscientiously preparing and checking the references. And finally, Colleen Sheedy and Sandra Roos helped in various phases of the project.

The publication of this collection of essays on the identity and equivalence problem in comparative politics is based on the presumption that trial and error is more important for the development of our discipline than neglect, avoidance, and underestimation. I am grateful to everyone who participated in this risky undertaking by sharing their doubts and hopes with me in an amiable and uncomplicated way.

Jan W. van Deth
Mannheim, January 1998

1   Equivalence in comparative political research

Jan W. van Deth[1]

A tricky problem

Tapping your finger against your temple can have remarkable effects. If you live in the Netherlands, people understand it as an indication of cleverness and insight. In Spain or France, however, it signals stupidity or craziness. Vice versa, the Dutch sign for suggesting stupidity or craziness is tapping your finger against your forehead, while Spaniards and French people understand this sign as a sign of intelligence. Although West European cultures have much in common, these identical gestures have opposite meanings in various countries. For people aware of these customs, avoiding embarrassing situations is simple: use *different* gestures if you want to signal the *same* meaning in dissimilar settings.

Examples of this problem can be found in many areas of comparative research. In their seminal work on sexual behaviour in the 1940s, Kinsey and his collaborators had to use different words for the same concepts among different groups. Even the order of the topics in their questionnaire could not be identical since some terms appeared embarrassing to some groups and other terms to other groups (Kinsey *et al.* 1948: 48–9). Anthropological research on family ties along the lines of Piaget's work in the 1920s has been confronted with severe problems because in many cultures the nuclear family in the Western sense does not exist. Even symmetrical relationships among brothers and sisters are not self-evident in cultures using different terms for older and younger brothers and sisters (LeVine and Price-Williams 1974: 27).

The field of comparative politics offers examples of the problem, too. For instance, the issue of corruption in the analyses of civil systems can be highly problematic. 'One observer's corruption is often another person's conception of acceptable behaviour, or perhaps even of proper and obligatory behaviour' (Peters 1996: 24). Moreover, these differences do not arise only in extreme cases of Third World countries. Another example is that patterns of majority-building in different political systems can be distinguished on the basis of their general policy content, which are in turn driven by different supply and demand functions. But these functions vary considerably between countries. In Israel, demand of religious parties is a strong factor, but in Scandinavian countries, the limited institutional supply of office benefits performs the same role (Strom 1990: 99). Only careful observation of strategically chosen political systems like Israel, Denmark, Norway, Ireland, and Italy enables us to use these different phenomena in the context of a common framework.

Research on political orientations and behaviour confronts similar problems. The term 'Bürgerinitiative' is closely related to, but certainly not identical with, the Dutch phrase 'inspraak', and comparisons of levels of participation should take these differences into account (van Deth 1986). Similarly, the measurement of concerns for pollution and ecological issues should not be based on the same set of items or topics in different countries since national restrictions and subsidies vary regarding car catalysts, wrapping, drainage water, and garbage discharge (Nas 1995). A crucial problem of comparative research, then, is the establishment of cross-culturally or cross-nationally valid and reliable instruments. If, on the one hand, we use culture- or nation-specific indicators for our concepts, we have problems tracing cross-cultural or cross-national differences. If, on the other hand, we construct identical instruments for various settings, we are unlikely to obtain an appropriate measure of national or cultural phenomena. How, then, are we to sail between the Scylla of losing national or cultural validity and the Charybdis of endangering cross-cultural or cross-national comparability?[2]

The problem of finding different indicators to compare the same concepts or phenomena is obvious to every novice in the field of comparative research, and many textbooks or overviews underline the importance of using equivalent instead of identical indicators.[3] Yet despite the striking consensus about the importance of the problem, the number of proposals to deal with it are rather limited, and attempts to handle equivalent indicators in comparative research are the exception, not the rule. This situation is due first of all to the complicated logical and empirical aspects of the identity-equivalence problem: that is, 'establishing credible equivalence is difficult, as "meaning" is contextual' (Teune 1990: 54). Indeed, the 'problems are severe and it is easier to explicate them than to suggests ways of dealing with them' (Verba 1969: 64).

Second, there are many situations where standardised, identical instruments do not present specific problems. In their seminal work on interview techniques, Maccoby and Maccoby (1954) remarked that for most research the problem is 'much less acute' than in the Kinsey case.[4] Moreover, they argued, one should consider whether 'the gains made by trying to get equivalence of one aspect [are] large enough to offset the non-equivalences of other aspects which almost inevitably accompany such an attempt' (Maccoby and Maccoby 1954: 453). A third reason for the scarcity of practical solutions to identity-equivalence problems in comparative political research is the fact that analysing relationships 'is assumed to be more important than the quality and reliability of the variables themselves' (Mair 1996: 327).[5] Finally, it can be argued that in identity-equivalence problems the traditional border between quantitative and qualitative approaches in comparative research must be crossed (Nießen 1982; Hartmann 1995). Apparently this challenge is still not very attractive for many researchers.

All of these factors – logical and empirical complexity, bounded necessity, focus on relationships instead of indicators, and the crossing of traditional borders –

have resulted in underestimating the tricky problem of comparing similar phenomena in different settings. The third point especially – the rather artificial
contrast between relationships and indicators – suggests a basic misunderstanding
of the nature of making valid comparisons. Contrary to the often practised
distinction between studying relationships instead of the quality of variables,
many approaches to the problem of identity and equivalence in comparative
research are based on an indissoluble connection between the meaning of specific
terms and concepts, on the one hand, and their relationships with other terms and
concepts, on the other. In the course of this introduction, this axiom will bring us
to a specific variant of similarity, the so-called *functional equivalence* of terms and
concepts.

The next two sections present a brief overview of several aspects of the ideas of
identity and equivalence. The remaining section of the introduction, as well as the
other contributions to this volume, address the practical complications of studying
similar phenomena in different settings and offer options for empirical researchers
of identity-equivalence problems in comparative politics. This implies that *a
posteriori* approaches in the context of secondary analyses are emphasised, and
that neither epistemological complications of 'travelling' theories and concepts,
nor practical problems of 'harmonising' existing data are our main concern. This
pragmatic orientation towards the equivalence issue is directly in line with Luhmann's statement that 'although the method of functional equivalence can be
abstractly developed as an analytical technique, it is not aimed to be applied in
emptiness' (1970: 38).

Identity and equivalence

The basic design of comparative research is simple and straightforward. In order
to reach insights not attainable in single-case studies, one examines either the
same phenomena in different contexts or different phenomena in similar contexts
(cf. Przeworski and Teune 1970: 31–46). For many purposes, a comparative
approach is preferred to single-observation studies and reasoning by analogy
(cf. King *et al.* 1994: 211–12),[6] although case studies clearly have their own merits
and advantages (cf. Feagin *et al.* 1991), and ingenious strategies have been offered
for a middle-of-the-road position (cf. Ragin 1987 and 1989; De Meur and Berg-
Schlosser 1994; Amenta and Poulsen 1994; Collier 1991). Be that as it may,
complex problems arise in comparative designs once we examine terms like the
'same phenomena' or 'different contexts'.

Problems in this field become clear when we start with the notion of identical
indicators. Two things are considered to be identical when they agree or are
exactly the same in every detail, or are similar in appearance. The term 'identity',
however, refers to absolute sameness or equality of two values. Ever since the
development of traditional logic in the Middle Ages, the principle of identity
('A = A'; 'Whatever is, is') has been a cornerstone of reasoning. But beyond the
scope of formal logic, the problematic nature of the principle immediately leads to

complicated questions and paradoxes, fascinating philosophers from Kant, Hume, Locke, and Leibniz, to Frege, Tarski, Wittgenstein, and many others.

The trivial version of the idea of identity states that two things are identical when they share all their qualities; that is, when all of their properties are the same. In other words, two objects are identical if for every class, one object belongs to the class if, and only if, the other does. This statement becomes a tautology, however, when the property of 'being identical with an object' is allowed to be a property of that very same object.[7] Leibniz used this line of reasoning to formulate an important conclusion based on a non-trivial version of the so-called principle of identity of indiscernibles (*principium identitatis indiscernibilium*). If two objects differ in quality, reasoned Leibniz, they must be two. That is, two distinct objects will differ in some intrinsic, non-relational property.

From these discussions, it is clear that identity is a complicated concept. As Hume indicated, 'the controversy concerning identity is not merely a dispute of words' (1969 [1739]: 303). Leibniz's conclusion of the inevitability of different intrinsic, non-relational properties of two objects has important implications. However, apart from this conclusion, the dispute does not help us much with the practical problems of comparative political research. The paradoxical nature of the identity problem has been formulated by Wittgenstein succinctly and conclusively: 'Roughly speaking, to say of *two* things that they are identical is nonsense, and to say of *one* thing that it is identical with itself is to say nothing at all' (1963 [1921]: 83; emphasis original).

Comparative research, then, must start from the axiom that even similar phenomena are never identical. The question is whether we can restrict the differences between the phenomena to intrinsic, non-relational properties irrelevant to the goal of our research. For instance, the fact that Italian and German Christian-Democratic parties differ in membership and organisational structure is evident; but the difference does not have to bother us in comparative studies on coalition strategies. Another example concerns the field of currencies and exchange rates. In order to see whether national currencies exist at a 'correct' level, one can use the so-called 'Hamburger Standard' or 'Big Mac Currency'. It is based on the idea that a Big Mac hamburger is made according to the same recipe in some eighty countries. The purchasing-power parity of the product can be computed by comparing its price in local currency to its price in dollars in the United States. The result is an assessment of the under- or over-valuation of the local currency. This assessment is based on the fact that all disturbing or irrelevant factors are controlled for (ingredients, weight, production, sales conditions, etc.), while the relevant property (local value) varies across nations.[8] In other words, comparisons become meaningful only if one distinguishes between relevant and irrelevant properties.

The search for (ir)relevant properties of distinct phenomena suggests a move from the idea of identity towards that of equivalence.[9] The concept of equivalence appears in fields as divergent as logic, informatics, physics, psychology, mathematics, electronics, finance, and civil and criminal law. Although the term has specific meanings in each discipline, broadly speaking we refer to the *equivalence* of two phenomena if they have the same value, importance, use, function, or result. Although the etymological origin of the term points in the direction of similarities,[10] the important aspect is the restriction of similarity to one or more specifically defined properties. We are willing to accept conclusions about coalition behaviour of clearly different Christian-Democratic parties in different countries if the parties manage to hold a centre position in various coalitions for many decades. Likewise, we are willing to assess the different purchasing powers of currencies if we can be sure that the appearance and taste of hamburgers are 'identical' in various countries. It is the *similarity* of the relevant properties of *different* phenomena that lies at the centre of the idea of equivalence in comparative research.

Obviously, the question of which properties are relevant cannot be answered in general terms. A property is not simply 'relevant' or 'irrelevant', but always relevant or irrelevant *for* something else. The more general question of 'What is comparable' can be answered only by 'putting the question in its proper form, which is: Comparable *in which respect?*' (Sartori 1994: 18; emphasis original).[11] By specifying several properties, we will – as Leibniz predicted – eventually find an intrinsic, non-relational property that establishes the difference between two phenomena. But it follows that extrinsic, relational properties can be used to obtain similarity. For this reason, many comparativists prefer the idea of *functional equivalence* to equivalence.

The idea of functional equivalence is based on the relevance of relationships instead of intrinsic properties of concepts. Especially in system theories as proposed by Luhmann, relationships provide the core and backbone of the argument. In this perspective, any comparison of systems will be confronted by the question of identity and functional equivalence:

> Every comparison of a system presupposes a preceding theoretical analysis of the systems involved, which clarifies its relational problem and possible solutions. It is possible that the comparison yields several variants of solutions for one and the same relational problem. In this way the hypothesis of its functional equivalence is verified. The question why single systems opt for different variants is then converted into concrete historical research, which always presupposes the determination of equivalences in case it should not be limited to the detection of facts only.
>
> (Luhmann 1970: 25)

Although very critical of traditional (American) functionalism, Luhmann's analyses show the opportunities for using the idea of functional equivalence in comparative research. His suggestion to study the historical development of existing systems provides a clear route for dealing with identity-equivalence problems. In more general terms, with respect to the problems faced by a system, several alternative ways to deal with the problems are available. It is the actual use of functionally equivalent concepts in historically oriented research that will help us answer the question of why different systems opt for different solutions. These indicators do not have to belong to a common set of indicators but can be attuned to the specific circumstances in each system.[12] It is this 'belonging' to a specific part of a system which makes concepts equivalent in comparative research. This suggestion can be rephrased as a general plea to rely on interpretations (or hypotheses) and auxiliary information in the course of assessing the similarity of (different) indicators used in different settings.

Equivalence and inference

The first problem encountered in international comparative research is the translation of terms and concepts. Even seemingly straightforward translations of single words provide complications due to different cultural meanings of the words. For instance, the translation of the English words 'friend', 'neighbourhood', and 'fatherland' into the German words 'Freund', 'Nachbarschaft', and 'Vaterland' poses difficulties. For identifying semantic errors in translations, several back-translation procedures can be used,[13] aiming at *lexical equivalence* or *linguistic equivalence* (cf. Osgood 1967: 17–20; Deutscher 1968). Translation is a common problem of virtually every international comparative project. Referring to survey research, Verba long ago remarked that 'literal equivalence, even if achievable, does not mean that the questions are equivalent in different languages' (1969: 63).

Although translations in comparative research are vital, we will not discuss them here as a separate strategy to deal with equivalence problems. Instead, we will emphasise the problems of actual research confronted with the complexities of using existing data collections.[14] From this mainly pragmatic perspective on secondary research, we will stress the relevance of functional equivalence. Functional equivalence refers to the requirement that concepts should be related to other concepts in other settings in more or less the same way. It is based on the notion that comparability 'cannot be conceived as an attribute of elements but as an *attribute of the elements' relationships to a more general point of reference*' (Nießen 1982: 86; emphasis original). Stated in this way, functional equivalence has much in common with reasoning by analogy. An analogy is based on the recognition or suggestion of similarity between two objects or two sets of objects. However, while analogies are based on similar relationships between different objects (i.e. A : B therefore C : D), functional equivalence refers to similar relationships between similar objects in different settings (i.e. A[i] : B[i] therefore A[j] : B[j]).[15] It is this last type of similarity between the theoretical or operational contexts ([i] and [j]) which provides clues for answering the question about which properties are considered relevant in our comparisons.

When we replace the requirement of identity by the search for equivalent indicators, opportunities for comparative research are substantially expanded. Indicators do not have to be similar at the operational level as long as we succeed in constructing instruments indicating similar concepts at a higher level of abstraction. This line of reasoning suggests a direct way of dealing with the problem of equivalent indicators in different settings: increase the level of abstraction of the concepts until cultural- or country-specific differences become irrelevant and can be ignored. This strategy requires extensive auxiliary information about the settings being compared as well as a sophisticated way of developing and demarcating our concepts. Although the intelligent use of auxiliary information is a *conditio sine qua non* for every type of comparative research and although a high level of abstraction is always desirable from a theoretical point of view, the risks involved in increasing the level of abstraction are evident. First, we risk the fallacy so nicely presented by Sartori (1970 and 1994b) that concepts can be 'stretched' in such a way that they lose virtually all their analytical and heuristic power. If the term 'constitution' is stretched to 'any state form', we have no way of testing the proposition 'constitutions obstruct tyranny'. The second risk in increasing the level of abstraction is, of course, the neglect of 'real' differences and the establishment of 'pseudo equivalence' (Niedermayer 1997: 92). For instance, an explanation of political campaigns in Europe and the United States can be highly misleading if the term 'political party' is not differentiated between the two political systems. Finally, it is clear that increasing the level of abstraction could come down to nothing more than a move of the equivalence problems from one level to another. Not much is gained if we have to assess the equivalence of the concept 'identification' instead of that of the stimulus 'being a member of a party'.[16]

The use of auxiliary information also provides the key for establishing equivalence in procedures not aiming at increasing the level of abstraction. The seminal work of Przeworski and Teune (1966 and 1970) contains a precise depiction of the basic structure of comparative analyses as well as a clear definition of the equivalence concept based on the idea that inference should guide attempts to solve the problems. Przeworski and Teune start with the general notions of validity and reliability, and use the phrase 'equivalent measurement' for observations that satisfy these two conditions. A measurement is equivalent, that is, when the indicators show 'validity in terms of each social system and reliability across social systems' (Przeworski and Teune 1970: 107). Next, they deny the importance of the equivalence of stimuli and stress that their concept of equivalence:

> does not refer to observations but only to the results of inferences made from those observations, that is, the inferred measurement statements. An instrument is equivalent across systems to the extent that the *results* provided by the instrument reliably describe with (nearly) the same validity a particular phenomena in different social systems. *Stimulus equivalence is an important problem only if measurement does not involve inference.*
>
> (Przeworski and Teune 1970: 108; emphasis original)

This statement rightfully emphasises the need for equivalence at the level of the results obtained with our measurements instead of concentrating on stimuli or items used in the phase of data collection. The term 'results', however, is ambiguous in this context. Przeworski and Teune argue within a framework of classical test and measurement theory and rely heavily on the distinction between direct and indirect measurement. But 'inference' can also be observed when we use some directly measured indicator in a wider theoretical setting and study its relationships with other factors. Some type of inference is always required in discussions about equivalence, whether in the form of constructing an instrument with a set of items or in the form of relating different indicators to each other in various settings. The measure under consideration has to be integrated into some structure (pattern, model, network, theory), and equivalence is established by assessing the degree to which these similar measures have the same position or play the same role within these structures.

In empirical-analytical approaches in comparative political research, the idea of functional equivalence is operationalised as construct validity; that is, as the satisfactory performance of indicators within some theoretical and operational context to which they refer.[17] From this demarcation of functional equivalence, it is clear that relationships (structures) are at the centre of the problems in comparative research. In *The Civic Culture*, Almond and Verba suggest an approach to the problem of different meanings of concepts in different settings in terms of a search for underlying patterns in the way so convincingly systematised by Przeworski and Teune:

> Though the judicious choice of indicators helps eliminate some of the problems of nonequivalence in cross-national research, perhaps the most important way in which such problems must be handled is in the analysis of the data . . . By phrasing the comparison *between* nations in terms of the similarities and differences in the *patterns* of relations *among* variables *within* each country, one controls somewhat for the difference in meaning that these variables may have from one nation to another.
>
> (Almond and Verba 1963: 70; emphasis original)

Unfortunately, many researchers – including Almond and Verba – seem to take this recommendation as an encouragement to study causal structures in several countries (e.g. explanations of voting behaviour), instead of developing indicators that could have the same meaning in different settings (e.g. the level of electoral participation).[18] But the idea of stressing 'similarities and differences in the patterns of relations among variables within each country' can be used to develop equivalent indicators more explicitly. In that case, the 'patterns' refer to the linkages between observed (or manifest) variables and unobserved (or latent) variables. Obviously, by developing this strategy we return immediately to the position taken by Przeworski and Teune: that the ultimate test of instruments is not to be found in a meticulous search for identical measures, but in '*the similarity of the structure of indicators . . . Equivalence is a matter of inference, not of direct observations*' (1970: 117–18; emphasis original). Though this procedure can rely on simple correlation coefficients, more sophisticated approaches have become available through techniques like confirmatory factor analysis (cf. Parker 1983) or (full) structural equation models (cf. Saris and Münnich 1995; van de Vijver and Leung 1997: 99–106). In any case, equivalence is not to be considered an intrinsic property of some measure or indicator, but, as van de Vijver and Leung put it unambiguously: *'Equivalence should be established and cannot be assumed'* (1997: 144; emphasis original).

From this repeated emphasis on inference in assessing the degree of equivalence, three important conclusions can be drawn about research strategies in comparative politics. First, if we wish to establish equivalence as the functional equivalence of some concept by analysing relationships in terms of underlying patterns, we must use at least two indicators for each concept in each setting, since the minimum requirement for any relationship is the existence of two objects or phenomena. It is the relationships between items which will provide information about the equivalence of the indicators selected. Second, we do not have to restrict our analyses to inferences based on a common set of stimuli, items, or indicators. Inference can be based on different stimuli, items, or indicators in various settings, and equivalence once again becomes a question of relationships. Third, if inference is stressed, we must distinguish between internal and external ways to infer conclusions about relational aspects of our observations or indicators. Internal consistency means that the stimuli or items used should show more or less the same structure in different environments; external consistency means that indicators are related in the same way to an element not belonging to the initial set of indicators. The question of whether a concept like party identification is equivalent in various settings has, then, no meaning. Only if we introduce relationships between two or more items to measure party identification or linkages between party identification and another concept can we discuss the degree of equivalence. These relationships can be conceptualised among a common set of stimuli or indicators, but different measures can be used in different settings.

Broadly speaking, we can divide the strategies for establishing equivalence in comparative research into two types: attempts to increase the level of abstraction and approaches based on some type of inference. Moreover, among the second type, we can distinguish between attempts based on common or on non-common sets of stimuli, items or indicators. Finally, we discriminate between establishing equivalence by way of referring to either internal or to external consistency.[19] These five main strategies can be summarised as shown in Figure 1.1.

Although the idea of equivalence can be used for each of the five types of strategies indicated, strictly speaking the idea of functional equivalence should be reserved for strategies relying on some kind of inference; that is, for strategies 2 through 5. The question of whether auxiliary information is required is irrelevant for this distinction. The intelligent use of auxiliary information is a necessary condition for the application of each type of strategy in comparative research.

Strategies in empirical research

The search for identical indicators and concepts is so popular that detailed explications are not required here. For each of the five main strategies described above, we present a short discussion. It should be noted, however, that we can place several examples in a single category and that frequently the criteria of

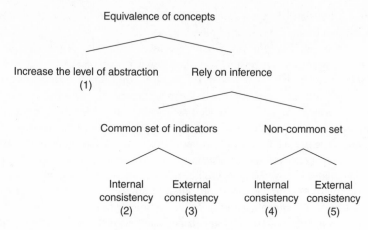

Figure 1.1 Main strategies for establishing equivalence

internal and external consistency are combined. The latter strategy is clearly evident in the revival of the so-called multitrait-multimethod approach.[20]

1 Increasing the level of abstraction

By increasing the level of abstraction of our concepts, we remove irrelevant or culture-specific properties from our analyses. In other words, we establish equivalence by ignoring specific properties, and we accept two indicators to be equivalent exactly because these properties are deleted.

Inglehart and Carballo (1997) illustrate this strategy in their global analysis of cross-cultural differences of coherent cultural patterns in several regions of the world. They use survey data collected in forty-three societies as divergent as Belarus, China, Argentina, and Denmark, and combine the individual-level data with economic, linguistic, religious, geographical, and political characteristics of the societies. The obvious question, of course, is whether the questionnaires applied have the same meaning to people in these widely different societies. The authors stress their co-operation with experts as well as extensive pilot testing of the instruments, and present a clear strategy to establish equivalence:

If we had asked questions about nation-specific issues, the cross-cultural comparability almost certainly would have broken down. In France, for example, a hot recent issue revolved around whether girls should be allowed to wear scarves over their heads in school (a reaction against Islamic funda-mentalism). This question would have had totally different meanings (or would have seemed meaningless) in many other societies. On the other hand, a question about whether religion is important in one's life is mean-ingful in virtually every society on earth, including those in which most people say it is not. The same is true of questions about respect for authority; or about how many children one would like to have; or whether or not one is satisfied with one's life as a whole.

(Inglehart and Carballo 1997: 40)

This strategy requires a high level of auxiliary information about the systems being compared in order to avoid the fallacies of 'conceptual stretching', 'pseudo equivalence', or simply shifting the problems. Whether Inglehart and Carballo succeed in avoiding these pitfalls remains to be seen. It is not self-evident that the equivalence of concepts like 'God' or 'authority' is less problematic than rules against overt religious practices like wearing a specific scarf. Furthermore, if 'God' can be interpreted by the respondents as anything ranging from Christ or Vishnu to the mysteries of the universe, the concept might have been stretched too far for analytical or heuristic purposes. Yet it is clear that the explicit neglect of specific characteristics certainly increases the opportunities for comparative research and that Inglehart and Carballo have presented an interesting example of dealing with similar instruments in widely divergent settings.

2 Using a common set of indicators: internal consistency

Instead of increasing the level of abstraction, alternative strategies can be based on the idea that inference is crucial in establishing functional equivalence. If we use a common set of indicators, the usual question is how to assess the equivalence of some given indicator. The strategy of using a common set of indicators and the criterion of internal consistency is meant to resolve this problem by analysing the structure among similar stimuli or items in various settings. Sophisticated methodological applications of this type of strategy have been proposed by Mokken (1971: 224–53), Saris and Münnich (1995), Saris (1997), and others.

A traditional example of this strategy is Rokkan's emphasis on so-called 'second-order comparisons' and its application in Almond and Verba's (1963) work on political culture in five countries. In that work, nations can be compared by emphasising patterns between indicators within different countries. Even if the cross-national validity of the indicators is questionable, the results obtained from the analyses of the relationships between the indicators provide the basis for accepting the equivalence of the phenomena (cf. Verba 1969). An identical position is taken by Inglehart in his analyses of the rise of postmaterialist value orientations in eleven countries in the early 1970s. He explicitly avoids discussions about different levels of postmaterialism between the countries and focuses on comparisons within given samples (Inglehart 1977: 37–8). Methodologically more sophisticated examples are the use of a multitrait-multimethod approach in the field of cross-national research on stereotype effects of the characterisations of nations (Hunyady and Münnich 1995) or the cross-national measurement of life satisfaction (Saris and Scherpenzeel 1995). Saris (1997) interviewed the same people twice in France, Belgium, and Spain with different techniques (that is, via personal and telephone interviews) and was able to show considerable cross-national differences in 'response probabilities' for a number of survey questions.

Van de Vijver and Leung (1997: 55) point to monotrait-multimethod approaches involving the use of multiple diverse measures to capture the same construct (so called 'triangulation').

These examples, however, already imply a shift from internal consistency towards strategies based on external consistency.

3 Using a common set of indicators: external consistency

As the examples of Almond and Verba, Inglehart, and others indicate, functional equivalence can be established by referring to relationships between the concept considered and one or more other concepts. In this strategy, a similar structure in different settings is accepted as evidence of the equivalence of the concepts.

This line of reasoning exists in several areas of comparative research. Gabriel (1998: 46–8) evaluated differences in the degree of national pride of West European countries by looking at the correlations with other indicators of attachment to the political system.[21] In order to deal with both longitudinal and cross-sectional comparisons, Clausen (1967) introduced the method of 'differential correlations' for establishing the equivalence of measures of voting behaviour in different sessions of the American Congress. Clausen asked, 'How do we know that the policy dimension being measured at time-one by scale X is the same as that being measured by scale Y at time-two?' (1967: 1020). He attempted to solve this problem with a set of items of similar content in four successive sessions of Congress and showed that the correlations within and between the sessions revealed a similar structure. This method of internal consistency was then expanded by computing the correlations between the instruments obtained in the first step with a number of other, theoretically relevant, variables. This second phase of external consistency confirmed the conclusion of the first phase and argued for the validation of the measures of the voting dimensions in different sessions of the American Congress.

The complications of analyses involving levels of education illustrate an example from another area of comparative research. Since national educational systems are very different, a straightforward comparison of levels of education is highly problematic. An attempt to resolve these problems uses directly related concepts like income and occupational status as 'criterion variables'. If nation-specific measures of the level of education appear related in a similar way to the other indicators, the functional equivalence of the indicator for education is established (Treiman 1975; Treiman and Terrell 1975). This example provides a clear strategy for basing equivalence on the idea of structural similarity and the use of inference. However, it also shows the weakness of the approach. As Müller (1997: 130) argues, the complications of establishing equivalence are simply moved from the concept of education to the concepts of income and occupational status, and differences in the impact of background factors may well modify the structure in different countries.[22] Similar objections can be raised against the study of political knowledge by Dimock and Popkin who rely on questions which are *presumed* to have 'roughly similar meanings across countries' (1997: 219) and which are simply related to media usage in various countries.

A last example of this strategy is somewhat different. While Przeworski and Teune and their followers stress the internal consistency of the same type of data, other researchers point to other possibilities by distinguishing between various levels in comparative research. Obviously, inter-level comparisons present additional, complicated problems, but a two-step strategy transforming indicators to a similar level in the first phase in order to perform intra-level comparisons in the second phase could be an interesting strategy for assessing equivalence.[23] For instance, micro-level data like survey responses could be aggregated into an 'opinion climate', which in turn could be related to economic or historical data characteristic of each society.[24]

An example of this strategy lies in the analyses of Kuechler (1991) who suggests using so-called 'contingency patterns' in his work on political support in Western Europe. In order to avoid the pitfalls in a comparison of the marginal distributions of survey questions (like the degree of satisfaction with democracy), he relates the developments of these marginals to the development of macro-economic indicators like inflation and unemployment rates in different countries. In this way, he is able to test several ideas about the relationships between the state of the economy and the level of mass support without relying on the assumption that the instrument applied has the same meaning in different countries. In other words, the macro-economic indicators serve as external points of reference to establish the equivalence of the instruments used in the questionnaires. Although this approach is quite different from the idea of internal consistency among a set of items or stimuli, the underlying argument in terms of inference is similar.

4 Using a non-common set of indicators: internal consistency

The use of internal consistency as the central criterion for equivalence among a set of non-common indicators is illustrated by looking at two applications of a method proposed by Przeworski and Teune (1966). The so-called *identity-equivalence method* relies explicitly on the idea that constraint among indicators does not imply using the same set of stimuli or items in each setting. The method starts with the search for a core set of identical stimuli or items which provide an anchor for evaluating the constraints of each measurement instrument (a so-called identity set). The next step is to add culture- or nation-specific stimuli or items in order to increase the validity of the instrument in a specific context. Finally, the instruments are applied in each setting and comparisons are based on the results obtained with these distinct instruments.[25]

An example is the search for equivalent measures for the concept of 'greenness' based on attitudes towards the environment (Nas 1995). Country-specific elements are obvious in this field. For instance, recycling bottles is everyday practice in some countries and not in others, and catalytic converters are obligatory in some countries and debated in others. On the basis of the 'identity-equivalence method', first a common structure is found in several West European countries by using the principal components model. Then the common components are enlarged with country-specific items. In that way, non-identical but equivalent measures are constructed.

Another example is the construction of equivalent measures for the concept 'political participation'. The level of political participation can be measured in several countries by constructing nation-specific instruments (van Deth 1986). On the basis of the identity-equivalence method, a common structure emerges in eight West European countries. This set appears to be a cumulative, one-dimensional scale in each country. The next step is the search for nation-specific additions to the common scale and the construction of non-identical, equivalent measures.

The strategy of relying on the structure between different sets of stimuli in different settings as a means of establishing equivalence seems to avoid 'conceptual stretching' as well as moving the problem of equivalence from one area to another.

5 Using a non-common set of indicators: external consistency

It is hard to find empirical examples of strategies based on a non-common set of indicators and the criterion of external consistency. In a study of role conflict, Ehrlich, Rinehart, and Howell (1962) collected data from two distinct populations and compared the results with those reported in the literature. They applied different measures for concepts like legitimacy and sanctions and analysed the internal structure of the measures as well as the behavioural consequences among different populations. From the fact that different stimuli showed a high degree of association and resulted in consistent predictions, the authors concluded that different questions were measuring the same dimensions (Ehrlich *et al.* 1962: 91, 93).

If we do not insist on strict empirical analyses, we can find an important recommendation for relying on a set of non-common indicators and external consistency in system theory as proposed by Luhmann. In this perspective, any comparison of systems will be confronted by the question of identity and functional equivalence. As indicated above, this 'belongingness' to a specific part of a system provides the key to establishing equivalence in comparative research. Only if we rely on auxiliary information can we assess the similarity of (different) indicators used in different settings.

Letting a hundred flowers blossom?

The problem of establishing equivalence is evident in all types of comparative research, be it cross-cultural, cross-national, or longitudinal. The five main strategies presented above include only the basic variants. Many specific and more sophisticated models can be easily developed when the restrictions are modified or different strategies are combined. In particular, (full) structural equation models provide the opportunity to combine strategies based on the idea of internal consistency with strategies based on external consistency. The number of research findings obtained this way, however, is remarkably limited, despite a revival of the multitrait-multimethod approach (Saris and Münnich 1995). Since this approach requires extensive or repeated measures, it can be used only in cases where equivalence problems have been recognised from the very beginning of the research design. This severely restricts its usefulness in existing projects and secondary analyses.

Although the tricky problem of identity and equivalence can spoil many attempts at comparative analysis, there is no need to overstate the difficulty. Establishing equivalence is not a goal in itself. As Maccoby and Maccoby pointed out in the 1950s, the cost of constructing equivalent indicators might easily destroy any advantage in using them. From this pragmatic perspective, all of the contributions in this volume concentrate on some theoretically relevant theme. Each one selects methods and techniques to resolve these problems, and the success of the attempts should be evaluated in terms of these interpretations and explanations. In additon, it should be remembered that none of the data collections presented has been specifically designed to deal with equivalence problems. Every contribution represents 'real' research and ongoing (secondary) analyses, not some methodological experiment.

The first set of contributions consists of approaches to equivalence problems of various political and societal orientations in the field of political culture. Starting from the assumption that both the limits and objects of *tolerance* are culturally and psychologically framed and can change over time, Bettina Westle discusses the problems of how attitudes of tolerance have developed in Western Europe since the early 1980s and how they can be compared to attitudes of tolerance in Eastern Europe (Chapter 2). For this purpose, she develops similar but not identical instruments for various settings. Ronald Inglehart shows the use of identical instruments in his contribution on *materialist–postmaterialist values* (Chapter 3). He explores the extent to which a battery of items designed to measure these values actually taps the same phenomenon in forty different societies. The third contribution in the field of political culture focuses on the comparisons of *religious orientations* in several European countries (Chapter 4). Using the frequency of church attendance as an indicator of church integration and traditional religiosity, Martin Feldkircher assesses the equivalence of this indicator via time-series analyses. The next contribution is a discussion of *gender-roles* by Michael Braun (Chapter 5). Gender-role attitudes have changed dramatically over time, making the problem of equivalent measurement especially urgent in this area of comparative research. Analysing cross-national data sets, Braun demonstrates the crucial importance of question wording and item formation. A more behaviourally oriented topic is presented by Jan W. van Deth and Frauke Kreuter in their comparison of *social participation and voluntary associations* in West European countries (Chapter 6). They demonstrate that involvement in voluntary associations depends on the kinds of organisations available as well as on the specific functions of the organisations in various cultural settings.

Political culture and political orientations are not the only sub-fields of comparative politics relevant to the problems of constructing equivalent indicators. In his analyses of *party organisations* in Western Europe, Thomas Poguntke starts from the well-known fact that the structure of parties and party organisations differs considerably in different settings (Chapter 7). Only by identifying relevant parties can we systematically compare the organisational structures of West European parties. In his contribution on *party positions*, Gábor Tóka discusses the question of how to obtain a cross-nationally valid measure of the overall degree of programmatic structuring in a national party system (Chapter 8). The empirical basis here is a cross-national comparison of results obtained from interviewing middle-level party activists in several East European countries. In the third contribution on parties and party systems, the focus is on *institutional regimes*. In Chapter 9, André Kaiser shows that new institutionalist concepts used for the comparative analysis of institutional regimes have considerable difficulty in attaining an acceptable level of generality. He presents an alternative analytical framework based on an analysis of the British political system.

The final chapter pays attention to the question of comparing clearly different newspapers and television programmes between different countries (Chapter 10). The analyses of *readers, viewers, and cat-dogs* by Rüdiger Schmitt-Beck underlines the need for equivalent measures of television and newspapers in a number of West European countries. By way of more detailed analyses of data from Germany, Spain, and the United States, he assesses the equivalence of media-related concepts by focusing on the information quality and societal reach of these media.

The contributions to this volume not only cover a wide area of substantive topics, they also differ in their approaches to equivalence problems and to types of data available. For instance, while possible solutions to the problems of comparing tolerance, religious orientation, and social participation are based on a search for country-specific indicators, the qualities of identical instruments are at the centre of analyses in the fields of value orientations or gender roles. Moreover, both the study of party organisations and of institutional regimes presented here require *a priori* conceptualisations of an analytical framework. On the other hand, several contributions do not start with such a framework but rely on a single conceptualisation. A combination of these approaches is presented in the chapter on mass media, where the results of an international comparison of media exposure in many countries are used in a first step and a typology of the media is used in a second step concerned with more detailed analyses in a restricted number of countries.

Although mass survey data appear in many chapters, they obviously do not exhaust the types of empirical information presented in this volume. Data here range from mass surveys on political orientations and behaviour to divergent types of information as elite interviews, organisational aspects of parties, figures on media exposure, and the properties of consociational democracies. The same diversity informs the selection of countries. Many chapters rely on data from West European countries, but comparisons are made with Eastern Europe in the chapter on tolerance. The chapter on value orientations presents information collected in no less than forty countries, and the chapter on mass media pays explicit attention to a comparison of findings in Europe and the United States.

The wide variety of topics, methods, data, and countries in this volume underlines the general nature of the equivalence problem in comparative research. The problem is evident in almost every aspect of such research and can be approached from very different angles. This does not lead, however, to 'letting a hundred flowers blossom and a hundred schools of thought contend' as Chairman Mao might have put it. On the contrary. Exactly because problems of equivalence are so complicated, there is no need and no place for simple experimentation or inductivism. What is needed are substantively guided analyses, clearly embedded in existing approaches, and related to substantive problems. Only thus can we assess the opportunities for dealing with a very thorny problem.

Notes

1 I thank the contributors to this volume as well as Hartmut Esser, Max Kaase, Daniela Mix, and Elinor Scarbrough for their helpful comments and stimulating criticism on several drafts of this chapter.
2 This dilemma is a more restrictive formulation of the fundamental problem of international comparative research in finding generalisations in a field where the 'uniqueness' of every setting is immediately apparent and where historic and idiographic factors cannot be neglected. The core of the problem is that 'reality seems to demand a configurative approach; generalizibility seems to demand a more analytical approach' (Verba 1967–8: 117; cf. Bendix 1963; De Meur and Berg-Schlosser 1994; Peters 1996).
3 To mention some examples: 'The most fundamental methodological issue is whether the concepts employed in the analysis are truly equivalent' (Kohn 1989: 84). 'If the first prerequisite of comparative legislative research is the further development of theory, the second condition is the attainment of cross-national equivalence in the measurement of those concepts which the theory employs' (Loewenberg 1972: 16). 'One of the most familiar problems in comparative analysis, but still one of the most important, is that of equivalence' (Peters 1996: 23; cf. Hartmann 1995; 44 or Gabriel 1998: 45).
4 Some authors take this situation for granted and simply announce that equivalence is no problem for their topic: 'We believe, however, that the advantages of comparability of an identically worded survey item across a number of systems clearly outweighs the disadvantages of potentially ambiguous meaning' (Anderson and Guillory 1997: 71). The rather naive suggestion underlying this 'belief' is that 'identically worded survey items' will not have 'potentially ambiguous meanings' in different settings – which is certainly not self-evident (cf. Crutchfield and Gordon 1947).
5 In general, one might say that the lack of attention to these problems is a manifestation of a much more fundamental problem of comparative research: 'Most would agree that measurement is problematic . . . The irony is that despite general acknowledgement of its deficiencies, measurement is a neglected area in macrocomparative research' (Bollen *et al.* 1993: 342).
6 This does not deny, of course, the specific value of single-observation studies or the opportunities for combining case studies in a comparative design (see King *et al.* 1994: 212; Price-Williams 1985: 997; Schmid 1995: 303–4; Ragin and Zaret 1983; Rose 1991: 447). The obligatory quotation here, however, is taken from Durkheim: 'La sociologie comparée n'est pas une branche particulière de la sociologie; c'est la sociologie même, en tant qu'elle cesse d'être purement descriptive et aspire à rendre compte des faits' (1981 [1895]: 137).
7 Proof of this trivial version: 'for any individuals x and y, if, for any property f, x has f if and only if y has f, then x is identical with y. Let the property f be the property of being identical with y. Surely y has it. But, then, if x has every property y has, then x has it also.

Hence, x is identical with y' (Honderich 1995: 391). See for a different approach Lowe (1989).

8 The Big Mac index was introduced by *The Economist* and has been published every year since 1986. Obviously, other 'identical' products like a pair of Levi 501 jeans or a bottle of Coca-Cola can perform the same function in comparisons of the purchasing power of currencies.

9 By 1977, Allerbeck observed that this conclusion has been accepted in survey research: 'A consensus has emerged among scholars engaged in cross-national survey research that the goal in such cases should be functional equivalence and not literal identity of indicators' (1977: 378). Considering the widespread use of identical measures to the present day, this conclusion was a bit too optimistic.

10 The word equivalence is a combination of the Latin words *aequus* (equal) and *valere* (to be strong; to be worth).

11 The question of whether two objects can be compared if, and only if, they belong to the same class, has given rise to an interesting debate on the nature of comparisons based on the seminal work of Kalleberg (1966–7). DeFelice presents a convincing attack on Sartori's (1970) position and stresses the fact that comparisons can be meaningful too if the objects do not actually share similar properties: 'comparison does not require that the same attributes be exhibited in all the things to be compared. Instead, to repeat, all that is necessary in this regard is that the things compared be capable of possessing the same attribute' (1980: 124).

12 For a similar line of reasoning based on clear functionalist notions, see the analyses presented by Patterson and Wahlke (1972) in the field of legislative behaviour or the proposals of Helms (1995) to the study of political parties.

13 Even if 'identical' instruments are the goal, designing or selecting instruments for use in many different countries places high demands on the skills of translators. Nobody is able to deal with 10–20 different languages at the level required for this type of work. Generally speaking, problems in translating terms are approached by procedures involving back-translations (both of the so-called parallel and the serial types, cf. Niedermayer 1997: 94). These procedures seem to solve most of the problems but are very time consuming and expensive. Other examples of efforts to deal with translating terms in comparative politics can be found in the activities of international task forces of scholars from several countries like the Political Action group, the World Values Surveys group, and the International Social Survey Program group. See Osgood (1967) for an early example of evaluating linguistic differences on the basis of cross-national consistency, and van de Vijver and Leung (1997: 35–51) for a more recent list of guidelines for translation and adaptation of instruments in comparative research.

14 As mentioned, neither epistemological questions about the complexities of 'travelling' theories and concepts, nor the practical problems of data 'harmonisation' (cf. Glover 1996: 33) will be discussed here.

15 See Hofstadter (1985) for a brilliant discussion of the usage of analogies and its complications.

16 The 'general tension between easy operationalizability and comparative adequacy' is discussed by Smelser (1973; cf. van de Vijver and Leung 1997), but the most elegant presentation of the problem is clearly Sartori's *Ladder of Abstraction* that can be climbed and descended in actual research (1970: 1041). For an impressive application of this idea to *coups d'état* in Africa, see O'Kane (1993).

17 In terms of research techniques, emphasis is placed on equal multiple correlation coefficients.

18 This development is based on the recommendation to study so-called 'second-order comparisons'. See Verba (1969) for a general discussion about the advantages of this strategy in international comparative research.

19 Van de Vijver and Leung present an interesting distinction between 'levels' of equivalence: 'construct (or structural) equivalence', 'measurement unit equivalence', and

'scalar equivalence (or full score comparability)' (1997: 8–9). Although this distinction is useful for their discussion of research methods, it is not very helpful in the present context which focuses on pragmatic strategies to deal with equivalence problems. The five main strategies presented here can be applied at each level distinguished by van de Vijver and Leung.

20 For this revival, see the volume edited by Saris and Münnich (1995), especially the discussion about the 'classical MTMM' design by Saris (1995) and De Wit and Billiet (1995). Unfortunately, this design requires extensive or repeated measures which are rarely available in secondary analyses of existing data sets.

21 This example once again shows that the line between strategies using external and internal consistency among a common set of indicators is not always very clear. If Gabriel had started with the aim of measuring the construct 'attachment to the political system' and had used his two questions as different indicators of this construct, his approach would have been an example of a monotrait-multimethod strategy as indicated by van de Vijver and Leung (1997: 55).

22 In addition, Müller (1997: 130) states that the argument becomes circular if we want to explain income and status on the basis of education if the relationships between these indicators are already used to establish equivalence. Although the implicit warning is important, this criticism seems to be based on a confusion of the phases of concept formation and measurement, on the one hand, and testing hypotheses or causal interpretations, on the other. As Jackman states, 'to identify and measure a variable is not to assume that it influences a second variable. Indeed, any such assumption would beg the question' (1985: 171). For this distinction, see also the concept 'structural equivalence' discussed by Esser (1996: 433–4).

23 On the distinction between inter-level and intra-level comparisons, see Eulau (1977: 51).

24 This two-step procedure must be distinguished from analyses that use macro-level concepts at the analytical level but restrict the empirical analysis to the micro-level. For instance, Kohn (1989) presents interesting findings based on the use of similar concepts in different settings in order to study the relationships between social structure and personality. His strategy is clearly based on the use of external consistency as a solution for the identity-equivalence problem.

25 A formal definition of this procedure is presented by Przeworski and Teune (1966: 557). See Westle (this volume: 26–7) for a more extensive discussion and application of their approach.

2 Tolerance

Bettina Westle

Introduction

Tolerance is not only a difficult topic for cross-national research, it is difficult to attain in our lives. Or is it? Aren't we all very tolerant persons? Aren't we much more tolerant than earlier generations? Aren't the people of Western democracies brighter examples of tolerance than others? Why, then, bother about it?

Though most people think of themselves as tolerant, everybody has limits to tolerance (McClosky and Brill 1983). These limits are culturally and psychologically framed and can change over time. Nowadays, tolerance is usually considered essential to peaceful social and political relations between and within nations. But this knowledge does not in itself create more tolerance. On the contrary, international observers believe that tolerance is on the decline. Thus, UNESCO declared 1995 the 'year for tolerance' (UNESCO 1994 and 1995). On the one hand, times of rapid change increase the need for tolerance; on the other, they threaten the ability to be tolerant. This creates a tolerance-gap – and serves as the subject of the next two sections of this chapter.

What is tolerance?

The Latin term *tolerare* originally meant the acceptance of something or someone we do not agree with. In this perspective, tolerance is not based on human nature but on self-discipline and carries with it the meaning of suffering. After Roman times, the meaning of tolerance changed, and now the word boasts a variety of definitions (Frenzel 1974; Wierlacher 1994). Historically, in Western Europe tolerance came into being as a rational calculus. In cases of armed conflicts without a clear winner, enemies agreed to tolerate each other when the price of ongoing battles seemed too high. Pragmatic motivation also underlay the relationship between a generally religious minority and a sovereign. Tolerance was practised when its social or economic profit seemed to outweigh the cost of suppression. Obviously, this kind of tolerance was precarious, since the cost–benefit calculus could easily deteriorate (Frenzel 1974; Fetscher 1990).

During the Enlightenment, the meaning of tolerance grew. The belief in human beings as creatures with dignity and the right to freedom led to the demand for tolerance as a human right. It was felt that humans should be tolerated as they are, no matter how different they might be. Tolerance thereby turned into a virtue and duty in religious, social, and political life (Fetscher 1990; Bielefeldt 1994). Whereas 'pragmatic-rational' tolerance demanded nothing other than the renunciation of violence and coercion, 'liberal' tolerance established the legitimacy of being different and required respect and equal rights for others. Nowadays, an even more demanding concept of tolerance is under discussion. This 'positive' concept requires solidarity and active engagement in improving the living conditions of those who are different (Baumann 1991; Wierlacher 1994).

The varying ethical meanings of tolerance are often thought of as hierarchical stages – in historical perspective, in respect to the extensiveness of demands on the tolerating subjects, and in reference to the consequences for the tolerated objects (Fritzsche 1995). However, whether these meanings represent a hierarchy or merely differ from one another is not always clear. In some aspects they even seem to be contrary. Authors who work on the problem of intolerance generally insist on disapproval and suffering as components of tolerance. They argue that when one does not disapprove of something, tolerance is not needed. This is why tolerance is so hard to achieve. In this perspective, a 'live and let live' attitude is not seen as tolerance but as indifference by a 'permissive society'. It is caused by a lack of value orientations or a lack of interest in others. This kind of indifference is often believed to hinder the development of active tolerance (Sontheimer 1974; Frenzel 1974; Oertzen 1974; Bielefeldt 1994; Wierlacher 1994; Fritzsche 1995). Thus the peaceful relations which have grown between Christian religions in the last centuries cannot be seen as tolerance but as indifference to religious questions. (Though no doubt it is a healthier state for mankind than the one before it.) Moreover, it seems unrealistic to demand active tolerance from people who are really suffering. Finally, low interest in the conditions of others and an attitude of 'live and let live' do not necessarily exclude support for the principle of tolerance as such, whatever its specific objects. In other words, the liberal concept of tolerance as acceptance of and respect for difference – though sometimes accompanied by indifference – might be a realistic aim.

But even if we accept the tolerance of 'live and let live', what about tolerance towards intolerance? This may be one of the most difficult questions. Can we in the social sphere, for instance, tolerate a religion which opposes our principles of freedom and equality for everyone or even opposes the principle of tolerance itself? Can we in the political sphere tolerate ideologies which aim at removing democracy?

Tolerance as a problem of cross-national research

In psychology, positive self-esteem is cited most prominently as a precondition of tolerance. Why? Because it is easier to respect the worthiness of others if one accepts oneself (Mitscherlich 1974; Thomas 1994). Since neither positive self-esteem nor tolerance fall from heaven but must be learned, long-term cultural factors play a central role in framing tolerance. Moreover, positive self-esteem is not independent of its context. Social and economic change can affect it – and this is where the short-term cultural factor comes in.

The first reason why tolerance attitudes are difficult to compare cross-nationally is because long-term cultural factors – i.e. the religious, social, political, and national history of a society – form cultural standards of acceptable behaviour and, as a result, form standards and limits of tolerance. Individual or group-specific tolerance may vary within the limits but rarely cross the borders. If they do, disagreement and sanctions are likely. Very few universal limits of tolerance exist, the most prominent being probably the incest taboo. And though the same cultural standards can be shared by different societies, they can be of different relevance and different reach. Individuals do not usually think about the standards of tolerance. In the case of successful socialisation, standards are not on the surface of consciousness.

Though societies condemn violations of their cultural standards, culture is not totally resistant to change. The second reason why tolerance attitudes are difficult to compare cross-nationally arises from the possibility of cultural change. Cultural standards may become a topic of debate and become fragile when challenged. A challenge can result from changing conditions of living, which alter the usefulness of cultural standards. Challenges of cultural standards can also arise from a strong deviant subculture, for which different standards of behaviour and tolerance seem acceptable. Crossing the cultural standards may have an innovative function in broadening tolerance. In such cases, rational-pragmatic motives might play a role. But development of tolerance is not a one-way street to wider areas and fewer limits. Tolerance can also become more restrictive. Contact with different cultures may well bring one's own standards of tolerance under scrutiny and may either weaken or strengthen them. According to the pragmatic concept, the standards of the stronger economic or social group will survive. According to social-psychological theories of group behaviour, the confrontation with differing cultural standards challenges one's own living conditions and self-esteem. This challenge provokes a counter-reaction, which posits the superiority of one's own standards (Tajfel and Turner 1986). This process is central to the vicious circle of the growing need for more tolerance and its increased challenge in times of rapid change and inter-cultural confrontation. In a longitudinal perspective, the faster social change occurs, the more our usual convictions become controversial. This might exhaust our ability and willingness to adapt. In inter-cultural perspective, the amount as well as the distance of the confronted standards of different cultures play a similar role in the danger of exhaustion and the growing need for tolerance.

Ongoing individualisation in the Western world, post-socialist transformations towards pluralism and democracy, increasing self-confidence of the Third World, and growing fundamentalism of Islam all form rapid changes in life. Moreover, the breakdown of the Iron Curtain amid high speed growth in communications and transport promotes cross-national contacts. The same applies to growing international migration. Therefore, we find ourselves in an era demanding more tolerance and finding it harder to achieve because everyone's living conditions and cultural convictions may be challenged.

From a philosophical and historical perspective, tolerance is strongly associated with democratic forms of government and politics. For this reason, this analysis of tolerance is based on a longitudinal comparison of societies with enduring democratic systems and a cross-national comparison of democratic and non-democratic societies. The process of European integration and the desire by Eastern countries to join the European Union can be seen as new challenges to tolerance, since societies with very different political, economical, and social backgrounds confront each other. In the following pages we will ask how attitudes of tolerance have developed in Western Europe since the early 1980s and how they can be compared to attitudes of tolerance in Eastern Europe.

Data base and approaches

Attitude-research in tolerance is not easy even within a single culture. Usually a high level of abstraction of the concept as well as in the concrete wording of questions is recommended for reaching cross-national comparability. A low level of abstraction can evoke culture- and situation-specific connotations, which endanger comparability. Yet with respect to tolerance a high level of abstraction is nearly unachievable. Since everybody thinks of himself and herself as being tolerant, we cannot simply ask 'are you tolerant?' Tolerance has to show itself not in abstract but in concrete terms. Therefore, we must enter a more concrete setting, presenting examples for possible objects of intolerance (Allport 1958; McClosky and Brill 1983). Working with concrete examples, however, raises the question of whether the examples represent relevant objects or whether other examples are more relevant.

In the cumulated *World Values Surveys I* and *II* used here, the operationalisation of tolerance relies on selecting examples from a pool of items. The items used in different surveys in various countries are summarised in Table 2.1.[1] The questions were asked in Western European democracies in 1981 and 1990, which allows for a longitudinal comparison, and in Eastern countries in 1990, which allows for a cross-national comparison between countries with very different political cultures.

A cursory look at the answers to the question (see Table 2.1) shows for most Western countries and both points in time rather few references to the items 'other race', 'foreigners' and 'large families', and rather few references in 1990 to 'Jews' and 'Muslims'. In most Western countries, in 1981 the item 'drinkers' is most frequently mentioned, followed by 'criminals' or occasionally by 'left-wing' or 'right-wing extremists'. In 1990 the new item 'drug addicts' is most frequently mentioned, generally followed by 'drinkers' and 'criminals' and occasionally by 'left-wing extremists'. The frequency of the other items lies in between, showing different orderings between countries as well as between points in time within single countries. The level of tolerance towards specific groups varies greatly between countries. Eastern countries reveal a similar ordering of 'drug addicts', 'drinkers', and 'criminals' as most disliked, followed by 'homosexuals'. In general,

Table 2.1 People that one would not like to have as neighbours (percentages and means)

Year/country	Right-wing extremists	Left-wing extremists	Other race	Foreigners	Muslims	Jews	Large families	Criminals	Drinkers	Unstable	Drug addicts	Homosexuals	Aids-sick	Mean no.
1981														
Norway	18	18	8	9			4	34	32	19				1.42
Sweden	17	21	6	4			5	27	44	12				1.36
Iceland	19	21	3	2			2	12	52	24				1.35
Ireland	16	21	7	5			3	44	33	23				1.52
North. Ireland	23	28	9	9			8	40	40	29				1.87
Great Britain	21	26	9	12			10	36	47	30				1.91
Denmark	3	6	3	10			5	16	28	9				0.80
Belgium	16	20	11	15			3	23	39	14				1.41
Netherlands	33	37	8	16			5	16	50	18				1.84
West Germany	44	48	10	20			8	26	66	28				2.50
France	13	9	5	6			4	10	44	8				0.99
Italy	39	35	6	3			12	36	43	28				2.03
Spain	24	25	8	2			4	35	37	21				1.57
1990														
Norway	22	19	12	16	21	9	6	37	32	22	55	19	25	2.97
Sweden	29	24	6	9	17	6	5	35	45	17	65	18	18	2.93
Iceland	29	30	8	8	12	7	2	24	61	32	74	20	18	3.24
Ireland	21	29	6	5	13	6	3	52	34	30	64	33	35	3.32
North. Ireland	29	35	7	7	15	6	9	46	43	23	59	48	28	3.53
Great Britain	27	33	8	11	16	7	10	41	49	28	64	33	24	3.51
Denmark	7	6	7	12	15	3	3	28	34	11	54	12	9	2.00
Belgium	39	35	17	20	27	13	10	30	49	22	53	24	24	3.63
Netherlands	52	47	7	9	14	3	8	28	60	18	73	11	15	3.46
West Germany	62	51	10	16	20	7	8	27	64	31	60	34	28	4.17
France	33	23	9	13	17	7	8	19	50	17	44	24	15	2.79

Table 2.1 continued

Year/country	Right-wing extremists	Left-wing extremists	Other race	Foreigners	Muslims	Jews	Large Families	Criminals	Drinkers	Unstable	Drug addicts	Homosexuals	Aids-sick	Mean no.
Italy	33	29	12	13	14	12	13	48	51	34	59	37	42	3.99
Spain	28	25	10	9	12	10	8	37	40	25	56	29	34	3.22
1990														
East Germany	70	58	12	18	20	8	7	34	72	20	59	34	20	4.32
Hungary	20	21	23	22	18	10	7	77	81	23	84	75	66	5.29
Czechoslovakia	36	38	31	34	49	23	15	72	74	33	81	59	64	6.07
Slovenia	33	31	40	40	38	37	40	37	45	36	47	43	41	5.06
Romania	42	45	28	30	34	28	22	67	79	64	76	75	66	6.57
Bulgaria	65	68	39	34	41	30	24	70	73	53	69	68	63	6.98
Belarus	42	40	17	17	24	21	16	72	82	63	82	79	73	6.27
Russia	40	41	11	12	15	13	12	63	82	51	86	81	68	5.75
Moscov	26	23	11	13	15	11	11	60	82	50	82	70	58	5.14

Note: See note 1 for selection of countries.

Eastern countries present a higher level of citations (see the higher average numbers of unwanted neighbours). These findings suggest that tolerance – as measured here – may cover more than one dimension.

The operationalisation of tolerance in this way raises several problems. First, the general stimulus 'neighbours' might carry different culture- and socio-structural connotations. For example, the meaning of 'neighbours' might differ in the countryside or in big cities. Also, the stimulus 'groups of persons' is problematic, some respondents may think of groups and others may think of individuals. (Living with an individual Muslim neighbour might differ, for example, from living in an area dominated by Muslims.)

The second (and central) problem here concerns whether items about different groups of people carry identical semantic meanings and weights as sensible objects of tolerance over time and across countries.

A third problem is a possible change in structures of perceptions caused by the addition of items in 1990; that is, has the addition of particular items changed the context of the other items?[2]

In testing the functional equivalence of items in a potentially multi-dimensional theoretical construct, Przeworski and Teune (1970: 113–31) propose three alternative approaches with explorative factor analysis dependent on the available item set. These approaches can be summarised as follows:

A   *Common items.* Here the aim is to find items which show an identical structure over all units of analysis. If unit-specific analyses yield an identical structure, the remaining items are analysed with all units pooled. If the structure in the pooled analysis differs, further exclusions of items become necessary. Indices for dimensions of the theoretical construct cover items which are commonly asked and represent the identical dimension in each unit of analysis.

B   *Common and different items.* Here Przeworski and Teune start with a pooled analysis of only common items. If we find an identity set, we may expand it by the time- and/or culture-specific different items in the next step. If these items show strong relationships to the items of the identity set, we add them to the respective dimension. Resulting indices are constructed out of common and culture-specific different items, but not out of common items which load on different factors in different units of analysis.

C   *Different items.* Here Przeworski and Teune propose unit-specific factor analyses tested against theoretical hypotheses on their factorial structure. If the theoretical assumptions are met empirically, we also test the resulting indices on external consistency.

In comparing these three approaches with respect to multi-dimensional constructs, a logical problem arises. In order to improve culture-specific validity, Przeworski and Teune accept denotatively different items in approaches B and C as possible functional equivalents. Therefore, these approaches follow the logic of optimising culture-specific validity. On the other hand, the logic of the search for an identity set in approaches A and B assumes that commonly asked items in different cultures must represent the same dimension of the theoretical construct. This assumption, however, reveals a different logic, namely that denotative linguistic identity must be the same as semantic equivalence in sociological terms. Following the logic of functional equivalence, however, we cannot *a priori* exclude the possibility that denotatively identical common items may carry culture-specific meanings – which would result in loadings on different factors – and are, in spite of this, valid culture-specific representations of those factors. Following the logic of approach A, we would have to exclude such items. But following the logic of approaches B and C, we may include such items on culture-specific different dimensions. This would form approach D. However, if we allow for different dimensional loading of one and the same item in different units of analysis, it seems advisable not to rely exclusively on internal consistency tests, but to add tests of external consistency and to compare the resulting indices of both approaches.

According to Przeworski and Teune, the following approaches are relevant here for the available data. For the longitudinal comparison of Western countries, we have 'common and different items', which leads to approach B with the possibility of item additions in 1990. For a comparison of Western and Eastern countries in 1990, we have 'only common items', which leads to approach A, the search for an identity set without country-specific deviations. Approach D affects both comparisons by allowing country-specific deviations of identical items.

Internal consistency

The first question to be dealt with is whether tolerance as measured with the reference to unwanted neighbours is a multi-dimensional construct. Therefore, we start the analyses without an *a priori* definition of the number of factors to be extracted. Table 2.2 summarises the results – with good and bad news. The good news is that we are indeed dealing with a multi-dimensional construct, since more than one factor is shown in every unit of analysis.[3] The bad news follows from the numbers of factors found. In the pooled analyses, three factors are extracted, but this structure is not repeated in each separate unit of analysis.

With different numbers of factors for the research units, we cannot find identity sets in all dimensions. Thus we can either restrict ourselves to countries which show a three-dimensional structure, or we can define *a priori* the number of factors. This latter strategy is more risky, because for the deviating cases we impose a somewhat differentiated structure of perception than really exists. Concerning a less differentiated structure, the probability increases that the dimensions originally obtained become less clear. Concerning a more differentiated structure, we create factors with an Eigenvalue below 1.00 – and it is questionable whether this is of much sense in respect to index construction of a dimension. In spite of these problems, we will define, first, a two-dimensional structure, since this may be the smallest common denominator of our units. Alternatively, we will define a three-dimensional structure, since this is the one most frequently found in the originally extracted structure.

Table 2.2 Number of factors extracted according to country, point in time, and set of items (principal components analysis; Eigenvalue > 1.0)

Year	1981		1990		1990		
Item set	1981		1981		1990		
Pool/country	2 factors	3 factors	2 factors	3 factors	2 factors	3 factors	4 factors
West 81 + 90				x			
West 90						x	
West + East 90				x		x	
Norway		x	x			x	
Sweden		x		x		x	
Iceland		x		x		x	
Ireland		x		x			x
North. Ireland		x	x				x
Great Britain		x		x		x	
Denmark	x			x		x	
Belgium	x		x			x	
Netherlands		x	x			x	
West Germany	x		x			x	
France		x	x				x
Italy		x	x			x	
Spain		x	x			x	
East Germany						x	
Hungary						x	
Czechoslovakia						x	
Slovenia						x	
Romania						x	
Bulgaria					x		
Belarus						x	
Russia						x	
Moscov						x	

The results of analyses with an *a priori* definition of *two dimensions and all items* is disastrous (data not shown). Comparison on the basis of the short item set shows for the pooled versions and for all countries very high loadings of both items about 'political extremists' on one factor. The second factor is formed in most countries by the items 'other race' and 'foreigners', in four countries additionally by 'large families', and in one country by 'unstable'. However, this picture is disturbed by Denmark 1981. To keep Denmark and stick to the criteria of Przeworski and Teune would result in just one factor of 'political extremists'. For most of the countries the longer item set in 1990 shows a clear factor of 'strangers', consisting of 'other race', 'foreigners', and 'Muslims', mostly accompanied by 'Jews', and in some cases by 'large families'. However, in this long item set, the factor of 'political extremists' is disturbed and the second dimension consists of a wide variety of different item-combinations.

The alternative solution of a *fixed three-dimensional structure and all items* reveals in all variants of the pooled analyses an identical and clearly interpretable structure (see Table 2.3). It contains one factor of 'political extremists' ('right-wing' and 'left-wing'), one factor of 'strangers' ('other race', 'foreigners', and, in 1990, 'Muslims' and 'Jews', whereas the item 'large families' does not fulfil the criteria in all cases), and a third factor with the remaining items (except for 'unstable' in the version with the long item set in 1990), a dimension which we call 'social deviants'.

Unfortunately, this structure does not repeat itself in all units (data not shown). If we stick to the procedure proposed by Przeworski and Teune and exclude all items which show a problem at least in one of the countries of comparison, the result is a single dimension of 'political extremists' on the short item set and two dimensions of 'political extremists' and 'strangers' on the long item set. This deviance between the two sets suggests that discarding all problematic items at once may lead to the unnecessary loss of the dimension 'strangers' on the short item set. Therefore, we try an alternative approach by excluding all items primarily associated with social deviance.

For all pooled versions as well as for all single units, this approach leads to one factor on 'political extremists' and a second factor built by all items on 'strangers', with only Denmark 1990 as deviant ('Jews' with a factor loading below 0.60). Excluding this item from all countries and pooled versions reveals clear identity sets for both dimensions. 'Political extremists' is formed by 'right-wing extremists' and 'left-wing extremists', and 'strangers' is formed by 'other race' and 'foreigners' in 1981 and by 'Muslims' in 1990 (data not shown).

On this basis, we reintroduce the items 'Jews' and 'large families' in some countries to the dimension of 'strangers'. This trial reveals that we can reach different results (data not shown). Taking the short item set, we can add 'large families' in four (1981) and in seven (1990) of the thirteen Western countries and eight of the nine Eastern countries. However, in only one of the Western countries is it the same country in 1990 as in 1981. This not only hints at an inter-cultural different meaning of the item, but also at a change of meaning within the same country over time. Taking the longer item set, we can either add 'Jews' in fourteen out of our twenty-two units or 'large families' in fifteen out of twenty-two units – but we can add both of them in only five cases. Moreover, these additions hint at artificial changes caused by the different context of the items within the smaller and larger item sets.

The total loss of the dimension 'social deviants' in a two-factorial solution is very unsatisfactory – especially because these items are frequently mentioned and because we have discovered a different solution with respect to the dimension 'strangers' when departing from the procedure of Przeworski and Teune. Therefore, we depart from their procedure again by attempting to exclude items hierarchically, beginning with the most problematic. Unfortunately, we cannot find an identity set within this dimension without disturbing the other two factors.

Our last attempt to find an identity set is born out of despair. We identify each possible item-combination within the remaining items; that is, eleven for the short item set and 120 for the long item set.[4] We define as reliable combinations those

Table 2.3 Factorial structure for pooled countries and points in time (principal components analysis; three factors extracted)

Pool-versions	Western countries 1981 + 1990, item set 1981			All countries 1990, item set 1981			Western countries 1990, item set 1990			All countries 1990, item set 1990		
Factors:	I	II	III	I	II	III	I	II	III	I	II	III
Right-wing extremists		0.91			0.91				0.90			0.91
Left-wing extremists		0.88			0.89				0.86			0.87
Other race	0.79			0.79			0.77			0.77		
Foreigners	0.80			0.79			0.79			0.77		
Jews							0.71			0.75		
Muslims							0.73			0.72		
Large families	0.63			0.72			*0.58*			0.64		
Criminals			0.69			0.75		0.63			0.65	
Drinkers			0.73			0.76		*0.57*			0.63	
Unstable			0.64			0.62		*(0.43)*			*(0.48)*	
Drug addicts								0.75			0.76	
Homosexuals								0.65			0.75	
Aids-sick								0.67			0.72	
Eigenvalue	2.60	1.31	1.02	2.74	1.36	1.11	4.17	1.63	1.33	4.32	1.88	1.37
Explained variance (%)	32.5	16.4	12.7	34.3	17.1	13.9	32.1	12.5	10.3	32.5	14.5	10.5
Total of explained variance (%)	61.7			65.3			54.9			57.5		

Note: Factor loadings below 0.60 are printed in italic; values resting on communalities below 0.40 are printed in brackets.

which do not disturb the factors of 'political extremists' and 'strangers', and fulfil the criteria of communalities higher than 0.39 and factor loadings higher than 0.59 for all included items. Our logic is that all items not strongly associated with either 'political extremists' or 'strangers' (but with one another) might come relatively close to what is defined as social deviance in some or all countries. With these criteria, at least one two-item solution is obtained in each country. In most countries, however, many different possible solutions exist (up to forty-three different versions in one country, data not shown). Comparing these solutions still reveals no identity set for 1981. On the basis of the longer item set in 1990, however, we reach an astonishing three different identity sets, namely 'criminals and drinkers', 'drinkers and drug addicts', and 'homosexuals and Aids-sick'. Though the first two identity sets partly overlap, they cannot be integrated into a three-item solution in several countries. Table 2.4 does not show the details of the factorial structures of the selected variants for all indices, but it summarises the item combinations.[5]

As Table 2.4 shows, the identity set for 'political extremists' covers 'right-wing extremists' and 'left-wing extremists'. The identity set for 'strangers' consists in 1981 of the items 'other race' and 'foreigners', and in 1990 (as an addition for the longitudinal comparison) the item 'Muslims'. For the dimension 'social deviance', there is no identity set in 1981 but three different identity sets in 1990.

Country-specific additions are possible for the dimension 'strangers', but we restrict ourselves to the time-specific identity sets because the addition of 'Jews' and/or 'large families' shows no substantively better measure of this factor (Eigenvalues and explained variances are no higher than without these items). With respect to the three identity sets on 'social deviants', we also decide against country-specific additions because of massive overlapping.

Theoretically, intolerance towards socially deviant persons might more plausibly be represented by quite different objects in different cultures, because – as said before – the definition of social deviance seems like the opposite of social tolerance standards. Therefore, we construct additional country-specific indices for this dimension.[6] Technically this means taking pro unit of analysis all items which fulfil the criteria of a clear third factor. Because more than one solution is possible in most cases, we select the variant with the highest Eigenvalue for the factor 'social deviance' (without pushing the Eigenvalues of the two other factors below 1.00).

Indices of tolerance

The mean-indices (see Table 2.5) for 'political extremists' reveal an enormous range of differences within Western countries: Denmark shows almost no rejection and West Germany shows a rejection by about half the population. In longitudinal perspective a small rise of disapproval appears in most Western countries, except in Italy. Only Belgium, France, the Netherlands, and West Germany show a substantial increase of rejection. The Netherlands and West Germany are countries with a relatively high level of disapproval of 'political extremists' in 1981, whereas France and Belgium belong to those with a low level of rejection in the

Table 2.4 Structuring of the dimensions 'political extremists', 'strangers', and 'social deviants' (summary of principal components analysis for pooled and country-specific data sets)

	Items
Identity sets	
Dimension 'political extremists'	
All countries 1981 + 1990, item set 1981	Right-wing extremists + Left-wing extremists
All countries 1990, item set 1990	Right-wing extremists + Left-wing extremists
Dimension 'strangers'	
All countries 1981 + 1990, item set 1981	Other race + Foreigners
All countries 1990, item set 1990	Other race + Foreigners + Muslims
Dimension 'social deviants'	
All countries 1981 + 1990, item set 1981	None
All countries 1990, item set 1990	1 Criminals + Drinkers
	2 Drinkers + Drug addicts
	3 Homosexuals + Aids-sick

Country-specific structure of dimension 'social deviants'	1981	1990
Norway	Criminals + Drinkers	Crim. + Drug addicts + Homo. + Aids
Sweden	Criminals + Drinkers	Crim. + Drinkers + Homo. + Aids
Iceland	Criminals + Drinkers	Crim. + Drinkers + Unstable
Ireland	Criminals + Drinkers + Unstable	Drug addicts + Homo. + Aids
Northern Ireland	Criminals + Drinkers + Unstable	Crim. + Drug addicts + Homo. + Aids
Great Britain	Criminals + Drinkers + Unstable	Crim. + Drinkers + Homo. + Aids
Denmark	Drinkers + Unstable	Crim. + Drinkers + Homo.
Belgium	Drinkers + Unstable	Drinkers + Unstable + Drug addicts + Aids
Netherlands	Drinkers + Unstable	Crim. + Drug addicts + Homo. + Aids
West Germany	Lge families + Unstable	Crim. + Drug addicts + Homo. + Aids
France	Drinkers + Unstable	Drug addicts + Homo. + Aids

Table 2.4 continued

Country-specific structure of dimension 'social deviants'	1981	1990
Italy	Drinkers + Unstable	Crim. + Drinkers + Drug addicts + Homo.
Spain	Criminals + Drinkers + Unstable	Crim. + Drinkers + Drug addicts + Homo. + Aids
East Germany		Drug addicts + Homo. + Aids
Hungary		Crim. + Drinkers + Homo. + Aids
Czechoslovakia		Drinkers + Drug addicts + Homo. + Aids
Slovenia		Crim. + Drug addicts + Homo. + Aids
Romania		Drinkers + Drug addicts + Homo. + Aids
Bulgaria		Crim. + Drinkers + Unstable + Aids
Belarus		Drinkers + Drug addicts + Homo. + Aids
Russia		Drug addicts + Homo. + Aids
Moskov		Crim. + Drinkers + Drug addicts + Aids

Table 2.5 Indices of tolerance (means)

Year/country	Political extremists	Strangers		Social deviance			Country and time-specific structure
	ID-set: Right-wing extremists + Left-wing extremists	ID-set item set 1981: other race + foreigners	ID-set 1990: item set 1990: other race + foreigners + Muslims	ID-set 1990: variant A: criminals + drinkers	ID-set 1990: variant B: drinkers + drug addicts	ID-set 1990: variant C: homosexuals + aids-sick	
1981							
Norway	0.18	0.09					0.33
Sweden	0.19	0.05					0.35
Iceland	0.20	0.03					0.32
Ireland	0.19	0.06					0.33
North. Ireland	0.26	0.09					0.36
Great Britain	0.24	0.11					0.38
Denmark	0.05	0.07					0.19
Belgium	0.18	0.13					0.27
Netherlands	0.35	0.12					0.34
West Germany	0.46	0.15					0.18
France	0.11	0.05					0.26
Italy	0.37	0.05					0.36
Spain	0.24	0.05					0.31
1990							
Norway	0.21	0.14	0.16	0.34	0.44	0.22	0.41
Sweden	0.27	0.08	0.11	0.40	0.55	0.18	0.29
Iceland	0.29	0.08	0.09	0.43	0.67	0.19	0.39
Ireland	0.25	0.06	0.08	0.43	0.49	0.34	0.44
North. Ireland	0.32	0.07	0.10	0.44	0.51	0.38	0.45
Great Britain	0.30	0.09	0.12	0.45	0.56	0.29	0.37
Denmark	0.06	0.09	0.11	0.31	0.44	0.10	0.24
Belgium	0.37	0.19	0.21	0.40	0.51	0.24	0.32

Table 2.5 continued

Year / country	Political extremists ID-set: Right-wing extremists + Left-wing extremists	Strangers ID-set item set 1981: other race + foreigners	Strangers ID-set 1990: item set 1990: other race + foreigners + Muslims	Social deviance ID-set 1990: variant A: criminals + drinkers	Social deviance ID-set 1990: variant B: drinkers + drug addicts	Social deviance ID-set 1990: variant C: homosexuals + aids-sick	Country and time-specific structure
Netherlands	0.49	0.08	0.10	0.44	0.66	0.13	0.32
West Germany	0.56	0.13	0.15	0.46	0.62	0.31	0.37
France	0.28	0.11	0.13	0.35	0.47	0.20	0.28
Italy	0.31	0.13	0.13	0.50	0.55	0.40	0.49
Spain	0.26	0.09	0.10	0.38	0.48	0.32	0.39
1990							
East Germany	0.64	0.15	0.17	0.53	0.65	0.27	0.38
Hungary	0.21	0.23	0.21	0.79	0.83	0.71	0.75
Czechoslovakia	0.37	0.33	0.38	0.73	0.77	0.61	0.69
Slovenia	0.32	0.40	0.39	0.41	0.46	0.42	0.42
Romania	0.44	0.29	0.31	0.73	0.78	0.71	0.74
Bulgaria	0.67	0.37	0.38	0.71	0.71	0.65	0.65
Belarus	0.41	0.17	0.19	0.77	0.82	0.76	0.79
Russia	0.41	0.11	0.13	0.72	0.84	0.74	0.78
Moscov	0.25	0.12	0.13	0.71	0.82	0.64	0.70

Note: Entries are mean scores of an additive index (for each item: 0 = tolerance and 1 = intolerance).

early 1980s. Perhaps historical experiences with political extremism are responsible for the different levels and context-effects for current developments. In West Germany, for example, both factors emerge when we think of Nazi history, left-wing terrorism during the 1970s, or the flickering right-wing extremism during German reunification. Eastern countries (except Hungary and Moscov) show a rather high rejection of 'political extremists' and clear differences as well with East Germany and Bulgaria at the top of rejection.

Intolerance towards 'strangers' measured on the basis of the identity set is rather low in Western countries in the 1980s, and shows only very small changes in 1990. A clearly higher level of rejection is found in Eastern countries. The addition of the item 'Muslims' leads in most countries to slightly stronger intolerance on this dimension. However, differences in the variants are so minimal as to carry no substantial change of content.

Comparing the three different identity sets of 'social deviants' in 1990 reveals substantial differences. Variant B 'drinkers and drug addicts' in all countries represents the least wanted, followed by variant A 'criminals and drinkers'. Variant C 'homosexuals and Aids-sick' clearly shows lower levels of rejection in Western countries. In most Eastern countries (except East Germany), these two latter variants experience rather close levels of intolerance. Within the variants, the range of differences between the countries is large but does not always reveal one country as most or least tolerant in all variants. Thus, Denmark is the most tolerant in all identity-set variants. The least tolerant country, however, differs between variants. Country-specific indices for 'social deviants' again show a higher level of intolerance in Eastern than in Western countries, but they again rank the countries differently compared to the identity sets.

For most countries, the three dimensions of tolerance are clearly rank ordered. The lowest intolerance is directed towards 'strangers', while the greatest is directed towards 'social deviance', especially towards 'drinkers and drug addicts'. It is also generally directed towards 'criminals and drinkers' and the country-specific representations of social deviance. Only in a few cases do 'political extremists' experience more rejection. The subdimension 'homosexuals and Aids-sick' experiences generally much less rejection.

In sum, the identity set dimension of 'political extremists' seems to fulfil the criteria of comparability and the 1990 addition within 'strangers' makes little difference. With respect to the dimension 'social deviance', we come to very different conclusions, depending on which identity set we use respectively if we use the country-specific indices.

We cannot decide on this basis which of the variants, if any, is most appropriate. Before we approach this question with external variables, we must look at the relationships between the indices to see whether we are dealing with different dimensions of the same theoretical construct. If we find zero or negative correlations between the indices of our dimensions, we will have strong evidence that we are dealing with different constructs or at least with different understandings of tolerance in general.

None of the correlations computed is negative and only very few are insignificant.

Links between 'political extremist' and 'strangers' as well as 'social deviance' are almost exclusively positive and weak-to-modest in strength. (Only in Iceland in 1981 is the correlation with 'social deviance' rather low.) In most cases the correlations of 'political extremists' are strongest for the country-specific representation of 'social deviance'. This might suggest the greatest validity of the country-specific version of 'social deviants'. Between 'strangers' and 'social deviants' in 1981 and in Western countries in 1990, we find exclusively moderate positive correlations. But some of the Eastern countries raise serious problems: in Belarus we see exclusively negative correlations between 'strangers' and 'social deviants'. In Bulgaria and Slovenia we find strong positive as well as strong negative and insignificant correlations between the two dimensions. In Slovenia, the different relationships vary with the different variants of 'social deviants'. This suggests two possible interpretations: a substantive interpretation (that tolerance towards 'strangers' and towards 'social deviants' tend to exclude one another in these countries) or a methodological interpretation (that we are not dealing with tolerance/intolerance in one of the dimensions but with something else).

Finally, the computations show clear differences between Western and Eastern countries. Western countries show the strongest correlation between 'strangers' and 'social deviants', whereas most Eastern countries show the strongest correlation between 'strangers' and 'political extremists'. Substantively, this hints at connotations between foreigners and deviant behaviour in the mind of respondents in the West – which points to cultural conflicts – and to a more independent position of 'political extremists'. In Eastern countries 'political extremists' are more associated with 'strangers'. This might be a consequence of transition processes in which ethnic conflicts are often transformed into political conflicts.

External consistency

In this section we test the indices of tolerance by external validation on the individual level. The assumption is that tolerance should be associated in all countries with similar characteristics of the respondents, namely attributes which can be assumed as another representation, associate, or determinant of tolerance. However, no definite result of the test is guaranteed. If no differences or country-specific differences between tolerance and external variables occur, we must ask whether insufficient cross-national comparability of tolerance or of the external variable is responsible for the outcome or whether some misspecified, culture-bound hypothesis is responsible.

Having these problems in mind, we look first at relationships between the tolerance indices and the attitudinal variables which are theoretically connected with tolerance in general. Second, we test links between the single tolerance dimensions and the attitudes which theoretically should be associated with the specific dimension. Finally, we ask whether some socio-demographic characteristics are connected systematically to the indices of tolerance.[7]

General associates of tolerance

'Good/Evil': Individuals who think that there are clear guidelines in life which apply to everyone at all times should be less tolerant than individuals who think that good and evil might depend on the circumstances. Thinking in 'black-and-white' categories should foster intolerance, while thinking in 'grey' categories should allow for more flexibility.

'Tolerance as an aim of education': Individuals who mention tolerance as an important aim of education should themselves be more tolerant than those who do not mention it.

'Social trust': Individuals who think that most people can be trusted should be more tolerant than those who think otherwise. The latter opinion articulates a generally suspicious, negative outlook towards others.

'Self-esteem': Individuals with high self-esteem should be more open to and more tolerant of the differences of others than individuals with low or negative self-esteem. According to social-psychology, individuals with low self-esteem reject human differences as a means of self-defence.

A straightforward test of these assumptions is rather disappointing (see Table 2.6). Generally low and insignificant correlations emerge among all external variables. In some cases, the same external variable shows differing relationships per country with the three dimensions of tolerance and, in a few cases, even to the different versions of the same tolerance dimension. The variable good/evil shows a few significant positive correlations and no negative correlations. Tolerance as an aim of education shows mostly positive correlations if any at all. Social trust shows the most positive correlations, especially with respect to 'strangers', 'social deviants/variant C', and the country-specific versions. In Northern Ireland, however, a negative correlation emerges with 'political extremists'. Self-esteem is more often negatively than positively correlated with tolerance towards each of the dimensions.

These results create more questions than they answer. In most cases our hypotheses are not strongly rejected – except for self-assertion – but in only a few cases they are strongly supported and these cases apply mostly to 'strangers' and 'social deviants', not to 'political extremists'. This could mean that tolerance attitudes towards 'political extremists' underlie characteristics different from those of other tolerance dimensions. Moreover, the weak correlations reveal that our assumptions and/or variables are not good enough for external validation. Finally, we observe that positive correlations are more frequent in the West than in the East. If we compare single countries, weak correlations and accidental distributions of positive correlations dominate the picture except in West Germany, where nearly all of our hypotheses are strongly supported. Our hypotheses on the relationships between tolerance and associated attitudes appear caught in our own cultural trap!

Associates of tolerance towards 'political extremists'

'Own ideological position': People who place themselves on a moderate position in the political left–right continuum should oppose 'political extremists' more than

Table 2.6 Relationships between dimensions of tolerance and other attitudes (Pearson's r)

	NOR	SWE	ICE	IRE	N. IRE	GB	DEN	BEL	NL	W. GER	FRA
1981											
Political extremism ID set and											
Good/evil (1 = circumstances, 2 = guidelines)	0.05	0.01	0.00	0.00	0.03	0.07	0.04	−0.01	0.01	0.08	0.02
Tolerance aim of education (0 = mentioned, 1 = not)	0.02	0.04	−0.02	−0.01	0.00	−0.04	0.00	−0.09	−0.05	−0.00	−0.06
Social trust (0 = trusted, 1 = careful)	0.00	0.00	−0.00	0.00	−0.14*	−0.03	0.04	0.04	−0.02	0.06	0.03
Strangers ID set and											
Good/evil	0.06	−0.01	0.01	0.09	0.07	0.11*	−0.03	0.10	0.05	0.16*	0.05
Tolerance as aim of education	0.09	0.09	0.01	0.07	0.19*	0.06	0.01	0.04	0.12*	0.17*	0.01
Social trust	0.14*	0.10	0.03	0.03	0.01	0.02	0.15*	0.07	0.14*	0.13*	0.14*
Soc. dev. C. spec. structure and											
Good/evil	0.06	−0.00	−0.04	0.12*	0.06	0.06	0.01	0.02	0.02	0.13*	0.06
Tolerance as aim of education	0.11*	0.11*	−0.01	−0.01	0.00	0.04	0.03	−0.12*	0.00	0.16*	−0.09
Social trust	0.15*	0.07	0.04	0.06	0.11*	0.09	0.10*	0.08	0.01	0.11*	0.03
1990											
Political extremism ID set and											
Good/evil (1 = circumstances, 2 = guidelines)	0.02	0.08	0.01	0.09*	0.13	0.07	−0.01	−0.01	0.06	0.06	0.00
Tolerance aim of education (0 = mentioned, 1 = not)	−0.02	−0.00	0.08	−0.06	−0.02	−0.04	−0.01	−0.04	0.00	−0.09*	−0.07
Social trust (0 = trusted, 1 = careful)	0.04	0.00	0.14*	0.05	−0.02	−0.02	0.04	0.05	−0.03	−0.01	−0.03
Self-assertion (0 = positive thru 8 = not pos.)	−0.10*	−0.01	0.13*	−0.06	0.00	0.15*	−0.07	−0.05	−0.11*	−0.09*	−0.11*

continued

Table 2.6 continued

	NOR	SWE	ICE	IRE	N. IRE	GB	DEN	BEL	NL	W. GER	FRA
Strangers ID set and											
Good/evil	0.04	0.03	0.08	0.07	0.09	0.05	0.06	0.08*	0.16*	0.13*	0.07
Tolerance as aim of education	0.12*	0.03	0.10	0.09	0.04	0.00	0.02	0.09*	0.08	0.18*	0.12*
Social trust	0.13*	0.13*	0.10	0.14*	0.15*	0.08	0.19*	0.11*	0.19*	0.17	0.15*
Self-assertion	−0.03	−0.01	−0.17*	0.04	−0.07	−0.04	0.00	−0.03	0.01	0.03	−0.10
Social deviance ID set A											
(criminals and drinkers) and											
Good/evil	0.07	0.04	0.02	0.12*	0.15	0.18*	0.06	0.07	0.13*	0.13*	0.10
Tolerance aim of education	0.08	0.03	0.00	−0.02	0.02	−0.00	0.00	−0.02	0.04	0.07	0.04
Social trust	0.18*	0.11	0.19*	0.07	0.11	−0.00	0.07	0.07*	0.12*	0.13*	0.08
Self-assertion	−0.01	−0.07	−0.10	−0.01	0.01	−0.07	−0.12*	−0.04	−0.04	0.03	−0.01
Social deviance ID set B											
(drinkers and drug addicts) and											
Good/evil	0.05	0.01	−0.01	0.07	0.17	0.09*	0.03	0.03	0.09	0.13*	0.03
Tolerance as aim of education	0.07	0.06	−0.01	−0.00	−0.01	−0.04	−0.02	−0.04	−0.02	0.04	0.08
Social trust	0.13*	0.06	0.18*	0.10	0.10	0.02	0.08	0.08*	0.07	0.12*	0.10
Self-assertion	−0.04	−0.07	−0.06	0.04	0.05	−0.04	−0.15*	−0.05	−0.04	0.01	−0.03
Social deviance ID set C											
(homosexuals and aids-sick) and											
Good/evil	0.13*	0.11*	0.13*	0.10*	0.12	0.11*	0.07	0.11*	0.23*	0.17*	0.13*
Tolerance as aim of education	0.12*	0.05	0.05	0.07	0.05	0.05	0.06	0.03	0.10	0.18*	0.11*
Social trust	0.19*	0.12*	0.17*	0.10	0.20*	0.08	0.11*	0.11*	0.17*	0.08	0.18*
Self-assertion	−0.04	−0.04	−0.08	0.04	0.03	−0.03	−0.02	−0.02	0.00	0.03	−0.02
Soc. dev. C. spec. structure and											
Good/evil	0.06	0.08	0.04	0.09	0.17	0.17*	0.07	0.07	0.19*	0.18*	0.11*
Tolerance as aim of education	0.08	0.05	0.01	0.04	0.05	0.03	0.02	0.02	0.06	0.18*	0.13*
Social trust	0.17*	0.14*	0.21*	0.13*	0.18*	0.05	0.09	0.13*	0.17*	0.14*	0.19*
Self-assertion	−0.03	−0.07	−0.12*	0.06	0.03	−0.07	−0.10	−0.03	−0.03	0.04	−0.03

Table 2.6 continued

	ITA	SPAIN	EGER	HUN	CZE	SLO	ROM	BUL	BEL	RUS	MOS
1981											
Political extremism ID set and											
Good/evil (1 = circumstances, 2 = guidelines)	0.10*	0.06									
Tolerance aim of education (0 = mentioned, 1 = not)	0.05	−0.03									
Social trust (0 = trusted, 1 = careful)	0.05	0.04									
Strangers ID set and											
Good/evil	0.06	0.05									
Tolerance as aim of education	0.09	0.04									
Social trust	0.05	0.04									
Soc. dev. C. spec. structure and											
Good/evil	0.03	0.14*									
Tolerance as aim of education	0.12*	0.02									
Social trust	0.11*	0.05									
1990											
Political extremism ID set and											
Good/evil (1 = circumstances, 2 = guidelines)	0.06	−0.01	0.07	−0.02	—	−0.02	−0.03	−0.08	0.05	0.03	0.02
Tolerance aim of education (0 = mentioned, 1 = not)	0.01	−0.05	−0.04	−0.01	−0.05	0.01	0.01	−0.01	0.01	−0.01	0.01
Social trust (0 = trusted, 1 = careful)	0.06	−0.01	−0.02	0.04	0.00	−0.08	−0.02	−0.01	0.06	0.05	0.08
Self-assertion (0 = positive thru 8 = not pos.)	−0.08*	−0.09*	−0.06	−0.06	−0.04	0.01	0.11*	−0.06	−0.09	−0.04	−0.09
Strangers ID set and											
Good/evil	0.04	0.04	0.04	0.00	—	0.03	−0.01	0.02	0.02	−0.01	−0.02

continued

Table 2.6 continued

	ITA	SPAIN	EGER	HUN	CZE	SLO	ROM	BUL	BEL	RUS	MOS
Tolerance as aim of education	0.09*	-0.03	0.14*	0.02	0.06	0.01	0.02	-0.00	0.02	0.04	0.06
Social trust	0.13*	0.07*	0.12*	0.15*	0.09	0.01	0.06*	0.05	0.10	0.05	0.10
Self-assertion	-0.06	-0.06*	-0.07	-0.08	-0.03	0.02	-0.09*	-0.08	-0.01	-0.03	-0.05
Social deviance ID set A (criminals and drinkers) and											
Good/evil	0.03	0.06*	0.04	-0.04	—	-0.02	0.02	-0.03	0.00	0.03	0.04
Tolerance aim of education	0.03	-0.01	0.07	-0.02	0.03	-0.05	0.03	-0.05	-0.05	-0.02	-0.07
Social trust	0.19*	0.07*	0.08	0.14*	0.04	-0.03	0.00	0.03	0.03	0.07	0.09
Self-assertion	-0.04	-0.06*	-0.08	-0.05	-0.06	0.04	-0.05	-0.04	0.02	0.00	-0.09
Social deviance ID set B (drinkers and drug addicts) and											
Good/evil	0.03	0.07*	0.04	-0.03	—	-0.05	0.03	-0.01	-0.00	-0.02	0.01
Tolerance aim of education	0.03	-0.01	0.05	-0.04	-0.02	-0.07	-0.01	-0.06	-0.07	-0.03	-0.11*
Social trust	0.17*	0.05	0.10	0.10	0.02	-0.05	0.04	0.04	0.04	0.07	0.07
Self-assertion	-0.05	-0.04	-0.09	-0.10	-0.09	0.05	-0.09	-0.06	0.02	-0.01	-0.09
Social deviance ID set C (homosexuals and aids-sick) and											
Good/evil	0.07	0.11*	0.09	-0.01	—	-0.05	0.06	-0.02	0.04	-0.02	-0.01
Tolerance aim of education	0.08*	0.02	0.23*	0.02	0.01	-0.06	-0.06	-0.05	-0.03	0.05	0.00
Social trust	0.20*	0.09*	0.15*	0.14*	0.08	-0.02	0.06*	0.07	0.04	0.06	0.14*
Self-assertion	-0.08*	-0.02	-0.08	-0.11*	-0.07	0.04	-0.11*	-0.03	-0.01	0.00	-0.06
Soc. dev. C. spec. structure and											
Good/evil	0.06	0.10*	0.09	-0.03	—	-0.05	0.05	-0.03	0.02	-0.01	0.01
Tolerance as aim of education	0.06	0.01	0.21*	0.00	0.00	-0.06	-0.04	-0.08	-0.05	0.03	-0.05
Social trust	0.22*	0.09	0.16*	0.18*	0.06*	-0.03	0.06	0.08	0.05	0.05	0.11*
Self-assertion	-0.06	-0.04	-0.09	-0.10*	-0.09*	0.04	0.11*	-0.05	0.01	-0.00	-0.10

Note: * = significant on level 0.001; — indicates missing indices or missing external variables.

those who place themselves at either end of the spectrum. An alternative hypothesis is that people who position themselves close to the left end of the political spectrum have the weakest reservations against 'left-wing extremists' and the strongest against 'right-wing extremists' (and vice versa). This case, however, hints at a strong component of sympathy/antipathy underlying tolerance.

Because of these differing hypotheses, we prefer means over correlations for a direct test. Our first hypothesis on the relation between tolerance towards 'political extremists' and ideological self-placement is rejected in most cases (see Table 2.7). Political moderates do not show the least tolerance. Instead, in Western countries those on the right end of the political spectrum, and in Eastern countries those on the left pole show the least tolerance.

The second hypothesis on the rejection of one's political opposite(s) finds support in most cases. Intolerance towards 'right-wing extremists' generally increases as respondents move to the left and vice versa. However, a few deviant cases of reverse relationships also appear: i.e. an increasing intolerance towards 'right-wing extremists' as respondents move to the right (Northern Ireland 1981, Iceland, Great Britain, Slovenia each 1990) and an increasing intolerance towards 'left-wing extremists' as respondents move to the left (Bulgaria). Since attitudes in these countries towards extremists on the 'other side' follow the usual pattern, a mistake of the left–right self-placement scale cannot account for this result. The mystery remains unexplained.

In sum, we conclude that the external tests hint at a relatively wide cross-national comparability on the dimension 'political extremists', but they also suggest a strong underlying component of sympathy/antipathy rather than neutral tolerance.

Associates of tolerance towards 'strangers'

'Respect for authority', 'obedience as an aim of education', and 'respect for parents': According to the psychology of the authoritarian personality (cf. Adorno *et al.* 1950), individuals who prefer greater respect for authority in society, who see obedience as an important aim of education, and who think parents should be respected regardless of their faults should exhibit more intolerance towards strangers than individuals who deny these opinions.

'National pride' and 'supranational identification': People with extreme pride in their nation and/or without any supranational identification are often seen as ethnocentric. Therefore, they should be more intolerant towards strangers than people with moderate national pride and/or with a supranational identification. However, prior research shows that national pride does not always carry ethnocentric elements (Westle 1996 and 1997). Moreover, national pride and supranational identification do not always exclude each other, but even can promote each other (Duchesne and Frognier 1995).

'Jobs to nationality': Because intolerance towards strangers is often fostered by fears of rivalry, the opinion that in time of need jobs should be given to one's own countrymen rather than to foreigners should be linked clearly with intolerance

Table 2.7 Relationships between tolerance towards 'political extremists' and ideological self-placement (means)

	NOR	SWE	ICE	IRE	N. IRE	GB	DEN	BEL	NL	W. GER	FRA	ITA	SPAIN	E. GER	HUN	CZE	SLO	ROM	BUL	BEL	RUSS	MOS
1981																						
Political extremism ID set and																						
Ideological self-placement																						
Left (1–3)	0.19	0.19	0.15	0.18	0.13	0.23	0.05	0.16	0.27	0.30	0.14	0.33	0.23									
Middle (4–7)	0.19	0.16	0.21	0.21	0.25	0.24	0.04	0.20	0.37	0.51	0.10	0.42	0.25									
Right (8–10)	0.20	0.29	0.22	0.23	0.39	0.33	0.09	0.23	0.46	0.49	0.17	0.40	0.42									
Right-wing extremists and																						
Ideological self-placement																						
Left (1–3)	0.29	0.22	0.21	0.23	0.16	0.34	0.09	0.19	0.35	0.47	0.23	0.44	0.30									
Middle (4–7)	0.19	0.15	0.20	0.19	0.24	0.22	0.03	0.18	0.35	0.48	0.11	0.42	0.24									
Right (8–10)	0.15	0.18	0.17	0.17	0.33	0.22	0.01	0.17	0.36	0.36	0.15	0.26	0.29									
Left-wing extremists and																						
Ideological self-placement																						
Left (1–3)	0.08	0.15	0.09	0.14	0.11	0.11	0.01	0.13	0.19	0.14	0.06	0.21	0.15									
Middle (4–7)	0.18	0.17	0.23	0.22	0.27	0.26	0.05	0.22	0.40	0.54	0.10	0.41	0.27									
Right (8–10)	0.25	0.40	0.28	0.30	0.44	0.43	0.17	0.29	0.56	0.63	0.19	0.54	0.54									
1990																						
Political extremism ID set and																						
Ideological self-placement																						
Left (1–3)	0.19	0.21	0.18	0.23	0.27	0.19	0.10	0.33	0.41	0.52	0.29	0.26	0.26	0.61	0.25	0.36	0.29	0.45	0.70	0.40	0.48	0.24
Middle (4–7)	0.20	0.25	0.30	0.27	0.28	0.31	0.06	0.39	0.52	0.58	0.31	0.33	0.28	0.66	0.22	0.38	0.35	0.44	0.68	0.42	0.42	0.26
Right (8–10)	0.24	0.36	0.36	0.22	0.49	0.40	0.08	0.39	0.58	0.63	0.30	0.35	0.30	0.59	0.20	0.37	0.34	0.49	0.64	0.46	0.46	0.27
Right-wing extremists and																						
Ideological self-placement																						
Left (1–3)	0.27	0.34	0.23	0.26	0.40	0.24	0.15	0.43	0.54	0.73	0.44	0.36	0.33	0.81	0.28	0.41	0.32	0.48	0.67	0.43	0.50	0.27
Middle (4–7)	0.22	0.28	0.29	0.23	0.25	0.28	0.07	0.41	0.54	0.62	0.35	0.35	0.29	0.71	0.22	0.38	0.36	0.43	0.67	0.41	0.42	0.26
Right (8–10)	0.22	0.30	0.32	0.16	0.43	0.29	0.05	0.35	0.53	0.56	0.22	0.27	0.26	0.50	0.15	0.29	0.38	0.39	0.62	0.45	0.45	0.29

Table 2.7 continued

	NOR	SWE	ICE	IRE	N. IRE	GB	DEN	BEL	NL	W. GER	FRA	ITA	SPAIN	E. GER	HUN	CZE	SLO	ROM	BUL	BEL	RUSS	MOS
Left-wing extremists and																						
Ideological self-placement																						
Left (1–3)	0.12	0.09	0.14	0.20	0.13	0.13	0.05	0.23	0.29	0.31	0.14	0.16	0.20	0.40	0.22	0.31	0.26	0.42	0.72	0.37	0.46	0.21
Middle (4–7)	0.18	0.22	0.31	0.30	0.32	0.35	0.05	0.38	0.50	0.53	0.28	0.32	0.27	0.61	0.23	0.38	0.34	0.45	0.69	0.42	0.43	0.26
Right (8–10)	0.27	0.42	0.39	0.27	0.55	0.51	0.11	0.43	0.63	0.70	0.39	0.44	0.33	0.69	0.25	0.44	0.30	0.60	0.67	0.48	0.47	0.25

towards 'strangers'. This should be the case regardless of the cultural context, although it could be affected by country-specific kinds of unemployment.

The analyses (see Table 2.8) do not contradict our hypotheses but show only weak correlations. Respect for parents clearly is the poorest indicator among those linking authoritarian attitudes and intolerance towards 'strangers'. This seems to say less about the validity of the tolerance indices, but rather it hints at a culturally different meaning of the indicator respect for parents. 'Respect for authority' and 'obedience as an aim of education' appear linked with intolerance towards 'strangers' in most Western countries and in East Germany, but not in all Eastern countries. This suggests that the psychological view is culture bound.

As expected, a similar problem applies to national pride. In some countries we find a strong link with intolerance towards 'strangers', in others none. The strongest correlations exist in both parts of Germany, which suggests that national pride, not tolerance, is responsible for country-specific relationships.

Supranational identification appears somewhat more regular despite rather weak correlations in the West in 1981, but it seems to lose its link with attitudes towards 'strangers' in some countries in 1990. It appears irrelevant in most Eastern countries. Perhaps it is a non-attitude in Eastern countries due to their foregoing isolation.

In contrast to the culture-bound external indicators, the opinion on to whom to give jobs clearly supports the validity of tolerance towards 'strangers'. The few exceptions in the Eastern countries may hint at non-attitudes in the job question because of non-salient rivalry.

On the one hand, these tests present a nice example of the problem of culture-bound hypotheses and/or external test variables which – if we lack information about the quality of the external variables and cannot test them all – may lead to the 'Münchhausen-attempt' to pull oneself out of the swamp by one's own pigtail. On the other hand, the culturally 'clean' indicator on jobs supports the validity of the tolerance dimension 'strangers'.

Associates of tolerance towards 'social deviants'

'Change': People who view changes in life anxiously are likely to be conservative, which also affects tolerance towards 'social deviants' in so far as social deviance is associated with societal change. We assume that this is primarily the case with respect to 'social deviants/variant C' ('homosexuals and Aids-sick') and country-specific representations of 'social deviants' which are also associated with these items. All other available indicators which may be linked with 'social deviants' refer primarily to single items of the deviance dimension.

'Fight criminality': Individuals who consider fighting against criminality an important aim of politics (in contrast to other aims) are more likely to be prejudiced or fearful towards people with a criminal record. Obviously, both attitudes might be affected heavily by the context of living. Indirectly, the option for fighting against criminality might also be linked to other objects of 'social deviants', as these are associated with illegal behaviour. The cultural context is

Table 2.8 Relationships between tolerance towards 'strangers' and other attitudes (Pearson's r)

	NOR	SWE	ICE	IRE	N. IRE	GB	DEN	BEL	NL	W. GER	FRA	ITA	SPAIN	E. GER	HUN	CZE	SLO	ROM	BUL	BEL	RUSS	MOS
1981																						
Strangers ID set and																						
Respect authority (1 = bad, 2 = neither, 3 = good)	0.10*	0.06	0.03	0.03	0.01	0.08	0.02	0.08	0.05	0.18*	0.05	0.08	0.02									
Respect parents (0 = earn it, 1 = always)	-0.01	0.00	0.07	0.07	-0.00	0.05	-0.03	0.05	-0.04	0.11*	0.00	0.07	0.02									
National pride (0 = not at all, 3 = very much)	0.16*	0.04	0.01	0.01	0.04	0.10	0.06	-0.01	0.03	0.18*	0.06	0.06	0.04									
Supranational identification (0 = yes, 1 = no)	0.05*	0.05*	0.05*	0.05*	0.05*	0.08*	0.05*	0.08*	0.05*	0.08*	0.08*	0.05*	0.05*									
1990																						
Strangers ID set and																						
Respect authority (1 = bad, 2 = neither, 3 = good)	0.11*	0.13*	0.03	-0.02	0.08	0.06	0.08	0.09*	0.15*	0.19*	0.16*	0.07	0.03	0.09*	0.05	0.01	-0.01	—	0.02	-0.05	-0.04	-0.03
Obedience = aim of education (0 = not, 1 = mentioned)	0.15*	0.11*	0.04	0.02	0.07	0.02	0.14*	0.07*	0.12*	0.16*	-0.05	0.16*	0.02	0.12*	0.04	0.10*	-0.01	-0.05	0.06	0.08	0.04	0.06
Respect parents (0 = earn it, 1 = always)	0.04	0.01	0.10	0.08	0.04	0.03	0.02	0.03	0.18*	0.12*	0.01	0.01	0.06*	0.03	-0.00	0.03	-0.08	0.06	0.02	-0.00	-0.02	-0.06
Jobs to nationality (1 = disagree, 3 = agree)	0.29*	0.35*	0.10	0.14*	0.27*	0.25*	0.31*	0.22*	0.31*	0.27	0.26*	0.14*	0.05	0.26*	0.12*	0.09*	-0.05	0.16*	0.05	0.03	0.10*	0.09
National pride (0 = not at all, 3 = very much)	0.06	0.08	0.06	-0.01	0.15*	0.09	0.08	0.03	0.11*	0.20*	0.06	0.09*	0.05	0.17*	0.07	0.01	-0.00	0.13*	0.11*	0.01	0.10*	0.02
Supranational identification (0 = yes, 1 = no)	0.08	0.08*	0.07	0.02	0.10	0.06	0.01	0.09*	0.09*	0.15*	0.14*	0.08*	0.04	0.14*	0.03	—	-0.03	0.04	0.12*	0.04	0.06	0.07

Note: * = significant on level 0.001; — indicates missing indices or missing external variables.

assumed to play a role here, since some of the items on 'social deviants' are surely illegal only in some of the countries.

'Sexual freedom': This question about individual sexual freedom might be linked primarily to all items of 'social deviants' associated with sexual behaviour. However, it also might represent one facet of generalised liberalism and thereby radiate upon other aspects of tolerance towards 'social deviants' as well.[8]

'Marijuana': Taking the drug marijuana is the closest indicator to 'drug addicts'. Again, problems of cross-national comparability appear. In some societies marijuana is illegal, in others not. So drug addiction as a problem differs between countries.

'Married have affair', 'homosexuality', and 'prostitution': These more concrete items on sexual behaviour shall be used for a comparison with the general question on sexual freedom and for evaluating subdimension C. The behaviours are universal, with culturally different legitimacy. Individuals who consider these acts indefensible should also be less tolerant of homosexuals than individuals with a less rigid sexual code. This link might also apply towards Aids-sick and drug addicts, depending on the inner link between the two. Again, culture is assumed to play an important role, because information about Aids and risk-groups varies widely between societies.[9]

In the case of 'social deviants', we are confronted with culture-specific differences. Therefore, we look not only at the rather improbable similarity of structures in links between dimensions and external variables (see Table 2.9), but we also look for a systematic pattern between the effects of a specific external variable on the single items of 'social deviants' which show country-specific structures.

The hypothesis of more tolerance among individuals unafraid of change is supported in around half of the Western but only in a few of the Eastern countries. Presumably this variable has other connotations in Eastern countries due to political transformations. Interestingly, if this external variable works at all in a specific country, it works mostly with respect to more than one of the variants of 'social deviants'. It usually works best for the country-specific representation and the identity set C (homosexuals and Aids-sick), but not as well with identity sets A and B (criminals and drinkers, drinkers and drug addicts). This hints at the existence of various degrees of modernisation underlying the 'social deviance' subdimensions.

The option 'fight criminality' links clearly in almost all Western countries with identity set A (criminals and drinkers) and links somewhat less well with the other two identity sets and the country-specific index. In all Western democracies, this option shows significant correlations if 'criminals' is included in the tolerance index. However, this is not the case in all Eastern countries. A closer look at the single items shows clear links between the option for fight against criminality and the item 'criminals', as well as in many cases with the items 'drug addicts', 'homosexuals', and 'Aids-sick', but in none of the cases with the items 'unstable' or 'large families'.

As expected, attitudes towards homosexuality and the tolerance-object 'homosexuals' show the highest correlations in almost all countries. Correlations are also

Table 2.9 Relationships between tolerance towards 'social deviants' and other attitudes (Pearson's r)

continued

	NOR	SWE	ICE	IRE	N. IRE	GB	DEN	BEL	NL	W. GER	FRA	ITA	SPAIN	E. GER	HUN	CZE	SLO	ROM	BUL	BEL	RUSS	MOS
	Crim+ Drink	Crim+ Drink	Crim+ Drink	Crim+ Drink+ Unstable	Crim+ Drink+ Unstable	Crim+ Drink+ Unstable	Drink+ Unstable	Drink+ Unstable	Drink+ Unstable	Leg fam + Unstable	Drink+ Unstable	Drink+ Unstable	Crim+ Drink+ Unstable									
1981																						
Country-specific structure and																						
Sexual freedom (1 = pro, 3 = anti)	0.08	0.02	0.11*	0.08	0.13	0.16*	0.03	0.10	0.12*	0.04	0.09	0.08	0.12*									
Marijuana (1 = justified, 3 = not justified)	0.12*	0.07	0.08	0.10*	0.09	0.03	0.08	0.06	0.18*	0.02	0.07	0.10	0.16*									
Married have affair (1 = justified, 3 = not justified)	0.18*	0.12*	0.00	0.04	0.05	0.09	0.09	0.10	0.09	−0.03	0.02	0.06	0.15*									
Homosexuality (1 = justified, 3 = not justified)	0.22*	0.15*	0.13*	0.11*	0.04	0.12*	0.08	0.06	0.10	0.09	0.05	0.14*	0.22*									
Prostitution (1 = justified, 3 = not justified)	0.14*	0.13*	0.10*	0.12*	0.00	0.08	0.08	0.09	0.14*	0.03	0.09	0.12*	0.20*									
Criminals and																						
Sexual freedom	0.10*	−0.01	0.07	0.09	0.06	0.12*	0.03	0.03	0.11*	0.17*	0.10	0.16*	0.14									
Marijuana	0.09	0.07	0.06	0.14*	0.12	0.08	0.12*	0.12*	0.10*	0.11*	0.09	0.18*	0.21*									
Married have affair	0.10	0.11*	−0.04	0.07	0.05	0.10*	0.07	0.10*	0.08	0.13*	0.09	0.18*	0.20*									
Homosexuality	0.16*	0.15*	0.10	0.14*	0.06	0.14*	0.14*	0.11*	0.15*	0.25*	0.16*	0.25*	0.26*									
Prostitution	0.17*	0.13	0.09	0.16*	0.08	0.12*	0.09	0.15*	0.13*	0.23*	0.14*	0.18*	0.22*									
Drinkers and																						
Sexual freedom	0.03	0.03	0.09	0.03	0.12	0.11*	0.05	0.08	0.13*	0.15*	0.11*	0.10*	0.09									
Marijuana	0.10*	0.05	0.06	0.07	0.07	0.08	0.11*	0.06	0.19*	0.12*	0.07	0.09	0.13*									
Married have affair	0.13*	0.09	0.02	0.04	0.09	0.09	0.10*	0.11*	0.13*	0.07	0.02	0.07	0.12*									
Homosexuality	0.15*	0.11	0.10	0.07	0.07	0.09	0.09*	0.06	0.10*	0.02	0.05	0.10*	0.14*									
Prostitution	0.19*	0.09	0.07	0.06	0.05	0.11*	0.11*	0.09	0.15*	0.04	0.10*	0.11*	0.14*									
Unstable and																						
Sexual freedom	0.04	−0.01	−0.02	0.04	0.10	0.11*	−0.03	0.08	0.05	0.01	−0.00	0.02	0.04									
Marijuana	0.04	0.02	0.02	−0.01	−0.00	−0.10*	0.00	0.03	0.09	0.01	0.01	0.07	0.01									
Married have affair	0.04	0.03	0.02	−0.03	−0.03	−0.00	0.02	0.03	−0.01	−0.03	0.01	0.02	0.01									
Homosexuality	0.05	0.07	0.01	0.00	−0.05	0.02	0.02	0.03	.05	0.08	0.02	0.13*	0.08*									

Table 2.9 continued

	NOR	SWE	ICE	IRE	N. IRE	GB	DEN	BEL	NL	W. GER	FRA	ITA	SPAIN	E. GER	HUN	CZE	SLO	ROM	BUL	BEL	RUSS	MOS
Prostitution	0.06	0.02	-0.02	-0.00	-0.12	-0.06	-0.00	-0.05	0.06	0.03	0.03	0.08*	0.07*									
Large families and Sexual freedom	-0.01	-0.04	-0.03	-0.02	0.02	0.06	-0.01	0.01	-0.01	0.07	-0.01	0.01	0.04									
Marijuana	-0.04	-0.04	-0.03	-0.03	0.05	-0.05	-0.04	0.02	-0.02	0.02	-0.09	-0.02	-0.07*									
Married have affair	-0.00	0.03	-0.08	-0.01	0.00	0.02	0.00	0.01	-0.03	-0.01	-0.06	-0.03	-0.03									
Homosexuality	-0.02	0.10	0.04	-0.03	0.08	0.05	0.01	0.02	0.06	0.05	-0.03	0.03	0.01									
Prostitution	0.07	0.09	-0.00	-0.05	-0.05	-0.00	-0.00	0.03	0.02	0.02	-0.06	-0.00	-0.00									
1990																						
ID set A (Criminals + Drinkers)																						
Change (1 = open to change, 10 = not open)	0.05	0.10	0.06	0.11*	0.09	0.08	0.02	0.06*	0.09	0.20*	0.10	0.10*	0.13*	0.07	0.02	0.11*	0.04	0.07	-0.02	0.01	0.08	0.04
Drink and drive (1 = justified, 3 = not justif)	0.05	0.00	0.07	0.13*	0.17	0.03	-0.01	0.10*	0.07	0.16*	0.13*	0.09*	0.04	0.06	0.10	—	-0.03	0.08	0.11*	0.04	0.06	-0.09
Marijuana (1 = justified, 3 = not justified)	0.05	0.02	0.08	0.15*	0.17	0.12*	0.11*	0.09*	0.17*	0.14*	0.11*	0.14*	0.09	0.03	0.04	0.15*	-0.05	0.10*	0.09	0.10	0.06	0.07
Sexual freedom (1 = pro, 3 = anti)	0.01	0.05	0.03	0.12*	0.07	0.13*	0.04	0.11*	0.18*	0.13*	0.10	0.14*	0.06	0.06	0.08	0.13*	-0.01	0.09	0.12*	0.03	0.06	0.06
Married have affair (1 = justified, 3 = not justified)	0.10*	0.04	0.10	0.14*	0.12	0.12*	0.07	0.11*	0.24*	0.16*	0.14*	0.12*	0.10*	0.10*	0.04	0.14*	-0.03	0.06	0.08	0.05	0.06	0.06
Homosexuality (1 = justified, 3 = not justified)	0.17*	0.14*	0.14*	0.22*	0.26*	0.18*	0.09	0.09*	0.18*	0.20*	0.15*	0.12*	0.15*	0.09	0.04	0.13*	-0.05	0.09	0.04	0.07	0.10*	0.06
Prostitution (1 = justified, 3 = not justified)	0.16*	0.08	0.15*	0.13*	0.25*	0.19*	0.18*	0.12*	0.20*	0.20*	0.17*	0.10*	0.14*	0.07	0.06	0.17*	-0.05	0.15*	0.03	0.12*	0.11*	0.13*
ID set B (Drinkers and Drug addicts) and																						
Change	0.02	0.08	0.07	0.07	0.03	0.07	-0.00	0.03	0.04	0.21*	0.15*	0.08*	0.13*	0.09	0.00	0.09*	0.05	0.10	-0.08	-0.00	0.04	0.07
Fight criminality	0.12*	0.14*	0.08	0.07	0.29*	0.12*	0.07	0.08*	0.13*	—	0.16*	0.10*	0.05	—	0.04	0.06	-0.03	0.12*	0.07	-0.05	0.06	0.02
Smoke marijuana	0.03	0.01	0.10	0.14*	0.16	0.11*	0.10	0.12*	0.17*	0.19*	0.15*	0.15*	0.09*	0.09	0.10	0.17*	-0.06	0.14*	0.09	0.14*	0.09*	0.10
Sexual freedom	0.03	0.02	0.08	0.09	0.12	0.13*	-0.01	0.11*	0.14*	0.16*	0.12*	0.13*	0.15*	0.03	0.04	0.11*	-0.02	0.14*	0.08	0.04	0.09*	0.06
Married have affair	0.07	0.00	0.09	0.14*	0.10	0.10*	0.04	0.10*	0.16*	0.16*	0.15*	0.09*	0.09*	0.06	0.04	0.12*	-0.09	0.11*	0.04	0.05	0.07	0.06
Homosexuality	0.15*	0.10	0.11	0.20*	0.24*	0.17*	0.09	0.10*	0.11*	0.20*	0.21*	0.12*	0.13*	0.11	0.09	0.08	-0.05	0.19*	0.08	0.06	0.10*	0.09
Prostitution	0.08*	0.05	11.00*	13.00*	0.25*	0.16*	15.00*	0.09*	0.12*	0.21*	0.21*	0.08*	0.12*	0.05	0.10	0.16*	-0.05	0.20*	0.05	0.11*	0.09*	0.12*

Table 2.9 continued

	NOR	SWE	ICE	IRE	N. IRE	GB	DEN	BEL	NL	W. GER	FRA	ITA	SPAIN	E. GER	HUN	CZE	SLO	ROM	BUL	BEL	RUSS	MOS
ID set C (Homosexuals and Aids–sick) and																						
Change	0.10*	0.17*	0.06	0.09	0.13	0.05	0.08	0.07	0.16*	0.22*	0.18*	0.10*	0.13*	0.08	0.01	0.13*	0.06	0.14*	-0.02	0.02	0.03	0.11*
Fight criminality	0.12*	0.16*	0.13*	0.09	0.15	0.14*	0.09	0.06	0.15*	—	0.15*	0.14*	0.06*	—	0.03	0.17*	-0.06	0.18*	0.07	0.09	0.12*	0.12*
Smoke marijuana	0.08*	0.03	0.12	0.14*	0.21*	0.16*	0.13*	0.07*	0.19*	0.13*	0.13*	0.18*	0.10*	0.06	-0.00	0.10*	-0.03	0.16	0.06	0.13*	0.02	0.04
Sexual freedom	0.00	0.03	0.04	0.14*	0.14	0.15*	0.11*	0.08*	0.17*	0.14*	0.20*	0.18*	0.19*	0.06	0.04	0.07	-0.04	0.21*	0.13*	0.06	0.07	0.00
Married have affair	0.13*	0.09*	0.10	0.12*	0.17	0.09*	0.12*	0.13*	0.19*	0.15*	0.15*	0.20*	0.13*	0.08	0.03	0.19*	-0.06	0.16*	0.11*	0.12*	0.12*	0.05
Homosexuality	0.34*	0.38*	0.40*	0.35*	0.42*	0.40*	0.36*	0.25*	0.48*	0.42*	0.40*	0.31*	0.29*	0.44*	0.09	0.39*	-0.00	0.30*	0.13*	0.15*	0.16*	0.19*
Prostitution	0.15*	0.09	0.16*	0.19*	0.31*	0.22*	0.22*	0.18	0.38*	0.30*	0.24*	0.19*	0.21*	0.19*	0.09	0.24*	0.03	0.28*	0.10	0.19*	0.11*	0.14*
	Crim+ Drink+ Homo+ Drug	Crim+ Drink+ Homo+ Aids	Crim+ Drink+ Unstable Aids	Drug+ Homo+ Aids	Crim+ Drug+ Homo+ Aids	Crim+ Drink+ Homo+ Aids	Crim+ Drink+ Homo	Crim+ Unstable + Aids	Crim+ Drug Homo+ Aids	Crim+ Drug+ Homo+ Aids	Drug+ Homo Aids	Crim+ Drink+ Drug+ Homo	Crim+ Drink+ Drug+ Homo+ Aids	Drug+ Homo+ Aids	Crim+ Drink+ Homo+ Aids	Crim+ Drink+ Homo+ Aids	Crim+ Drug+ Homo+ Aids	Drink+ Drug+ Homo+ Aids	Crim+ Drink+ Unstable + Aids	Drink+ Drug+ Unstable Homo+ Aids	Drug+ Homo+ Aids	Crim+ Drink+ Drug+ Aids
1990																						
Country-specific structure and																						
Change	0.04	0.16*	0.04	0.08	0.12	0.08	0.04	0.09*	0.15*	0.26*	0.21*	0.12*	0.15*	0.10*	0.02	0.13*	0.04	0.13*	-0.01	0.01	0.02	0.08
Fight criminality	0.13*	0.17*	0.16*	0.10	0.23*	0.16*	0.07	0.08*	0.18*	—	0.18*	0.12*	0.06*	—	0.04	0.14*	-0.06	0.17*	0.08	0.08	0.13*	0.06
Smoke marijuana	0.05	0.03	0.04	0.17*	0.24*	0.17*	0.13*	0.11*	0.23*	0.18*	0.17*	0.19*	0.12*	0.09	0.02	0.15*	-0.05	0.17*	0.09	0.14*	0.05	0.07
Sexual freedom	0.03	0.05	0.03	0.13*	0.14	0.13*	0.07	0.09*	0.20*	0.16*	0.20*	0.18*	0.19*	0.05	0.07	0.11*	-0.02	0.20*	0.13*	0.05	0.09*	0.04
Married have affair	0.09	0.07	0.08	0.14*	0.19	0.13*	0.10	0.11*	0.21*	0.17*	0.17*	0.17*	0.14*	0.08	0.05	0.18*	-0.06	0.16*	0.11*	0.10	0.13*	0.07
Homosexuality	0.17*	0.30*	0.15*	0.35*	0.41*	0.35*	0.21*	0.17*	0.37*	0.39*	0.40*	0.24*	0.24*	0.40*	0.08	0.30*	-0.01	0.27*	0.07	0.12*	0.16*	0.11*
Prostitution	0.13*	0.10	0.12	0.20*	0.34*	0.24*	0.23*	0.15*	0.30*	0.30*	0.26*	0.15*	0.20*	0.17*	0.10	0.24*	0.01	0.27*	0.06	0.17*	0.12*	0.16*
	Crim+ Drink+ Homo+ Drug	Crim+ Drink+ Homo+ Aids	Crim+ Drink+ Unstable Aids	Drug+ Homo+ Aids	Crim+ Drug+ Homo+ Aids	Crim+ Drink+ Homo+ Aids	Crim+ Drink+ Homo	Crim+ Drink+ Homo+ Aids	Crim+ Drug Homo+ Aids	Drug+ Homo+ Aids	Crim+ Drink+ Drug+ Homo Homo+ Aids	Crim+ Drink+ Drug+ Homo	Crim+ Drink+ Drug+ Homo+ Aids	Drug+ Homo+ Aids	Crim+ Drink+ Homo+ Aids	Crim+ Drug+ Homo+ Aids	Crim+ Drug+ Homo+ Aids	Drink+ Drug+ Homo+ Aids	Crim+ Drink+ Unstable Homo + Aids	Drink+ Drug+ Homo+ Aids	Drug+ Homo+ Aids	Crim+ Drink+ Drug+ Aids
Criminals																						
Fight criminality	0.10*	0.08	0.17*	0.15*	0.15*	0.14*	0.14*	0.06	0.11*	—	0.14	0.08*	0.05*	—	0.03	0.12*	-0.04	0.10*	0.06	0.05	0.05	0.03
Marijuana	0.06	0.02	0.08	0.15*	0.18	0.12*	0.09	0.07*	0.14*	0.10*	0.09	0.13*	0.09*	0.01	0.01	0.11*	-0.03	0.09	0.08	0.06	0.05	0.05
Sexual freedom	0.01	0.06	0.00	0.11*	0.04	0.08	0.09	0.08*	0.16*	0.09*	0.09	0.12*	0.12*	0.04	0.08	0.08	0.01	0.10	0.14*	0.02	0.05	0.04
Married have affair	0.09*	0.05	0.11	0.11*	0.14	0.08	0.09	0.09*	0.18*	0.10*	0.13*	0.12*	0.12*	0.12*	0.06	0.12*	0.02	0.04	0.10	0.04	0.07	0.04
Homosexuality	0.15*	0.12*	0.15*	0.22*	0.24*	0.16*	0.13*	0.12*	0.18*	0.21*	0.17*	0.15*	0.17*	0.16*	0.02	0.17*	-0.02	0.05	0.03	0.06	0.10*	0.07
Prostitution	0.18	0.08	0.13*	0.13*	0.22*	0.15*	-0.04	0.14*	0.18*	0.18*	0.13*	0.11*	0.16*	0.09*	0.06	0.15*	-0.01	0.11*	0.05	0.12*	0.12*	0.13*

continued

Table 2.9 continued

	NOR	SWE	ICE	IRE	N. IRE	GB	DEN	BEL	NL	W. GER	FRA	ITA	SPAIN	E. GER	HUN	CZE	SLO	ROM	BUL	BEL	RUSS	MOS
Drinkers																						
Fight criminality	0.08	0.12*	0.07	0.04	0.22*	0.06	0.05	0.05	0.10	—	0.10	0.05	0.03	—	0.03	0.04	-0.02	0.07	0.05	0.03	0.01	-0.03
Marijuana	0.02	0.02	0.06	0.07	0.10	0.08	0.03	0.08*	0.13*	0.12*	0.08	0.09*	0.07*	0.04	0.06	0.13*	-0.05	0.08	0.09	0.10	0.05	0.07
Sexual freedom	0.01	0.03	0.04	0.08*	0.07	0.12*	0.10	0.10*	0.12*	0.11*	0.08	0.10*	0.12*	0.05	0.04	0.13*	-0.02	0.05	0.07	0.03	0.04	0.05
Married have affair	0.07	0.01	0.06	0.11*	0.05	0.11*	0.06	0.08*	0.19*	0.15*	0.09	0.07	0.07*	0.04	-0.00	0.11*	-0.07	0.06	0.04	0.04	0.01	0.05
Homosexuality	0.13*	0.12*	0.09	0.12*	0.17	0.12*	0.16*	0.03	0.10	0.11*	0.08	0.04	0.08*	-0.03	0.04	0.03	-0.06	0.11	0.04	0.05	0.05	0.02
Prostitution	0.08	0.05	0.11	0.07	0.18*	0.14*	0.02	0.04	0.14*	0.14*	0.14*	0.05	0.08*	0.01	0.04	0.13*	-0.06	0.13*	0.00	0.05	0.05	0.07
Unstable																						
Fight criminality	0.02	0.03	0.11	-0.05	0.09	0.01	-0.00	0.02	0.07	—	0.08	0.03	-0.01	—	0.03	0.06	-0.07	0.02	0.06	0.01	-0.01	-0.04
Marijuana	-0.01	-0.05	-0.04	0.02	0.03	0.02	0.01	0.01	0.06	0.05	-0.00	0.05	-0.01	-0.03	-0.02	0.06	-0.03	0.02	0.07	0.05	-0.07	-0.04
Sexual freedom	-0.05	0.00	0.02	0.05	0.02	0.06	0.00	0.03	0.02	0.01	-0.00	0.05	0.05	-0.00	0.02	0.03	-0.01	0.01	0.04	0.04	-0.05	-0.04
Married have affair	0.01	0.01	0.02	-0.02	0.04	0.03	0.06	0.01	0.07	0.01	0.01	0.02	-0.01	-0.05	0.01	0.14*	-0.06	-0.03	0.06	0.03	-0.05	-0.05
Homosexuality	0.07	0.02	0.09	0.02	0.08	0.03	0.09	0.06	0.12*	0.09*	0.03	0.01	0.04	0.07	0.03	0.16*	-0.05	0.04	0.08	0.05	-0.06	0.01
Prostitution	-0.00	-0.02	0.02	0.03	0.09	0.02	0.01	0.01	0.08	0.02	0.01	0.03	0.03	-0.01	0.03	0.14*	0.00	0.03	0.04	0.06	-0.04	-0.05
Large families																						
Fight criminality	0.02	0.06	0.02	-0.05	0.03	0.04	0.00	0.01	0.03	—	0.03	0.01	-0.04	—	0.01	0.04	0.00	0.00	-0.02	0.03	0.00	-0.00
Marijuana	-0.03	-0.02	-0.09	-0.11*	-0.11	0.02	0.07	-0.03	-0.04	0.04	-0.02	-0.02	-0.01	-0.03	0.02	-0.02	-0.02	-0.04	0.02	-0.09	0.01	-0.05
Sexual freedom	-0.04	0.07	-0.03	-0.02	0.07	0.05	0.03	-0.03	0.02	0.01	-0.00	0.02	0.00	0.05	0.02	-0.03	0.00	-0.05	0.02	0.03	-0.07	-0.00
Married have affair	0.00	0.02	0.02	-0.05	-0.00	0.04	0.09	-0.00	-0.03	0.02	-0.01	-0.02	0.01	0.02	0.06	0.03	-0.02	-0.03	0.04	-0.08	-0.04	0.02
Homosexuality	0.10*	0.10	0.12*	0.00	-0.04	0.06	0.03	0.01	0.08	0.12*	0.02	0.02	0.06*	0.04	0.04	0.07	0.04	0.00	0.10	-0.07	-0.03	0.04
Prostitution	0.03	0.03	0.07	-0.01	-0.02	0.07	0.04	0.02	0.05	0.06	0.02	0.01	0.05	-0.00	0.03	0.03	0.01	0.03	0.04	-0.09	-0.03	-0.02
Drug addicts																						
Fight criminality	0.13*	0.13*	0.07	0.07	0.25*	0.13*	0.08	0.08*	0.12*	—	0.16*	0.11*	0.06*	—	0.03	0.05	-0.03	0.13*	0.08	0.05	0.10*	0.05
Marijuana	0.04	0.00	0.12*	0.15*	0.16	0.10*	0.03	0.13*	0.16*	0.18*	0.16*	0.16*	0.09*	0.10	0.10	0.15*	-0.06	0.16*	0.07	0.14*	0.09	0.11
Sexual freedom	0.05	0.01	0.10	0.07	0.13	0.08	0.08	0.09*	0.10	0.15*	0.13*	0.11*	0.13*	0.00	0.03	0.05	-0.01	0.19*	0.07	0.04	0.12*	0.05
Married have affair	0.06	-0.01	0.10	0.12*	0.11	0.05	0.09	0.09*	0.08	0.12*	0.15*	0.08*	0.09*	0.05	0.07	0.09	-0.08	0.12*	0.04	0.05	0.11*	0.05
Homosexuality	0.13*	0.06	0.09	0.20*	0.22	0.14*	0.11*	0.13*	0.08	0.21*	0.27*	0.15*	0.14*	0.18*	0.11*	0.11*	-0.02	0.21*	0.10	0.06	0.12*	0.12*
Prostitution	0.05	0.04	0.08	0.14*	0.23*	0.10*	-0.04	0.11	0.05	0.19*	0.20*	0.08	0.13*	0.07	0.12*	0.14*	-0.02	0.21*	0.08	0.11*	0.10*	0.13*
Homosexuals																						
Fight criminality	0.07	0.15*	0.12	0.11*	0.09	0.13*	0.07	0.05	0.11*	0.14*	0.12*	0.10*	0.04	0.05	0.01	0.15*	-0.05	0.15*	0.06	0.05	0.05	0.11*
Marijuana	0.08	0.02	0.10	0.13*	0.19*	0.14*	0.12*	0.06	0.18*	0.15*	0.13*	0.17*	0.10*	0.03	-0.00	0.12*	-0.04	0.15*	0.08	0.11*	0.02	0.07
Sexual freedom	0.00	0.02	0.07	0.11*	0.16	0.14*	0.11*	0.08*	0.13*	0.15*	0.19*	0.18*	0.16*	0.03	0.04	0.07	-0.04	0.19*	0.09	0.04	0.06	0.02
Married have affair	0.12*	0.08	0.10	0.13*	0.15	0.09	0.37*	0.12*	0.16*	0.17*	0.17*	0.23*	0.13*	0.06	0.03	0.18*	-0.05	0.13*	0.05	0.08	0.08*	0.03

Table 2.9 continued

	NOR	SWE	ICE	IRE	N. IRE	GB	DEN	BEL	NL	W. GER	FRA	ITA	SPAIN	E. GER	HUN	CZE	SLO	ROM	BUL	BEL	RUSS	MOS
Homosexuality	0.37*	0.39*	0.44*	0.37*	0.40*	0.43*	0.21*	0.26*	0.50*	0.46*	0.43*	0.33*	0.30*	0.45*	0.10	0.42*	0.02	0.32*	0.18*	0.15*	0.15*	0.24*
Prostitution	0.15*	0.11*	0.15*	0.18*	0.24*	0.23*	-0.00	0.18*	0.35*	0.31*	0.26*	0.19*	0.21*	0.15*	0.09	0.23*	0.03	0.27*	0.10	0.16*	0.06	0.12
Aids-sick																						
Fight criminality	0.13*	0.11*	0.10	0.05	0.17*	0.11*	0.09	0.05	0.14*	—	0.14*	0.14*	0.05*	—	0.05	0.15*	-0.07	0.17*	0.07	0.11*	0.14*	0.10
Marijuana	0.06	0.04	0.11	0.11*	0.17	0.14*	0.09	0.07	0.15*	0.08*	0.09	0.14*	0.08*	0.05	0.00	0.05	-0.02	0.14*	0.03	0.11*	0.01	-0.01
Sexual Freedom	0.00	0.03	0.01	0.12*	0.08	0.11*	0.11*	0.06	0.15*	0.07	0.16*	0.13*	0.16*	0.08	0.04	0.05	-0.02	0.19*	0.14*	0.06	0.05	-0.02
Married have affair	0.11*	0.08	0.07	0.07	0.13	0.06	0.23*	0.10*	0.17*	0.08*	0.07	0.11*	0.11*	0.07	0.03	0.14*	-0.06	0.14*	0.13*	0.13*	0.12*	0.05
Homosexuality	0.24*	0.25*	0.27*	0.21*	0.30*	0.25*	0.17*	0.16*	0.34*	0.23*	0.24*	0.21*	0.21*	0.26*	0.05	0.26*	-0.03	0.21*	0.04	0.12*	0.12*	0.08
Prostitution	0.11*	0.04	0.13*	0.13*	0.29*	0.14*	-0.01	0.12*	0.30*	0.19*	0.13*	0.13*	0.16*	0.17*	0.08	0.19*	0.02	0.24*	0.07	0.18*	0.11*	0.11*

Note: * = significant on level 0.001; — indicates missing indices or missing external variables.

high with other items referring to sexual behaviour. This picture suggests that, on the one hand, the moral code of sexuality is a rather good substitute for liberalism/conservatism, and that, on the other hand, in nearly all of our countries complex links exist between all the items of 'social deviants' except for 'large families' and 'unstable'. Other peculiarities also exist. Almost exclusively in the Western countries, the item 'drinkers' shows remarkable links with the criteria variables. Therefore, we should be cautious about the indices including this item in the East. Second, in Hungary, Belarus, Russia, and Moscov nearly all links are low or insignificant and – even more strangely – are negative and near zero in Slovenia. Apparently, either the question on tolerance or the questions on deviant behaviour or both have not worked in the Slovenian survey.

In sum, we cannot reach a firm conclusion about the relative quality of the different index variants of 'social deviants', because of the suboptimal quality of our criteria variables. However, most of the criteria variables – if they work at all – work fairly well for all subdimensions of 'social deviants'. This suggests using the country-specific representations of this factor as functionally equivalent.

Tolerance and socio-demographic characteristics

In seeking systematic relationships between socio-demographic characteristics and tolerance are we now moving from slippery to safe ground? Unfortunately, no. For example, being 70 years old is biologically but not socially invariant to culture because of wide variations in the role of the elderly in different cultures. We must therefore be cautious in hypothesising links between such variables and tolerance.

'Sex': Attitudes should not differ between men and women towards 'political extremists' and 'strangers' except for a possible indirect effect of job rivalry in the latter, articulating stronger among men because of unequal employment of the sexes. Intolerance towards 'social deviants' might be more frequent among women, especially in more traditional cultures, because their role is usually more traditionally defined than that of men. Moreover, most of the items referring to socially deviant behaviour seem to be more frequent among men. However, 'social-deviants/identity set C' ('homosexuals' and 'Aids-sick') should be an exception because heterosexual men may still deny homosexuals more than women do, especially in modern countries with less rigorous sexual morality.

'Age' and 'education': In general we expect greater intolerance with increasing age caused by declining flexibility. However, this hypothesis should apply more to 'strangers' and 'social deviants' than to 'political extremists', since revolutionary ideas more likely attract younger people than older. On the other hand, a higher level of education, which is more frequent among the young, should transport the value of democracy and should, therefore, lead to a stronger denial of political extremism among them in Western countries. With respect to 'strangers', we expect more openness from the young, although this should apply primarily to Western countries because of greater democratic education and increased intercultural contacts. Concerning 'social deviants', we expect more tolerance from the young and higher educated because they usually have less rigid moral codes. They often seem to form an avant-garde in changing standards of social deviance.

The results of our analyses mostly support these hypotheses (see Table 2.10). With respect to sex we find no clear contradictions but mostly weak or null relationships. In only a few countries do men articulate more reservations towards 'political extremists' and 'strangers' than women. Women's greater intolerance towards 'social deviants' or 'criminals', 'drinkers' and 'drug addicts', especially in the Eastern countries, supports our expectations. The same applies to their tolerance of 'deviants' consisting of 'homosexuals and Aids-sick'.

Concerning age and education, our expectations are met in most cases. A link between increasing age and more denial exists with 'political extremists' in about half of the Western countries at both points in time but in only two Eastern countries. In a few Western countries (and in East Germany too), 'political extremists' are denied more by people with higher education. Tolerance towards 'strangers' is more frequent among the younger and better educated in almost all Western countries but in only a few Eastern countries. A similar structure applies to 'social deviants' of all variants. The younger and better educated articulate more tolerance, especially in the West.

In sum, no strong evidence exists against the assumed link between these socio-demographic characteristics and the tolerance dimensions. Our expectations are generally if not always met.

Conclusion

What can we learn from the foregoing analyses? The question can be answered by looking at the operationalisation of our measures, the validation procedures, and the instruments obtained from a methodological perspective. In addition, it can be answered from a substantive point of view.

First, with respect to the *operationalisation* of attitudinal topics such as tolerance in cross-national comparison, it is wiser to work with concrete than abstract objects. Concrete objects allow for better internal and external validation. However, listing concrete objects calls for broad *a priori* knowledge of the time- and culture-specific comparability of the objects. And even with this knowledge, there is no certainty that an identical list (or even different lists) of objects can catch all the relevant topics. Therefore, when extensive pre-tests are impossible, it might be useful to add a question about a relevant object. For instance, one might ask an open question like this: 'Which other group of people would you most dislike to have as a neighbour?'

In any case, there is no way out of the dilemma of comparability. With respect to culture-bound topics, culture-specific items seem more appropriate than identical objects. This structural problem underlines the necessity of internal and external tests of cross-national comparability. In addition, with questions like the one on tolerance, working with scales instead of a selection of items is recommended to reduce the effects of institutes and/or interviewers. In combination with an open

Table 2.10 Relationships between the different dimensions of tolerance and socio-demographic variables (Pearson's r)

	NOR	SWE	ICE	IRE	N. IRE	GB	DEN	BEL	NL	W. GER	FRA	ITA	SPAIN	E. GER	HUN	CZE	SLO	ROM	BUL	BEL	RUSS	MOS
1981																						
Political extremism ID set and																						
Sex (1 = male, 2 = female)	−0.19*	−0.11*	−0.14*	−0.06	−0.04	−0.13*	−0.07	−0.02	−0.14*	−0.04	−0.02	−0.07	−0.01									
Age (in years)	0.06	0.14*	0.08	0.06	0.05	0.18*	0.04	0.08	0.05	0.17*	0.10*	0.16*	0.06									
Education (1 = low, 10 = high)	0.00	0.01	0.04	0.11*	0.12*	0.04	0.05	0.03	0.12*	0.03	0.04	−0.07	0.01									
Strangers ID set and																						
Sex	−0.06	−0.05	−0.02	−0.08	−0.05	−0.04	0.04	0.06	−0.03	0.05	−0.03	−0.03	0.03									
Age	0.22*	0.16*	0.14*	0.16*	0.01	0.14*	0.04	0.12*	0.13*	0.19*	0.04	0.13*	0.11*									
Education	−0.11*	−0.08	−0.07	−0.07	−0.04	−0.10*	−0.05	−0.09	−0.08	−0.15*	−0.06	−0.11*	−0.08*									
Soc. dev. C. spec. structure and																						
Sex	0.06	−0.01	0.11*	0.05	0.05	0.01	0.06	0.12*	0.07	0.04	0.15*	0.02	0.11*									
Age	0.21*	0.20*	0.10*	0.11*	0.02	0.26*	0.08	0.08	0.12*	0.11*	0.12*	0.15*	0.14*									
Education	−0.15*	−0.12*	−0.06	0.03	0.07	−0.08	−0.03	−0.04	−0.08	−0.05	0.00	−0.10*	−0.06									
1990																						
Political extremism ID set and																						
Sex	−0.19*	−0.11	−0.12	−0.07	−0.05	−0.17*	−0.08	−0.06	−0.14*	−0.01	−0.09	−0.08*	−0.06*	−0.11*	−0.11*	−0.03	0.01	−0.05	−0.05	−0.08	−0.03	−0.06
Age	0.09*	0.14*	0.22*	0.09	0.27*	0.19*	0.05	0.10*	0.13*	0.07	0.07	0.15*	0.09*	−0.01	0.05	0.12*	−0.04	0.07	0.04	0.11*	0.04	0.08
Education	−0.06*	−0.06	0.01	−0.02	−0.05	0.02	0.01	0.03	0.09	0.03	0.10	−0.03	0.03	0.11*	0.05	0.06	0.04	0.07	−0.06	0.03	0.06	0.03
Strangers ID set and																						
Sex	−0.13*	−0.09	−0.09	−0.06	−0.14	−0.05	−0.12*	−0.02	−0.02	−0.01	−0.04	−0.01	−0.02	−0.03	0.02	0.05	0.02	−0.01	0.02	0.02	0.03	−0.01
Age	0.20*	0.06	0.21*	0.14*	0.26*	0.18*	0.09*	0.11*	0.22*	0.14*	0.11	0.16*	0.14*	0.12*	0.14*	0.10*	−0.04	0.07	0.11*	−0.01	0.03	0.11
Education	−0.16*	0.01	0.10	−0.21*	−0.13	−0.10*	−0.01	−0.10*	−0.15*	−0.17*	−0.17*	−0.12*	−0.07*	−0.18*	0.00	−0.10*	−0.01	−0.05	−0.02	−0.02	−0.06	0.02
Social deviance ID set A																						
Sex	−0.00	−0.00	0.00	0.07	0.05	0.02	−0.00	0.06*	0.07	0.14*	0.08	0.07	0.04	0.11*	0.12*	0.16*	0.03	0.13*	0.05	0.12*	0.17*	0.23*
Age	0.15*	0.05	0.05	0.18*	0.34*	0.28*	−0.01	0.11*	0.11*	0.24*	0.13*	0.14*	0.17*	0.15*	0.13*	0.17*	−0.05	0.12*	0.05	0.04	0.10*	0.11*
Education	−0.10*	−0.01	0.02	−0.14*	−0.07	−0.07	−0.03	−0.05	−0.10	−0.11*	−0.14*	−0.08*	−0.07*	−0.09*	−0.05	−0.05	0.03	−0.09	−0.05	0.01	0.02	0.04
Social deviance ID set B																						
Sex	−0.05	−0.05	0.00	0.04	0.03	0.02	−0.08	0.04	0.05	0.11*	0.08	0.02	0.03	0.04	0.11*	0.15*	0.03	0.10*	0.07	0.10	0.14*	0.17*
Age	0.09	−0.00	0.05	0.12*	0.32*	0.22*	−0.05	0.08	0.10	0.22*	0.11	0.15*	0.19*	0.14*	0.06	0.11*	−0.03	0.14*	−0.01	0.01	0.04	0.07
Education	−0.06*	−0.00	0.03	−0.17*	−0.08	−0.08	−0.03	−0.02	−0.11*	−0.12*	−0.12*	−0.09*	−0.07*	−0.05	−0.05	−0.03	0.04	−0.09	−0.06	0.02	0.03	0.02

Table 2.10 continued

	NOR	SWE	ICE	IRE	N. IRE	GB	DEN	BEL	NL	W. GER	FRA	ITA	SPAIN	E. GER	HUN	CZE	SLO	ROM	BUL	BEL	RUSS	MOS
Social deviance ID set C																						
Sex	−0.14	−0.12*	−0.16	−0.05	0.05	−0.11*	−0.10*	−0.03	−0.07	−0.04	−0.01	−0.03	−0.03	−0.06	0.02	0.06	0.01	0.06	0.01	0.02	0.08	0.06
Age	0.20*	0.13*	0.25*	0.19*	0.33*	0.28*	0.15	0.17*	0.24*	0.25*	0.17*	0.22*	0.23*	0.20*	0.02	0.12*	−0.02	0.18	0.03	0.07	0.08*	0.07
Education	−0.18*	−0.03	−0.01	−0.23*	−0.20	−0.20*	−0.02	−0.15*	−0.18*	−0.22*	−0.23*	−0.17*	−0.14*	−0.18*	−0.03	−0.16*	−0.02	−0.19	−0.06	−0.04	−0.05	0.03
Soc. den. C. spec. structure and																						
Sex	−0.03	−0.07	−0.06	−0.04	0.03	−0.06	−0.04	0.01	−0.02	0.01	0.00	0.01	0.00	−0.07	0.08	0.12*	0.01	0.09	0.02	0.06	0.08*	0.18*
Age	0.13*	0.11	0.00	0.18*	0.38*	0.33*	0.03	0.13*	0.20*	0.27*	0.16*	0.20*	0.24*	0.19*	0.09	0.14*	−0.03	0.18*	0.05	0.05	0.07	0.13*
Education	−0.09*	−0.03	0.02	−0.24*	−0.21*	−0.16*	−0.03	−0.10*	−0.17	−0.23*	−0.22*	−0.14	−0.13*	−0.16*	−0.04	−0.12*	0.01	−0.16*	−0.05	−0.01	−0.04	0.04

Note: * = significant on level 0.001; − indicates missing indices or missing external variables.

question on the most disliked group, this may anchor the country/time-specific relative level of intolerance.

Second, the *procedures of internal validation* proposed by Przeworski and Teune should be supplemented with an approach that allows for the combination of country-specific similar as well as different items. Methodologically, the identification of different identity sets on the basis of all possible combinations is questionable in explorative factorial analyses.

Third, our tests of *external validation* show the problems of culture-bound hypotheses and/or culture-bound external test indicators. These problems seem to increase with the level of abstraction of the external variables and/or theoretical concepts. They are less sharp when relatively concrete external variables are available, though these sometimes do not apply the same way to all indicators of an index. Therefore, we recommend including concrete external test variables more than variables which try to catch theoretical concepts about the explanation of the formation of attitudes.

From a substantive perspective, it is clear that tolerance is a more dimensional construct due to different types of disliked persons. But the level of tolerance also seems to be defined by more general psychological and social characteristics which are historically shaped and culture-specific. The main impression of the analyses is one of little contradictory evidence of the cross-national and longitudinal validity of the tolerance-dimensions and of more or less strong evidence of their validity. Unfortunately, this picture is disturbed by many weak and insignificant relations. But a missing link can also indicate a low salience of the respective tolerance-dimension or a country-specific difference in salience of the external variable for the respective tolerance-dimension. Moreover, in the case of external variables which are to be seen less as a different expression of the same tolerance-dimension or a correlate but more as some explaining variable, this might hint at the inappropriateness of the assumptions concerning the formation of intolerance. In some of our cases, the latter might be more likely than an insufficient cross-national comparability of the tolerance-dimensions.

We conclude that tolerance towards 'political extremists' and 'strangers' in most countries is represented quite well by the identity sets. Because of different cultural histories and different actual experiences with political extremism, immigrants, and inter-cultural contacts, it is plausible that both dimensions might be of a different centrality and therefore are sometimes linked with varying saliency to external variables.

Tolerance towards 'social deviants' appears to be the most problematic category because of widely differing levels of intolerance for the different subdimensions and for the country-specific structure of the dimension. The definition of social deviance is probably culture-bound and the dimension is therefore extremely sensible for the problem of catching the most relevant objects. In our case, the different identity sets seem to catch subdimensions which stand for different components of deviant behaviour, whereas the country-specific differing structures of this dimension seem to integrate these components according to their culture-specific centrality. Thus, if we are interested in tolerance towards social deviance in general, country-specific representations may give the best picture.

Finally, reminding ourselves that articulating tolerance is easy in the abstract but harder in the concrete, we should not be too surprised about various degrees in links with external variables. On the contrary, the links may hint at different situations which affect tolerance in concrete cases. We conclude, therefore, that the discussed operationalisation catches two aspects of tolerance: a general, culturally framed level and a situation-specific level. In any case, we can expect a higher level of intolerance when the concrete situation provokes the cultural standards.

Against this background, we can ignore small differences in tolerance levels because they are probably caused by differing actual situations. The general pattern of more frequent intolerance on all dimensions in the Eastern countries – especially on the dimension 'social deviants' – suggests culturally framed standards. In the midst of ethnic and national conflicts in the East, relatively low intolerance towards 'strangers' may come as a surprise. Can it be that the items do not tap the ethnic groups in conflict? Even if that is not the case, these distributions may show only the general level and we should expect a rise of intolerance towards strangers with increasing inter-cultural contacts between these countries. Moreover, almost all Western and Eastern countries show strong links between the dimension 'strangers' and 'social deviants'. This means, in conclusion, that intolerance may easily be transferred from one object to another and might become politicised, thereby creating a highly dangerous climate.

Notes

1 The main criterion for the inclusion of Western European countries was that the question must have been asked at both points in time (resulting in the exclusion of Portugal 1990, Austria 1990, Switzerland 1990, and Turkey 1990). For Eastern European countries, the question must have been asked in 1990 (resulting in an exclusion of Poland 1990). Since we wanted to analyse an identical set of items in 1990, further exclusions became necessary: Finland 1981 and 1990 (because of doubts about correct interviewing of the question); Lithuania 1990, Latvia 1990, and Estonia 1990 (because the item 'extremists' was asked instead of 'left-wing extremists' and because the item 'people of other nationalities' was asked instead of 'right-wing extremists'). In the cases of Slovenia and Romania, documentation of the World Values Surveys reveals that the item 'Gypsies' was replaced by 'Hindus'. In the case of Romania, the file contains no answers on this item. And in the case of Czechoslovakia, the frequencies lead one to suspect that 'Gypsies' was asked instead of 'Hindus'. Since the exclusion of all these cases would have led to a remarkable under-representation of Eastern European countries, we decided to exclude the 'Hindus/Gypsies' item instead.

2 A strict test of changes in perceptions caused by the differing context of items in 1981 and 1990 is not possible. However, the variation of the analyses with the item set of 1981 for both points in time may hint at the problem. A further problem is caused by the answering format through selection. There is no way to observe the intensity of possible differences or changes, and there is no great range for variance. Besides, the format is very sensitive to interviewer reliability (for example, by allowing respondents enough time for selection or by forcing them to select more than one item).

3 Moreover, if we force a one-dimensional solution, the results are very poor. In the pooled versions, only about 30 per cent of the variance are explained, and in the time- and country-specific versions, 25–41 per cent is explained. This is clearly below the values of around 70 per cent reached in a two- or three-dimensional solution.

4 Surely this strategy cannot be recommended as a normal procedure because with an increase in the numbers of items, possible item-combinations grow enormously.

5 Extensive tables and details about these analyses can be obtained from the author.

6 Of course, we can think of a variety of ad hoc combinations which suggest more specific dimensions. For example, the combination of 'drug addicts', 'homosexuals' and 'Aids-sick' clearly hints at an Aids-associated factor; the combination of 'drinkers', 'unstable', 'drug addicts' and 'Aids-sick' hints at an underlying dimension of illness; the combination of 'criminals', 'drinkers' and 'drug addicts' hints at a fear factor, and so on. But these ad hoc interpretations cannot constitute a systematic interpretation of the third factor, which is applicable to the cross-national comparison.

7 Obviously, we must restrict the test of our hypotheses to those characteristics on which we have data.

8 The following variables, which might work as external criteria, stem from an item-battery which could be called 'attitudes towards deviant behaviour'. Unfortunately, this item-battery cannot be used as an index, because the list has enormous problems of cross-national comparability. Instead, we pick out a few single items which could be linked with our tolerance-objects.

9 Because of an extremely one-sided distribution, we recode the eleven-point scale in three steps, leaving the category 'never' with one single point. Remaining variance problems: Norway, Sweden, Northern Ireland, East Germany, Romania, and Russia.

3   Political values

Ronald Inglehart[1]

Introduction

A fundamental and recurring question in comparative research is 'Do given words or questions have comparable meanings in different societies?'. Unless this question can be answered satisfactorily, comparative research may be futile.

The question of comparability was particularly acute in the 1990–93 World Values Surveys, which interviewed people in forty-three widely varying societies using thirty-one different languages. Our questionnaire was designed to cope with the problem of cross-cultural equivalence. Built on extensive previous cross-national survey research and extensive pilot testing, with input from social scientists on five continents, it was designed to ask questions that share meaning across many cultures. But how do we ask such questions?

This chapter argues that we must start by asking the right kind of questions – which means asking questions at a relatively high level of abstraction. If we seek cross-cultural comparability, we should ask questions dealing with broad concerns that are meaningful across a wide range of settings. Conversely, we should avoid asking questions that evoke situation-specific factors.

Having designed questions to tap broad, general concerns, our next step is to test the degree to which the questions actually mean what they are intended to mean in another language, through the standard procedures of back-translation and pre-testing. But this is not enough. The final test of comparability takes place after we have carried out cross-cultural fieldwork. At this point, we can examine the degree to which the questions evoke similar concerns and images in different societies, by analysing the structure, the connotations, the demographic correlates, and the crystallisation of the responses given by people in different societies.

At this stage, we will almost certainly find anything from subtle to gross differences in the connotations and structure of responses in different societies. Given words almost never mean *exactly* the same thing in different settings or different languages. They don't even have exactly the same meaning from one person to another within the same society – or even for the same individual over time. As Zeno pointed out long ago, 'You can't step into the same river twice.' Strictly speaking, there is no such thing as posing identical questions to two different people, even within the same culture. We can only attain reasonably close approximations.

But this does not mean that we must abandon all hope for cross-cultural research. Though subtle differences in meaning will always be present, shared meanings are often close enough that we can communicate the essential point. For example, last year a colleague sent me the message, 'Meet me at the Rathauspark Hotel in Vienna at 9 a.m. on 11 June to discuss our project'. On 11 June, people from Australia, Austria, Brazil, Canada, Germany, Japan, Norway, Switzerland, and the United States showed up at the Rathauspark Hotel and discussed the project. The Rathauspark Hotel probably carries different connotations for each of these people, Vienna probably conveys different images, and June probably carries different meanings for a Norwegian (for whom it comes in spring) and a Brazilian (for whom it comes in the autumn). But in spite of these differences, the basic meaning of the message was clear enough to achieve its purpose. A meeting of minds took place.

Thus, the fact that a given question evokes somewhat different connotations and concerns in different societies does not mean that we must renounce comparative research. It does mean, however, that we must be aware of these differences when we interpret the results. Sometimes the differences are so small that we can ignore them for all practical purposes. Other times they are very large – so large that the meaning of a given question in one society may be its polar opposite in another society.

This chapter will focus mainly on analysing and interpreting cross-cultural differences in one specific case: the meaning and structure of the items used to measure materialist–postmaterialist values in forty societies. But first let us say a little more about how to deal with cross-cultural comparability in general.

Establishing cross-cultural comparability

In his introduction to this volume, van Deth refers to a controversy over head scarves as an example of a situation-specific question. Let us consider this case in more detail, for it illustrates the importance of asking questions at a relatively general level.

Recently, a hot political issue in France concerned whether girls should be allowed to wear scarves over their heads in school. Relatively conservative and traditional members of the French public opposed the practice in reaction against the penetration of Islamic fundamentalism into their society. If we were carrying out a one-country survey of French social or political life, asking one's position on this issue would be a meaningful and useful question. But in many societies, from Japan to Chile, the question would seem absurd, evoking the response 'Why on earth *shouldn't* girls be allowed to wear scarves if they wish to?'. On the other hand, in Turkey precisely the same question has also been recently at the centre of a heated political conflict – one in which those with traditional religious views *favour* allowing girls to wear head scarves. Secular political forces oppose it. In France by contrast, opposition to head scarves is an indicator of traditional religious views –

and secular forces favour allowing it. Clearly, we would not use this item as an indicator of cultural conservatism in a global survey.

The question about head scarves may carry totally different meanings (or may seem pointless) as we move from one society to another. But a question about whether religion is important in one's life is meaningful in virtually every society on earth, including those in which most people say it is not. Analysis of the data from the World Values Surveys indicates that this question taps a major dimension of cross-cultural variability (Inglehart 1997). It is understood throughout the world, and the ideological and demographic correlates of being religious (or not religious) show an impressive degree of similarity across more than forty societies.

This approach can be formulated as part of a more general strategy: Design broadly relevant questions – but when you have asked them, examine to what extent their structure, connotations, demographic correlates, and degrees of constraint are cross-culturally similar.

In this chapter we will examine the degree to which a battery designed to measure materialist–postmaterialist values taps similar concerns in a variety of cultural settings. In doing so, we will examine four aspects of the battery's structure and connotations. First, we will look at the structure of the battery itself (at what van Deth calls 'internal consistency'). Second, we will consider the connotations of the index with other variables that might logically be used to validate it ('external consistency'). Third, we will analyse the demographic correlates of the battery. This might be considered a special case of what van Deth calls external consistency; but as we shall see, the theoretical status and the implications of demographic correlates are distinctive from other types of external consistency. In the case at hand, the relevant theory postulates that throughout advanced industrial society younger and better educated respondents should be more likely to have postmaterialist values. As we shall see, this expectation proves to be true in most but not all societies, and the exceptions are theoretically significant. Finally, we turn to the concept of crystallisation, or degree of constraint. We are not only interested in whether given orientations are correlated in a consistent fashion, but also in whether these orientations are tightly constrained or only weakly correlated.

The case of the materialist–postmaterialist value dimension

Let us now apply these tests of cross-cultural comparability to evaluate the cross-cultural meanings of materialist–postmaterialist values. In our survey, we measured materialist–postmaterialist value priorities by asking the respondents a series of questions that began as follows:

> There is a lot of talk these days about what the aims of this country should be for the next ten years. On this card are listed some of the goals which different people would give top priority. Would you please say which one of these you,

yourself, consider the most important? And which one would be the next most important?

Twelve goals were ranked, but in order to reduce the task to manageable proportions, we presented them in three groups of four items. Each set of four goals contained two items designed to tap materialist priorities, and two designed to tap postmaterialist priorities.[2]

The choices deal with broad societal goals rather than the immediate needs of the respondent. We wanted to tap long-term concerns, not one's response to the immediate situation. Among the twelve goals, six items were intended to emphasise survival needs: 'rising prices', 'economic growth', and 'stable economy' being designed to tap emphasis on economic security; and 'maintain order', 'fight crime', and 'strong defence forces' being designed to tap emphasis on physical security. These items tap two distinct types of needs, but both groups are 'materialist' in that they relate directly to physiological survival. We hypothesised that they would tend to go together. Conversely, people who feel secure about the satisfaction of both sets of needs would take them for granted and tend to give top priority to belonging, self-expression, and intellectual and aesthetic satisfaction – postmaterialist needs that the remaining six items were designed to tap. Our expectation, therefore, was that emphasis on the six materialist items would tend to form one cluster, and that emphasis on the postmaterialist items would form another.

Thus, our theoretical framework predicts that we will find a specific structure underlying the responses to these items: emphasis on economic security and on physical security will tend to go together. Why? Because they are survival needs, and those who feel insecure about them will have a fundamentally different outlook and political behaviour from those who feel secure about them. Those who feel secure about survival will tend to take it for granted, and may give top priority to non-material goals such as self-expression, belonging, and intellectual or aesthetic satisfaction.

Emphases on economic and physical security were expected to go together, because from a macrosocietal perspective war tends to produce both economic and physical insecurity – both hunger and loss of life. Consequently, generations who have experienced war are likely to feel less secure about both. By the same token, from a microsocietal perspective, poor individuals tend to be exposed to both economic and physical insecurity – both poverty and relatively high crime rates. The more affluent have resources that shield them, to some extent, from both.

Satisfaction of the survival needs, we hypothesised, leads to a growing emphasis on non-physiological or 'postmaterialist' goals. Today, a large share of the public in Western societies have been socialised in an environment that provides unprecedented certainty that one's physiological needs will be met. Consequently, Western public responses should tend to polarise along a materialist–postmaterialist dimension, with some individuals consistently emphasising materialist goals and others giving priority to postmaterialist goals.

Will we actually find the expected structure – and will we find it consistently, across cultures? In order to answer these questions, we performed principal components analyses of the rankings of these goals in each of the countries surveyed. For this analysis, each item was recoded as a separate variable with codes ranging from '1' to '3', indicating whether the item was ranked as most important in its group of four items, as second most important, or as one of the two least important items.

The expected structure emerged when these items were first tested in 1973, and the materialist–postmaterialist dimension has proven to be remarkably robust over time. As Figure 3.1 demonstrates, factor analyses of survey data from the nine member countries of the European Community in 1973 reveal two clear clusters: at the top of the continuum, five postmaterialist items cluster together, showing positive polarity, and at the opposite pole of the continuum, all six postmaterialist items cluster together, showing negative polarity. This pattern is remarkably uniform across all nine nations (detailed country-by-country results appear in Inglehart 1977: 44–7). Moreover, this battery was used again in a subsequent survey in the same countries in 1978, and as Figure 3.1 reveals, the results were strikingly similar to those from 1973. The results show a cross-national consistency

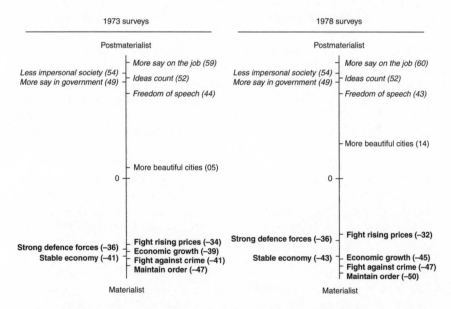

Figure 3.1: Stability over time: the materialist–postmaterialist values dimension in nine Western European nations, 1973 and 1978

Source: Inglehart (1990: 140).

Notes: Mean factor loadings from each of the nine European Union countries surveyed in September 1973 and October–November 1978. Items with materialist polarity are in bold; items with post-materialist polarity are in italic. Based on principal components analysis of rankings of the twelve goals.

that is truly remarkable. In survey after survey, five items – the same five items in every country – cluster near the positive end of the continuum. On the other hand, six items – again, the same six in every country – are grouped near the negative pole. The remaining item falls near the midpoint.

The items that cluster towards the negative pole are the six materialist items. And five of the six postmaterialist items fall into the opposite group. A single item – the one concerning 'more beautiful cities' falls into neither cluster. This item does not behave according to our expectations, a fact that we must explore in more detail. But the other eleven items live up to expectations to an almost uncanny degree. The consistency of responses to these items cannot be attributed to common sources of spurious correlation such as response set, which often occurs when respondents rate a series of items as either 'good' or 'bad' (or 'very important' or 'less important') or when respondents give similar ratings to a whole series of items. In the present case, this is impossible. One must rank each goal as being *more* important or *less* important than the others in a format that gives no cues to the 'right' answer.

Given respondents tend to be preoccupied with a consistent set of needs located on either the materialist or postmaterialist side of the continuum. Eleven of the twelve items fall into two separate clusters, reflecting materialist and postmateri- alist priorities, respectively. The item designed to tap aesthetic needs fits into neither cluster. With the same consistency by which the eleven other items fit into their expected places, this one fails to show a strong positive loading in any of these countries. Why?

The answer is that this item does not simply evoke aesthetic needs as intended. Instead, it also taps an urban/anti-urban dimension on which collective economic development is seen as conflicting with one's personal security. On this dimension, the item shows a surprisingly strong relationship with the safety needs (see Inglehart 1977: 45–50). For many people, the term 'cities' evokes fear of crime.

The relationship between aesthetic concerns and postmaterialist values is clar- ified by another analysis utilising the Rokeach Terminal Values survey (see Rokeach 1973) together with the materialist–postmaterialist battery, both of which were included in the American component of the Political Action study (Barnes *et al.* 1979). Factor analysis of the twelve-item materialist–postmaterialist battery plus the eighteen–item Rokeach battery reveals an interesting structure. A materialist–postmaterialist dimension is clearly recognisable, and several of Rokeach's items show substantial loadings on it. In the postmaterialist cluster of this dimension, we find Rokeach's items 'Equality' and 'Inner Harmony', plus a pair of items relating to intellectual and aesthetic needs – 'Wisdom' and 'A World of Beauty'. Ironically, the item designed to tap aesthetic needs fails to show the expected empirical relationships. Conversely, 'A World of Beauty', the item devel- oped by Rokeach, does. Our own item concerning 'more beautiful cities' had an unexpected tendency to be linked with emphasis on 'the fight against crime'. Including the word 'cities' in this context seems to evoke a concern with safety among some respondents. For them, cities are 'unbeautiful' not only because they are dirty but because they are dangerous. Rokeach's item makes no reference to

Table 3.1 The materialist–postmaterialist dimension in fifteen Western nations, 1990 (loadings on first principal component)

Less impersonal society	0.60
More say on job	0.62
More say in government	0.50
Ideas count more than money	0.51
Freedom of speech	0.34
More beautiful cities	0.18
Strong defence forces	−0.26
Fight rising prices	−0.28
Fight against crime	−0.39
Maintain order	−0.55
Economic growth	−0.59
Maintain stable economy	−0.63

Source: 1990–91 World Values Survey data from France, Britain, West Germany, Italy, the Netherlands, Denmark, Belgium, Ireland, Norway, Sweden, Spain, Finland, Iceland, Canada, and the United States.

Notes: Items with materialist polarity are in italic; items with postmaterialist polarity are in roman.

cities and evokes aesthetic concerns in unmixed form – and consequently falls into the postmaterialist cluster, as the need hierarchy hypothesis would suggest. The anomalous results obtained from this item seem to reflect imperfect formulation of our 'aesthetic' alternative rather than an indication that aesthetic concerns are not part of the postmaterialist syndrome. For when unambiguously formulated, they *are*.

The pattern found in both 1973 and 1978 continues in the 1990s. The loadings on the first factor in fifteen Western countries are shown in Table 3.1. (Detailed results for each country are shown in Abramson and Inglehart 1995.) In this table, the goals designed to tap materialist priorities appear in the lower part of the table; the goals intended to tap postmaterialist priorities appear in the upper part. With almost incredible consistency, in nation after nation, emphasis on the six items designed to tap economic and physical security forms a coherent materialist cluster. Vice versa, in every case, emphasis on the five items designed to tap belonging, self-expression, and intellectual satisfaction forms a clearly defined postmaterialist cluster.

The postmaterialist dimension in global perspective

The 1990 World Values Survey measured materialist–postmaterialist priorities in more than forty societies, using the ranking method. As we have seen, the results from fifteen Western democracies show remarkable cross-national similarity. The materialist–postmaterialist battery seems to tap a cross-nationally comparable phenomenon throughout the Western world. But is it merely a Western phenomenon – or (as the theory implies) does it emerge in any society undergoing an intergenerational shift towards higher levels of prosperity and security?

Do the people of other societies see things from a similar perspective? Apparently they do. Four Latin American societies were included in the 1990–91 World Values Survey, and the same basic structure applies (see Table 3.2). Some variations emerge from the pattern found in advanced industrial societies: 'more beautiful cities', already known to be a deviant item, shows negative polarity here, and 'economic growth' links only very weakly with the materialist cluster. But all five of the postmaterialist items show positive polarity and fall into the predicted cluster.

Even more significantly, the overall pattern in Japan and South Korea is practically identical to that of Western Europe and Latin America. Although these two East Asian societies have profoundly different cultural traditions from those of the West, they have both become advanced industrial societies – and their publics respond in a fashion almost indistinguishable from that of Western respondents. As Table 3.3 demonstrates, the five postmaterialist items cluster at one pole, and the six postmaterialist items cluster at the opposite pole. Moreover, the item concerning 'more beautiful cities and countryside', which gave ambiguous results in the West, shows a clear postmaterialist polarity in both Japan and South Korea. The two East Asian countries not only conform to theoretical expectations, they actually fit the theory slightly better than do most Western countries. This is a very interesting finding. It indicates that the emergence of a polarisation between materialist goals and postmaterialist goals is not uniquely Western. It is a phenomenon of advanced industrial society that emerges with high levels of economic development – even among societies that started from very different cultural heritages.

There are societies in which the polarisation between materialist and postmaterialist values is less distinct, but the division is not between Western and non-Western cultures. The countries that deviate most from the materialist–postmaterialist configuration are the ex-socialist countries, even those with historically close ties to the

Table 3.2 The materialist–postmaterialist dimension in four Latin American countries (loadings on first principal component)

More say in government	0.67
More say on job	0.60
Less impersonal society	0.52
Freedom of speech	0.36
Ideas count more than money	0.34
Economic growth	−0.15
Strong defence forces	−0.27
More beautiful cities	−0.27
Maintain stable economy	−0.31
Fight rising prices	−0.37
Fight against crime	−0.49
Maintain order	−0.56

Source: 1990–91 World Values Survey data from Mexico, Argentina, Brazil, and Chile.

Notes: Items with materialist polarity are in italic; items with postmaterialist polarity are in roman.

Table 3.3 The materialist–postmaterialist dimension in East Asia (loadings on first principal component)

Less impersonal society	0.70
More say on job	0.60
More say in government	0.50
More beautiful cities	0.38
Freedom of speech	0.45
Ideas count more than money	0.24
Fight against crime	−0.30
Fight rising prices	−0.31
Strong defence forces	−0.45
Maintain order	−0.50
Maintain stable economy	−0.61
Economic growth	−0.62

Source: Pooled 1990–91 World Values Survey data from Japan and South Korea.

Notes: Items with materialist polarity are in italic; items with postmaterialist polarity are in roman.

West. The 1990–91 World Values Survey includes samples from eleven societies of the former Soviet bloc, as well as China. In eleven of these twelve countries, the five postmaterialist items cluster together in one group. Poland is the sole exception. Thus, even in most communist and ex-communist societies, we find a clear and consistent postmaterialist cluster. But there is a tendency for emphasis on 'economic growth' to fall into the postmaterialist cluster, as Table 3.4 demonstrates. (For detailed country-by-country results, see Abramson and Inglehart 1995: Chapter 7.) This is a striking anomaly from what we find elsewhere. Nevertheless, within the societies that have had state-run economies, it is understandable. 'Economic growth'

Table 3.4 The materialist–postmaterialist dimension in eleven ex-socialist or socialist countries (loadings on first principal component)

More say in government	0.73
Less impersonal society	0.46
More say on job	0.44
Freedom of speech	0.27
Economic growth	0.18
Ideas count more than money	0.17
Maintain stable economy	−0.02
Strong defence forces	−0.37
More beautiful cities	−0.38
Fight rising prices	−0.43
Maintain order	−0.50
Fight against crime	−0.57

Source: Pooled 1990–91 World Values Survey data from Belarus, Bulgaria, China, Czechoslovakia, East Germany, Estonia, Hungary, Latvia, Lithuania, Poland, Russia, and greater Moscow.

Notes: Items with materialist polarity in Western countries and East Asia are in italic; items with postmaterialist polarity in Western countries and East Asia are in roman.

(like almost anything connected with the economy) has fundamentally different connotations in a state-socialist society than it has in a market economy.

The socialist societies had authoritarian political systems and state-run economies that had become stagnant to the point of paralysis. By 1990, the system of state controls had widely come to be seen as incompatible with economic growth. Even in China, which continued to experience rapid growth, the growth was entirely in the private sector. State-run industries were stagnant. In this context, as of 1990 economic growth was believed to be attainable only by breaking free from the massive and sclerotic state bureaucracy and turning the economy over to individual initiative. In contrast to the West, where an emphasis on economic growth was linked with loyalty to the established order, the state-socialist world often viewed economic growth as a goal achievable only through radical socio-economic changes. Moreover, the changes were closely linked with the post-materialist emphasis on individual autonomy: they required the liberation of the individual from state authority. Hence, in most of the former state socialist societies and China, we find that respondents who gave high priority to economic growth were the same people who emphasised 'giving the people more say in government', 'more say on the job', 'freedom of speech', and 'a less impersonal, more humane society'.

Further analyses support the conclusion that in these societies postmaterialist values are linked with support for reduced government involvement in the economy. In the 1990–91 World Values Survey, respondents were asked to place themselves on a ten-point scale measuring their attitudes towards governmental versus private ownership of business and industry. In the non-socialist countries, people with postmaterialist values tend to be slightly more favourable to the idea of a state-run economy than are those with materialist values. This reflects the traditional ideological heritage of the left.

The situation is dramatically different in Eastern Europe, the former Soviet Union, and the People's Republic of China. In all twelve of these societies, people with postmaterialist values are *less* favourable to a state-run economy than are the materialists. The polarity of 'progressive' values has reversed. Throughout these societies, people who place themselves on the left and people with postmaterialist values reject the idea of a state-run economy.

Figure 3.2 compares the results from twenty-eight non-socialist societies with those from eleven former Soviet bloc societies plus China. Across the twenty-eight non-socialist societies as a whole, little relationship appears between attitudes towards private ownership and postmaterialist values. But among the twelve socialist and ex-socialist societies, a very strong relationship exists between attitudes towards privatisation and postmaterialism. Among materialists, only a third of the group favour privatisation. Among those with Mixed values, about half do. And among postmaterialists, seven out of ten favour moving towards private ownership of business and industry.

The 'beautiful cities' item has different associations in different societies in the World Values Survey, and the variations follow a consistent pattern. In the 1990 surveys in Western societies, the item has a mildly postmaterialist polarity. It has

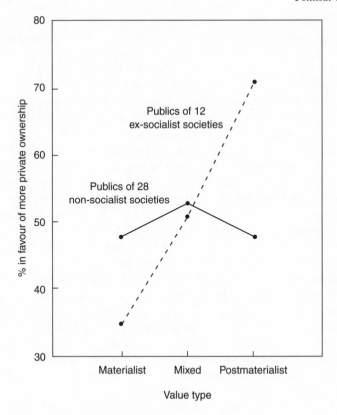

Figure 3.2 Values and attitudes towards private ownership

Source: 1990–91 World Values Survey.
Notes: Percentage in favour of privatisation of business and industry by materialist–postmaterialist values among twenty-eight non-socialist and twelve socialist or ex-socialist societies, 1990–91. Based on the four-item values index. Percentages shown are those placing themselves at points 1–4 on a nineteen-point scale on which 1 = 'private ownership of business and industry should be increased' and 10 = 'government ownership of business and industry should be increased'.

an even clearer postmaterialist polarity in Japan and South Korea. In the four Latin America countries, on the other hand, the goal of 'more beautiful cities' emerges as a materialist value; and it is even more clearly a materialist goal in the societies of the former Soviet bloc.

In the West this goal, originally designed to tap aesthetic values, now appears to be performing its original mission, though still only weakly. The fact that the item falls into the materialist cluster in Eastern Europe seems to reflect severe environmental deterioration in these societies (see Inglehart and Abramson 1992). In these societies, environmental pollution is far more severe than in the West. By 1990 it had become a massive and life-threatening problem. In the former state socialist countries, pollution is not perceived primarily as an aesthetic problem but as a life-threatening one. This perception is far from groundless. Death rates in some regions of Russia, former East Germany, Poland, and former Czechoslovakia are shockingly high due to massive industrial pollution. In the West, the goal of 'more beautiful cities' taps aesthetic needs to some extent, with secondary connotations of urban disorder and crime. In Japan and Korea, the item unequivocally taps postmaterialist concerns. But in the former Soviet bloc countries, with life-threatening levels of pollution, it tends to tap basic materialist concerns for the effects of industrial pollution on human survival.

In the former communist world, economic and physical security can not be taken for granted to the same extent as it can be in the rich industrial societies of the West and East Asia. Hence, as one might expect, the materialist–postmaterialist dimension is less consistent and less clearly crystallised in the ex-socialist societies than it is in the West and East Asia. Though a recognisable materialist–postmaterialist dimension does emerge in the former Soviet bloc, it accounts for less variance than it does in richer, advanced industrial societies. And in three of these societies (Lithuania, Czechoslovakia, and Hungary), the dimension emerges only as the second principal component in the factor analysis.

The postmaterialist phenomenon is only marginally present in such low-income societies as India and Nigeria, both of which had per capita incomes of approximately $300 in 1990. As the theory implies, few postmaterialists exist in these countries, and mass values do not crystallise along this dimension as strongly as they do in richer societies. (See Abramson and Inglehart 1995 for country-by-country results.) A recognisable materialist–postmaterialist dimension emerges in India, but it accounts for less variance than in almost any other country, and it is the second principal component instead of the first (see Table 3.5).

Although interesting cross-national differences in the structure of these values exist, evidence suggests that the core meaning of materialism–postmaterialism is

Table 3.5 The materialist–postmaterialist dimension in India (loadings on second principal component)

More say in government	0.61
Less impersonal society	0.58
More say on job	0.43
Ideas count more than money	0.38
Freedom of speech	0.06
Strong defence forces	−0.01
Economic growth	−0.08
Maintain order	−0.19
Maintain stable economy	−0.34
More beautiful cities	−0.35
Fight rising prices	−0.46
Fight against crime	−0.49

Source: 1990–91 World Values Survey data India.

Notes: Items with materialist polarity are in italic; items with postmaterialist polarity are in roman. In India, the first principal component reflects a polarisation between emphasis on economic priorities and emphasis on maintaining military and domestic order: all of the postmaterialist items are neutral on this dimension.

similar across this wide range of societies. The quest for economic security is much more politicised in societies with state-run economies than in societies with market economies, which gives a distinctive meaning to items that refer to the economy. Apart from this fact, however, the materialist goals show consistent results, and the five postmaterialist items behave in a similar way in all types of societies, East and West, as well as North and South. The results indicate that an additive index, based on summing up the five postmaterialist items (producing an index with scores ranging from 0 to 5) can be used in virtually any of the forty-three societies included in the World Values Survey. On balance, the cross-national similarities are far more pervasive than the differences.

Connotations of postmaterialism

Inglehart (1997) demonstrates that postmaterialists are relatively supportive of homosexuality, abortion, divorce, gender equality, the environmentalist movement, aid to developing countries, and numerous other orientations. By comparison with materialists, postmaterialists place relatively heavy emphasis on friends and leisure activities and less emphasis on family and religion. In fact, postmaterialist values prove to load highly on one of the two key dimensions used to map the cultures of the world (Inglehart 1997: Figure 3.2). These values show cross-culturally consistent relationships with a wide range of other values and preferences, constituting part of a postmodern world view. Nevertheless, we find one interesting exception to this pattern: in Western market societies, postmaterialists are slightly more favourable to state ownership than are materialist – but in ex-socialist societies as of 1990, postmaterialists were much more favourable to *private* ownership.

Demographic correlates of postmaterialism

The relevant theory implies that younger and economically more secure members of society should be most likely to have postmaterialist values. Here, we limit ourselves to examining the relationship with date of birth. To what extent does this relationship appear, and is it cross-culturally consistent?

Though the highly industrialised democracies of Western Europe and North America historically led the shift towards postmaterialist values, our theory implies that this process should also occur in other nations that develop high levels of prosperity and advanced social welfare networks. Consequently, it should be at work in East Asia (parts of which have now attained Western levels of prosperity) and even in Eastern Europe. The value change theory implies that we should find a higher proportion of postmaterialists among the younger cohorts than among the old in *any* society that has had sufficient economic growth since the Second World War so that the younger cohorts experienced substantially greater economic security during their pre-adult years than did their forebears.

At first glance, it might seem unlikely that intergenerational value change would be at work in East European countries, since they are far less prosperous than

Western Europe and the United States, and their economies are currently in decline. But a country's absolute level of wealth is not the crucial variable. The value change thesis implies (1) that countries with high levels of prosperity should have relatively high levels of postmaterialist values, and (2) that countries that have experienced relatively high rates of economic growth should show relatively large differences between the values of young and old, reflecting the fact that the formative conditions of the respective generations have undergone relatively large amounts of change.

Thus, we would expect Russia and other East European countries to show relatively low absolute levels of postmaterialism. But they should also show substantial intergenerational change in these values, reflecting the massive differences between the conditions shaping those who grew up during the First World War, the Great Depression and the Second World War and those who grew up subsequently. The crucial factor governing the emergence of postmaterialist values is whether one experienced a sense of economic and physical security during one's formative years. Accordingly, we would expect postmaterialist values to have developed since the end of the Second World War in Eastern Europe and the former Soviet Union. Though their GNP per capita lags behind that of Western countries, it is far above the subsistence level (and several times as high as that of such countries as China, Nigeria, or India). As of 1990, throughout the ex-Socialist world, the younger birth cohorts had generally experienced greater security during their formative years than had older ones.

In the Russian case, for example, those born in 1920 experienced the civil war and mass starvation linked with forced collectivisation during the 1920s, the terror and Stalinist purges of the 1930s, and the mass starvation and loss of 27 million lives in the Soviet Union during the Second World War. The 1950s and 1960s, by contrast, were an era of recovery and rapid economic growth at rates exceeding those of most Western countries. This was the era that led Khrushchev to boast 'We will bury you' economically, a claim that many Western observers thought plausible at the time. Recent years have been calamitous, creating a period effect that tends to drive all Russian cohorts downward towards the materialist pole. But the formative years of the younger cohorts were far more secure than those of the older cohorts, and if the intergenerational differences reflect differences in pre-adult experience rather than current conditions, we would indeed expect to find evidence of intergenerational change in Eastern Europe.

From 1945 to about 1980, most East European countries had impressive rates of economic growth, and in the early decades it seemed that they would overtake the West. Since 1980, their economies have decayed, but there is no question that the average Pole or Russian experienced far greater economic and physical security during the era from 1950 to 1980 than during the period from 1915 to 1945. East Asia is the opposite. At the end of the Second World War it was far less developed than Eastern Europe. As recently as 1950, Japan's annual per capita income was only a fraction of that in Czechoslovakia, Poland, or Hungary – and the Chinese and South Korean per capita incomes were a fraction of Japan's. But in recent decades, East Asia (including China, since the pragmatists took power in

1976) has shown the most rapid economic growth rates in the world. By 1990, per capita income in South Korea and Taiwan had reached East European levels and Japan was one of the richest countries in the world. Even China was experiencing annual growth rates of around 10 per cent, enough to double GNP every seven years.

Thus, the older East Asian birth cohorts grew up under conditions of extreme scarcity, while the younger cohorts have experienced relatively secure circumstances throughout their formative years. Consequently, we would expect these countries to show low proportions of postmaterialists overall, but relatively steep rates of intergenerational change. The East European countries should be the opposite. Since they started out at much higher economic levels but have grown less rapidly, we would expect to find higher proportions of postmaterialists but less intergenerational change. Figure 3.3 shows the value differences across the respective birth cohorts, using 1990–1 World Values Survey data from countries in Eastern Europe and East Asia, together with the European Union and the United States, using the twelve-item values indicator.

As Figure 3.3 illustrates, the younger birth cohorts do, indeed, show considerably higher proportions of postmaterialists than the older cohorts in most of the societies. The intergenerational shift from materialist to postmaterialist values is not limited to Western democracies. It is found among advanced industrial societies with a wide variety of political and economic institutions and a wide variety of cultural traditions. Though the richer countries have much higher absolute proportions of postmaterialists than do poorer ones, we also find a steep slope reflecting intergenerational value differences in poor countries that have experienced a rapid increase in prevailing standards of living during the past several decades.

Results from several European Union countries are combined into a single line in Figure 3.3 to simplify the picture. Overall, the European Union shows the highest proportion of postmaterialists, with the United States and Japan also ranking high. Even the oldest birth cohorts in these advanced industrial societies rank higher than the youngest cohorts in most other countries. But an upward slope, reflecting a rising proportion of postmaterialists to materialists as one moves from old to young cohorts, is also found in Eastern Europe and East Asia.

In virtually every case, from North America to Western Europe to Eastern Europe to East Asia, as we move from the oldest cohorts at the left of the figure to the youngest cohorts at the right, the ratio of postmaterialists to materialists rises. This is exactly what we would expect to find if intergenerational value change were occurring. To prove that it is, we would need data from a long time series, and thus far such data are available only for Western Europe and, to a lesser extent, in the United States and Japan. But in every country for which substantial time series data *are* available, the evidence indicates that these age differences reflect intergenerational change rather than lifecycle effects. There is no tendency for given birth cohorts to become more postmaterialist as they age. Furthermore, as this finding implies, the ratio of postmaterialists to materialists has gradually risen over time. We believe that the other countries in Figure 3.3 are on a

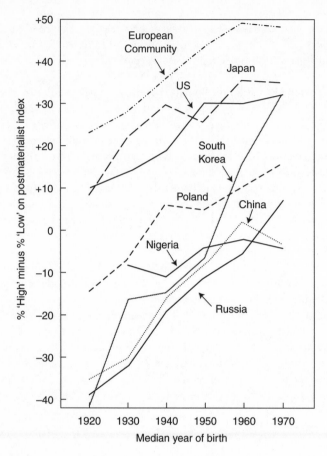

Figure 3.3 Values by birth cohort in Western democracies, Eastern Europe, East Asia, and
        Africa

Source: 1990–91 World Values Survey.
Notes: Respondents are classified as 'high' on the twelve-item materialist–postmaterialist values index
used here if they gave high priority to at least three of the five postmaterialist goals (ranking them
among the two most important in each group of four goals). They are classified as 'low' if they gave
high priority to none of the five postmaterialist goals.

trajectory similar to the one on which Western nations and Japan have been
travelling in recent decades.

Figure 3.3 presents a great deal of information, reflecting the twentieth century
history of each nation, and could be discussed at considerable length. The data
reveal huge cross-national differences. Thus, there are far more postmaterialists in
the United States and the European Union than in South Korea, but the slope
rises steeply in South Korea, suggesting a very rapid process of intergenerational
change. Since the 1970s, only one country in the world (Singapore) has had a
higher rate of economic growth than South Korea, which shows the steepest slope

in the figure. Among Singapore's oldest birth cohort there are literally no post-materialists; 70 per cent fall into the pure postmaterialist category and 30 per cent are mixed types (producing an index of -40 on the vertical axis). Among Singapore's youngest cohort, materialists outnumber postmaterialists by only ten points.

If postmaterialist values simply reflected current conditions, one would not expect to find a shift from materialist to postmaterialist values in such countries as Russia and Poland, which experienced economic stagnation during the decade preceding these surveys and suffered economic collapse by 1990. But the theory postulates a long-term process of intergenerational change based on the differences experienced during a given cohort's pre-adult years. From this perspective, we would expect to find intergenerational value differences in Eastern Europe, for it is clear that the formative experiences of the cohorts born in the 1950s, the 1960s, and the 1970s experienced far more secure circumstances than those born during the traumatic upheavals of the 1920s, 1930s, or 1940s. And we do find evidence of intergenerational change. As Figure 3.3 demonstrates, the Russian results show an upward slope. Though the Russian cohort line starts and ends at a level far below that of the richer countries, intergenerational differences in Russia are even steeper than those found in Western Europe, the United States, or Japan.

China shows an equally steep slope, reflecting sharp intergenerational differences that may have contributed to the spring 1989 clash between young intellectuals and the ageing leadership still in control of the army. These intergenerational differences reflect massive differences between the formative experiences of the older generation in China, who lived through an era of mass starvation and civil war almost continuously from 1920 to 1949, and the younger generation brought up in conditions of relative stability and prosperity (broken only by the severe but relatively brief upheavals of the Great Leap Forward and the Cultural Revolution in the late 1960s). China has had a series of wild swings since 1949, including periods of very rapid economic growth and periods of severe economic decline. As recently as 1959–60, millions of people starved to death, but this was a relatively brief period compared with the decades of slaughter and starvation that dominated the period of the war lords, the Civil War, and the Second World War. By these standards, the communist victory in 1949 brought a distinct improvement. Since the late 1970s, China has experienced exceptional economic growth, at an average rate higher than Japan's. Our data reflect these facts. China starts out with an extremely low proportion of postmaterialists among her oldest cohorts, but then shows a steep upward slope (though not as steep as South Korea's) as we move to her younger cohorts. Though her absolute level of postmaterialism remains far below that of most Western countries, China seems to be on a similar trajectory, and (as we will argue in the following section) further economic development should increase mass support for democratisation.

European Union countries show a steeper rate of change than does the United States, reflecting their higher growth rates since the Second World War. While among the older West European cohorts, materialists substantially outnumber postmaterialists (and thus fall well below the zero level), all three of the cohorts born after 1945 are positioned above this threshold. Indeed, the two youngest European Union cohorts rank well above their American counterparts.

The value differences across birth cohorts are greater in Western Europe than in the United States, which implies that Western Europe manifests a more rapid rate of value change over time. This has indeed been the case. In 1972, when the American public was first surveyed, it showed a considerably higher proportion of postmaterialists than did the combined six European Union countries for which data were then available. Subsequently, Western Europe has caught up but the United States has nevertheless shown a significant movement in the predicted direction.

Figure 3.3 would be unreadable if it included the results from all of the societies for which data are available, but we should note that two important countries show no indication of intergenerational change: India and Nigeria. Data for Nigeria are plotted on Figure 3.3, with an almost horizontal line reflecting virtually no intergenerational change. Data for India are not shown here, but as Figure 3.4 demonstrates, the relationship between values and date of birth is even weaker there, with younger groups being slightly *less* postmaterialist than older groups. A combination of relatively slow industrialisation and rapid population growth during most of 1945–90 kept India from developing at anything approaching the East Asian rate. Nigeria has had virtually no increase in GNP per capita since 1965, and its public also shows a flat relationship between date of birth and values. These findings indicate that intergenerational value change is not inherent in the human condition. As our theory implies, we find it in countries where the formative years of younger cohorts are shaped by significantly higher levels of economic security than are those of older cohorts. In countries that have not experienced economic development, intergenerational value differences are absent.

The value change thesis implies that large amounts of intergenerational change will be found in countries that have experienced relatively high rates of economic growth. Figure 3.4 tests this hypothesis against all of the societies for which we have data and not just the selected examples just discussed. In order to present the findings from more than forty societies on one graph, Figure 3.4 condenses the relationship between date of birth and values for each country into a single coefficient. As this figure demonstrates, the selected examples shown in Figure 3.3 reflect the overall pattern: intergenerational value differences tend to be largest in countries that have experienced the greatest amounts of economic growth since the 1950s. Accordingly, the correlation between date of birth and values is strongest in such countries as South Korea and China and weakest (or even negative) in such countries as Nigeria and India – which have not only experienced much lower rates of economic growth than China or South Korea, but which also have much more unequal income distributions, so that many people live at the edge of starvation.

Note that intergenerational value differences are also relatively weak in the United States. While this country has a relatively high absolute level of postmaterialism, the rate of intergenerational change is relatively small. Although the

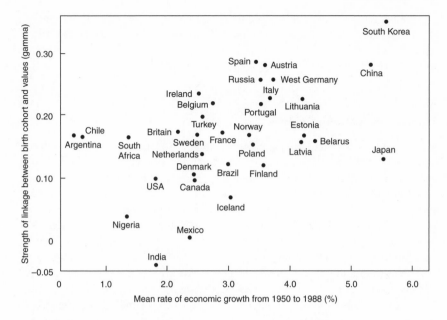

Figure 3.4 Societies with fast-growing economies have relatively large differences between the values of birth cohorts

Source: 1990–91 World Values Survey. Based on the twelve-item materialist–postmaterialist values index.

Note: Data on economic growth were not available for several Eastern European countries.

United States has been one of the world's richest countries since the nineteenth century, it has not experienced dramatic changes between the formative experiences of younger and older cohorts like those found in Europe and East Asia. The United States has been a relatively rich country throughout the lifetime of everyone in the sample and was not devastated by the Second World War. In the decades preceding this survey, however, the United States has had relatively slow growth.

As usual, we find some deviant cases. Argentina and Chile are 'overachievers' showing larger intergenerational differences than their economic growth rates would predict. By the same token, Japan is an 'underachiever'. But overall, the pattern fits our theoretical expectations. High rates of economic growth tend to go with large intergenerational value differences.[3]

The tendency for the young to be more postmaterialist than the old is not universal. As already noted, the young are not more postmaterialist in Nigeria. As Figure 3.4 demonstrates, the linkage between values and date of birth in Nigeria is virtually zero. The same also holds true in India and Mexico. The Mexican case is anomalous: we would expect some shift towards postmaterialism there. And in India, the relationship is actually negative: the young tend to be slightly *less* postmaterialist than the old. Both Nigeria and India are exceptions that fit the theory: their societies experienced virtually no increase in per capita GNP during the decades preceding the survey (though India has begun to experience rapid economic growth more recently). We would not expect to find much evidence of an intergenerational shift towards postmaterialist values in these countries – and we do not.

The crystallisation of values

Although there is remarkable consistency in the way people respond to these values across forty societies, the degree to which this structure is crystallised into a strong materialist–postmaterialist dimension varies cross-nationally. In four countries (Lithuania, the former Czechoslovakia, Hungary, and India), the materialist–postmaterialist dimension did not emerge as the first principal component. In all four cases, however, a clearly recognisable materialist–postmaterialist dimension appears as a second principal component that explains only slightly less variance than the first.

On the whole, the degree to which these items are crystallised into a materialist–postmaterialist dimension varies according to the degree of economic development. For example, though the materialist–postmaterialist dimension emerges as the first component even in such poor countries as China and Nigeria, on the whole the structure of these values is more strongly crystallised in richer and more secure countries. Although choice among national goals throughout the world tends to reflect the same pattern as in Western nations, choice among the goals is less structured in poorer countries. In Denmark, South Korea, West Germany, Italy, and Sweden, the first principal component explains 24 to 27 per cent of the variance. In India, China, Nigeria, South Africa, Portugal, Brazil, Mexico, and in all of the Eastern European and former Soviet societies except the former East Germany, Russia, and the Moscow region, this dimension explains 17 to 19 per cent of the variance.

As Figure 3.5 demonstrates, the materialist–postmaterialist dimension is significantly less crystallised in poor countries than in rich ones. Our figure shows the percentage of the variance explained by the materialist–postmaterialist values dimension in our principal components analysis in each of these forty societies, controlling for their per capita gross national product. In a few countries – such as Japan and the former Czechoslovakia – these values are less highly structured than one might expect based upon their wealth. Conversely, the mass publics of South Korea and Argentina have more highly structured values than one might expect. Overall, however, there is a strong and statistically significant relationship.[4] Clearly, values are more highly structured in relatively wealthy societies than in relatively poor ones.

Theoretically, postmaterialism emerges when relatively high levels of existential security are attained in advanced industrial society. Consequently, we would not expect low income societies to polarise strongly along this dimension – and they do not. But does this finding reflect the fact that the postmaterialist phenomenon has not yet emerged in these countries or the fact that these societies tend to have

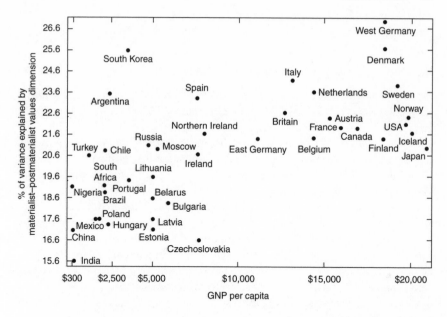

Figure 3.5 Percentage of variance explained by materialist–postmaterialist values dimension, by GNP in forty societies, 1990–91. Based upon a principal components analysis of the twelve-value items

Source: 1990–91 World Values Survey. Economic data are from World Bank reports.

low levels of formal education? A conclusive answer to this question will require additional research.

We suspect that both factors are at work. For relatively low levels of crystallisation are not the only indication that postmaterialism has not yet emerged as a major phenomenon in India and Nigeria. Our measurements indicate that there are very few postmaterialists in these societies, and the few that we detect may be partly due to measurement error. Some degree of random answering is present in any mass survey. This, plus coding error, would produce at least a few apparent postmaterialists in any sample. The structure of the battery in India indicates that the materialist–postmaterialist dimension is relatively weak; and the fact that in both Nigeria and India, the young are no more postmaterialist than the old suggests that the intergenerational changes that give rise to postmaterialism have not yet begun to reshape the world views of these societies. Various indicators converge in suggesting that genuine postmaterialism is very rare in Nigeria and India. The situation is slightly different in our third low-income society, China. Although our measurements indicate that there are very few postmaterialists there, and responses to the battery are weakly crystallised, a sharp difference exists between the positions of young and old on this dimension. China has experienced extraordinarily rapid economic growth in recent decades, and intergenerational polarisation along these lines may be beginning to emerge. If so, it is still at a very early stage.

Developing a twelve-item index for global use

On the whole, the battery designed to measure materialist–postmaterialist values functioned as intended, but significant differences exist between what it taps in the former socialist societies and the rest of the world and between industrial and low-income societies. Nevertheless, treating the 'more beautiful cities' item as neutral, one can use this battery to construct an index of materialist–postmaterialist values. Some individuals might give high priority to any one postmaterialist goal for idiosyncratic reasons or even by random answering. However, those who consistently favour all of the postmaterialist goals over all of the materialist ones (or vice versa) are not likely to be answering idiosyncratically. They are probably responding to a meaningful materialist–postmaterialist dimension. Further indications that the responses are meaningful and comparable emerge from the demographic correlates of the measure built from this set of values. As Inglehart demonstrates (1977 and 1990), there are cross-nationally consistent and theoretically predictable generational and socio-economic differences between post-materialists and materialists.

Our factor analyses demonstrate that a cross-culturally consistent measure can be constructed on the basis of the twelve-item battery. For although the items concerning economic growth and a stable economy are not cross-nationally consistent, and the item concerning 'more beautiful cities' has been problematic from the start, all five of the items designed to tap postmaterialist priorities show a high level of cross-national consistency. All five of the items loaded in a post-materialist cluster in thirty-nine out of forty societies, as the country-by-country results in Abramson and Inglehart (1995) demonstrate. This is a remarkable degree of cross-cultural consistency, and the materialist–postmaterialist values index used for global comparisons is based on the responses to these five items.

If we were constructing a measure that focused only on developed societies, we might score the 'beautiful cities' item as a postmaterialist value. Likewise, if we were studying materialist–postmaterialist values only in Eastern Europe or in China, we might develop a measure that scored 'economic growth' as a post-materialist value.

Our goal, however, is to build a measure that can be used across all of these societies. Our analyses demonstrate that five goals – 'more say on the job', 'less impersonal society', 'ideas count more', 'more say in government', and 'freedom of speech' – have postmaterialist polarity in thirty-nine out of the forty societies. (Even in the 40th case, three of the five items show a postmaterialist polarity.) Consequently, for cross-national comparisons on a global basis, we constructed an index based upon how many of the items are given a high priority. Scores range from a low of 0, in which respondents choose none of the five goals, to 5, in which all five are selected.

In any interpretation of the results, one must bear in mind that this index does not measure exactly the same thing in all societies. Postmaterialism has a distinct flavour in certain societies, especially the former state socialist societies. And it is clear that postmaterialism scarcely exists in the three low-income societies, China, India, and Nigeria.[5] Nevertheless, low-income societies fall into the right ball park, ranking near the low end of the continuum on this variable. At the other end of the developmental spectrum, we are on firmer ground. Our measures are relatively consistent in structure, have remarkably consistent connotations and demographic correlates, and are well crystallised. And as the theory implies, postmaterialists are much more numerous in rich societies than in poor ones.[6] The evidence points to the conclusion that throughout advanced industrial socie-ties – in East Asia as much as in the West – the postmaterialist phenomenon is well developed.

Assessing comparability

We have examined the extent to which a battery of items designed to measure materialist–postmaterialist values actually taps the same thing in a wide variety of cultures. In doing so, we have dealt with several different aspects of comparability. Let us review them.

As we have suggested, one never attains perfect comparability: cross-culturally identical questions do not exist. As van Deth (this volume: 4) puts it, 'Comparative research, then, must start from the axiom that even similar phenomena are never identical. The question is whether we can restrict the differences between the phenomena to intrinsic, non-relational properties irrelevant to the goal of our research.' The crucial issue is whether the questions one asks show relatively high or relatively low degrees of similarity from one setting to another.

Assuming that one has asked broadly relevant questions, interpreting the results still requires an awareness of differences in meaning from one society to another. This is something that must be examined even after one has carried out fieldwork. In this chapter, we examined four different types of indicators to determine whether a given concept has comparable meanings in surveys carried out in different societies.

The first step is to examine the structure of the battery itself (what van Deth calls 'internal consistency'). With an isolated item, it is virtually impossible to determine whether or not it taps similar meanings cross-culturally. The face content of the questions may look similar, but the underlying meaning may be entirely different. Using multi-item indicator variables enhances accuracy in any case, but it is especially valuable in cross-cultural research because it enables one to examine the structure of the indicators: if they tap the same meaning in different societies, they should show a similar configuration. Our examination of materialist–postmaterialist values on five continents provides a detailed illus-tration of this approach. We find that the core meaning of this battery is, on the whole, cross-culturally similar, but there are significant differences in structure and connotations. These differences are especially pronounced as we move from the former socialist world to market-oriented societies. Surprising as it may seem, the structural differences between the responses from East Asian and Western societies are relatively small. There are enormous cultural differences between the two groups of societies, but their peoples respond to this particular battery in quite similar ways.

The next step is to examine the connotations of one's index with other variables that might logically validate it ('external consistency'). If it is an important variable, it will almost certainly be related to other attitudes in the study. The question is: 'Are these correlates similar from one society to another?' If not, this suggests that the variable has significantly different connotations in different societies. Inglehart (1997) demonstrates that materialist–postmaterialist values are closely linked with a wide range of other attitudes in a cross-culturally consistent fashion, constituting part of a postmodern world view. Nevertheless, in ex-socialist societies, postmaterialist values show a different relationship to support for state ownership of industry from the one they have in the rest of the world. This is almost inevitable. Until about 1990 (when these surveys were carried out), the economic reality to which these items refer fundamentally differed in socialist and market societies. Consequently, any item that refers to the economy will, almost necessarily, carry different meanings in the two societies. On the whole, the connotations of materialist–postmaterialist values show a remarkable degree of cross-cultural similarity, but they are not identical.

A third step is concerned with the study of demographic correlates. In almost any study, the relevant theory usually implies that the key variable should show some specific linkage with social class, religion, gender, or some other demographic variables. The question is: 'Is the direction and strength of this relationship uniform across all societies?' Any substantial deviations from the expected relationship require interpretation. They may reflect substantive differences between the given societies, or they may reflect different interpretations of the question. In the case of materialist–postmaterialist values, the theory postulates that, throughout advanced industrial society, younger and better educated respondents should be more likely to have postmaterialist values. As we have seen, this expectation proves to be true in most but not all societies, and the exceptions are theoretically significant.

Finally, crystallisation or degree of constraint should be used in assessing the equivalence measures. We not only examined whether given orientations are correlated in a consistent fashion, but also whether the orientations are tightly constrained or only weakly correlated. A highly crystallised structure, based on relatively strong correlations between attitudes, suggests that the given phenomenon is salient and generally understood. The interpretation is complicated by the fact that, in general, more educated respondents show more highly crystallised orientations. Consequently, one might expect to find less tightly structured orientations among societies with relatively low levels of formal education. But, other things being equal, weakly structured attitudes suggest that the concept is meaningless to many people, or that attitudes do not polarise along the expected dimension.

Our findings indicate that the materialist–postmaterialist construct is relatively clearly structured across advanced industrial societies, both East and West, but that it is so weakly crystallised as to scarcely exist in India and Nigeria.

Notes

1 This chapter utilises examples from previously published material. Figure 3.4 appeared in Inglehart (1990), Figure 3.5 in Abramson and Inglehart (1995), and the remaining figures and tables in Inglehart (1997).
2 These twelve goals are shown in abbreviated form in Figure 3.1. The full text of this battery appears in Inglehart (1997: Appendix 2).
3 $r = 0.52$, statistically significant at the 0.001 level.
4 $r = 0.61$, statistically significant at the 0.0001 level.
5 Our index gives them low scores, although it probably inflates them somewhat, counting some weakly crystallised and spurious postmaterialist responses as genuine.
6 The correlation with GNP per capita is 0.68.

4 Religious orientations and church attendance

Martin Feldkircher

Introduction

When studying the development of Christian religion and the position of the church in Western Europe, one is struck by the assertion of modern research that traditional religion has lost its course in society (Laeyendecker 1989: 13) and its function of holding society together (Neuhold 1988: 51). Institutions have forfeited their religious legitimation as well as their deep, eternal, and overall character (Swanson 1960). Furthermore, the influence of the church is more and more diminished, with the consequence that the church has become only one institution or subsystem among others (Luhmann 1977; Dobbelaere 1984).

These are common, well-documented claims in many countries. In the context of institutional change, research focusing on religious orientations and their change over time is not surprising. Social sciences, which try to explain our contemporary world in terms of 'rationalisation', 'modernisation', 'secularisation', and 'individualisation', must come to a micro-social level in order to understand the concrete results of the primary macro-level processes. Thus the change of religious orientations can be seen as a consequence of macro-societal processes labelled 'secularisation' or, more generally, 'modernisation'.[1]

Religious studies should not be limited to an exclusive macro- or meso-perspective of society. The change of individual beliefs, attitudes, and values is often embedded in social change. A closer look at religious orientations, then, not only emphasises the personal view of the world and the individual 'compensators' (Stark and Bainbridge 1987) for the essential needs and questions of life, it also allows us to clarify the meaning of traditional Christian religions in our society and gives us a deeper insight into behaviour. Thus, on an individual level, we can determine whether religious motivation and religious norms have lost their meaning for the conduct of life (Neuhold 1988: 51).

Research on religious orientations is important beyond this micro–macro perspective. Religious orientations by no means represent only the consequences of macro-societal processes; they also can be understood as explanatory variables in other fields. According to van Deth and Scarbrough (1995a: 44–5), religious or secular–religious orientations are, together with left–right materialist and materialist–postmaterialist value orientations, the central motives for political

change. These value orientations do not cover every politically relevant orientation, but they outline the major aspects of value change in modern industrialised
nations. Therefore research on religious orientations is useful due to its meaning
for other orientations and behaviour in spheres of society like politics (Harding *et
al.* 1986: 64–5).

In this chapter we are interested in the inter-cultural change of religious
orientations, more precisely church integration and traditional religiosity. We
will describe and compare the development of these orientations in five specific
European countries via the construct 'church attendance'. Our main question
concerns comparability or equivalence: does 'church attendance' measure church
integration and traditional religiosity in every country in the same way? If we can
find empirical support that it does, we can interpret church attendance as a crude
indicator for inter-cultural change of at least one dimension of religious orientations. In this context, we will first discuss the concept of religious orientations and
the problem of equivalence. Next, we will describe the countries and time points
of our analyses. Since this chapter covers the empirical study of cross-national
equivalence of church attendance, we will end the analysis with a short description
of the inter-cultural change of traditional religiosity in the last decades, and reflect
critically on the problem of equivalence in the analysed context.

The concept of religious orientations

Religious orientations can be understood as value orientations which indicate the
condition of a society or of a special sub-population on a micro-societal level. Values
constitute the core of every culture and every society (Hillmann 1986: 54). In the
course of historical processes within a culture, they achieve a specific emphasis,
peculiarity, and relevant behavioural force. At the same time, they solidify in ideas,
symbols, norms, and behavioural rules, so that specific aspects of the culture
correspond to the character of its summarised values. To measure religious
orientations means to measure value orientations in the sense of a latent, not
directly observable, social construct which must be seen in its social context.[2]
Nevertheless, one must be aware that religious orientations are only one part of
the spectrum of value orientations, namely those which concentrate on aspects
connected with the central views of life.

Although many have tried to depict the culture-specific influences of, and
changes within, religious orientations, no general definition exists. The construct
of religious orientations could be described as a subsuming of all orientations which
express the different dimensions or levels of cognitive, ideological, or emotional
religiosity of the individual. According to Haller and Janes (1996: 244–7), it is not
easy to define 'religiosity', for it consists of different dimensions and, from a
sociological viewpoint, does not represent a clearly defined phenomenon. This
fact is confirmed in the literature. One can find innumerable aspects of religiosity
or religious orientations which differ considerably with regard to the operationalisation of the relevant constructs (for instance, Felling *et al.* 1987; Eisinga *et al.*
1990; Berthouzoz 1991; Dobbelaere 1995a; Dobbelaere and Jagodzinski 1995).

Some dimensions of religious orientations are traditional or Christian religiosity, general religiosity, orthodox religiosity, church competence, church integration, confessional attachment, and confessional distance. Obviously these dimensions are interdependent. For some of them the differences are only marginal; for others they are fundamental in nature or consequences.[3] Above all, with regard to the formation of and growing interest in new religious movements, substantial differences exist between traditional Christian religiosity and any other kind of religiosity (for instance, cultural syncretism or non-Christian transcendent religiosity). In most cases, however (as when we focus on church integration and orthodox or traditional religiosity), the differences are primarily analytical.

Given the manifold dimensions of religious orientations, we must first decide which dimension to choose when studying changes of religious orientations over time and the differences between countries. If we had high quality data for all points in time and for all countries, no other problem would exist. But unfortunately we do not. Hence, we must find a construct so general that it appears in most of our data sets and yet reflects at least one dimension of religious orientations. One such variable is church attendance. It is very simple, can be found in most cross-national data sets, and correlates strongly with other constructs measuring religiosity more directly. Jagodzinski and Dobbelaere (1995) propose using church attendance as a central variable for constructing a useful indicator for a relevant dimension of religious orientations. On the basis of the World Values Surveys they show with (external) constructs like the importance of God and the subjective religiosity of the respondents, that church attendance as a:

> crude index of church integration is an excellent indicator of church religiosity. It is not a direct indicator because it measures reported behaviour; but, indirectly, it reflects the degree of individual religiosity. However, our measure [of church religiosity] is clearly an excellent indicator of the religious beliefs and attitudes of our respondents. Hence, this measure of church religiosity is used to operationalize religious–secular orientations.
>
> (Jagodzinski and Dobbelaere 1995: 90)

With a simple indicator like church attendance, we should be able to describe the development of church integration and church religiosity, which can easily be regarded as a form of traditional Christian religiosity.[4] In this sense, the degree of church attendance can be viewed as an expression of faith in the Christian God, belief in the dogma, and acceptance of the church as the institution which represents God on earth.

Surely, this approach for measuring religious orientations is very restrictive. Values are operationalised without taking individual orientations or attitudes into consideration. But the relationship between church attendance as an indicator for church integration and traditional religiosity is mainly an empirical question (Jagodzinski and Dobbelaere 1995: 86). We shall see that church attendance, although restricted exclusively to behavioural aspects, is a good indicator for at least one dimension of religious orientations, namely traditional religiosity. Nevertheless, we must discuss and empirically confirm problems of equivalence before inter-cultural time analyses of a construct like church attendance can provide deeper insight into the change of value orientations.

Since we are interested in inter-cultural change, we must rely on secondary analyses of existing surveys. We must focus on the comparability of data in the last phase of a study: data analysis.[5] Two problems of equivalence are of prior interest: the equivalence of the indicator 'church attendance' across nations and across points in time. In order to secure long, country-specific time series, we must fall back on very different national and cross-national data. These data are usually characterised by very diverse thematic focuses and by different item selections, item operationalisations and item constructions. As a consequence, we must determine differences in the meaning of the selected indicator. In other words, the main problem of equivalence with 'church attendance' is clearly whether it measures church integration and traditional religiosity for all countries and points in time. The advantage of this variable is that it expresses reported behaviour and thus reduces the risk of country- and time-specific comprehension. But for the respondents this behaviour can mean very different things (Kelley and de Graaf 1997: 645). For example, in one country, church attendance may express predominantly social or cultural localism (Eisinga *et al.* 1990) or social pressure; in other countries, it may express traditional religiosity. The problem is that we would measure a form of socially motivated religiosity, on the one hand, and a 'true', internally motivated religiosity, on the other. However, 'church attendance' is an 'excellent indicator of church religiosity' as proclaimed by Jagodzinski and Dobbelaere (1995: 90), only if its meaning is similar in all considered countries. So we must confirm the equivalence of church attendance before picturing the country-specific developments in traditional religiosity. This strategy is by no means self-evident, because in research on religious orientations and their effects, it is easy to find cases where concepts of religious orientations within comparative research are used without questioning country- and time-specific meanings (for instance, Meulemann 1993).

Country selection and data available

For theoretical reasons, we have restricted the examination of cross-national changes and differences in traditional religiosity (as a dimension of religious orientations) on the basis of church attendance to five countries. They have been selected according to their special historical and structural characteristics; that is, by their especially high degree of social integration of their political subcultures, at least until the beginning of the 1960s. These are the 'pillarised' societies of the Netherlands, Belgium, Austria, and Switzerland, and the society of Italy. Characteristically, their historical processes have solidified the subcultures on a structural level via the upgrading and strengthening of intermediary organisations. Each of the countries has a more or less strong Catholic subculture.[6] Because of this, they differ from other Western European countries insofar as historical processes led to a cultural segmentation and not just to a cultural diversity (Obler *et al.* 1977: 8).

The specific constellations of these countries also had implications on the political level, where political behaviour or decision-making were characterised by 'consociational politics' (Lijphart 1977; Obler *et al.* 1977) to guarantee peaceful relations among the subcultures.[7] In each country (at least since the 1960s), particular tendencies of change have been observed on the macro-, meso- and micro-level. These changes had fatal consequences for the existence of subcultures, and their decay (reflected in the organisational structure and the commonly shared orientations of their members) has been shown by various authors (Steininger 1975; Middendorp 1991). We selected these countries for our analysis because macro-societal processes like modernisation and secularisation have more far-reaching consequences here than in any other Western European country.

If we are willing to rely on an indicator which is very simple and is generally implemented in a number of data sets, many different national and cross-national surveys are at our disposal in the five countries selected. But for our analysis of equivalence it does not seem wise to use all available data. The more we consider different surveys with divergent qualities concerning the constructs used for testing the equivalence of church attendance, the more complex and less comparable the results will be. To reduce that complexity and to secure an 'identity set' of questions, we will use only a limited set of comparative designed surveys for our tests of equivalence. The primary advantage is that we can consider similar variables with similar response categories for all countries within such 'international' surveys. Thus, we will enhance the comparability of different constructs, render the results easier to interpret and, last but not least, make the test for equivalence more reliable. The surveys which represent different periods, which take our country sample into account, and which contain other relevant constructs for an external validation of church attendance are these: the Political Action Study (PAS) for the mid-1970s, the World Values Surveys (WVS) for the early 1980s and 1990s, and the International Social Survey Program (ISSP) for the beginning of the 1990s.

Equivalence of church attendance

Our analysis of the inter-cultural equivalence of 'church attendance' as a measure for traditional religiosity follows Jagodzinski and Dobbelaere (1995). Via correlations with a set of different variables theoretically representing the construct 'traditional religiosity' more directly, we can see if the meaning of 'church attendance' is similar for all points in time and for all countries. According to the distinction of methods used to test and solve the problems of equivalence introduced by van Deth (this volume), our strategy tests for external consistency. In contrast to Jagodzinski and Dobbelaere (1995), we will use this method explicitly to handle the equivalence problem.

First, we must specify our central variables. 'Church integration' is measured on an ordinal scale where the highest value assigns a regular churchgoer as one who attends church at least once a week. According to Jagodzinski and Dobbelaere (1995: 86), the index for church integration is a combination of church attendance and the denomination of the respondent. The lowest value on the scale is assigned to 'unchurched' respondents who do not report or assign themselves to any denomination. Evidence suggests that this population is most distant from the church although some members are quite religious and sometimes go to church.[8] Therefore, non-churchgoers with a nominal denomination are ranked higher than the 'unchurched'. Note that the question for church attendance and its response categories differs somewhat in the used data sets, but no homogenisation is carried out. Instead, we prefer the use of the survey-specific indices of church attendance to exhaust their full variance. Nevertheless, all of our scales follow the same logic: the higher the score on the index of church integration, the more frequently one attends church, the more one is integrated into church, and the more one is traditionally religious.

After designing our central variable, we must choose constructs to use for its external validation. The variables used by Jagodzinski and Dobbelaere (1995: 86) which are more directly linked to church religiosity are 'subjective religiosity', 'subjective importance of God', 'number of religious beliefs', and 'type of God one believes in'.[9] In analysing the equivalence of church attendance we have added several indicators for the test of external consistency which were available in part for only some of the surveys.[10] They include the 'degree of voluntary membership in religious or church organisations', the 'application of the Ten Commandments', the 'confidence in the church and religious organisations', the 'feelings about the Bible', the 'to base right and wrong on God', and the 'meaningfulness of life (death and suffering) due to God'. The assumed relationships between church attendance and the external variables are all the same: they must be positive – the higher the extent of church attendance, the higher the degree of consent of the external variables – and relatively strong (above 0.40 as an essentially arbitrary reference value).[11]

As seen in Table 4.1, for most of the calculated correlations both requirements are fulfilled. With only a minor share of exceptions each r_s indicates a very strong positive relationship. Rarely does r_s drop below 0.40. Besides the unsatisfying results with the membership variable – due possibly to problems reported by van Deth and Kreuter (this volume)[12] – only the correlation of church attendance with 'importance of God' in the Austrian sample is somewhat deviant. By no means are the reported correlation coefficients the same. For some countries and some points in time, differences between correlation coefficients over 0.20 can be found (for instance, between the Netherlands and Austria for the WVS90 and the external variable 'subjective religiosity'). But these variations are negligible compared to the striking consistency of the results: a similar relationship exists between both countries and time periods.

However, this interpretation is not self-evident and one can argue against it in two ways. First, one can question whether the differences in the correlation coefficients are really insignificant, since some of them can also be seen as signs of non-equivalence. No clear answer is possible since no reference value exists to

Table 4.1 Relationships between church attendance and various external indicators of traditional religiosity in five European countries (Spearman's r_s)

Country	Study	Subjective religiosity	Membership in religious organisations	Type of God	Importance of God	Confidence in church and religious organisations	Right/Wrong based on God's law	Feelings about Bible	Life is meaningful because of God	Life, death, suffer are meaningful because of God	Number of religious beliefs	Application of Ten Commandments
Netherlands	PAS	0.64	0.18	—	—	—	—	—	—	—	—	—
	WVS80	0.61	0.60	0.60	0.63	—	—	—	—	—	0.73	0.65
	WVS90	0.68	0.69	0.58	0.75	—	—	—	0.56	0.57	0.73	—
	ISSP	0.69	—	—	—	0.59	0.61	0.54	0.63	—	0.67	—
Belgium	PAS	—	—	—	—	—	—	—	—	—	—	—
	WVS81	0.54	0.29	0.47	0.63	—	—	—	—	—	0.65	0.56
	WVS90	0.67	0.34	0.63	0.70	—	—	—	0.54	0.57	0.68	—
	ISSP	—	—	—	—	—	—	—	—	—	—	—
Italy	PAS	0.53	0.12	—	—	—	—	—	—	—	—	—
	WVS81	0.44	0.26	0.40	0.55	—	—	—	—	—	0.59	0.57
	WVS90	0.48	0.36	0.56	0.63	—	—	—	0.53	0.57	0.64	—
	ISSP	0.58	—	—	—	0.52	0.56	0.45	0.50	—	0.55	—
Switzerland	PAS	0.45	0.19	—	—	—	—	—	—	—	—	—
	WVS81	—	—	—	—	—	—	—	—	—	—	—
	WVS90	0.46	0.31	0.37	0.50	—	—	—	—	—	0.52	—
	ISSP	—	—	—	—	—	—	—	—	—	—	—
Austria	PAS	0.61	0.14	—	—	—	—	—	—	—	—	—
	WVS81	—	—	—	—	—	—	—	—	—	—	—
	WVS90	0.45	0.27	0.46	0.12	—	—	—	0.47	0.53	0.58	—
	ISSP	0.62	—	—	—	0.57	0.53	0.44	—	—	0.50	—

Sources: Political Action Study 1974–76 [PAS]; World Values Survey 1981–83 [WVS81]; World Values Survey 1990–91 [WVS90]; International Social Survey Program 1991 [ISSP] (unweighted samples).

tell us in which cases a difference between correlation coefficients signals non-equivalence. Although a large number of our items for external validation show strong correlations with church attendance, their power of persuasion is limited. A second objection to our interpretation is related to the method itself. As van Deth notes in the introduction to this volume, the test of external consistency is problematical. Ultimately, the problem of equivalence is not really solved by this method but rather moved to another level. Testing the validity of a construct via an external variable implicitly assumes that the variable measures similar things in all samples. If we want to test the equivalence of the external variable via another test of external consistency, we will endlessly test for validation. For every external validation, we must ensure the equivalence of the external construct. Only the hypothesis that the constructs used for external validation are equivalent justifies the general interpretation of the results in Table 4.1.

Because of these problems with a simple test of external consistency, we will want to enhance the validity of the equivalence analysis. We can do so in an elegant way which by no means solves the problem totally but strengthens the previous results. The central idea is that a shift of the equivalence problem to another level must happen only once. This means that before an indicator is used for external validation of church attendance, we must prove its 'internal consistency' (see van Deth, this volume) for all countries. Therefore we must use an external construct which represents, on the one hand, a more direct measurement of traditional religiosity as church attendance and, on the other, is measured with a set of different variables. In this way, we make explicit the implicit idea that the external variables have the same meaning in all countries and on all points in time.

A construct which fits the above mentioned conditions is the subjective competence and legitimation one assigns to the religious institution 'church'. This latent construct can be seen as a reflection of the meaning the respondent assigns to the Christian church. It can also be viewed as the degree of identification with the church, which at least partly expresses identification with central traditional religious values. Because the indicator emphasises a dogmatic orientation of the respondent with respect to a central religious institution, it can be interpreted as an operationalisation for a traditional Christian world view and the religiosity of the respondent. Therefore, we may suppose that if 'church attendance' is a good indicator for traditional religiosity in all countries and for all points in time, it must correlate highly with the respondent's assignment to competence and legitimation for the church.[13]

Although using this construct clearly makes theoretical sense, we also need an adequate measure. Unfortunately, only the WVS includes variables which can serve as indicators for the subjective competence and legitimation one assigns to the religious institution 'church'. In total, fourteen items may be used for a cross-national test for equivalence of church attendance. The respondents are asked whether the church gives adequate answers to, and may legitimately speak out on, various aspects of life. For both types of questions, the WVS provides a distinct set of items, with the response categories of 'yes', 'no' and 'don't know':

Generally speaking, do you think that your church is giving, in your country, adequate answers to:

- The moral problems and needs of the individual
- The problems of family life
- People's spiritual needs
- The social problems facing our country today?

Do you think it is proper for churches to speak out on:

- Disarmament
- Abortion
- Third World problems
- Extramarital affairs
- Unemployment
- Racial discrimination
- Euthanasia
- Homosexuality
- Ecology and environmental issues
- Government policy?

In the WVS90, these fourteen items were used for all countries except Switzerland. In the Swiss survey only the first eight items of the second item pool were included. The WVS81 – which considers only the Netherlands, Belgium, and Italy – has only a very reduced instrument for measuring our central construct, namely the first three items concerning adequate answers from the church.

Although both pools of items show similarities, they certainly do not have the same meaning. The first pool theoretically represents to a high degree what is understood by the term 'competence'. It emphasises the qualification, capability, and responsibility of the church to give advice (indicated by the word 'adequate' in the first question). The second pool has a somewhat different emphasis which we describe as 'legitimation'. Its focus lies on the authorisation and assignment of the right to express a position in public independent of the qualification. Competence is only one reason for legitimation besides tradition or tolerance.

Whether respondents distinguish between the pools and the concepts in the same way in an interview cannot be easily ascertained. Although the meaning of both aspects is hard to separate analytically, they can easily be viewed as general reflections of the meaning the church has for the respondents as a (social) institution.

To see if a substantial separation exists between competence and legitimation[14] – as well as between second-order dimensions concerning distinct social issues – we must take a closer look at the structure of the items.[15] For testing internal consistency (or construct validity), we use explorative factor analysis. In the same way as several other contributors to this volume (for instance, Westle; van Deth and Kreuter), we follow the suggestions of Przeworski and Teune (1970). First, we search for a common identity set of items before extracting the additional country-specific, non-common items. For the identification of the identity set, we calculate a principal components analysis (PCA) with an oblimin rotation for the pooled data set using all surveys of the WVS90 except the Swiss. Before analysing the Swiss data as a special case, we search all the identical and country-specific (but equivalent) items and structures for the Netherlands, Belgium, Italy, and Austria. Since only a fraction of the items can be used for the WVS81, a separate analysis for these data sets concludes the test of internal consistency.

In the pooled analysis we clearly get four components, which explains about two-thirds of the total variance.[16] All items except one achieve component loadings above 0.70, and communalities are distinctly greater than 0.50. The only exception is the item 'disarmament' which shows two loadings of about 0.45. Excluding this item, the results clearly fit the condition of an identical set of items (and structures) for a pooled analysis. We test the remaining set of items, secondly, in country-specific analyses. This leads to a further exclusion of items, partly because the country-specific structures differ from the pooled structure. So the items 'euthanasia' and 'government politics' are deleted from the common set of items as they do not fit either in Austria or Italy with our criteria concerning component loadings.[17] For the WVS90, we then have an identical set of items consisting of eleven variables representing four non-orthogonal dimensions both for the country-specific and the pooled data. The outcomes show high main loadings on the same components, low rest

Table 4.2 Identity set of items concerning the subjective competence and legitimation of the religious institution 'church' (principal components analysis; pooled data set)

	Church legitimation concerning sexuality and life	*Church competence*	*Church legitimation concerning disadvantaged*	*Church legitimation concerning general political issues*
Extramarital affairs	−0.86			
Abortion	−0.80			
Homosexuality	−0.77			
Moral problems		0.83		
Family life		0.81		
Spiritual needs		0.72		
Social problems		0.72		
Third World			0.82	
Racial discrimination			0.74	
Ecology				0.80
Unemployment				0.76
Eigenvalues (before rotation)	1.05	1.66	0.85	4.32

Source: WVS90 (n = 6,790).

Notes: Only loadings > 0.40 are considered; negative loadings have no substantial meaning if the main loadings of the entire column got negative signs; those cases can be interpreted as positive loadings as well. Kaiser–Meyer–Olkin Measure of Sampling Adequacy: 0.86; communalities > 0.60; explained variance: 71.6 per cent; inter-factor correlation < 0.35.

loadings, and a satisfactory explanation of variance. Table 4.2 shows the results of the pooled analysis.

These four extracted components reflect the presumed separation between both item pools. On the one side, a single factor represents the general social and political competence of the church; on the other, three components represent the assigned legitimation to the church.[18] These components show a second-order dimensionality: the individually assigned legitimation of the church to speak out on sexuality and life, on the societally disadvantaged, and on general political issues.

On the dimension of the *general social and political competence of the church*, all items of the first pool achieve high loadings. In addition to the substantive and technical reasons mentioned above for establishing a single dimension for these four items, several more must be mentioned. All four items have a general character, while the others refer to more specific issues. For example, the item 'the social problems facing our country today' covers all single issues of the second item pool. Moreover, the items labelled with 'general (social and political) competence of the church' emphasise primarily more personal aspects of (church) belief: moral, individual, and spiritual needs These are aspects closely linked to the function of religion and religiosity.

The next dimension is composed of items which can be subsumed by the label *personally assigned legitimation to the church to speak out on issues concerning sexuality and life*. The items are 'abortion', 'extramarital affairs', 'homosexuality', and, for most countries, 'euthanasia'. All of the items refer unambiguously to basic individual decisions in border areas of human life. They express an immediate personal view of life or represent a self-concept of the individual. Furthermore, because they focus on issues concerning the beginning and end of life, the connection to church is relatively close. Fundamentally, these items cover aspects which tend to be prescribed and sanctioned by Christian religious dogma and the church (Eisinga 1995: 84–5).

The third dimension is labelled *personally assigned legitimation to the church to speak out on issues concerning general political issues*. It consists of the items 'unemployment', 'ecology', and, for most countries, 'government politics'. The emphasis here is on general and traditional political topics. The connection between the church and the items is rather indirect and cannot be derived directly from Christian religious dogmas.

The last dimension, personally assigned legitimation to the church to speak out on issues concerning disadvantaged, covers the issues 'Third World problems' and 'racial discrimination'. Both items refer to topics about the disadvantage of distinct populations or subgroups. Although clearly political, this dimension differs from the previous one in that it refers directly to relevant issues and interests of the church (for instance, charity).

After having searched for an identical measure of subjective competence and legitimation assigned to the religious institution 'church' in all analysed countries, we enlarge this by culture-specific non-common items and consider again the previously deleted items for each country. The results are quite satisfactory. In

Table 4.3 Equivalence set of items concerning the subjective competence and legitimation of the religious institution 'church' (principal components analysis; country-specific data sets)

	Netherlands				Belgium			
	(1)	(2)	(3)	(4)	(1)	(2)	(3)	(4)
Extramarital affairs	0.79				0.78			
Abortion	0.85				0.86			
Homosexuality	0.75				0.69			
Euthanasia	0.84				0.79			
Moral problems		0.83				0.82		
Family life		0.86				0.83		
Spiritual needs		0.74				0.70		
Social problems		0.73				0.70		
Third World			0.84				0.81	
Racial discrimination			0.75				0.71	
Ecology				−0.73				0.76
Unemployment				−0.70				0.77
Government policy				−0.76				0.75
Eigenvalues (before rotation)	4.71	2.32	1.24	0.90	5.09	1.76	0.97	1.18

	Italy				Austria			
	(1)	(2)	(3)	(4)	(1)	(2)	(3)	(4)
Extramarital affairs	0.79				−0.81			
Abortion	0.80				−0.74			
Homosexuality	0.73				−0.71			
Euthanasia	0.71							
Moral problems		−0.85				−0.80		
Family life		−0.78				−0.79		
Spiritual needs		−0.76				−0.70		
Social problems		−0.76				−0.68		
Third World			0.77				−0.78	
Racial discrimination			0.76				−0.72	
Ecology				0.82				0.73
Unemployment				0.79				0.69
Government policy								0.70
Eigenvalues (before rotation)	4.83	1.63	0.91	1.14	1.08	1.45	1.03	4.39

Source: WVS90 (n_{NL} = 947; n_B = 2,392; n_I = 1,900; n_A = 1,460).

Notes: Only loadings > 0.40 are considered; negative loadings got no substantial meaning if the main loadings of the entire column got negative signs; those cases can be interpreted as positive loadings as well.

	NL	B	I	A
Kaiser–Meyer–Olkin Measure of sampling adequacy	0.86	0.88	0.87	0.87
Communalities	> 0.55	> 0.58	> 0.60	> 0.60
Explained variance	70.5%	69.2%	70.9%	66.3%
Inter-factor correlation	< 0.42	< 0.39	< 0.42	< 0.34

Legend
(1) Church legitimation concerning sexuality and life
(2) Church competence
(3) Church legitimation concerning disadvantaged
(4) Church legitimation concerning general political issues

every data set, we can add country-specific items to the sample to serve as non-common indicators for the specific unfolded four components structure (see Table 4.3). Again, the most problematic item is 'disarmament'. For three of four countries, the main loading is below 0.60 and the rest loading is relatively high. However, the basic reason for removing this item is its divergent structuring in the single countries.[19] Apart from this measure, only two other items are removed from the country-specific item set because they do not fit our criteria: 'government politics' in Italy, and 'euthanasia' in Austria. Finally, we can add two non-common items to the identity set of the Netherlands and Belgium ('euthanasia' and 'government politics'), one non-common item to the identity set of Italy ('euthanasia'), and one non-common item to the identity set of Austria ('government politics'). In so doing, it is clear that 'euthanasia' loads high on the dimension representing the 'church legitimation concerning sexuality and life', while 'government politics' can easily be assigned to the political issue dimension.[20]

In addition to these basic results, can similar interpretations be made for the Swiss sample and for the WVS81 data? As mentioned previously, the data for Switzerland include only a reduced set of items. If we look at the results of Table 4.4, we see that two components – though highly correlated – can be extracted. In

Table 4.4 Equivalence set of items concerning the subjective competence and legitimation of the religious institution 'church' for Switzerland (principal components analysis)

	Step 1		Step 2		Step 3	
	(1)	*(3)*	*(1)*	*(3)*	*(1)*	*(3)*
Extramarital affairs	0.84		0.85		0.85	
Abortion	0.92		0.92		0.93	
Homosexuality	0.83		0.85		0.86	
Euthanasia	0.83		0.83		0.81	
Third World		0.91		0.90		0.93
Racial discrimination		0.80		0.82		0.85
Disarmament		0.87		0.86		
Unemployment		0.56				
Eigenvalues (before rotation)	4.86	1.00	4.30	0.99	3.80	0.84

Source: WVS90 (n = 1,400)

Notes: Only loadings > 0.40 are considered; negative loadings got no substantial meaning if the main loadings of the entire column got negative signs; those cases can be interpreted as positive loadings as well.

	Step 1	Step 2	Step 3
Kaiser–Meyer–Olkin Measure of sampling adequacy	0.90	0.87	0.85
Communalities	> 0.64	> 0.67	> 0.67
Explained variance	73.3%	75.5%	77.4%
Inter-factor correlation	0.62	0.61	0.58

Legend
(1) Church legitimation concerning sexuality and life
(3) Church legitimation concerning disadvantaged

line with the previously reported results, these two dimensions reflect 'personally assigned legitimation to the church to speak out on issues concerning sexuality and life' and 'personally assigned legitimation to the church to speak out on issues concerning disadvantaged'. However, two items are removed. With a component loading below 0.60, the item 'unemployment' does not fit our criteria. After removing it, however, 'disarmament' still achieves high loadings on the 'disadvantaged' dimension. To retain an item set highly comparable to the empirical structures so far, we remove 'disarmament' too.[21] Thus we obtain a structure with six items reflecting two dimensions which can also be found in the other four countries.

Besides the Swiss data, we have data concerning the subjective competence assigned to the religious institution 'church' for the early 1980s in several countries, but only three items were used. On the basis of our previous empirical results, it is not very surprising that a PCA with these three variables results in a single component. Table 4.5 shows the results of the pooled and country-specific analyses. Clearly, these three items also reflect our previously detected 'general competence of the church' dimension, where the first three items represent our identity item-set for this component.

With all analyses we have ensured the equivalence of the external constructs, reflecting subjective competence and legitimation assigned to the religious institution 'church'. Now we can test the equivalence of church attendance as a measure of traditional religiosity and make use of a more reliable test of external consistency. As we have found different underlying components, we will want to analyse the relationship with 'church attendance' in terms of these dimensions rather than in terms of the separate variables. For this purpose we create so-called factor scales or factor scores.[22] Table 4.6 shows the correlations between the index of church attendance and the calculated factor scores for each country and each component. Clearly, the relationship is strongest between general competence of the church and the degree of church attendance, although it is only a moderate relationship. Remarkable are the nearly equal correlations for the measures in the 1980s, which indicates equivalence of this dimension over time. A similar relationship exists for the assigned legitimation of the church to speak out on issues concerning sexuality and life itself. In comparison, the other two components

Table 4.5 Identity set of items concerning the subjective competence and legitimation of the religious institution 'church' (principal components analysis; country-specific data sets)

	Pooled	*Netherlands*	*Belgium*	*Italy*
Moral problems	0.87	0.84	0.88	0.88
Family life	0.87	0.85	0.88	0.87
Spirtual needs	0.84	0.80	0.85	0.85
Explained variance	74.5%	69.9%	76.6%	76.2%
n	3,437	1,075	1,110	1,252

Source: WVS81.

Notes: Kaiser–Meyer–Olkin measures of sampling adequacy > 0.70.
Communalities > 0.65.

Table 4.6 Relationship between church attendance and subjective competence and legitimation of the religious institution 'church' (Spearman's r_s; country-specific data sets)

| | Church competence | WVS90 Legitimation of the church to speak out on: | | | | WVS81 Church competence | |
		sex and life	poli. issues	disadvant.	n		n
Netherlands	0.30	0.26	0.09	0.07	944	0.30	1,066
Belgium	0.42	0.36	0.06	0.13	2,389	0.43	1,099
Italy	0.48	0.47	0.13	0.12	1,969	0.41	1,252
Austria	0.44	0.34	0.09	0.10	1,455		
Switzerland		0.24		0.10	1,373		

Source: WVS90; WVS81.

Note: All correlations are significant at the 0.05 level (2–tailed).

or dimensions – the assigned competence of the church to speak out on general political issues and on topics concerning the societal disadvantaged – show lower relationships with church attendance. A polarisation within the four dimensions appears with respect to the levels of correlations. But this result is no surprise. If church attendance is really a crude measure for traditional religiosity, it must correlate highly with both first dimensions – general competence of the church, and church legitimation concerning sexuality and life – because they have substantial meaning for individual respondents, while more general political topics lack such personal involvement. The immediate concern of the dimensions to the respondents' world view (and of course to their traditional religiosity) results in correlations like these.

Nevertheless, the cross-national differences are only marginal. In general, Italy shows the strongest relationships while the Netherlands shows somewhat lower ones. Irrespective of these differences between correlation coefficients, all countries reveal similar relationships between church attendance and the external constructs (see Table 4.1). All in all, the findings support our general assumption. Although we cannot solve every problem with the test of external consistency, we can strengthen the statement that the substantial meaning of 'church attendance' in all countries is more or less the same. The findings also show consistent support for the assumption that church attendance is a crude, but nevertheless adequate, indicator of traditional religiosity.[23] Although we can make only restricted interpretations about a time-dependent equivalence – due to the marginal measurement of our central external construct in the WVS81 – we can see a distinct tendency. Together with the results of the first tests of external consistency, we have obtained some empirical evidence for the hypothesis that church attendance is an equivalent measure of traditional religiosity over time. With these restrictions in mind, we will describe country-specific developments briefly in the next section.

Inter-cultural change of traditional religiosity

For our five countries, which can be characterised by their formerly strong denominational subcultures, the general research question can be formulated more precisely: do these countries show a parallel development on the level of the entire society? In other words, has traditional religiosity decreased for each population in the last few decades?

To examine this question we must use a set of very mixed data to get information for many different points in time. Two divergent empirical time series are used in this context to describe changes in traditional religiosity: (1) a set of very different national and cross-national surveys, and (2) a time series of various Eurobarometer surveys. These two sets of data are analysed separately for various reasons. The advantage of Eurobarometer time series over the single surveys lies clearly in its roughly identical questionnaires concerning church attendance. Results based on this data are more reliable, because they reduce the possibility of artefacts due to variant survey design, different degrees of representativeness, and divergent construction of the central construct. But Eurobarometer surveys are available for only three of the five countries: the Netherlands, Belgium, and Italy. As a consequence, we must first use the data sets which give us information on all countries. That is, the surveys for which we have made the test for equivalence plus additional specific national surveys (see Figure 4.1).[24]

The development of traditional religiosity is operationalised by the change of the proportion of respondents who attend church at least once a week. Although we lack equally distributed information over time for all five countries, three out of five countries reveal a clear decline of traditional religiosity (see Figure 4.1). From the starting point of the nation-specific time series, we see this distinct tendency for the Netherlands, Belgium, and Austria. At the first available point in time, the percentage of regular churchgoers is more than ten points higher than at the last.[25] For Italy, we obtain a somewhat divergent finding. After a decline in traditional religiosity until the mid-1980s, weekly church attendance – and therefore traditional religiosity – became more important at the beginning of the 1990s. The development of traditional religiosity clearly deviates from the pattern found in the other three countries.[26] Though we can make plain statements at the level of entire societies for almost all countries, the Swiss case is an exception. Here no clear tendency can be seen. While a comparison of the cross-national surveys (PAS and WVS90) suggests no change, the additional consideration of the two national surveys resists this interpretation. One can think of an artefact due to the divergent orientations of both denominations in Switzerland, but separate analyses reveal no theoretically acceptable explanation.[27]

If we consider the data of the Eurobarometer surveys, all countries show a striking confirmation of our previous results (see Figure 4.2). A clear and continuous decline of the share of respondents who attend church at least once a week is visible in the Netherlands and Belgium. Both populations show an almost parallel development over time, with Belgium's results slightly higher. The Italian sample also reveals the previously stated deviations. After the decline of traditional religiosity until the early 1980s, a plain increase is visible. This confirms that traditional religiosity in Italy has undergone a kind of 'renaissance'.

It should be noted that for the index of church attendance all unchurched

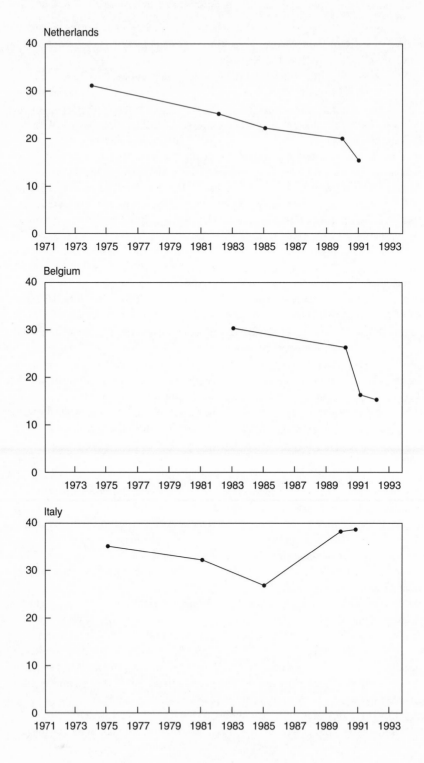

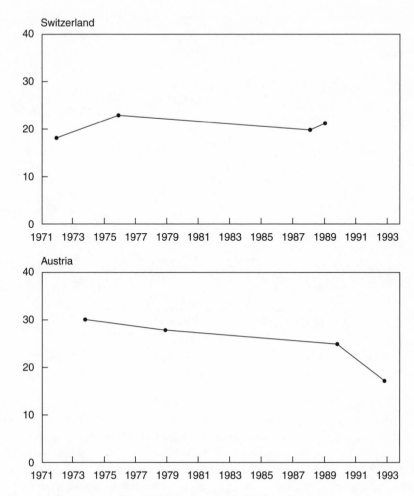

Figure 4.1 Proportions of respondents who attend church at least once a week
(percentages; various surveys)

Sources: Political Action Study (NL/A: 74; I: 75; CH: 76). World Values Survey (NL: 82/90; B: 83/90; I: 81/90; CH: 89; A: 90). International Social Survey Program (NL: 91; I: 90; A: 93). Social and Cultural Developments in the Netherlands (NL: 85). General Election Study Belgium (B: 91/92). Political Culture of Southern Europe (I: 85). Pulse of Europe (I: 91). Swiss Voting Study (CH: 72). Pluralité confessionelle, religiosité, identité culturelle en Suisse (CH: 88). IFES 7930 (A: 79).

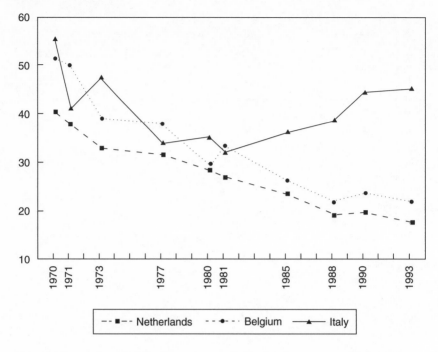

Figure 4.2 Proportions of respondents who attend church at least once a week (percentages; Eurobarometer data)

respondents – those without a denomination – are treated as valid cases. Therefore, one can object that the previous analyses merely measure the increasing proportion of respondents without denomination, and so cover the marginal (or no-) change in traditional religiosity of respondents assigned to a denomination. One could argue, for instance, that even if church attendance within denominations were constant over time, the proportion of regular churchgoers would decrease if unchurched respondents simultaneously increased.

Two arguments counter this objection. First, we have defined the unchurched population as the one most distant from church. They therefore represent the population with the weakest traditional religiosity, and their relative growth is a clear sign of decreasing traditional religiosity. This is exactly what we want to measure. Second, while the proportion of unchurched respondents has certainly risen over time in all countries (especially in the Netherlands and Belgium)[28] a decline in traditional religiosity in specific subgroups is evident, too. If we decompose our sample to such relevant populations (that is, to the denominational groups in the mixed-confessional countries), we gain additional information. Focusing on the development of church attendance in the Netherlands clearly supports our hypothesis (see Figures 4.3 and 4.4).

The Catholic sub-population shows a massive and constant decline in tradi-

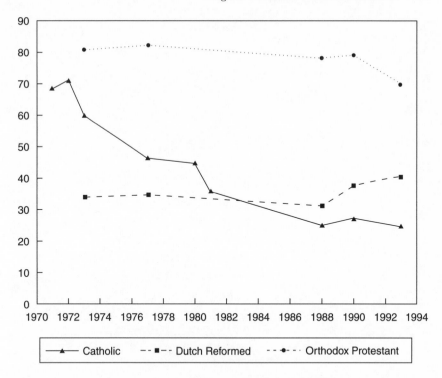

Figure 4.3 Proportions of Dutch respondents who attend church at least once a week (percentages; by denomination; Eurobarometer data)

tional religiosity in both figures. Church attendance and traditional religiosity of Orthodox Protestants (*Gereformeerd*) is on a clearly higher level than that of both other important denominations in the Netherlands. And it is more or less constant over time with a moderate decline in the 1990s. A totally different finding emerges for the Dutch Reformed sub-population (*Nederlands Hervormd*). While the Eurobarometer time series shows a widely unchanging traditional religiosity until the 1990s, Figure 4.4, which is based on various surveys (PAS, WVS, SOCON, ISSP), indicates a plain increase over the last few decades.[29] Regardless of which interpretation fits reality best, a greater percentage of Protestants go to church more regularly now than Catholics do (Felling *et al.* 1987: 68). And this means that the religious orientations of Dutch Protestants are now more traditional than those of Catholics.

Though denomination groups differ in their development, it is evident that at least the Catholic population experiences the change of traditional religiosity depicted in Figure 4.1. Although not shown here, it is true for Catholics in all of the countries considered. Therefore, the clear change in traditional religiosity reported for the Netherlands, Belgium, and Austria is due to a growing number of

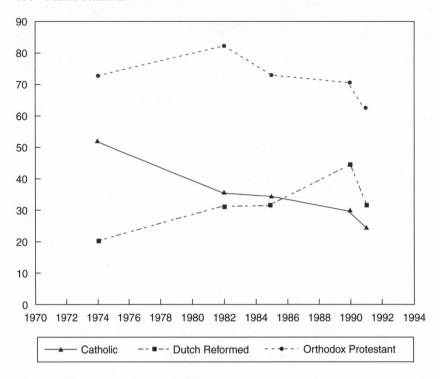

Figure 4.4 Proportions of Dutch respondents who attend church at least once a week
(percentages; by denomination; various surveys)

unchurched *as well as* to a decreasing share of (nominal) Catholics who attend
church regularly.

Conclusion

Although this chapter describes the development of religious value orientations in
five different countries, research on the basis of cross-national time-series analysis
on a micro-level creates severe problems. For this reason we have used the simple
index 'church attendance' as an indicator for religious value orientations, namely
traditional religiosity. Our empirical analyses show that this indicator is a crude
but adequate indicator for describing general developments in traditional religiosity. All of our findings point out that 'church attendance' is equivalent in all
countries.

Regrettably, the use of this index is not trouble free. If we want to know whether
one concept – 'church attendance' – is equivalent to a much broader concept –
'traditional religiosity' – the opportunities for testing are clearly restricted. No
available survey indicates whether its respondents go to church regularly due to
their religious orientations, habits, cultural localisms, or social pressures. In
secondary analyses, the only strategy which might clarify the matter is a test of

external consistency. If one accepts the test as a way to analyse the inter-cultural equivalence of a construct, convincing results can only rarely be expected. Too many difficulties – some of them mentioned above – reveal this.

We have therefore strengthened the results of simple tests for external consistency by verifying the internal consistency of our constructs. This strategy helps us to obtain clearer and more reliable findings concerning the equivalence of 'church attendance'. In the end, however, our interpretations must rely on correlations between church attendance and other external concepts. And unless a clear frame of reference tells us what country-specific differences in the correlations we should accept, we will always have a hard time justifying our interpretation. For that reason, we must accept inter-cultural differences in the relationship between our relevant indices, look carefully for tendencies, and put together several indicators for external consistency analyses. Only then will we be able to say that 'church attendance' is a proper instrument for measuring traditional religiosity in cross-national and longitudinal research.

Notes

1 One must keep in mind that these macro-societal processes are by no means unitary phenomena. Not every dimension of religious orientations is equally subject to the forces of secularisation (Harding *et al.* 1986: 33).
2 For the detailed conceptualisation of value orientations, see Feldkircher (1997: 206) and, above all van Deth and Scarbrough (1995a).
3 Schmitt (1985), for example, shows that church integration has much in common with the confessional attachment of the individual. But he also points out that both constructs affect voting behaviour differently in different denominations.
4 Although not exactly the same, the concepts 'church religiosity' and 'traditional (Christian) religiosity' are used interchangeably here.
5 This in no way means that equivalence and identity at the first stages of a study are less important (Halman and de Moor 1993) or are free of serious methodological difficulties. Comparability of data during conceptualisation, operationalisation, and sample drawing is the precondition for equivalence of data on the level of analysis. But once these phases are finished, mistakes can be discovered only by putting the question of equivalence on the level of data analysis.
6 Members of those subcultures share common world views and value orientations which result in some kind of self-identification. On a regional level these subsocieties are held together by a network of intermediate organisations (for instance, political parties, trade unions, recreational associations) which is multi-faceted and penetrated and propped by all life situations. This organisational structure 'ties' members together and operates as a cognitive support or intensifier of existing orientations for every participating member of the subculture. The subculture of our country sample is Catholic. The organisations are either ecclesiastic (for instance, old peoples' homes), or they have more or less informal relationships with the church elite (for instance, denominational political parties).
7 Italy is an exception. The consideration of the Italian sample is substantiated mainly for its formerly powerful Catholic subculture (Fix 1995: 190–2). Italy therefore was a country with a strong social basis of closed Catholicism on which the church previously relied (Furlong 1988: 131).
8 In the pooled data of the World Values Survey 1990, about three-quarters of all respondents without any reported denomination never attend church. Most of the remaining population attend church at best several times a year, mainly on holy days.

Although this population is not homogeneous and the assignment is somewhat restrictive, we categorise the respondents without denomination as 'unchurched' as do Jagodzinski and Dobbelaere (1995: 86). But one must notice that the percentage of respondents without denomination depends on the question format (Eisinga and Felling 1990). In addition, the surveys used differ slightly in the question concerning denomination (for instance, the WVS81–83 and 90–91).

9 While 'subjective religiosity' more or less measures general religiosity independent of Christian linkage, the last three constructs reflect religiosity referring to a God. The 'number of religious beliefs' and the 'type of God one believes in' clearly intend to measure a more orthodox aspect of personal religiosity, so these are the most direct indicators of traditional religiosity.

10 The extent of the linkage between the (external) variables and traditional religiosity varies, too.

11 For all these indicators of traditional religiosity, we use Spearman's rank correlation coefficient (r_s). This measure is recommended for correlations if both variables are an ordinal scale (Bortz 1989: 283–4). Church attendance is in a strict sense merely an ordinal scale, like most of the external variables. To secure a high degree of comparability between the measurements, r_s was also calculated for metric variables. In contrast to Jagodzinski and Dobbelaere (1995), we follow somewhat stricter assumptions concerning the statistics used. Criticism of the quality of a measure like r_s, (Benninghaus 1989: 2–3) notes that the results of the relationships measured with other statistics for ordinal scales (for instance Tau *b*) lead to the same conclusions. In general, they indicate a slightly weaker relationship than Spearman's rank correlation coefficient does.

12 The huge differences in the measured relationships for PAS and WVS may lie in divergent questioning. The question concerning membership in a religious organisation in the PAS emphasises the extent of activity, while the WVS explicitly substantiates this activity – doing unpaid work for the organisation.

13 We assume that the respondents do not assign a strong competence to church when their church attendance is primarily the reflection of social localism or social pressure. This hypothesis is not free of conflicts. Conceivably, church attendance alone influences the consciousness (church competence) no matter what the behaviour constitutes (church religiosity or social localism). But this cannot be empirically analysed with the available instruments and data sets.

14 Besides the substantive arguments mentioned, the structural separation between both item pools can be due to 'technical' reasons. One potential cause are the somewhat differing question anchors. In the first item pool the question refers to the country-specific church of the respondent's own denomination; in the second, the question refers to church (as an institution) in general. A second reason is the well-known methodological artefact that respondents incline to answer the items of one pool homogeneously. So a kind of intra-item-block acquiescence may be responsible for a structural separation of items.

15 For the analyses, the response categories of the fourteen variables are changed. To make use of the full variance, the category 'don't know' was not coded as a missing value but as an explicit measurement of an intermediate response category (as it probably is). Hence, wavering respondents were coded between a negative and a positive answer concerning the various items of church competence or legitimation. The explicit consideration of these respondents does not change the results significantly. The empirical deviation is marginal both on the level of principal components analysis and on the level of correlations.

16 The criteria for the factor extraction is the so-called scree test proposed by Cattell (1966). The recommendation for the number of components extracting is to retain all those Eigenvalues (and hence components) in the sharp descent before the first one on the line where they start to level off (Stevens 1992: 378). This means that Eigenvalues

(or components) can also be extracted which does not fit the Kaiser-criteria. In general the extraction results of the scree test are quite accurate although the criterion is more subjective (Kim and Mueller 1978: 45; Stevens 1992: 379). In our analyses the decisions according to the scree test clearly indicate a four components model, as every additional change in the Eigenvalues is only marginal in character. In all further results of the PCAs, the respective structure fits the criteria of the scree test.

17 Criteria of an item exclusion are a component loading below 0.60 and/or a communality below 0.40.

18 This interpretation can be strengthened even more if the number of components extracted is restricted to two. A model of this kind results in a clear distinction between the two item-batteries both in the pooled data and in the later country-specific analysis (with the exception of Italy, where some differences can be found).

19 'Disarmament' has its main loading only in Italy and Austria on the dimension labelled 'church legitimation concerning general political issues'. In the other two countries the item loads high together with 'Third World' and 'racial discrimination' on one component. Because of this inconsistent structuring, it is advisable to remove this item completely to obtain clearer structures.

20 It is important to note that the dimensions are in no way independent from each other. As can be seen in Table 4.3, the components correlate up to 0.43. This can be interpreted as *ex post* justification for rotating the component structure non-orthogonally or obliquely, although an orthogonal procedure is sometimes preferred for group comparisons.

21 As reported previously, this item is very problematic for a comparative structuring of items. Perhaps its loadings in the Swiss data result from the lack of the two other items reflecting general political issues. Perhaps this is also the explanation for the loadings of the item 'unemployment'.

22 The method calculating the factor scale used here is Bartlett's criterion. According to Kim and Mueller (1978: 69), the real choice between the methods for creating adequate factor scales lies between Bartlett's and the regression method. In terms of the correlation between the underlying factor and its respective scale, they are superior in comparison to other methods. But if one wants to use the factor to estimate the underlying correlations between the hypothesised and the outside variables – as we plan to do – the regression method does not work as well as the others (Tucker 1971).

23 Additional analyses of relevant sub-groups would enhance the validity of these interpretations. By no means would the relationships have to be the same over groups of different denominations. Therefore, separate analyses for the Catholic and Protestant populations of each country would bring more evidence. This would surely be a fine strategy if our sample consisted of mixed religious countries, but only Switzerland and the Netherlands can be ascribed in this way. For the other three merely homogenous Catholic countries separate analyses do not make too much sense. As Jagodzinski and Dobbelaere (1995: 117) point out, the correlation coefficients would not be stable for the minority religion (in this context, Protestants) while the coefficients for the majority religion (Catholics) would be almost identical to the ones calculated for the entire population. Because of this, we avoid additional separate analyses here.

24 This strategy is preferred instead of a pooled analysis of all available surveys. If all used surveys equally represented the population and all questions concerning church attendance included the same response categories, there would be no problem in analysing all surveys together. But unfortunately this is not the case. Even for the Eurobarometer surveys, the questionnaires and the response categories differ slightly over time. While we tolerate this deviation in the case of the sole analysis of Eurobarometer data, we are not willing to water down the findings in a pooled analysis.

25 These findings are similar to those of other researchers, for instance, Becker and Vink (1994) for the Netherlands, Dobbelaere (1995b) for Belgium, or Zulehner *et al.* (1991) for Austria.

26 Jagodzinski and Dobbelaere (1995: 103–4) establish similar results for Italy without well-founded explanations.

27 Though the Protestants' traditional religiosity slightly rises on a low level over the years the Catholic population shows a similar ambiguous development to the entire society.

28 For the Netherlands the proportion of unchurched increased from about 33 per cent in 1973 to 51 per cent in 1993 and for Belgium from 14 per cent to 29 per cent (Eurobarometer data). In the other three countries, the increase was less than ten points. One reason for this cross-national difference is of course the varying meaning of nominal denomination in the Netherlands and Belgium.

29 An increase of traditional religiosity for the Protestant sample and a decrease for the Catholic sample can also be found in analyses of the other mixed-confessional country, Switzerland.

5 Gender roles

Michael Braun

Introduction

In few areas has social change been more dramatic in recent decades than in the relationship between men and women. Legal status, social relationships, self-concepts, and behaviour have altered in many areas: political participation, family relations, labour-force participation, and more. Attitudes have changed, too, as a prerequisite (or consequence) of behavioural change (Alwin *et al.* 1992; Braun *et al.* 1994; Höllinger 1991; Hoepflinger 1987; Lupri 1983; Thornton 1989; Thornton *et al.* 1983).

Many measurement tools have been created to capture gender-related attitudes. In this chapter, I restrict myself to the attitudes related to the global division of labour between men of women in the areas of household and paid work. Thus, I ignore, for instance, the role of the two genders in politics – which has become less and less controversial (see Alwin *et al.* 1996; Ferree 1974) – or gender roles with regard to sexuality. I hold that the questions revolving around the division of labour are in some sense primordial, that they drive changes in other areas more than they are driven by them.

Attitudes of the kind considered here have been measured in national general social surveys[1] on a regular basis for several decades, though international comparisons are more recent. The American General Social Survey (GSS, see Davis and Smith 1996) has used the same four-item battery since 1977, when it was adapted from other American studies on special groups (Cherlin and Barnhouse Walters 1981; Helmreich *et al.* 1982; Mason and Bumpass 1975; Mason *et al.* 1976; Mason and Lu 1988; Thornton and Freedman 1979). The German ALLBUS (Braun and Mohler 1991) adopted the GSS battery in 1982 and added two items; the British Social Attitudes Survey took up the American measure in 1984; and the Polish General Social items (PGSS) at its beginning in 1992 introduced the items in order to increase comparability with both the American and German surveys.

The GSS/ALLBUS measure was then used as the basis for constructing a gender-role battery in the 1988 study of the International Social Survey Program (ISSP, see Braun 1994; Davis and Jowell 1989) on 'Family and Changing Gender Roles' (Zentralarchiv 1991). The response scale was changed, however, as was the phrasing of items, and the number of items was increased. In the 1994 replication of this study (Zentralarchiv 1997), one of the 1988 items was dropped and three were added, leading to a net increase in the number of items over the original study. 'Family and Changing Gender Roles' is now awaiting its second replication in the early twenty-first century.

While other large-scale projects like the World Values Surveys (WVS) have also used their own gender-role items, I focus here on the ISSP because it offers several advantages with regard both to the construction and evaluation of functionally equivalent measures. The ISSP is a co-operative effort between national general social surveys of different countries which annually prepare a questionnaire for one thematic topic and conduct their surveys in a similar manner. To date the ISSP has twenty-nine members around the world, including:

1   European Community: Austria, Britain, France, Germany, Ireland, Italy, the Netherlands, Portugal, Spain, Sweden.
2   Other European countries: Bulgaria, Czech Republic, Cyprus, Hungary, Latvia, Norway, Poland, Russia, Slovak Republic, Slovenia.
3   Asia: Bangladesh, Israel, Japan, the Philippines.
4   America: Canada, Chile, United States.
5   Australia and New Zealand.

New topics selected for inclusion in the ISSP are handed over to a drafting group which ideally consists of a microcosm of the membership. In this phase, first-hand knowledge of the topic is advantageous and so is knowing the peculiarities of individual countries and the problems of asking questions in an inter-culturally comparable manner.

The ISSP emphasises the 'literal' replication of questions which may (though not necessarily) turn out to be functionally equivalent replications (Alwin *et al.* 1994). Only if a question will not be understood in a country can it be left out or replaced by an 'equivalent' question. An alternative to literal replication is to ask different questions in different countries with the aim of capturing common, underlying concepts. The main problem with this 'conceptual equivalence' approach, however, is that it is unclear – especially in this substantive field – how to construct items which differ in their manifest content but are functionally equivalent in their theoretical dimension.

Thus, the data base I am dealing with consists of a common set of indicators – at least in theory. In practice, due to translation errors in some of the national surveys, one ends up with a partially incomplete common set of indicators. Unfortunately, the country-specific 'deviations' are not the result of an attempt to reach comparability on the conceptual level by using country-specific indicators. Another characteristic of my approach is the focus on internal consistency. As gender-role attitudes are likely to be in flux in most of the countries and the level of traditionality and rate of change differ markedly, similar structures between the concepts considered here and, say, socio-demographic variables can hardly be expected.

Theoretical background

During the 1960s when gender-role attitude items were constructed in the United States, the benefits to women coming from the traditional, gendered division of labour were seen to be rapidly declining (Mason *et al.* 1976): the rise in returns for female labour on the market, the decline in desired and actual family size, and the rise of divorce rates increased costs for traditional homemakers. In accordance with this changed opportunity structure, female behaviour changed, too. Inequalities between the genders in education were markedly reduced, and female labour-force participation rose. At roughly the same time, the women's movement generated public discussions of the role of women. The question was then whether the changed opportunity structure for women, their changed behaviour, and the women's movement also produced changes in attitudes which could help promote less-traditional gender roles.

Inasmuch as the most dramatic change in family and gender roles in the 1960s occurred in the behaviour of women – while apparently the need for men to change was neither perceived nor even considered possible – it comes as no surprise that most items for measuring gender-role attitudes focused on women. As we shall see, this might have been a considerable weakness when comparing attitudes across time and culture.

The GSS measure for gender-role attitudes[2] takes into consideration two theoretically discernible dimensions: 'consequences of (female) labour-force participation for the family' and 'gender ideology'. Both dimensions were thought to be related, for if maternal employment was seen as detrimental to children, a strong argument could be made for the traditional division of labour between the genders.

The International Social Surveys Program 1988 added another dimension related to the 'economic consequences of (female) work' and increased the number of items for the two other dimensions.[3] In 1994, one item of the 1988 battery was dropped and three were added – one related to the 'economic consequences of (female) work' and one related to the role of men for each of the two other dimensions. These items are discussed in great detail in the next section (see the list of ISSP 1994 items with their respective factor loadings in Table 5.1). However, there is no reason to assume that the dimensions which can be empirically found across time and place will always be the same as those derived from theoretical considerations.

These items have been criticised for a variety of reasons. They are phrased around a traditional role of woman that is increasingly less common in industrial countries. This has two consequences. First, the questions are less and less accepted by respondents, which creates difficulties in the administration of the surveys. Second, important differentiations cannot be reflected in the data (see Braun *et al.* 1994). For example, the item regarding the suffering of a child in the case of a working mother confounds two distinct aspects: does the child suffer if *no* parent is around during the day? And if so, does it matter whether the mother or father is absent from the home? Both aspects fall together only if it is the norm (statistically, as well as otherwise) that women stop working but men continue to work after the birth of a child. In this case it can be assumed that only the behaviour of the mother matters. If both aspects fall apart, however, the item becomes two-dimensional and respondents who believe that children suffer if both parents are absent, but do not necessarily want the mother to stay home, are confused and do not know how to respond. Another criticism concerns the omission of the role of the man in the battery of 1988, where it is implicit in nearly all of the items. This suggests that only women have to change, not men.

Keeping items which are biased in this sense is justified as long as traditional response alternatives remain relatively popular and as long as disagreeing with the items constitutes an egalitarian stance. However, the strong liberal trend observed in Western industrialised countries like the United States, Britain, and Germany (Braun *et al.* 1994) makes it likely that several of the items will soon become ineffective in measuring social change.

Moreover, when it comes to cross-national comparisons, the reverse might also apply. Though countries like Sweden have often been less traditional than both Germany and the United States, in some countries even traditionally biased items might not differentiate between degrees of traditionalism. Why? Because they might still be perceived as too liberal by the overwhelming majority of respondents – as in fundamentalist Islamic countries or rural Catholic societies.

In terms of comprehension problems, however, the liberal-traditional dimension is not the only relevant one. The role of objective reality for the understanding of questions must be regarded much more generally. Items may be especially misunderstood, for instance, if they are not matched to the social or economic reality of a country and are, therefore, incongruent with the experiences of respondents. Additional complications arise when questionnaires must be translated for inter-cultural research. Obviously, even a 'perfect' translation cannot handle a mismatch between the social reality of a country and the elements of an item. But a poor translation can worsen the mismatch.

In the following, I will give relatively short shrift to blatant translation errors and concentrate on more subtle things; that is, where different social realities cause different interpretations of items, where cognitive structures seem to differ between populations of different countries, and where seemingly innocuous (and difficult to detect) variations in item formulation cause different framings of the underlying problem and thus different interpretations of the meaning of an item.[4]

Conceptual problems and ambiguity of items

In the previous section, I have discussed three dimensions of gender-role attitudes. I will now examine the items of these dimensions with regard to potential intrinsic difficulties. Then I will discuss these difficulties on the basis of empirical evidence for a reduced number of problems.

Consequences of (female) labour-force participation for the family

A working mother can establish just as warm and secure a relationship with her children as a mother who does not work may focus on the emotional needs of the child or on the capabilities of the mother (Braun *et al.* 1994). Both the ALLBUS/GSS time series and the ISSP data show that Germans tend to have less traditional opinions with regard to this item than do Americans and British. (With the following, related items, however, it is the other way round.) Given the ambiguity of the item, Germans may tend to evaluate the capabilities of a mother, while Anglo-Saxons evaluate the needs of the child. The effect is that the German responses appear to be less traditional than the Anglo-Saxon. However, the reason may lie in the difficulty posed by the term 'secure', which is difficult to translate in an equivalent manner. In the German version, 'secure' was rendered by *vertrauensvoll* (which resembles 'trusting').[5] Yet *vertrauensvoll* may be much weaker for the needs of the child than 'secure', because the former refers more to the capabilities of the mother and less to the reaction of the child.

A pre-school child is likely to suffer if his or her mother works. As discussed above, this item confounds two aspects: whether a child suffers if its parents work and, if so, whether the presence of the mother is of special importance. However, additional problems lie in this item which concern virtually every part of the sentence. First, what is meant by 'pre-school'? In a country in which no mother dares to leave a less than 1-year-old child alone, respondents will automatically think of a 5- or 6-year-old child. In another country, where women are obliged to resume work almost immediately after giving birth to a child, respondents will probably think of a very young child. Second, what does 'suffer' mean? Does it include some form of permanent damage or is it 'just' an emotional state of aversive stimulation? Third, what about the father? In most cases he is probably assumed to work, too. But this might differ in countries with high unemployment or in rural societies.

Finally and most importantly, if it is assumed that both parents work, where does the child stay during the day? Very few respondents might assume that the child is left completely alone, but beyond this assumption many possibilities exist, including kin, day-care facilities, baby-sitters, etc. What makes international comparisons difficult is that respondents in different countries might think of completely different solutions to which they attribute different qualities. In Southern Italy, for example, the absence of the mother might not pose any problems, because children are assumed to stay with relatives and not necessarily with the nuclear family. In communist countries day-care facilities were virtually all-encompassing, although their quality was evaluated very differently from country to country. After the collapse of communism, the provision of childcare was drastically reduced in some countries. Western countries, too, differ sharply in the availability, quality and flexibility of day-care facilities. Thus, the question of whether the absence of the mother is important is not only dependent on the role of the father but on the society in which it is expressed. Moreover, an evaluation of the absence of mother and/or father can only be judged in the light of the institutional support of the respective countries. In turn, this makes conclusions from the responses to this item all but straightforward.

All in all, family life suffers when the woman has a full-time job is likely to tap several dimensions: the consequences of working women on family life, gender-role ideology and the possible contribution of a second income to the economy of the family. Different translations are likely to emphasise one dimension more than others even if they are not blatantly 'wrong' in a narrow sense. Indeed, some translations render 'when the woman has a full-time job' as 'when the woman works' (Braun 1993; Braun and Scott 1998). Thus, while the original English wording may invoke in some respondents a comparison of employment and unemployment (rather than a comparison with the voluntary chosen homemaker role), it may invoke the concept of self-actualisation in other countries.

Family life often suffers because men concentrate too much on their work is one of the 'male items' introduced in 1994. The main problem with this item seems to be the term 'because' which has been more or less deliberately translated in some countries by 'if'. Apparently, researchers/translators found it more natural not to assume that men in fact act in the way described. Another weakness lies in the phrase 'concentrate on their work'. Probably nobody doubts that men should concentrate on their work while at work. But what the item actually expresses is that men either work overtime, invest too much time in their careers, or give their careers a higher preference than their families. However, these are options largely restricted to flourishing economies and/or middle-class environments.

Gender ideology

Gender ideology in the sense used here refers to the beliefs about the 'nature' of women (and to some degree men) and about what women 'really' want. In this sense, it is more 'ideological' than perceptions of the consequences of labour-force participation for the family. Gender ideology items are mostly framed in a traditional point of view and are therefore likely to arouse the protest of respondents, men as well as women.

A job is all right, but what most women really want is a home and children has problems at once. First, the meaning of 'all right' is not entirely clear (whether it means 'good' or just 'acceptable', for instance), and the meaning of 'job' is questionable. Is the emphasis on 'to have a job' or on 'to work'? Dependent on the answers to these questions emphasis will be on unemployment or the voluntarily chosen role as a homemaker.

Being a housewife is just as fulfilling as working for pay poses the same problem. As long as 'working for pay' is read as 'having a paid job' the focus is likely to be unemployment and not the chosen role as a homemaker. However, the item can also be read as referring to the possible benefits of a job outside the home (social contacts, intrinsic motivation). Obviously, translations which present exactly the same ambiguity are hard to achieve and, thus, any translation will confer a different meaning of the item to the respondent.

It is not good if the man stays at home and cares for the children and the woman goes out to work, added in 1994, is the only 'male item' for this dimension. Significantly, it is also phrased in the traditional sense. A positive formulation might have appeared to be too 'modern' in some countries. However, the real problem with this item is located on a different level. When the item was drafted, it was intended as a 'modern' solution in which the woman gets rid of her traditional role by merely changing roles with the man. The implicit assumption is that one parent should stay at home and care for the children. However, if this assumption is not shared by the respondents, who might hold that there is no need for one parent to stay at home, problems will arise in answering the question. In fact, the item can be agreed with for two opposite reasons: either because it should be the woman who stays at home or because both should work. As we will see later, respondents in some socialist countries with traditionally high levels of both female and male labour-force participation have the greatest problems with this item.

Economic consequences of (female) work

The third dimension consists of a collection of three rather heterogeneous items. I give them less attention because they are not central to gender-role attitudes.

Having a job is the best way for a woman to be an independent person leaves unclear whether independence is meant mainly in financial terms (Braun *et al.* 1994). In addition, the item leaves unclear how responses to the question should be interpreted. First, some people may not want women to be independent. How would they answer? Second, some people may think that, though having a job is 'all right', a job itself does not lead to independence, inasmuch as patriarchal thinking is still deeply rooted in society. Finally, some people might argue that women who have a (dependent) job cannot be independent, as they are subject to the restrictions such a job implies. Hence, negative answers might mean different things for different respondents.

The meaning of gender-role items

After briefly sketching the methods and looking at the dimensionality of the gender-role items, I now present empirical evidence for some of the problems mentioned above: the interpretation of a 'warm and secure relationship', the conditions determining the suffering of the child, the differential impact of using 'when the woman has a full-time job' versus 'when the woman works', and the workings of the two male items.

Basically, I use two distinct analytical strategies here. The first is made up by a secondary analysis of the ISSP 1994 data. Starting with the common factor-analytic solution for all countries, I switch to multi-dimensional scaling (MDS, see Borg and Shye 1995; Borg and Groenen 1997). This method allows me to present the results in a much more comprehensible way than factor analysis. What MDS technically does is graphically represent the intercorrelations of the items in a multi-dimensional space. Correlations correspond to the distances between the items which are drawn as points. The interpretation of the MDS representation focuses on the correspondence between geometrical characteristics of the config-uration and the substantive characteristics of the items. The lines entered into the MDS representations are theoretically derived dividing lines between items. Ideally the partitions of the space should be achieved by straight lines.

The second strategy was pursued by a methodological study conducted in only one country, Germany, in early 1997 (see Braun 1997; Thoma and Braun 1997). A series of methodological experiments was nested in three modes (CSAQ, CATI, and PAPI).[6] The study was administered on randomised groups selected on the basis of a quota sample in which age, gender, and education were controlled. The sample reflects the distribution of these socio-demographic variables for the respondents in German national social surveys.

The dimensionality of gender-role attitudes

Table 5.1 shows the factor-analytical solution for the gender-role battery for all countries together with the mnemonics of the items as they are used in the following MDS representations of the intercorrelations of the gender-role items. It becomes obvious that both 'male items' have comparatively low loadings. However, the same applies to some degree to *warm relation, housework as fulfill* and two of the three items in the economic-consequences dimension. If we compare the factor-analytic results with the MDS representation of the inter-correlations[7] of the gender-role items in Figure 5.1 we see the same structure represented in a different way.

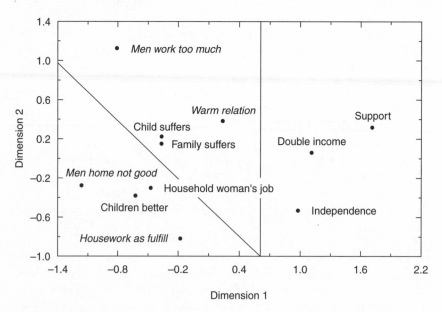

Figure 5.1 MDS representation of intercorrelations of gender-role items: all countries
Source: ISSP 1994.
Notes: N = 33,590. Stress = 0.04.

Table 5.1 Dimensionality of gender-role attitudes (factor-analytic solution; all countries; oblique rotation)

	F1	*F2*	*F3*
Consequences for the family			
Warm relation: A working mother can establish just as warm and secure a relationship with her children as a mother who does not work			0.62
Child suffers: A pre-school child is likely to suffer if his or her mother works			0.73
Family suffers: All in all, family life suffers when the woman has a full-time job			0.72
Men work too much: Family life often suffers because men concentrate too much on their work			0.54
Gender ideology			
Children better: A job is all right, but what most women really want is a home and children	0.76		
Housework as fulfill: Being a housewife is just as fulfilling as working for pay	0.68		
Housework woman's job: A man's job is to earn money; a woman's job is to look after the home and family	0.79		
Men home not good: It is not good if the man stays at home and cares for the children and the woman goes out to work	0.61		
Economic consequences			
Independence: Having a job is the best way for a woman to be an independent person		0.66	
Support: Most women have to work these days to support their families		0.67	
Double income: Both the man and woman should contribute to the household income		0.75	

Source: ISSP 1994.

Notes: N = 33,590. Only highest loading per item is presented.

What is striking in Figure 5.1 is that two items which belong to each of the regions 'consequences of (female) labour-force participation' and 'gender ideology' are located at an equal or even greater distance to the two remaining items of the respective clusters than the distance between these remaining items of the two regions. In addition to the 'male items' (for which I expected some irregular behaviour), two items – *warm relation* and *housework as fulfill* – which I expected to be somewhat central for their respective clusters, are the relative outliers. This has already become visible by the factor-analytic solution.

What deserves special attention, too, is the fact that the three regions – especially the first two (on the left side of the figure) – are not neatly separated. That is, if we consider all countries together, the items form something of a continuum on the cognitive map of the respondents. That this is not necessarily the case in the single countries is shown in the MDS for Japan in Figure 5.2.

With the exception of only two items (which are likely to have been translated

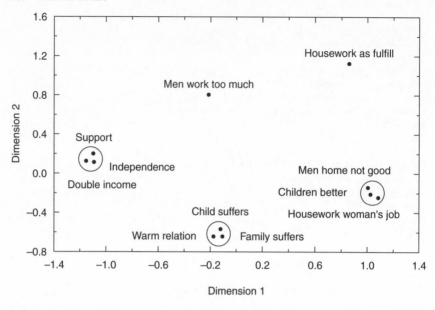

Figure 5.2 MDS representation of intercorrelations of gender-role items: Japan

Source: ISSP 1994.
Notes: N = 1,307. Stress = 0.07.

inadequately), the Japanese organise gender-role attitudes into three neat clusters which are perceived as clearly distinct from each other and for which the connectedness of the constituent items is acknowledged by the respondents. Basically, the United States (not displayed) is the opposite of Japan regarding the equality of the distribution of the items over the space. In the United States, respondents make no principal distinction between the three regions, but highly differentiate between the items constituting the single dimensions. The remaining countries fall more or less in between both extremes. In a certain sense, there is a parallel to this with factor analysis which may produce two to four factors depending on the country.

The Anglo-Saxon countries (Figure 5.3) show two characteristic deviations from the model for all countries. While *warm relation* is better integrated in the consequences dimension (where *child suffers* and *family suffers* have essentially the same point representation), *housework as fulfill* has basically left the gender-ideology region in the direction of the economic-consequences dimension. I will come back to the interpretation of these results when I discuss the implications of the MDS for the concrete problems I have sketched above.

In striking contrast to the Anglo-Saxon countries, both of these items behave in the opposite manner in West Germany and Austria (Figure 5.4). *Warm relation* is further apart from the other items in the consequences dimension, but *housework as fulfill* has its natural home in the gender-ideology region. Also, *men home not good* is perfectly understood by the respondents in Germany and Austria as being part of the gender-ideology dimension, as intended when the questionnaire was drafted.

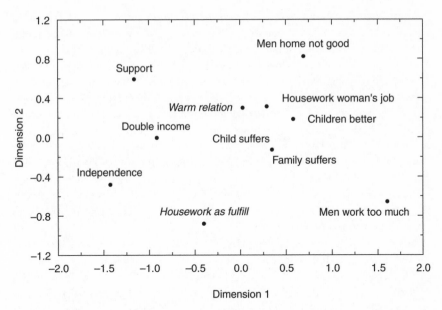

Figure 5.3 MDS representation of intercorrelations of gender-role items: Anglo-Saxon countries

Source: ISSP 1994.
Notes: N = 8,282 (Great Britain, Nothern Ireland, Ireland, United States, Canada, Australia, New Zealand). Stress = 0.10.

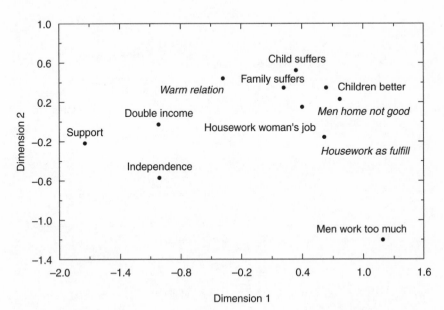

Figure 5.4 MDS representation of intercorrelations of gender-role items: West Germany and Austria

Source: ISSP 1994.
Notes: N = 3,301. Stress = 0.10.

Unfortunately, in the case of the former socialist countries many kinds of deviations exist from the model for all countries. We can only speculate about the reasons, one of which might be the relatively high proportion of inadequate translations. Most of the former socialist countries share a Slavic language which is less akin to English than are German and the Scandinavian languages. In addition, bilingual translators are hard to come by in these countries. Therefore, I restrict myself here to only one pattern found in these countries and which is shared by East Germany, Poland, and Slovenia. Two peculiarities of Figure 5.5 deserve mentioning. First, *men home not good* is not perceived as a central part of the gender-ideology cluster, especially in East Germany. In this case we can probably exclude linguistic reasons for the deviation compared to West Germany. Second, while *housework as fulfill* is regarded as integral to the gender-ideology dimension, the central item of the economic-consequences dimension, *double income*, moves close to the gender-ideology cluster.

Figures 5.6 and 5.7 display the MDS representations of the intercorrelations for Italy and Spain. Both countries are included here to show both an example of a blatant translation error and the possible consequences of slight variations in the emphasis of an item. At the outset, it could be expected that these two Mediter-ranean 'cousins' would not differ much from each other. To a relatively high degree, their development of family and female labour-force participation has been parallel in recent decades. In addition, both are Catholic and both have

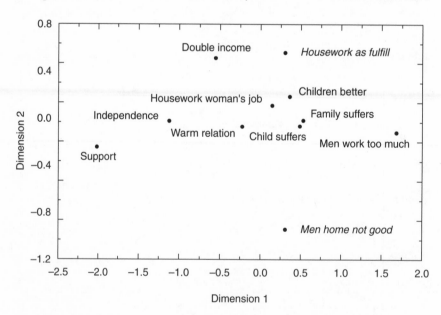

Figure 5.5 MDS representation of intercorrelations of gender-role items: East Germany, Poland, Slovenia

Source: ISSP 1994.
Notes: N = 3,726. Stress = 0.05.

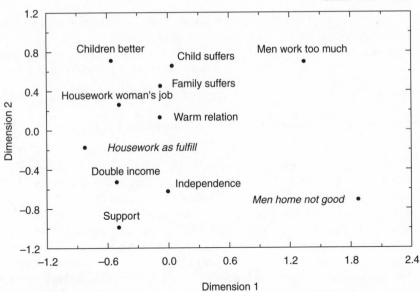

Figure 5.6 MDS representation of intercorrelations of gender-role items: Italy

Source: ISSP 1994.
Notes: N = 1,018. Stress = 0.09.

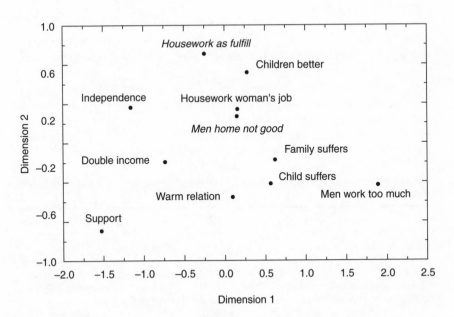

Figure 5.7 MDS representation of intercorrelations of gender-role items: Spain

Source: ISSP 1994.
Notes: N = 2,494. Stress = 0.09.

experienced industrialisation relatively late compared to other Western and Central European countries. Translation is the cause for the different positioning of *men home not good*; that is, the Italians omitted the word 'not'. The more interesting result, however, concerns *housework as fulfill*, where the Italians seem to put a slightly different emphasis. I will come back to this later.

Consequences of (female) labour-force participation for the family

In order to check whether translation of the first item of the consequences dimension – a 'warm and secure relationship' – might be at the core of the differences between Germany and the Anglo-Saxon countries, I included two versions of the item: the traditional German rendering and a variant in which 'secure' is translated as *sicher* (Braun 1997). The results show that Germans appear to be slightly more traditional when 'secure' is rendered by *sicher*. Regardless of item formulation, however, the differences are too small to exclude the possibility that Germans refer more to the 'capabilities of the mother' than do Anglo-Saxons.

Methodological research on the second item of this dimension (child suffers) proves very telling for Germany and also sheds light on the entire 'consequences of (female) labour-force participation' dimension (Braun 1997). I designed a battery of six items in the form of vignettes (Rossi and Nock 1982) in which respondents had to evaluate the potential suffering of a 3-year-old child when his or her mother and father worked to different degrees: full-time, part-time and not at all. In one split-version I used the sequence presented on the left hand side of Table 5.2 which shows average values for the two versions. In the other split, 'mother' and 'father' appeared in the reversed order (but exactly the same structure was preserved).

As two-thirds of the respondents did not know in advance – with the exception of the paper-and-pencil survey – how many and which situations they had to evaluate, and as the sequence was reversed in the two split-versions, I am confident that the results cannot be explained by a conscious tendency to treat mother and father equally. This is the more the case as the scale was rather complicated (a

Table 5.2 Mean values for the suffering of a child dependent on labour-force participation of parents

Split 1			Split 2
Mother and father full-time	4.9	5.0	Father and mother full-time
Mother full-time, father part-time	3.6	3.6	Father full-time, mother part-time
Mother full-time, father not	2.4	2.2	Father full-time, mother not
Mother part-time, father full-time	3.1	3.0	Father part-time, mother full-time
Mother and father part-time	2.8	2.8	Father and mother part-time
Mother not, father full-time	2.3	2.8	Father not, mother full-time

Source: Attitudes towards family and society in Germany (Thoma and Braun 1997).

Note: N = 302, all modes combined.

seven-point scale with labelled end-points) and the respondents did not always answer consistently (see Braun 1997 for a detailed analysis and discussion of these inconsistencies).

Obviously, German respondents barely differentiate between both genders when it comes to the importance of mother and father for the child. They prefer that one parent be exclusively at home, but whether this is the mother or the father is not as crucial as might be expected. What is also striking is the high level of 'suffering' which Germans attribute to the child, even if only one parent is at work.[8]

The male item in the 'consequences of (female) work for the family' dimension (*men work too much*) is close to the other items in some MDS representations and further apart in others. The reason is likely because of the ambiguity of this item. Agreeing with it is in some sense indicative of positive attitudes towards a more equal sharing of the household burden by both genders. On the other hand, it also means that the absence of one parent is seen as detrimental to the child. Both aspects – having egalitarian gender-role attitudes and optimism about the consequences of labour-force participation for the child – are highly correlated. However, the two aspects have opposite consequences with regard to answering the male item.[9] Due to the high correlations between the other items of the consequences and gender-ideology dimensions, this drives the 'male item' far from both dimensions.

It is only in countries where the 'male item' is not seen to be related to both dimensions that it comes close to the consequences dimension. This is the case of at least some of the socialist countries. In these countries, too, people who think that the child will not suffer also think that the family will not suffer because men concentrate too much on their work. However, they do not establish a relationship to the gender-ideology dimension. The emancipation of women is not expected to be reached by changed conduct in men but by the intervention of the state (in the form of childcare facilities etc.) in reducing the burden of having to juggle job and family. Thus, the positioning of this 'male item' tells us something more complex, and it is hard to interpret in the sense in which it was intended.

Gender ideology

Given the fact that many of the items of the gender-ideology dimension are highly ambiguous and that respondents might – because of this or because of other reasons – differentiate among them, it is very hard to establish whether patterns of inconsistent answers exist which create bad data. Probably many respondents answer inconsistently. This could mean that on a five-point scale average values around 4 mean total disagreement and values of 5 could possibly never be reached empirically due to data errors. If this is true, two of the four gender-ideology items are close to their ceiling in Germany, and further change cannot be monitored. Methodological studies need to find out to which degree that is true. If it turns out to be true, one alternative might be to rephrase the gender-role items by substituting man for woman in the gender-ideology dimension in the following way:

1   A job is all right, but what most men really want is a home and children.
2   Being a house-husband is just as fulfilling as working for pay.
3   A woman's job is to earn money; a man's job is to look after the home and family.
4   It is not good if the woman stays at home and cares for the children and the man goes out to work.

Speculating on how these items might be interpreted by the respondents might be helpful for a better understanding of how the ISSP measures work. The most 'unnatural' item would be number 3 which would boil down to a mere change of the traditional gender roles of men and women and as such would not present a modern solution. Number 1 sounds strange, too, because it either presupposes that an ideology in this sense exists, or it would be answered in the sense of a lack of work motivation (an explanation which, astoundingly, does not easily come to mind in the case of women). Numbers 2 and 4 seem perfect at a first glance. However, number 2 might pose a problem in countries with high unemployment where the item might be regarded as cynical. In such countries, number 4 would be uniformly understood in the sense that both partners should work. A possible change of roles would not come to mind (as in the original item where the positions of man and woman are reversed).

The empirical analysis partly supports the above interpretation with regard to the difference between using 'when the woman has a full-time job' and 'when the woman works', especially with regard to *housework as fulfill*. ISSP data of 1988 demonstrate (see Braun and Scott 1998) that while the Italians generally show very traditional gender-role attitudes, they turn out to be the least traditional nation on this item. The same trend is also visible within Italy, with Southern Italians appearing to be slightly less traditional than Northern Italians and, for related questions, clearly more traditional. Thus, basically (some of) the Italians may answer a different question and a comparison with the remaining nations could hardly be recommended without taking this into account. It is worth noting that the English version uses 'to work' for some items and 'to have work' for others. It is only in the two cases where the Italian version deviates in this way from the English version (that is, where the Italian questionnaire refers to 'to have work' instead of 'to work') that striking results appear.

Similar insights can be obtained by comparing the English and French versions of the Canadian study. The French questionnaire nearly always employs 'works' when the English uses 'has a job' and vice versa. While English and French respondents are generally identical with regard to their degrees of traditionality, the French turn out to be more liberal than the English whenever the French version employs 'has a job' and less where it employs 'works'.

We see the same tendency when comparing the Italian and Spanish MDS representations. The Spanish use an equivalent of 'to work' and the Italian use 'has a job'. As a consequence, *housework as fulfill* is located in the gender-ideology region in Spain but in the economic consequences of (female) work region in Italy.

As observed by Braun and Scott (1998) genuine country differences exist which are unrelated to translation issues and which are responsible for different interpretations of *housework as fulfill*. Thus, in the Anglo-Saxon countries, this item is located somewhere between the gender ideology and the economic consequences of (female) work regions. In other countries, its natural home is in the gender ideology region. Only if the translation deviates from the English in emphasis does it move into the economic consequences of (female) work region.

The 'male item' for the gender-ideology dimension, *men home not good*, works quite well in most of the countries. However, it seems to behave the opposite of the 'male item' in the consequences dimension, *men work too much*. While the latter works only in the socialist countries, the former does not work there at all. The reason is obvious. People do not see any advantage in men changing roles with women. Both should work and the state should care for the children. In socialist countries, the item is therefore not interpreted along a liberal-traditional dimension as was intended.

Comparing gender-role attitudes across countries

The conclusion of the methodological considerations seems to be that in order to construct truly comparable measures, problematic items should be eliminated from the respective indices. For the consequences dimension this leads to dropping *warm relation* and the male item and keeping only *child suffers* and *family suffers*. Thus, this dimension gets a much clearer interpretation, and it should now measure the consequences of (female) labour-force participation for the family and the children in a much more literal sense. In such a revision, the *gender-ideology dimension* would be measured only by *children better* and *housework woman's job* and by dropping *housework as fulfill* and the male item which proved problematic in several countries. Finally, for the economic consequences dimension only the item *double income* would be selected for a clear interpretation.

Tables 5.3 and 5.4 show how indices based on the full set of items which constitute the single dimensions differ from the reduced indices which should perform better as inter-culturally comparable measures. Table 5.3 covers the countries we have discussed above, and Table 5.4 gives the full picture for all the countries included in ISSP 1994.

Although the comparable set uses only half or fewer of the original items, the means for all countries are much the same as with the full set. This is a purely technical observation having to do with similarities in the distribution of the items, but it makes deviations for the single countries or groups of countries easier to observe. Changes from the full to the comparable indices are bold if, after considering the change of the mean for all countries, their net amount is bigger than 0.3. Given this criterion, for the groups of countries only two pairs of means deserve mentioning. With regard to the consequences dimension, Germany and Austria appear clearly more traditional than before, and the same applies to Italy

Table 5.3 Means of gender-role attitude indices for selected countries (groups of Figures 5.1–5.7)

	Consequences		Gender ideology		Economic consequences	
	Full	*Compar.*	*Full*	*Compar.*	*Full*	*Compar.*
All countries	2.9	2.8	3.0	3.0	3.8	3.8
Anglo-Saxon countries	3.0	3.1	3.3	3.4	3.6	3.5
Germany and Austria	**2.7**	**2.3**	3.0	3.1	3.9	3.8
East Germany, Poland and Slovenia	2.9	2.8	2.9	2.9	3.8	4.0
Japan	3.3	3.2	2.7	2.9	3.6	3.5
Italy	2.7	2.4	**3.4**	**3.1**	3.8	4.0
Spain	2.8	2.7	3.0	3.0	3.8	4.0

Source: ISSP 1994.

Note: N = 33,590. Full: index with all indicators; Compar: comparable index with reduced number of indicators.

Table 5.4 Means of gender-role attitude indices for all countries

	Consequences		Gender ideology		Economic consequences	
	Full	*Compar.*	*Full*	*Compar.*	*Full*	*Compar.*
All countries	2.9	2.8	3.0	3.0	3.8	3.8
Great Britain	3.1	3.1	3.2	3.4	3.7	3.7
Northern Ireland	3.1	3.1	3.1	3.2	3.8	3.8
Ireland	2.9	2.9	3.0	3.1	3.8	3.9
United States	3.2	3.2	3.2	3.3	3.6	3.6
Canada	3.3	3.4	3.6	3.8	3.6	3.7
Australia	2.8	2.9	3.2	3.2	3.4	3.3
New Zealand	2.8	2.9	3.4	3.5	3.3	3.2
West Germany	**2.8**	**2.3**	3.0	3.2	3.8	3.7
Austria	**2.7**	**2.3**	2.8	2.8	4.0	4.0
Netherlands	3.0	2.9	3.4	3.4	3.0	2.9
Norway	3.0	3.1	3.5	3.5	3.5	3.6
Sweden	3.3	3.3	3.4	3.5	4.0	4.1
East Germany	3.4	3.3	3.6	3.8	4.2	4.4
Poland	2.7	2.5	2.4	2.4	**3.8**	**3.4**
Slovenia	2.7	2.5	2.8	2.7	**4.0**	**4.3**
Czech Republic	2.8	2.7	2.7	2.5	4.1	4.3
Bulgaria	2.4	2.2	2.1	2.2	4.5	4.6
Russia	**2.7**	**2.1**	2.2	2.3	4.0	3.8
Hungary	2.4	2.1	2.2	2.1	4.0	4.1
Italy	2.7	2.4	**3.4**	**3.1**	3.8	4.0
Spain	2.8	2.7	3.0	3.0	3.8	4.0
Israel	2.7	2.9	3.2	3.2	**3.9**	**4.2**
Japan	3.3	3.2	2.7	2.9	3.6	3.5
Philippines	2.9	2.7	2.4	2.2	3.9	4.0

Source: ISSP 1994.

Note: N = 33,590. Full: index with all indicators. Compar.: comparable index with reduced number of indicators.

with regard to the gender-ideology dimension. This has been expected from the direction in which the defective items deviated in these countries from their intended meaning.

Some additional insights are possible when we turn to the individual countries. This is mostly because, even if net differences between the full and comparable indices are not large, the observation of the same tendency in a group of countries might be significant. With respect to the consequences dimension, it is obvious that *all* Anglo-Saxon countries improve their relative position by showing more liberal attitudes with the reduced index. Moreover, in addition to West Germany and Austria, all Eastern European countries lose ground, Russia even more than West Germany. In the gender-ideology domain, there is hardly any change, except for Italy which appears more traditional with the comparable index, all Anglo-Saxon countries stay where they are or slightly improve their positions. Meanwhile, some Eastern European countries end up with slightly higher index values, some with slightly lower and others stay where they are. Finally, with respect to the economic consequences dimension, two countries end up with clearly higher and one with lower values. Given the heterogeneity of the full set of items, however, an interpretation of this result makes hardly any sense.

Comparing the means of the full and comparable sets of items, one might infer that the differences are not dramatic and that it does not matter whether the methodological considerations outlined above are observed when constructing comparable measures. However, the following should be borne in mind. First, even entirely different questions may produce numerically equal means and, second, survey research favours – for good reason – items which are not very skewed and which, as a consequence, yield similar mean values. In fact, as the figures in Table 5.4 aptly show, nearly all means range from 2 to 4. Moreover, the variation of means for the single dimensions is even more restricted. For the full set of the consequence dimension, for example, the means for the different countries vary only from 2.4 to 3.4. Given that fact, the difference for Russia of 0.5 (after correcting for the reduced overall mean for the comparable set) is a big drop, indeed.

In addition, Figures 5.8 and 5.9 show that the selection of an index also affects the correlation with age. Using the comparable index for the consequence dimension, for example, increases the correlation both in the Anglo-Saxon countries and in West Germany and Austria (see Figure 5.8). Nevertheless, the effect on the mean in the latter group of countries is clearly more significant.

Figure 5.9 does not pit the comparable set against the full set for gender ideology in Italy and Spain. As mentioned above, two items of the full set were affected by problems in Italy, one of which was the omission of 'not' in the male item. As this is a trivial error, it makes little sense to take the full set for comparison; rather, we shall take an intermediate set where the affected item has been eliminated for both countries.

As Figure 5.9 shows, in Spain the intermediate index practically coincides with the comparable one with regard to the correlation with age, but in Italy the intermediate index produces a weaker correlation. Moreover, for the comparable

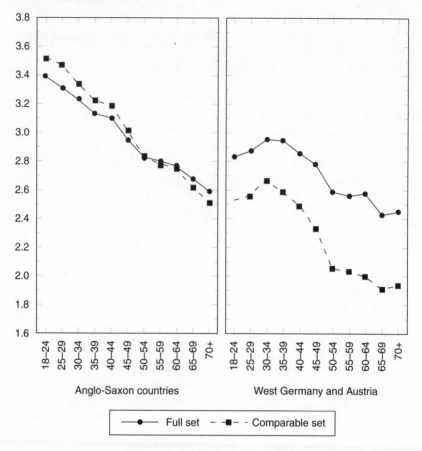

Figure 5.8 Consequences dependent on age group

Source: ISSP 1994.
Note: N = 11,583.

set, Italy and Spain display a nearly identical pattern which is not the case for the intermediate index.

Comparing the working of different indices with regard to third variables can be seen as a first step in external validation. However, it should be emphasised that external validation of the gender-role scales is in general rather difficult. From Figure 5.10, which presents means of the gender-role ideology index for different age groups in five countries, it is obvious that the relationship between age and attitudes is not similar across countries.

Hardly any association exists between age and gender-role ideology in Russia and the Philippines, and the curves of both Germanys and the United States show at least several differences in important details. The United States is closest to a linear relationship with age over the entire range, that is, every age group is slightly less traditional than its predecessor. Moreover, while for the groups below age 45 or so,

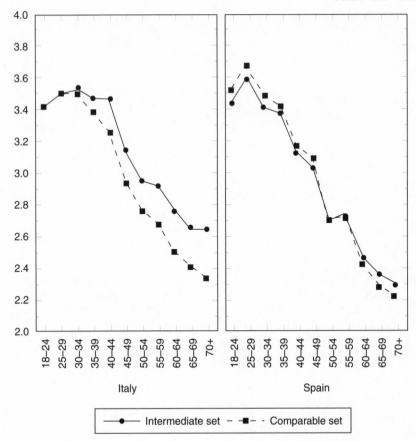

Figure 5.9 Gender-role ideology dependent on age group

Source: ISSP 1994.
Note: N = 3,512.

the Americans are hardly less traditional than corresponding groups in Germany, the gap between both countries widens, especially for age groups of 45–64, and shrinks again for groups above 65 years. In West Germany, age groups below 40 hardly differ from each other, and in East Germany the same applies to age groups of 25–49 and, somewhat less, for all age groups below 64. It is only from the age of 40 in West Germany and 65 in East Germany that a clear linear trend emerges. It is also from age 65 that the trend in the United States becomes more pronounced.

Does this mean that the gender-role ideology is still (that is, after having eliminated two problematic items) not measured in a functionally equivalent way in the different countries? Or is it that the patterns of change in each country differ from each other? Though I intuitively prefer the latter explanation, conclusive proof is hard to come by. For the Philippines and Russia we do not even know whether gender-role attitudes have changed, since the questions were asked only once. If change has occurred, it would have been within age groups and not

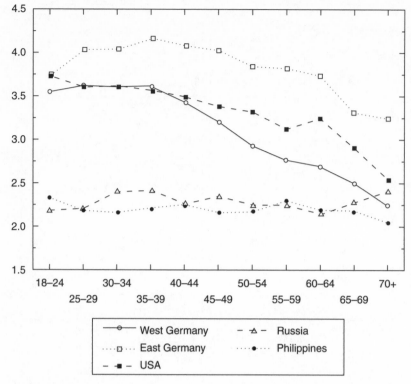

Figure 5.10 Gender-role ideology by age group in five countries

Source: ISSP 1994.
Note: N = 8,066.

produced by cohort succession. For Western countries, we know that considerable change has occurred in a liberal direction since the 1970s and that it has been due more to change within groups than to cohort succession – though the latter has accounted for one-third to one-half of the total change (Braun *et al.* 1994). From Figure 5.10 one can conclude that the proportion of change explained by cohort succession in East Germany should have been clearly smaller.

What is the meaning of all this? In a nutshell, it means that the available data are compatible with the hypothesis that social change is shaped by different patterns in different countries.

Discussion

Attitudes towards gender roles are difficult to measure – and even more so when international comparisons are at stake. As could be shown, even the most frequently used measurement device in international comparative research has serious shortcomings. This is not to criticise the researchers of ISSP who presumably did their best. The lesson we learn is this: that in order to design adequate measurement instruments we need considerable empirical research on existing data and an incremental process of improving the instruments.

However, as researchers are interested above all in substantive questions and not only in methodological issues, relegating substantive conclusions to the future is clearly no alternative. I would suggest that dealing with partially defective data be pursued as a multifold strategy until 'perfect' measurement devices and 'perfect' data become available. First, data should be routinely checked for problems of functional equivalence using a variety of statistical procedures. In this chapter I have advocated multi-dimensional scaling, but this is clearly not the only useful method. In addition, if deemed necessary, I would recommend an *ex post* translation of the foreign-language questionnaires back into their original tongue. Both the back translations and the MDS representations of the single countries might then yield information on which items are most error prone, whether they are badly translated or whether they are interpreted differently in different countries for other reasons. While we probably could not do very much about the effects of bad translations during data analysis (unless it were possible to do additional research in the respective countries to gauge the direction and the magnitude of the error produced by translation problems), problems of functional equivalence due to other reasons might be interesting as such. Differences in understanding items, whether due to systemic differences between countries, to differences with regard to social and economic indicators and their change, or to the overall level of traditionality of attitudes, should be regarded as part of the explanation and included in the report of substantive results.

Substantive analyses – especially when comparing marginals which are methodologically the most problematic, if also the most interesting, aspect of data analysis – would then be based on the core of the hopefully less error-prone items.

Notes

1 General social surveys are research projects designed to collect and distribute social science data for academic research and teaching. Since 1972 the American General Social Survey (GSS) and since 1980 the German ALLBUS have been conducted annually or every second year. The British Social Attitudes Survey began in 1983.

2 The GSS items are:

- A working mother can establish just as warm and secure a relationship with her children as a mother who does not work.
- It is more important for a wife to help her husband's career than to have one herself.
- A pre-school child is likely to suffer if his or her mother works.
- It is much better for everyone involved if the man is the achiever outside the home and the woman takes care of the home and the family.

3 The items asked in the ISSP 1988 study are:

- A working mother can establish just as warm and secure a relationship with her children as a mother who does not work.
- A pre-school child is likely to suffer if his or her mother works.
- All in all, family life suffers when the woman has a full-time job.

- A woman and her family will all be happier if she goes out to work (dropped in 1994).
- A job is all right, but what most women really want is a home and children.
- Being a housewife is just as fulfilling as working for pay.
- Having a job is the best way for a woman to be an independent person.
- Both the husband and the wife should contribute to the household income.
- A husband's job is to earn money; a wife's job is to look after the home and family.

4 An overview of translation errors and other problems with functional equivalence for the 1988 study can be found in Braun (1993).

5 This happened in the early 1980s, when the items were adopted from the American GSS, and the translation has never been changed, partly in order to preserve comparability over time. However, Germany was not the only country to deviate from a 'literal' translation. Thus, 'secure' was rendered by '*stabile*' in the Italian and '*szoros*' in the Hungarian versions, which resemble 'stable' and 'tight', respectively.

6 CSAQ = Computerised self-administered questionnaire; CATI = Computer-assisted telephone interview; PAPI = Paper and pencil interview.

7 The MDS items had to be recoded so that high values indicate non-traditional responses. The following variables were recoded: *warm relation, independence, support,* and *double income.*

8 I could have included the situation where neither parent works, but I was afraid that this might provoke a different understanding: e.g. the unemployment of both parents and, thus, economic hardship.

9 For this reason, recoding the 'male item' in the sense that agreeing with the position that family life suffers because men work too much is regarded as a non-traditional response, does not help.

6 Membership of voluntary associations

Jan W. van Deth and Frauke Kreuter[1]

Introduction

The development of modern societies seems to be characterised by an ongoing differentiation, fragmentation, and individualisation. A virtually endless list of authors has pointed out the dangers inherent for societies to integrate their members amid increasing distinctions and the loss of 'natural' relationships. In the context of theories of mass society (Kornhauser 1959), voluntary associations are singled out as intermediating organisations between individual citizens and primary groups like families, on the one hand, and central organisations like state agencies, on the other. Participation in intermediary organisations, then, is crucial for the functioning of modern societies.[2]

Broadly speaking, the fact that individual citizens are disrupted from their social rootedness is a crucial consequence of the development of mass society. Yet participating in voluntary organisations should remedy the threat (cf. Berry 1969; Cutler 1973; Berger 1977). Formulated in a more positive way, voluntary organisations provide 'free spaces' for the development of civil skills and more assertive group identities (Evans and Boyte 1992). The relevance of voluntary organisations has been stressed in debates on proposals by Communitarians to stimulate small-scale alliances between citizens to further the virtues of citizenship (cf. Etzioni 1993; 1997) and by the introduction of the concept of social capital (Coleman 1988; Putnam 1993; 1995a; 1995b) emphasising the need for social contacts, norms, and trust among citizens in civil society. Following a clear Tocquevillean line of arguing, many authors consider these organisations a *conditio sine qua non* for political decision-making in democratic societies and for political involvement of individual citizens (cf. van Deth 1997).

Although the importance of voluntary associations for the development of modern societies and the opportunities for democratic decision-making is widely recognised, the empirical record on membership in voluntary organisations is ambiguous. First, very crude measures show impressive cross-national variation in the membership rates of voluntary associations, which are only barely related to socio-demographic differences between countries. Relatively high proportions of populations of English speaking countries and several north-western European countries like Denmark, the Netherlands, and Luxembourg belong to a wide variety of organisations. Citizens of southern European countries like Spain and Italy, on the other hand, appear much less attracted to them (Curtis *et al.* 1992; Wessels 1996; van Deth 1996).[3] These differences between countries have been discussed from a broad cross-cultural perspective by Fukuyama (1995).

In addition to these differences, empirical analyses suggest changing levels and modes of voluntary association membership within countries. For instance, the panel study of Babchuk and Booth (1969) has indicated clear changes in 'membership profiles' accompanied by moderate changes at the aggregate level due to multiple membership ties of many respondents. Researchers have found small but noteworthy increases in the percentage of American adults belonging to voluntary associations (Hyman and Wright 1971), but others do not confirm this increase. In Europe, no clear change in the number of people joining unions or new social movements has been observed in the last decades (Aarts 1995). In discussing the change and persistence of voluntary association membership, Putnam (1995a; 1995b) has argued that a decline in active participation can be observed in the United States. People still join organisations but are increasingly 'bowling alone'. This last thesis underlines the need for a distinction between the modes and level of participation in voluntary associations.

This chapter limits its analyses to membership of citizens in voluntary associations in several European countries. Since cross-national or cross-cultural differences are likely to be expressed in membership of different *kinds* of organisations in various settings, the practice of constructing simple additive scales based on the average number of memberships of respondents is questionable.[4] If the number of memberships – irrespective of the kinds of organisations involved – is to serve as an indicator for social integration and involvement, we must start with a closer look at the relationships between memberships of different kinds of organisations. On the basis of these relationships, we will investigate the opportunities for constructing an equivalent instrument of voluntary organisation membership in cross-national research. First, we will search for internal consistency among a common set of indicators used in several countries in a similar way and for one or more cross-national measures of membership. Second, we will assess the validity of our measures by looking at external consistency; that is, by analysing their relationships with several social-structural antecedents as well as their performance in models on the stability of democratic political systems. Our indicators are straightforward questions on membership of voluntary associations included in a set of large-scale representative surveys among the populations of a number of countries. Although we will incidentally refer to results from other cross-national surveys, our search for equivalent measures will be based on the analysis of the so-called World Values Surveys (1990–93).[5]

Measuring membership

Estimates of the roles and functions of voluntary associations are usually based on membership surveys among citizens. In this type of research, respondents are asked to indicate which organisations they support by becoming a member or by providing resources like time or money. Other ways include questions on the degree of involvement or commitment, the positions people have held in organisations, the kind of work they are doing, their motives for becoming involved, and the like (cf. Scott 1957; Babchuk and Booth 1969; Hyman and Wright 1971; Curtis *et al.* 1992). Research on the motivation of participants takes place by interviewing members or volunteers within specific organisations (Gaskin and Smith 1995; van Deth and Leijenaar 1994). Obviously, this research is relevant only for those organisations with membership or with opportunities for volunteering.[6]

In several surveys, respondents are confronted with a list of organisations and asked to identify which, if any, they belong to.[7] The number of memberships provides a simple measure of the *degree of individual organisational participation.* Table 6.1 summarises the results of several large cross-national surveys since the 1970s. Entries in this table show the percentage of people who belong to at least one organisation in each country and the average number of memberships per respondent. Although question wordings, question formats, and coding schemes differ between surveys, the general conclusions presented by Curtis, Grabb, and Baer (1992) are confirmed. Cross-national differences in the average level of social participation are substantive (and consistent). As already mentioned, the highest levels of involvement are in countries like Denmark, Luxembourg, and the Netherlands, with much lower levels in southern European countries. The scope of participation – as indicated by the average number of organisational memberships per citizen – shows the same pattern.

In spite of these clear differences, Table 6.1 shows large variations within countries that cannot easily be explained. For instance, in Belgium what accounts for a figure of 58 per cent membership in at least one organisation in 1975 and 71 per cent in 1977? These fluctuations do not seem to reflect real changes and a search for possible trends among them does not look very promising.

The conclusions of clear cross-national differences combined with fluctuations within each country can also be based on an analysis of the results of a subset of the countries included in Table 6.1 (van Deth 1996: 17–20). Broadly speaking, on the overall level of social participation, three categories of countries emerge. Denmark, Luxembourg, and the Netherlands are in the first category with over 70 per cent of their populations belonging to at least one organisation or association. In the middle category, with 50–60 per cent participation, are Ireland, Northern Ireland, Great Britain, Belgium, and Germany. In the third category, with approximately 30 per cent participation, are the more southern countries of France, Italy, Portugal, Greece, and Spain. The relatively large standard deviations (not shown here) indicate the fluctuations already mentioned within each country, but the fluctuations do not affect the ordering of the countries by their average level of membership. Moreover, a test on the similarities of the rankings of countries within each survey yields highly significant results and underlines the validity of the orderings of the countries (van Deth 1996: 19).

It is unlikely that organisational membership within countries fluctuates

Table 6.1 Membership of voluntary associations in Europe, 1974–93 (percentages and means)

Country	1974[a] $\%^d$ m^e		1975[b] % m		1977[b] % m		1981[c] % m		1983[b] % m		1987[b] % m		1990[b] % m		1990[c] % m	
Austria	45	0.7	—	—	—	—	—	—	—	—	—	—	—	—	53	1.1
Belgium	—	—	58	1.0	71	1.4	41	0.6	44	0.7	51	0.9	56	1.1	57	1.4
Bulgaria	—	—	—	—	—	—	—	—	—	—	—	—	—	—	41	0.7
Denmark	—	—	64	0.9	75	1.4	64	1.0	65	1.1	84	1.8	86	1.8	81	1.8
Estonia	—	—	—	—	—	—	—	—	—	—	—	—	—	—	73	1.2
Finland	63	0.9	—	—	—	—	40	0.4	—	—	—	—	—	—	77	1.8
France	—	—	50	1.0	63	1.0	27	0.4	44	0.7	44	0.7	42	0.7	38	0.7
East Germany	—	—	—	—	—	—	—	—	—	—	—	—	70	1.0	84	1.7
West Germany	36	0.5	53	0.9	53	0.9	48	0.7	57	1.0	45	0.7	57	1.0	67	1.4
Great Britain	44	0.6	52	0.8	54	1.0	52	0.9	58	1.0	61	1.1	61	1.1	52	1.1
Greece	—	—	—	—	—	—	—	—	32	0.5	22	0.3	25	0.3	—	—
Hungary	—	—	—	—	—	—	—	—	—	—	—	—	—	—	50	0.7
Iceland	—	—	—	—	—	—	82	1.6	—	—	—	—	—	—	90	2.4
Ireland	—	—	59	1.1	54	1.0	52	0.8	55	1.0	65	1.2	56	0.9	49	1.0
Northern Ireland	—	—	59	0.8	54	0.9	66	1.0	60	1.0	67	1.2	70	1.2	56	1.2
Italy	7	0.1	35	0.4	46	0.7	24	0.3	36	0.5	36	0.5	38	0.6	34	0.6
Latvia	—	—	—	—	—	—	—	—	—	—	—	—	—	—	68	1.2
Lithuania	—	—	—	—	—	—	—	—	—	—	—	—	—	—	60	0.8
Luxembourg	—	—	71	1.3	71	1.9	—	—	69	1.5	77	1.8	77	1.6	—	—
Netherlands	44	0.6	63	1.4	80	2.4	61	1.2	78	1.7	72	1.5	74	1.5	84	2.7
Norway	—	—	—	—	—	—	61	1.0	—	—	—	—	—	—	81	2.0
Portugal	—	—	—	—	—	—	—	—	—	—	31	0.4	25	0.3	33	0.6
Romania	—	—	—	—	—	—	—	—	—	—	—	—	—	—	30	0.4
Russia	—	—	—	—	—	—	—	—	—	—	—	—	—	—	71	1.0
Slovenia	—	—	—	—	—	—	—	—	—	—	—	—	—	—	39	0.6
Spain	—	—	—	—	—	—	31	0.4	—	—	18	0.2	27	0.3	23	0.4
Sweden	—	—	—	—	—	—	67	1.1	—	—	—	—	—	—	85	2.1
Switzerland	47	0.7	—	—	—	—	—	—	—	—	—	—	—	—	43	0.7

Notes:
[a] Political Action Study.
[b] Eurobarometers.
[c] World Values Surveys (1981–84 and 1990–93).
[d] Percentage of the respondents being member of at least one association.
[e] Average number of memberships among respondents.

to the degree indicated by Table 6.1 and we must conclude that measurement problems are responsible for the fluctuations. Since differences in question format and sample design are usually reduced in the context of international comparative projects, a major source of the fluctuations might stem from the use of a straightforward question on membership. Apart from the possibility that similar associations might perform different tasks in different countries, collecting information this way presents at least two serious complications.

First, the lists presented to the respondents usually contain a remarkably heterogeneous set of organisations, ranging from unions to sports clubs to cultural organisations. Distinct categories on the lists are very different and very difficult to compare. For instance, the category 'religious or church organisations' covers different organisations and is more ambiguous than the category 'trade unions'. While selecting a relevant union is obvious for most respondents, selecting a religious or church group might include church activities for the elderly, contributions of money to missions in Central Africa, or a Bible course for young parish members. Moreover, for some organisations in several countries attending or contributing to these activities might not be understood as 'membership'. By including specific and unspecified types of organisations in the questionnaires, large fluctuations might result from small differences in question format and question wording.

A second complication follows directly from the first. By simply adding the number of associations to measure individual organisational participation, we assume implicitly that each type of membership contributes the same weight to the single score for social involvement of each respondent. This seems a rather bold assumption given the heterogeneity of the set of organisations. Distinct categories vary in their 'coverage' of groups of organisations as the example of unions and religious associations shows.[8] In other words, it is not self-evident that membership in organisations as different as sports clubs, trade unions, and health organisations can be simply added in order to measure the degree of social participation. A dimensional analysis which uncovers the structure of the different kinds of memberships might help us design more adequate measures.

A common membership structure?

It is hard to accept the inconsistent results obtained from widely used questions on the organisational participation of citizens. Simple additive measures are clearly problematic. The question, then, is whether we can construct a more sophisticated instrument to compare differences in social involvement within and between countries in the existing data. We start by analysing the structure underlying membership items. The following question in the World Values Surveys has been applied identically in many countries:

Please look carefully at the following list of voluntary associations and activities and say (1) which, if any, do you belong to, and (2) which, if any, are you currently doing unpaid voluntary work for:

- Social welfare services for elderly, handicapped or deprived people
- Religious or church organisations
- Education, arts, music, or cultural activities
- Trade unions
- Political parties or groups
- Local community action on issues like poverty, employment, housing, racial equality
- Third World development or human rights
- Conservation, the environment, ecology
- Professional associations
- Youth work (e.g. scouts, guides, youth clubs, etc.)

- Sports or recreation
- Women's groups
- Peace movement
- Animal rights
- Voluntary organisations concerned with health
- Other groups.

Responses to these questions have been analysed by several researchers. Confronted with the same problem of finding a latent structure underlying these items, Wessels (1997) attempted to reduce the possible modes of associational participation to a limited number of theoretically relevant types. First, he constructed an involvement index based on a combination of the answers to the questions of whether the respondent was a member of a specific type of organisation and whether the respondent performed activities for the organisation.[9] On the basis of a principal components analysis of data for several countries,[10] he proposed three distinct dimensions: one for *traditional political associations* (unions, professional organisations, political parties); one for *new social movements* (environmental organisations, peace groups, Third World and human rights organisations, animal protection groups); and one for *social organisations* (welfare organisations, religious groups, community groups, youth organisations, women's organisations, sports clubs, health organisations, educational organisations). This three-dimensional space exists when the structure is limited to three dimensions and a so-called oblique rotation of the solution is applied (Wessels 1997: 200).

For some reason, a replication of Wessels' analyses for the pooled set of countries does not result in identical findings. It reveals a different placement for sports clubs (Wessels' traditional political associations) and for community activities (Wessels' new social movements). The first dimension to appear in our computations of the same data set is a new social movement dimension with high loadings for associations active in the fields of Third World, environment, peace, and animal rights (18.6 per cent of the variance before rotation). A second dimension consists of traditional political associations like unions, parties, and professional organisations, but also of sports clubs and cultural and educational organisations (7.6 per cent variance). Finally, a third dimension consists of welfare organisations, religious organisations, and organisations for young people and for women (7.2 per cent variance). This solution clearly deviates from Wessels' and is harder to interpret.

Applying a fixed three-dimensional space with oblique rotation to each separate country shows large and unambiguous differences between them. Here are a few examples. The dimension for new social movements includes political parties in the United States and Canada, and women's organisations in Spain. The dimension for traditional political organisations includes cultural and educational organisations in Portugal, Spain, and Belgium, but not in the other countries. And remarkable differences appear between countries for organisations belonging to the area of welfare and social support. In short, we find no similar structuring of the items in each – or even in the majority – of the countries considered by

Wessels. Several modifications of the specifications of our analyses result in different solutions – none of which avoid the conclusion that clear cross-national differences exist in the underlying structure of these items.[11]

This disappointing attempt to reduce the items to a few general types of organisational participation requires modifications. A closer look at the distributions of simple membership figures in European countries suggests why we cannot find a similar structure in various countries. The only unambiguous answer to the very heterogeneous items lies in respondents who belong to no organisation at all. Cross-national differences are very impressive in this category of people. With respect to the large differences between countries, we must question the straightforward application of factor analysis to the complete set of respondents. For instance, in Spain in 1990 only 23 per cent of the respondents belong to an organisation (see Table 6.1) and only about 7 per cent belong to three or more. In countries like France, Italy, and Portugal, figures for multiple membership are equally low. In a pooled data set, somewhat less than 50 per cent of the respondents are organisationally inactive. With such severe limitations on the variance of distinct countries, it is clear that structures distracted are greatly determined by those belonging to at least one organisation. It follows that in the search for structure, the results for inactive people should be distinguished from those for active people.

Two additional modifications of our research strategy seem necessary. Since cross-national differences are now evident, we restrict our analyses to a limited set of *European* countries: Sweden, Norway, Denmark, the Netherlands, Belgium, East Germany, West Germany, Britain, Ireland, France, Italy, Spain, and Portugal.[12] Beside, using the complete set of sixteen distinct types of voluntary associations appears problematic, and deleting specific items might result in more acceptable structures among the remaining associations.

On the basis of these three considerations – distinguishing between active and inactive people, reducing the number of countries, and reducing the number of items – we reconsider the results of a dimensional analysis of voluntary association membership. Using a simple dichotomy between people who belong and people who do not belong to an organisation, a principal components analysis indicates relatively low communalities (<0.30) for community work groups, health organisations, and other associations among the total samples.[13] This result is easy to understand. Diseases are distributed among the population in ways independent of the willingness to be involved in voluntary associations, and community organisations (especially 'other' associations) are apparently too heterogeneous to find a clear place among voluntary associations. We delete these three items from the analyses. Among the remaining items, several also appear problematic with respect to their positions or loadings. After rotating the structure to improve the distinctions between the obtained dimensions, sports clubs still find a place on two dimensions, while youth clubs and educational organisations show relatively low loadings (<0.40). For these reasons, we delete these three items, too.

For the remaining set of ten types of voluntary associations, we compare the structures obtained for all respondents and for people belonging to at least one

Table 6.2 Factor structures of association memberships (pooled data; rotated component matrix of selected items)

	All respondents			At least one membership		
	1	2	3	1	2	3
Environment	0.72			0.71		
Animal rights	0.68			0.61		
Third World	0.57			0.56		
Peace movement	0.52			0.49		
Religious or church		0.69			0.65	
Women's groups		0.66			0.61	
Social welfare services		0.57			0.53	
Professional organisations			0.73			0.70
Political parties and groups			0.69			0.67
Variance explained	18.3%	14.8%	13.1%	17.5%	13.7%	12.5%

Source: World Values Survey 1990–93 (France, Belgium, W. Germany, E. Germany, Italy, the Netherlands, Denmark, Britain, Spain, Ireland, Norway, Sweden, Portugal).

Notes: Principal components analyses; Varimax rotation; N = 21,398 and 11,367.

organisation. For both categories of respondents, the two structures are remarkably similar. The only clear deviation is trade union membership which has an ambiguous position (that is, high loadings on two dimensions) and a different place in the structure among activists. Deleting this item has virtually no impact on the remaining structures (see Table 6.2). In a pooled set of data for the European countries, then, we find very similar three-dimensional structures for activists and for the population, explaining about 44 per cent of the variance among the first group and 46 per cent among the latter.

The three-dimensional structure presented in Table 6.2 can be interpreted like Wessels' (1997) above. The first factor extracted consists clearly of themes belonging to a *new politics agenda*, with references to concerns about the environment, animal rights, the Third World, human rights, and peace. The second dimension indicates activities in the field of *social welfare*, with high loadings for religious, social, and women's organisations. And the third dimension involves *traditional interest groups* like professional organisations and political parties.

Although the substantive interpretation of these three-dimensional structures differs little from interpretations discussed earlier, it should be noted that our solution is based on a restricted but unambiguous set of items. The crucial question, however, is whether the result obtained for the pooled data set can be found within each country separately.

Constructing equivalent measures

The structure underlying the nine items selected to measure associational membership in Europe (see Table 6.2) is technically, as well as substantively, satisfying. It seems to be a very good starting point for constructing cross-national equivalent measures. If a similar structure can be found within each country and in the pooled data set, evidence will exist that our indicators reflect a similar construct. Following the so-called identity-equivalence procedure proposed by Przeworski and Teune (1966), we will construct an identity set: that is, a set of identical items structured similarly in various countries and in the pooled data set. Then we will explore opportunities for adding country-specific additions. The combination of a common-core set of items and specific additions can be considered a cross-nationally equivalent measure of social involvement.

The search for similar structures within each of the countries proves extremely complicated. The structure underlying the subset of nine items in the pooled data set can be reproduced in only two countries (Belgium and West Germany), with a very similar structure in East Germany. In the remaining ten countries, different structures clearly exist. Applying the three-dimensional structure underlying the pooled data set to measure membership within countries, then, definitely implies the use of inappropriate instruments. What is required is a further reduction of the subset of items in order to find a similar structure among a common set of items both within countries and in the pooled data set. Unavoidably, we cannot use the structure summarised in Table 6.2 as a starting point for the construction of equivalent measures. We must search for a common structure among a reduced set of items.

In a large number of explorative analyses of the membership data, no single identity set could be constructed with a reasonable number of items.[14] Even a reduction to four or five items does not result in similar structures within various countries. In an attempt to rely on a more systematic approach, we select an alternative strategy based on a clear reduction of the number of items included in a limited identity set. We obtain this set by selecting two items from each of the three factors which show the highest correlation in the pooled data set. This new set of six items (environment and Third World from the first factor, welfare and religious from the second, and professional and parties from the third) represents a single dimension (that is, only one component is subtracted with an Eigenvalue >1.0). Yet a three-dimensional structure can be found easily in the pooled data set when the dimensionality of the final solution is fixed at that number.

Can this simple structure be used as an identity set for the construction of equivalent measures? Again, we must conclude that the structure found in the pooled data set cannot be reproduced within the countries. Obviously, the country-specific nature of voluntary association membership cannot be covered by a similar, valid cross-national structure among a limited set of items. With respect to the items used in large-scale surveys, this conclusion hardly comes as a surprise. Church organisations, trade unions, animal rights groups, and the like are almost by definition imbedded in specific societies. And it is certainly not self-evident that behind the same labels similar organisations (or even organisations performing similar functions) can be found. Heroic attempts to construct equivalent measures in this area are probably based on a clear underestimation – or even misunderstanding – of the problems encountered in empirical comparative research. Either we have to drop the idea of constructing equivalent measures for voluntary association membership or we have to accept less demanding criteria.

In order to avoid the conclusion that voluntary association membership cannot be validly measured in cross-national research, we give up the idea of a common space among the complete set of items. Instead we consider distinct analyses for the three subsets of items which appeared in the factor analysis of the pooled set of data (see Table 6.2), and we select the two items with the highest inter-correlation as starting points for three separate analyses. If we obtain no similar structures for the complete set of indicators, we might be able to use the notion of various clusters of types of voluntary association membership as an alternative. So we use the three pairs of items mentioned as three distinct identity sets, and we use each pair for a search of nation-specific additions. In this way, we abandon the idea of a common space underlying the complete set of items and retreat to the much less demanding assumption of three distinct clusters of items.

Since we have, initially, only two items available for each type of voluntary association membership, the number of nation-specific items to be added must be very limited in order not to lose the opportunity to interpret these types unambiguously. For this reason, we restrict the potentially relevant set of items for each of the three clusters to those items which have already shown some relationship to the six items included in the three distinct identity sets. For instance, we restrict the search for nation-specific additions to the identity set for membership of social movements (consisting of the items environment and Third World) to memberships of peace groups and animal rights groups, because these two items can be found on the same factor as the initial pair of items in the common structure (see Table 6.2). In the same way, we explore opportunities for a nation-specific addition of women's groups to the identity set of social participation (welfare and religious organisations), and trade unions to the identity set of interest groups (professional organisations and parties). We base acceptance of an item to the final scale on the requirements that (1) the resulting structure remain one dimensional, and (2) none of the loadings for the items included be relatively low.[15] Table 6.3 summarises the results of these computations.

For movement membership, we can obtain nation-specific additions for all countries except Portugal. In eleven countries, peace groups belong to this type of voluntary association membership, as do animal groups in ten countries. Similarly, women's groups are closely tied to membership of socially active voluntary associations in twelve countries. Finally, trade unions are an aspect of membership of interest groups in ten countries. In this way, we measure three distinct types of membership in voluntary associations in a cross-nationally valid way by using nation-specific additions for each type of membership. Although our procedure clearly differs from analyses presented by other researchers, the results are in part identical. Like Wessels (1997), we find three types of membership, two of which are partly based on the same items (interest membership and movement membership).[16] Differences are evident especially with respect to the composition of the organisations covered by the label social movements.

The three equivalent measures obtained for the types of voluntary association

Table 6.3 Factor structures of three types of association memberships

	Fr	GB	W. Ger	Ital	Neth	Den	Bel	Sp	Ire	Nor	Swe	E. Ger	Por	Pooled
Movement membership														
Third World	0.53	0.63	0.71	0.46	0.69	0.54	0.74	0.68	0.41	0.67	0.66	0.61	0.71	0.67
Environment	0.75	0.77	0.67	0.70	0.74	0.69	0.74	0.71	0.65	0.72	0.73	0.71	−0.71	0.72
Peace groups	0.66	0.63	0.75	0.63	0.51	0.69	0.62	0.74	0.73	0.42	0.57	0.63		0.59
Animal rights		0.52		0.66	0.65		0.54	0.69	0.60	0.43	0.49	0.54		0.59
Variance explained	42.5	41.5	50.7	38.2	42.7	41.4	44.2	49.6	37.0	33.0	38.5	39.0	50.3	41.3
Social membership														
Social welfare	0.77	0.51	0.65	0.77	0.68	0.72	0.67	0.65	0.60	0.56	0.75	0.73	0.78	0.66
Religious groups	0.74	0.72	0.68	0.77	0.66	0.53	0.76	0.69	0.76	0.55	0.54	0.53	0.63	0.69
Women's groups	0.48	0.72	0.64		0.60	0.59	0.64	0.62	0.66	0.71	0.57	0.58	0.40	0.63
Variance explained	45.8	43.2	43.4	58.9	42.1	38.3	48.0	42.2	45.8	37.3	39.3	38.3	38.9	43.6
Interest membership														
Political parties	0.72	0.67	0.68	0.70	0.41	0.76	0.73	0.73	0.72	0.59	0.63	0.75	0.51	0.66
Prof. associations	0.63	0.73	0.63	0.44	0.73	0.76	0.59	0.55	0.72	0.73	0.66	0.75	0.72	0.65
Trade unions	0.72	0.48	0.60	0.75	0.72		0.60	0.75		0.66	0.63		0.74	0.65
Variance explained	47.8	40.6	40.5	41.6	40.6	57.8	41.6	46.4	51.3	44.0	41.1	56.3	44.1	42.7

Source: See Table 6.2.

Notes: Principal components analyses; listwise deletion of missing data; N = 21,398.

membership can be used for cross-national comparisons. For each country we compute the average level of participation based on simple additive scores (corrected for different numbers of items). Since participation in many countries is rather limited, we dichotomise those resulting scores with people who belong to at least one organisation versus people who belong to none. Table 6.4 shows the rankings of each country based on the percentages of people involved in voluntary associations. The first column shows the rankings based on the undifferentiated set of all items used for Table 6.1. The three additional columns contain the results obtained with the three distinct, but equivalent, measures developed here.

In general, these computations confirm the relative positions of the countries. The correlation coefficients at the bottom of the table are all positive and five out of six are significant. A remarkable similarity appears for the positions of countries based on the simple additive index of all items and the much more limited measure of movement participation.[17] Only very small deviations occur here, most notably the relatively low number of people in the Netherlands participating in social movements. A different picture arises when we look closely at the right side of Table 6.4. Social participation is relatively high in the Netherlands and Great Britain, while Sweden and East Germany move to the middle of the lists. Although the measure of participation in interest groups quite clearly reflects

Table 6.4 Membership of voluntary associations for distinct types of participation (percentages, rankings, and correlation coefficients)

Country	Total set %	Rank	Equivalent measures Movement part. %	Rank	Social memb. %	Rank	Interest memb. %	Rank
Sweden	85	1	64	1	16	8	22	2
Netherlands	84	2	33	5	43	5	35	1
East Germany	84	3	63	2	27	2	6	8
Denmark	81	4	58	3	11	10	15	3
Norway	81	5	53	4	21	4	10	5
West Germany	67	6	27	6	20	5	7	7
Belgium	57	7	23	8	20	6	15	4
Ireland	56	8	16	9	18	7	5	11
Great Britain	52	9	24	7	22	3	7	6
France	38	10	10	11	11	11	6	9
Italy	34	11	13	10	11	12	6	10
Portugal	33	12	10	12	13	9	1	13
Spain	23	13	6	13	7	13	3	12

Correlation (Spearman's rho):

Total set			0.91[a]		0.60[b]		0.81[a]	
Movement part.					0.60[b]		0.78[a]	
Social memb.							0.40	

Notes:
[a] Significant at 0.01 level (1-tailed).
[b] Significant at 0.05 level (1-tailed).

participation in movements and participation with the unspecified additive measure, social participation and interest group participation differ markedly. From a comparative perspective, we see that the simple non-equivalent index covers what is also registered equivalently with the index for movement participation. The other two equivalent indexes, however, uncover different types of participation unmeasured by the simple index. In other words, the common usage of the simple additive index for a large number of voluntary association memberships reflects participation only in social movements in a cross-nationally equivalent way. Cross-national comparisons of social memberships and interest group participation require the application of particular measures.

External validation

Despite the concise analysis of cross-national differences in voluntary association membership above, we must look closer at the validity of our instruments. Certainly, the fact that the three distinct measures could not be based on an uncomplicated extension of some identity set calls for subsequent testing. We will concentrate here on the construct validity of our measures and approach the validity problem from two very different perspectives. First, we use the three measures as dependent variables in a micro-level analysis of social-structural antecedents of participation. Second, we assess the quality of these measures as independent variables in a macro-level model explaining the stability of democratic political systems.

Social-structural antecedents

Since people differ in resources, interests, skills, motivation, and social positions, participation across activities is not equally distributed. In many countries research has long shown that, on average, women, the young and old, the lower educated, and the lower status groups are less involved than men, the middle-aged, the higher educated, and the higher status groups, respectively. Without going into detail here, these differences can usually be explained in straight-forward ways (cf. Milbrath and Goel 1977; Verba *et al.* 1995).

Differences in participation between men and women generally correspond to differences in traditional role patterns, with women mainly responsible for home, and men mainly responsible for external contacts. Although these patterns have changed rapidly with the second wave of female emancipation, traditional roles are still traceable. The relatively low levels of participation among the very old and the very young are due to physical hindrances as well as to declining social contacts in the old and high mobility levels in the young. The fact that the higher educated and the higher social-status groups display high levels of participation is usually ascribed to their command of resources (time, money, contacts) and specific skills (verbal and cognitive). These factors are not independent. For instance, on average, young women are more highly educated than old women;

old people often lack resources; and men reach higher social status levels more easily than women.

An empirical test of the social-structural antecedents of participation must consider the specific nature of the problem. That is, the method should be appropriate for: (1) the measurement of participation as a dichotomous dependent variable,[18] (2) non-linear relationships between participation and the independent variables, and (3) multivariate effects of these independent variables. In addition, the evident differences in participation rates for different countries should not bias the results. A logistic regression model for subgroups according to country and different types of participation meets these criteria.

Table 6.5 summarises the results of a large number of logistic regression analyses. Since our main objective here is to assess the cross-national validity of the relationships between participation and several social-structural antecedents, figures for the fit of the models are secondary. The same applies to the exact value of the regression coefficients. We do not claim that the independent variables we use provide a comprehensive explanation of participation – they don't, as the 'power' of the models in terms of statistical explanation is not very impressive. But for a validity test of well-known social-structural antecedents of participation this approach suffices. Hence, Table 6.5 contains symbols reflecting the differences between the coefficients and not the exact magnitudes. In this way, a large number of detailed results is conveniently rearranged in order to focus on the core information required.

In the last column of Table 6.5, the results for the pooled data set indicate that the chance for women to participate in social movement organisations is lower than for men. The same applies to age groups up to 55 years, each of which shows a higher level of participation than among younger age groups, while the oldest group clearly participates less. The coefficients for the level of education indicate that participation increases with education. As expected, social status is related to participation, and belonging to a lower status group decreases the chances of participation. For the pooled data, then, these findings clearly support the common interpretations of participation in Western European countries. But perhaps the most interesting part of Table 6.5 is that these results can be easily traced in virtually every country for all variables with only minor exceptions. This outcome strengthens the conclusion that our measure of movement membership taps a specific mode of cross-national participation.

These results are obtained only partly for the two other variants of our measure of voluntary association membership. For membership of social organisations (the middle of Table 6.5), women participate more than men, and do so increasingly as their age, education, and social status increase. The first of these results – referring to older women – are not in line with standard explanations but can hardly surprise us if we know that membership of women's organisations and of social welfare groups are included in our measure. Much more important is the man-ifestation of remarkable cross-national similarities in the findings. Minor devia-tions are registered for only the oldest age groups in several countries. In terms of

Table 6.5 Social-structural antecedents of social participation (logistic regression)

	Fr	GB	W Ger	Ital	Neth	Den	Bel	Sp	Ire	Nor	Save	E Ger	Por	Pooled
(a) Movement membership														
Participation (%)	10.2	24.4	26.6	13.0	33.2	16.6	22.5	6.2	8.5	52.4	63.7	15.5	9.8	20.35
Gender	w < m	w < m	w < m	w < m	w < m	w < m	w < m	w < m	w = m	w < m	w < m	w < m	w < m	w < m
Age 26–35	<	<	<	<	<	<	<	<	<	<	<	=	<	<
36–45	<	<	>	>	<	<	<	>	>	<	<	=	>	<
46–55	>	>	=	=	<	<	=	>	=	<	—	=	=	>
56–65	>	>	=	=	>	>	=	=	=	>	>	=	=	>
66+	>	=	=	=	>	>	=	=	=	>	=	=	=	>
Education	<	<	<	<	<	<	<	<	<	<	=	<	<	<
Social status: middle	>	>	=	>	>	m.d.	=	>	=	m.d.	m.d.	=	=	>
skilled	—	>	>	>	>	m.d.	=	>	>	m.d.	m.d.	>	>	>
unskilled	>	>	>	>	>	m.d.	>	>	>	m.d.	m.d.	>	>	>
(b) Social membership														
Participation (%)	11.1	23.3	23.1	12.0	45.3	12.5	24.7	7.9	20.3	22.2	18.05	30.9	13.3	18.6
Gender	w > m	w > m	w > m	w > m	w = m	w > m	w > m	w > m	w > m	w > m	w > m	w > m	w > m	w > m
Age 26–35	=	=	=	=	=	=	<	=	=	=	=	=	<	<
36–45	=	<	<	=	<	=	<	=	<	=	=	<	>	<
46–55	<	<	<	=	<	=	<	<	<	=	=	<	>	<
56–65	<	<	<	=	=	=	<	<	<	>	<	>	=	<
66+	<	<	<	<	=	=	<	<	<	=	<	=	<	>
Education	=	=	=	<	=	m.d.	=	>	=	m.d.	m.d.	=	<	>
Social status: middle	=	=	=	=	=	m.d.	=	>	=	m.d.	m.d.	=		>
skilled	=	>	=	>	=	m.d.	=	>	>	m.d.	m.d.	=		>
unskilled	=	>	=	=	>	m.d.	=	>	>	m.d.	m.d.	=		>

continued

Table 6.5 continued

	Fr	GB	W Ger	Ital	Neth	Den	Bel	Sp	Ire	Nor	Swe	E Ger	Por	Pooled
(c) Interest membership														
Participation (%)	6.3	7.3	6.9	5.0	34.5	15.4	14.9	2.8	4.6	10.2	21.6	6.3	1.3	9.2
Gender	w = m	w = m	w = m	w = m	w > m	w = m	w = m	w < m	w = m	w = m	w = m	w < m	w = m	w = m
Age 26–35	=	=	=	=	<	<	<	=	=	=	=	=	=	<
36–45	=	=	=	=	<	<	<	=	=	=	<	=	=	<
46–55	=	<	>	>	<	>	<	<	=	<	<	=	=	>
56–65	=	<	=	>	<	—	=	=	=	<	=	=	=	<
66+	=	=	=	>	>	=	=	=	=	=	=	=	=	>
Education	<	=	<	<	<	<	<	<	<	<	<	=	<	<
Social status: middle	=	>	=	=	>	m.d.	=	>	>	m.d.	m.d.	=	m.d.	>
skilled	=	>	=	=	>	m.d.	=	>	>	m.d.	m.d.	=	=	>
unskilled	=	>	=	=	>	m.d.	=	>	>	m.d.	m.d.	=	>	<

Notes:
Gender: man/woman.
Age: reference category 17–25 years.
Education: age leaving school in years.
Social status: reference category upper status.
For the first group after the reference category: ∨ means a lower probability, ∧ larger and = equal.
For all following categories the comparisons refer to the previous category (| means equal odds rates).
m.d.: missing data.

cross-national equivalence, the measure of social membership obviously behaves in more or less the same way in different countries.

Unfortunately, the outcomes of our analyses for the third measure are confusing and disappointing. As the lower part of Table 6.5 shows, the pattern mirrored by the regression coefficients is neither consistent with our expectations nor among the countries. Clearly, for interest group participation, the cross-national validity of our measure is dubious.

This brief discussion of the results of country-specific logistic regression analyses of the social-structural antecedents of participation ignores many interesting findings for particular countries. Nevertheless, the information provides a provisional answer to the question of the cross-national validity of our three distinct measures. The measures for movement membership and social membership are both related plausibly and consistently to gender, age, education, and social status. These two measures provide excellent starting points for a more thorough comparative study of specific aspects of voluntary association membership. From a similar perspective, it follows that the measure for participation in interest groups is problematic.

The stability of democratic systems

Since Tocqueville's visit to the United States, membership in voluntary associations is considered important for democratic political systems. These organisations provide citizens with opportunities to develop their skills and contacts and to experience the need for modesty and compromise in social decision-making processes (cf. van Deth 1997). This line of reasoning has been revived in debates on the problems and prospects of democratic political systems in terms of 'social capital' (cf. Putnam 1993; 1995a; 1995b). Among others, Inglehart (1997) has urged that 'cultural' factors be included in models explaining the stability of these systems. As a second way to obtain information on the validity of the three measures for voluntary association membership developed here, we will replicate Inglehart's analyses.

Summarising a long practice in political science, Inglehart designed a model to explain the stability of democracy which he operationalises as the number of years of democracy in a country or as the shift in the level of democracy from 1990 to 1995. In several multiple regression models at the macro-level he includes cultural variables (level of subjective well-being, interpersonal trust, support for change), social-structural variables (share of the service sector, higher education, income inequality), and an indicator for economic development (GNP per capita). Finally, he introduces a measure of social participation apparently based on a simple addition of membership scores for the same list of organisations presented above (Inglehart 1997: 197–205).

Since Inglehart summarises the arguments in the literature on the stability of democratic systems, we need not do so here. It suffices to know that modernisation theories, in particular, have created the expectation that economic development is a precondition for democracy (cf. Przeworski *et al.* 1996). In addition, at least since the days of Almond and Verba's *The Civic Culture* (1963), the relevance of cultural factors for the stability of democracy is undisputed. Inglehart combines various lines of reasoning in a strong appeal to disentangle the impact of these different factors on empirical grounds. For our discussion here, his conclusion about the additional value of including a measure of organisational membership is especially relevant. He reports that the inclusion brings a remarkable change in the explained variance: the adjusted R-square of a model including a simple additive measure of voluntary membership is about twice as high as a model lacking that variable (Inglehart 1997: 204–5).

In order to assess the cross-national validity of our three measures of voluntary association membership, we have replicated Inglehart's macro-level model for the countries discussed here.[19] If these measures function as predicted by a Tocque-villean argument, we should find positive correlations between membership and the stability of democracy, just as Inglehart did. Table 6.6 reveals the results of our analysis, with the first column showing the regression coefficients and the variance explained for a baseline model including social variables (subjective well-being and interpersonal trust), social-structural variables (share of the service sector and spread of higher education), and an economic variable (GNP/capita). The remaining four columns include the results if this basic model is extended with, respectively, the index used by Inglehart or by one of the three equivalent measures designed here. The dependent variable is the number of years of stable democracy in the countries.[20]

With respect to the distributions of several variables, we should interpret the coefficients in Table 6.6 very cautiously, but comparisons between the general pattern of the columns is what is relevant. The first thing to note is that movement membership has a clearly *negative* impact on the stability of democracy after entering the other variables in the model. Yet this does not seem to affect the way other variables perform (compare the coefficients for the columns for the cumulative index and for the movement membership).[21] Second, both measures

Table 6.6 The impact of social, cultural, and economic variables on the stability of democracy (multiple regression; N = 13; beta-coefficients and explained variance)

| Variables | Basic model | Voluntary association membership | | | |
| | | | Equivalent measures | | |
		Add. index	Movement	Social	Interest
Subj. well-being	1.00	0.97	1.10	0.90	1.17
Trust	−0.10	−0.10	−0.10	−0.04	−0.38
Service sector	0.13	0.15	0.14	0.18	0.15
Higher education	−0.26	−0.26	−0.25	−0.26	−0.32
GNP/capita	0.09	0.08	0.09	0.12	0.02
Membership		0.06	−0.14	0.08	0.26
R-squared	0.89	0.89	0.90	0.90	0.91

Sources: WVS and Inglehart (1997).

of social membership and interest group membership behave very differently than the two other measures. Including social membership in the model virtually neutralises the impact of inter-personal trust, indicating that these two aspects of 'social capital' are strongly connected. On the other hand, interest group membership is a strong competitor for the economic indicator in the model, while the impact of trust increases considerably when we use this measure of social participation. In addition, the beta-coefficient for this measure suggests a substantial influence on the dependent variable.

The analyses summarised in Table 6.6 – coarse and simple as they are – provide exactly the kind of information relevant here. The three distinct measures for voluntary association membership uncover different impacts on the stability of democracy in ways that cannot be seen if we use a simple additive index. So the benefit of using the three distinct measures instead of the index is apparent. Apart from the advantage that our measures are cross-nationally equivalent, the substantive gains are remarkable. Obviously, participation in social organisations and interest groups has a positive relationship with the stability of democracy, while participation in social movements shows a rather opposite impact. Since our social movement indicator performed best in our previous analyses (see Tables 6.4 and 6.5), more sophisticated analyses could reveal important modifications or specifications of the Tocquevillean argument. These potential gains are not available if we follow the common practice of using bare additive measures of voluntary association membership.

Conclusion

This chapter has evaluated the opportunities for developing a cross-nationally valid instrument to measure membership of voluntary associations in several countries. Ordinarily, this type of social involvement is measured by a simple additive index based on the number of associations a respondent belongs to. Broadly speaking, the results obtained this way in a number of large-scale surveys reveal large cross-national differences and large, unusual, temporal fluctuations. The main objective of our analyses is to improve the measurement of voluntary association membership within the context of secondary analysis.

The task of constructing an equivalent measure seems extremely complicated. Among a number of indicators for membership of various associations, we cannot find a so-called identity set useful for country-specific extensions. In order to avoid the conclusion that constructing an equivalent measure for voluntary association membership is impossible, we present a pragmatic solution instead. This alternative approach weakens the conditions implied in the Przeworski–Teune approach by abandoning the requirement of a single space for different measures. Instead, we explore three distinct clusters of indicators and construct three cross-nationally equivalent measures. We assess the validity of these measures by analysing their function as dependent variables in analyses of social-cultural antecedents and as independent variables in analyses of the stability of democratic systems.

Two of our three measures (participation in movements and in social organisations) function plausibly and consistently in cross-national analyses, while the third (participation in interest groups) is rather disappointing. In addition, applying these three measures as alternatives for the simple additive index in macro-level analyses of the stability of democratic systems achieves only partly satisfactory results. Instead of trying to solve these problems by increasingly sophisticated forms of number crunching, we should develop more theoretically sound concepts based on the motives and interests of people for different modes of participation. These concepts, however, do not seem to underlie the instruments used in data sets available for secondary analyses in this field.

Participation in voluntary associations, then, is a complicated concept both theoretically and empirically. The complications are shown clearly in the analyses presented here, and our results should be seen more as an invitation to further research than as a solution to the problems encountered. Plain additive measures of voluntary association membership do not meet minimal standards of cross-national equivalence. As a result, their widespread use should be taken as a mark of naivety which leaves much to be desired.

Notes

1 We thank the contributors to this volume – particularly Rüdiger Schmitt-Beck – for their helpful comments on earlier drafts of this chapter.

2 Terms to identify these organisations vary widely: interest groups, voluntary associations, intermediary organisations, social movements, civic associations, third sector organisations, non-governmental organisations, non-profit organisations (cf. Kuhnle and Selle 1992; Anheier and Seibel 1990; van Deth 1997). We use the term 'voluntary association' here for organisations to be mentioned below (see the section on measuring membership).

3 A similar conclusion can be based on an extensive overview of 'volunteering' in Europe presented by Smith (1993).

4 See van Deth (1997) for examples of this practice.

5 The World Values Surveys consist of two waves in the early 1980s and the early 1990s. Chairman of the international group of researchers responsible for collecting these data is Ronald Inglehart. Data can be obtained from the ICPSR in Ann Arbor, Michigan (Study Number 6160).

6 For the problems related to survey questions on social participation and organisational membership, see Parker (1983), Baumgartner and Walker (1988), and the discussion following this last article (Smith 1990; Baumgartner and Walker 1990).

7 Notice that this straightforward method already presents problems of comparison since some questionnaires use the phrase 'membership', while other use the non-formal phrase 'belong to'.

8 This question not only implies problems between but also within categories. For instance, a member of one sports club gets the same score on this item as a member of three different sports clubs.

9 Categories of this involvement index are: (1) belong to *and/or* active in organisation; (2) do not belong to *and* no activities for this organisation.

10 In addition to the member states of the European Union, Wessels included Finland, Norway, Austria, the United States, and Canada in his dimensional analyses.

11 Alternative specifications included variants of the index for involvement, restriction of the analyses to respondents belonging to at least one organisation, or varying the number of dimensions to be extracted.

12 In order to avoid additional problems by mixing information from clearly different cultures, we treat East and West Germany as two different 'countries' here.

13 The application of factor analytical techniques for dichotomous data has been disputed. However, the results obtained with this straightforward indication of membership do not differ from the results obtained with more complicated scales used by Wessels or with a three-point scale. For this reason, the analyses presented in the remaining part of this contribution are based on these dichotomies unless otherwise indicated. Furthermore, in order to make cross-national comparisons somewhat easier, only orthogonal solutions are distracted.

14 Exploring the chances for all permutations of sixteen items to be structured in a similar way within thirteen countries and the pooled data set is virtually impossible. After inspecting the correlation matrixes, we explored a large number of potentially promising combinations of items.

15 In technical terms these requirements imply that (1) only one Eigenvalue is larger than 1.0, and (2) no factor loading coefficient is smaller than 0.40.

16 This empirical distinction between 'interest membership' and 'movement membership' is an almost perfect replication of the theoretical distinction between 'traditional' and 'new' political organisations proposed by Roller and Wessels (1996: 11).

17 The percentages as well as the rankings for these two measure are very similar (Pearson's r = 0.89 and Spearman's rho 0.95, respectively). They are also, of course, highly significant (<0.000, 1-tailed).

18 As indicated above, we dichotomised the three participation measures to avoid complications with extreme skewness.

19 A close replication of Inglehart's analyses is not possible here. The main difference between our two analyses is that we restricted the number of countries to the ones we treated in the previous sections. In addition, our dependent variable is the number of years of stable democracy and not the shift in the level of democracy in the early 1990s. Using Inglehart's dependent variable for our set of countries results in very severe problems with the estimation of our model.

20 The use of this dependent variable presents very serious complications due to a highly skewed distribution. Since many cases show the highest value (75 years), the indicators of the variance explained should be treated with care. Moreover, deleting specific cases (like Spain and Norway) shows the dependence of our results on the selection of countries involved in the analyses.

21 Since the confidence intervals of these coefficients are relatively large, this conclusion should not be overestimated.

7 Party organisations

Thomas Poguntke[1]

Introduction

Parties are intermediaries, establishing linkages between societies and the institutions of democratic government. To perform this function, they need to be anchored in both arenas, that is, in state institutions (such as parliaments, governments, and bureaucracies) and in society. While it has been suggested that their relationships with the state may have grown too large for democratic governance (Katz and Mair 1995), it has become increasingly obvious since the 1970s that their stable anchorage in society can no longer be taken for granted. Social modernisation and changing values have increasingly undermined the stable relations of mass parties with their electorates, loyal supporters, and even party members (Inglehart 1977 and 1990). Processes of electoral dealignment (Dalton *et al.* 1984), increasing levels of volatility (at least within political camps) (Bartolini and Mair 1990; Pedersen 1983), and challenges from new social movements and citizen initiatives (Dalton and Kuechler 1990) are symptoms of weakening linkage between parties and society. Much of this literature, particularly the perspective taken by electoral research, examines changes on the individual level: individuals are more prone to loosen their traditional ties to parties – or less likely to establish them in the first place – because they are better informed and better educated, have moved into social categories other than their parents', or have undergone similar processes of social mobility and individualisation.

The *organisational* dimension of linkage, however, is frequently not given adequate attention. Parties have, in principle, two ways of establishing stable organisational linkages with relevant segments of society; that is, directly, through their own membership organisation, and indirectly, through organisational co-operation with various kinds of collateral organisations. Organisational linkage can take two forms: formal and informal. Formal linkage between parties and collateral organisations is codified in statutes and guarantees specific co-determination rights of these organisations within the party organisation (or vice versa). Informal linkages are informal exchange relations sometimes built on overlapping mass membership or on tacit agreements about the mutual (or unilateral) representation of elites in the party's decision-making bodies (or vice versa). Although informal linkages may fulfil functions like those guaranteed through formal linkage, they suffer from a decisive disadvantage from the party's point of view: they are highly contingent upon political circumstances, even upon leadership personalities, and they are therefore less reliable and stable than formal linkages. It follows that they exercise considerably less control over relevant segments of the electorate by party elites, which means that they are less relevant for a political party's organisational viability.

This last consideration explains why the study used in this chapter as an example of the intricacies of comparative and longitudinal research on political parties concentrates on formal linkages between parties and collateral organisations. It can draw upon a unique data base of the formal aspects of party organisations in Western Europe and the United States from 1960 to 1990 collected by a cross-national team directed by Richard S. Katz and Peter Mair. The project included the collection of rules on the formal intra-organisational distribution of power as it is mainly codified in party statutes. In addition, it compiled all available data on party membership, organisational density, and party finance (Katz and Mair 1992a).[2]

Party statutes are the most authoritative source for analysing the development of formal organisational linkages over time. They represent the 'official' story of organisational exchange between political parties and collateral organisations. Together with informal linkages they make up the 'real' story of organisational linkage between parties and their organisational environment (Katz and Mair 1992b: 6–8). Although the latter are of secondary importance for political parties (see above), it would be desirable to measure both over time in order to arrive at a complete picture. Nevertheless, what Katz and Mair say about party rules in general is also true for this particular aspect of party organisation: 'Changes in rules also reflect the resolution of real conflicts and struggles within the party, and will inevitably map the changing balance of intra-organisational power' (1992b: 7). Furthermore, the material used for this analysis is 'hard' data. Party statutes were analysed and summarised by acknowledged country experts, which means that inaccuracies in the translation into English language and through the synopses of complicated party statutes are likely to be small. In addition, ambiguities in the original tables could generally be resolved through feedback from the primary researchers and through their discussion of the data in Katz and Mair (1994).

The entirely different nature of political parties in the United States, particularly the absence of party membership in the European sense (and hence the absence of a membership organisation), suggests excluding the United States from the present study. This leaves us with seventy-seven political parties[3] in eleven countries, which amounts to almost all relevant parties in Western European party systems with uninterrupted party political development since the Second World War. The core data base of our analysis is represented by a detailed coding of the party statutes, which distinguishes between types of organisations linked to different party arenas and the organisational levels of linkage. When coding party statutes, adequate identification of equivalent party arenas across time and space represents a serious methodological problem. Following a brief presentation of the theoretical aspects of linkage between parties and collateral organisations, this chapter discusses the problems of comparing party organisational structures. It also gives several examples of satisfactory solutions, and it concludes with empirical results and the evaluation of the presented methodology.

Parties and their organisational environment

The concept of linkage refers to all processes of two-way communication between parties and society. Because parties provide 'a substantive connection between rulers and ruled' (Lawson 1980: 3), it is important to see linkage as a connection open to input from both ends. Parties need stable means of communication with their electorates in order to identify, select, and aggregate relevant grievances, communicate them to the higher echelons, and strive for policies which take them into account. At the same time, though this is trivial, parties need to be able to explain and justify their actions *vis-à-vis* their constituency. Whereas the first aspect of linkage needs organisation, the latter aspect can, to some extent, be fulfilled by the media, where parties interact with individuals without linking organisations. However, the media cannot aggregate demands; that is, no organised interaction and competition exists between a multitude of groups who articulate different, sometimes mutually exclusive, demands. No doubt organisational linkage provides another kind of linkage, because built-in organisational thresholds and formalised procedures of decision-making serve to select and aggregate demands and channel them to party elites.

The functionality of linkage depends, however, on the kind of organisations that are linked – and those have changed fundamentally over the past decades. Ongoing social differentiation, even individualisation (Beck 1986), along with processes of cognitive mobilisation (Dalton 1984) and value change – better yet, pluralisation (Inglehart 1977 and 1990; van Deth and Scarbrough 1995b) – have seminally weakened traditional interest organisations. Trade unions, to use an obvious example, have begun to develop from collective actors with a high degree of symbolic integration and a coherent ideological base into little more than insurance companies, whose organisational survival depends increasingly on the provision of selective incentives (Streeck 1987: 474–82; Wessels 1991: 457; Rucht 1993: 271–92). As a result, union members may increasingly resent exclusive co-operation of their union with a particular party, or even the use of trade union funds for political purposes. They may consider themselves no longer members of the labour movement but employees in a modern society who need to join an organisation which works for the enhancement of their working conditions and pay levels. In general terms, intra-organisational resistance against exclusive linkages with one party is likely to rise as the intra-organisational coherence of ideology and interest declines. At the same time, parallel processes are at work inside political parties – and it depends on the organisational adaptability of the parties and the interest organisations whether or not the changes lead to organisational friction or organisational decline.

The disintegration of traditional mass organisations means that they increasingly lose their capacity for the integration of sizeable segments of society. This means, in turn, that they are increasingly less capable of aggregating interests and delivering votes for 'their' political party, while the continuation of close ties limits the party's freedom to manoeuvre. To be sure, beyond a certain degree of disintegration of modern society, exclusive and obvious connections between party and interest organisations may be detrimental for both partners. What used to be a happy symbiosis in the days of mass politics has increasingly become a burden in the age of individualistic society (Kirchheimer 1965).

So far we have implicitly referred to interest groups which organise *external interests*; that is, interests, which exist independently of, and mostly prior to, a political party (for example, religious interests, economic interests, ecological interests). *Internal interest organisations*, on the other hand, are created through organisational activity by the party. Strictly speaking, there is no pre-existing social group like the Christian Democratic women or Social Democratic teachers. Parties create satellite organisations with a view to gaining a hold on sizeable segments of the electorate with specific socio-economic interests and common political preferences. Such 'target group' strategies strive to create organisational forums for potential interests. Since organisational strategies are strongly influenced by a party's history (cf. Panebianco 1988: 17–20), parties with a strong tradition of organisational mobilisation are particularly prone to pursuing these target group strategies once their linkages with external interest groups begin to weaken. In other words, the decline of traditional social organisations may encourage political parties to develop their own, increasingly differentiated, capillary system of collateral organisations.

The prospects for this organisational strategy are limited, however. Processes of social change, as outlined above, have not only undermined the homogeneity of traditional interest organisations, they have given rise to a powerful competitor for political parties. Now single issue initiatives and new social movements compete with parties for a limited pool of potentially active citizens (cf. Barnes *et al.* 1979; Jennings *et al.* 1990: 369). This challenge would be less serious for political parties if they could, in principle, establish stable linkages to potentially supportive segments of the so-called movement sector. Yet a low degree of formalisation typically inhibits such linkages. In addition, empirical research shows that single issue initiatives and new social movements tend to regard governments and parliaments as more promising for their activities than political parties (Dalton 1994).

The preceding discussion suggests that the frequency of formal linkages based on external interests between political parties and organisations should have declined since the 1960s. Alternatively, the linkages may have been devalued; that is, they may have been moved from the centres of intra-party power to more deliberative bodies like the party council or the party congress. To compensate for losing hold of traditional interest organisations, parties are likely to have expanded their system of party-sponsored collateral organisations; that is, organisations based on internal interests.

Comparing party bodies

The problem of comparison

Empirical evidence for the previous contentions can be found only through a longitudinal, cross-national research design. The development of formal linkage patterns between party organisations and various kinds of collateral organisations can be measured through the analysis of the overlapping of formal elite and mass membership between the organisations as they are codified in party statutes. In a nutshell, this calls for a detailed analysis of representation and delegation rights of collateral organisations *vis-à-vis* the most important party bodies.

Obviously, a thorough analysis of linkage patterns between parties and collateral organisations should account for the relative importance of party bodies to which collateral organisations have access. In more concrete terms, representation of a collateral organisation in a party's executive committee demonstrates a stronger linkage than the right to send guests to the party congress. It follows, therefore, that accurately identifying party bodies across space and time is crucial for meaningful comparative analyses (cf. Mair 1996: 326–8). In attempting to make such identifications, the researcher is confronted with the following problems. First, party bodies may change their function and position within the party organisation without changing their name. At the most obvious level, this may be caused by changes of the membership of a national executive. More substantially, rule changes may result in a new distribution of formal powers between existing party bodies. Second, parties within the same national party system may vary formally. Thus the function and position of particular party bodies may also vary, despite having similar or even identical names across the system. Third, parties in different party systems may differ systematically with regard to both the name and position of their central party bodies.

To summarise, two comparative perspectives create problems of identifying the adequate objects of comparison: (1) comparison over time, and (2) comparison across cases (which includes two subcategories: comparison within and between national party systems; that is, between organisational cultures).

These sources of variation illustrate that, strictly speaking, the search for identical objects of comparison is futile (van Deth, this volume). When it is debatable whether the leadership body of a party is identical to that of the previous year, we must identify properties of party bodies relevant to our comparative inquiry rather than try to find bodies identical in every respect. In methodological terms, we must elevate the level of abstraction (Sartori 1970: 1040–6) to a point where 'cultural- or country-specific differences become irrelevant and can be ignored' (van Deth, this volume: 6–7). In our example, we must focus on the formal internal distribution of power and competence between a party's principal bodies; that is, on the relative positions of the bodies within the party structure and the potential changes over time. This requires us to develop criteria of equivalence which permit the categorisation of party bodies. Such bodies may look very different and have very different names, but nevertheless have the same function within given party organisations. A suitable starting point for this search is some general consideration of the functional requirements of party organisations and the concomitant organisational differentiation.

A basic organisational map of party organisations

Democratic organisations, like societies as a whole, need a certain degree of functional differentiation (cf. Rothstein 1996: 133–4; Mayntz and Ziegler 1977: 35). They need a rule-making body in charge of formulating binding decisions for the collectivity (that is, party organisation). Primarily, this involves decisions on basic procedural rules (that is, party statutes) and on basic policies (that is, political principles usually codified in basic programmatic documents). Depending upon the degree of grassroots control of party policies, the powers of the rule-making body will extend to decisions about specific policies, coalition agreements, and the control of the party budget. Most important, the rule-making body will have the right to select the party's top leadership unless that right rests with the membership at large, which may have the right to select the party leader and/or the prime ministerial candidate via the ballot.

Since large organisations cannot be steered by a large rule-making body, one or several smaller committees (that is, executive bodies) are needed for day-to-day management and for decisions on short-term policies. Finally, some kind of arbitration body is needed for settling controversies between executive bodies (like a clash over interpreting party rules) or for disciplining party factions or individual dissenters. Frequently, parties set up some kind of court structure. However, since parties are voluntary organisations and members are free to leave in case of fundamental disagreement, a strict separation of powers is usually not considered necessary. Hence, many parties leave arbitration tasks to either a select committee or to the party congress, depending on the issue at stake.

Obviously, this basic dichotomy of rule-making and executive bodies inadequately describes the (functionally induced) common core structure of modern democratic party organisations. Political parties are not self-contained organisations operating independently of their social environment. On the contrary, as discussed earlier, their organisational success is highly contingent upon their ability to forge stable relations with their environment (cf. Panebianco 1988: 33–6; Mayntz and Ziegler 1977: 49). This may induce parties to create a network of more or less dependent collateral organisations which must be adequately represented within the main party structure. Depending on a party's degree of organisational differentiation, its party bodies must reconcile two principles of representation: territorial representation of its membership at large, and functional representation of its collateral organisations. In conjunction with the imperatives of size, this is likely to result in further functional differentiation, which will be discussed in the following sections.

Convening a party congress is costly in large states and large parties. Nevertheless, democratically minded parties are reluctant to leave the bulk of decisions to their executive bodies. To do so, inevitably involves the power to influence even fundamental policy decisions through the capacity to define situations (Poguntke 1994: 208). Hence, parties often establish a smaller rule-making body, which is easier to convene. It is capable of meeting more frequently and can decide questions of fundamental political importance, which would ideally be decided by a party congress. Significantly, such bodies are often called 'small party congresses'. Furthermore, since party congresses tend to be composed on the basis of territorial representation, such bodies can more easily deviate from the prevailing democratic principle. Instead, they can also guarantee the adequate representation of collateral organisations. Hence, in addition to the imperative of size, 'small party congresses also owe their existence to the need to integrate and balance diverging functional interests within parties.

Similarly, the composition of executive bodies is guided by two contradictory imperatives: the principles of efficiency and representativeness. A party executive should integrate representatives of all important party factions (cf. Herzog 1997: 303), regional entities, and sub-organisations. This means that it should contain both territorial and functional representation. Normally, this is achieved through seat guarantees for delegates (mostly the chairs) from regional parties or collateral organisations. In addition, it should be large enough to permit the representation of political tendencies independent of territory or function but small enough to permit efficient discussion, decision-making and, above all, implementation. The need to reconcile these contradictory requirements frequently leads to the creation of a smaller executive body, usually a sub-committee of the national executive. This body is in charge of day-to-day leadership.

It follows from this concise depiction of rule-making and executive bodies that two important criteria normally facilitate the identification of the top leadership body; that is, size and seat guarantees. The viability of a party body (that is, its capacity to act efficiently day to day) is primarily a function of its size, and it declines with increasing size. Hence, in cases where the proliferation of party bodies has unclearly distributed formal powers between them, smaller bodies can normally be regarded as the more powerful. From this perspective, it is plausible to distinguish between decision-making bodies and legitimising bodies, even those on the executive level (cf. Müller 1996: 290–1). Similarly, the absence of seat guarantees can be used to identify the top leadership body. Although parties tend to consider regional and functional proportionality when selecting inner leadership bodies, they rarely make it explicit. Otherwise the selection of top leadership would be seriously constrained by the need to achieve proportional representation of various intra-party sections – or it would inevitably lead to an inflation of its membership. Explicit seat guarantees are therefore typical of less selective bodies, that is, national executives.

Defining the criteria in the real world

Guided by this 'functional map' of party organisation, we can categorise concrete party organisations through the following three steps, which eventually lead to operational definitions of party bodies.[4]

First, we analyse party organisations separately in order to establish the relative position and function of their relevant party bodies according to the theoretical framework discussed above.

Second, we compare party organisations of national party systems. Since contextual conditions (language, historical traditions, systemic constraints, etc.) are likely to mould national party organisations in a similar way, it should be relatively easy to establish functional equivalence between the party bodies of parties of the same nation.

Third, once we have identified comparable party bodies in national party systems, we can identify the core attributes of each type of party body. These attributes must focus on the specific functions of a given party body and its relative position within the overall party structure, that is, 'a more general point of reference' (Nießen 1982: 86). This will permit comparability across parties within the same nation and in different national party systems over time.

Methodologically, this approach combines deduction and induction. Initially, we deduct a general core structure of party organisation by theoretical reasoning; that is, by increasing the level of abstraction. Then, we use empirical investigation to develop inductively the indicators which define party bodies by their relationships to other bodies; that is, by focusing on their position and function within a party structure. In this way, we ascertain functional equivalence and hence comparability.

The description of our approach indicates immediately why we cannot follow a purely quantitative strategy. The nature of the data requires a circular process in order to arrive at a common set of indicators for the classification of party bodies. Starting from the analysis of individual party organisations, we widen the scope to a national and then a cross-national perspective in order to develop a common set of indicators. Then we apply the indicators to individual cases again. At this stage, the approach is akin to the logic of internal consistency (van Deth, this volume), because it focuses on the relation of indicators to one another. Yet the criteria which define these relationships are not quantitative (as, for example, are responses to standardised survey questions). Instead, they are deducted from a theoretical argument at a higher level of abstraction.

A strictly quantitative approach is also not possible once the set of indicators has been developed. There are cases where the relevant party bodies exist but where some of the indicators are missing or do not fit well (due to organisational idiosyncrasies of a given party). Such cases require qualitative judgement with a view to maximising the closeness of the categorisation to the theoretical concepts which initially guided the development of the indicators. In other words, in pragmatic decisions about the classification of party bodies, the relative position of the bodies within the party structure is the overriding point of reference. We will illustrate the logic of this approach below, but first we will discuss the common set of indicators for each type of party body. In other words, we will present the operational definitions of the party bodies which specify the essential attributes characteristic of each type.

An operational typology of party bodies

Executive committee (presidium)

In cases where parties have a dual leadership structure, the executive committee is the top-level body in charge of day-to-day political and organisational leadership. Usually, it is a sub-committee of the national executive with approximately fifteen to twenty members. The selection of the executive committee is normally not constrained by seat guarantees, but it may contain one or several ex officio members, like the general secretary of the party.

National executive

This is the extended national leadership and usually comprises a larger number of people. Although the frequency of meetings is still high, this body tends to be more involved in fundamental political debates about party ideology and strategy and tends to leave everyday management to the executive committee. In order to fulfil its executive function, it should normally be closer to fifty (or less) than to 100 members and meet regularly, that is, normally at least once per month. If a party uses seat guarantees to select some of its top leadership, it is normally reserved for the national executive (and not for the executive committee). Obviously, the competences of an ideal-typical executive committee rest with the national executive in parties which have no executive committee. Such parties may achieve efficient day-to-day management through either a comparatively small executive or through informal leadership circles.

Party council

This body is sometimes called the 'small party congress' and meets only several times a year to co-ordinate policies between various organisational levels and decide about general policy guidelines. Frequently (and in accordance with its label of 'small party congress'), this body has the right to decide all matters not decided by the previous party congress. It is the highest party body between national party congresses, which implies that it meets more frequently than the party congress.[5] It is typical of parties in federal political systems and can contain several hundred members who are frequently selected on the basis of a combination of territorial and functional principles. It is mainly a discussion and guideline-issuing body and is neither the principal rule-making body nor a truly executive and leading body.

As an intermediate body located between the party congress and the level of executive decision-making, the party council is notoriously hard to define. Hence, an important additional indicator is the relative position of given party bodies. As a general rule, the following procedure applies: in cases where there are only two relevant party bodies above the party congress and where the highest party body is very small (15–20 members), the highest party body is categorised as executive committee and the second highest body as national executive. There may be cases (for example, the Italian PCI) where the national executive is obviously far too large to perform real executive functions (that is, the Comitato Centrale). In such cases it is assigned to the category of party council although these bodies may originally have been created as national executives (see below).

The frequency of meetings is an important criterion, but not necessarily decisive. The example of the Belgian VU (see below) shows that the national congress can in fact function as a party council although it meets only once a year. Meanwhile, the party council is effectively the highest rule-making body despite a higher frequency of meetings. In short, a party council is primarily a consultative assembly which normally (but not necessarily) meets more often than the party congress and which may or may not have decision-making powers. In any case, its decision-making powers are subject to the jurisdiction of a party congress.

Party congress

The party congress (or, in some cases, the general assembly) is the formal party sovereign. Fundamental policy decisions are normally referred to the congress and the selection of the party leadership is ultimately legitimised by it. This can be achieved in two ways: (1) through direct election of the party leader and the national executive by the party congress; and (2) through the election of an intermediate body (like the party council), which then elects the party leadership and the national executive. The methods can be combined, but the indirect election is the exception rather than the rule. In most cases, party leadership and national executive (or most of its members) are directly elected through the party congress.

To summarise, a party congress must have two functions: it is the ultimate sovereign on deciding fundamental policies and on selecting the leadership. However, one necessary qualification exists: in recent years, 'direct democracy' has become increasingly widespread among West European parties, and powers which formerly rested exclusively with the party congress may have been shifted to the party membership at large. Examples are membership ballots and the direct election of the party chairperson. But as long as these powers are not given to another party body, the categorisation of the party congress is unproblematic.

Analysis

This section demonstrates the empirical application of the typology to a number of problematic cases, including instances where classifications based on a common set of indicators had to be complemented by qualitative judgement. In the vast majority of cases, however, party bodies could be classified unambiguously according to the operational typology. This means that the party structures of most Western European parties conform to the expected dichotomy of rule-making and executive bodies, frequently modified by an intermediate assembly (the party council) and an additional smaller executive body (the executive committee). In addition, the categorisation of individual party bodies within a party's overall structure is straightforward except for two complications. First, individual party bodies may be difficult to classify because they deviate in one or more important ways from our operational definition though their overall party structure conforms to the model. Second, specific organisational traditions may lead to a proliferation of party arenas. The Austrian SPÖ, for example, has had four national party leadership bodies (see below). In this case, the need for systematic comparison across time and space requires the identification of those bodies which primarily fulfil the above-mentioned functions. Furthermore, there are some cases where party bodies have existed only briefly. This itself is a strong indication of the secondary role of such a body in the power structure of a party and justifies its exclusion from the analysis.

The categorisation of all problematic cases is discussed below.[6] As far as possible, the relevant information is summarised in several tables and additional explanations only are given in the text. In most ambiguous cases, a decision had to be made about how to assign two or more bodies of a given party to two adjacent types of party bodies. This means that indicators in the tables are designed to capture the specific kind of comparison at stake. Hence, they describe two given types of party bodies only in comparison to each other; that is, they focus on their relative positions instead of providing a complete list of their attributes.

The first task encountered is the distinction between national leadership bodies. In the Austrian case, the categorisation of party leadership bodies is problematic for two reasons. First, some of the leadership bodies have ceased to exist and/or have been fundamentally reorganised or renamed. Second, there are more leadership bodies than in all other countries, especially among the Social Democrats (SPÖ) (cf. Müller 1996: 251–6, 291–4; Müller 1992). Throughout the period of analysis, the SPÖ had four national leadership bodies. Until a fundamental reorganisation in 1967, two of them, the Parteikontrolle and the Parteivertretung,[7] played only a secondary role and could therefore be excluded from the analysis (see Table 7.1). Both party bodies had only inferior competences *vis-à-vis* the remaining two party bodies, which could unambiguously be classified as national executive and executive committee.

After the reorganisation of 1967, the situation became somewhat more complicated: one of the party bodies excluded from the analysis (the Parteivorstand) gained additional powers. The party statutes simply mention that the Parteivorstand runs the party and decides all matters not explicitly designated to other party bodies. However, there are two reasons to disregard the Parteivorstand also after 1967: according to the logic of the distribution of power between leadership bodies within an organisation, executive power is concentrated at the top; that is, it tends to rest primarily with small bodies capable of meeting frequently (cf. Müller 1996: 294). This indicates that the Erweitertes Parteipräsidium was the true national executive (see Table 7.1). Furthermore, the 'small party congress', the Parteirat, was also clearly designated in the party statutes. Presumably there was not much real power left for the Parteivorstand, which is located between Parteirat and the Erweitertes Parteipräsidium. Hence, for reasons of cross-national comparability, this body was excluded from the analysis.

Table 7.1 Party organisation of the Austrian Social Democrats (SPÖ)

Name of party body	Parteikontrolle	Parteivertretung	Parteivorstand	Parteiexekutive	Kontrollkommission[a]	Parteivorstand[b]	Erweitertes Parteipräsidium[c]	Parteipräsidium
Period of time	-1966	-1966	-1966	-1966	1967-89	1967-89	1967-89	1967-89
Type / **Attributes**								
Executive committee								
Smallest leadership body (15-20)	No (20-25)	No (40-50)	No (15-20)	Yes (6-10)	No (10)	No (54-65)	No (15-20)	Yes (6-10)
No seat guarantees	Yes	No	No	Yes	Yes	No	No	Yes
Day-to-day management	No	No	No	Yes	No	No	No	Yes
National executive								
Larger than smallest leadership body (around 50)	Yes	Yes	Yes	No	Yes	Yes	Yes	No
Seat guarantees (optional)	No	Yes	Yes	No	No	Yes	Yes	No
Strategic leadership	No	No	Yes	No	No	Within limits	Yes	No
Classification	Excluded from analysis	Excluded from analysis	National executive	Executive committee	Excluded from analysis	Excluded from analysis	National executive	Executive committee

Notes:
[a] Former Parteikontrolle.
[b] Former Parteivertretung.
[c] Former Parteivorstand.

Until 1980, the ÖVP leadership structure was unambiguous (see Table 7.2). In 1980, a third national leadership body was created, the Erweiterter Bundesparteivorstand, which consisted of the Bundesparteivorstand and all Land party chairmen. However, this party body was given few explicit powers. The general phrase that it should 'decide questions of particular importance' indicates no clear transfer of power. In addition, the powers of the Bundesparteileitung (national executive) remained virtually untouched. This changed fundamentally in 1989, when three things occurred: the Erweiterter Bundesparteivorstand was renamed the Bundesparteivorstand; the body was enlarged to integrate the chairpersons of the sub-organisations; and, above all, executive powers were transferred from the Bundesparteileitung to the Bundesparteivorstand. Consequently, the Bundesparteivorstand was coded as national executive in 1989 and the Bundesparteileitung was not coded thereafter.

The example of the ÖVP illustrates that the decisive criterion for the classification of party bodies is their relative position within the overall power structure (that is, leadership power). Size and seat guarantees are additional indicators used to make a safer judgement. In the case of a functionally highly fragmented party like the ÖVP, however, all party bodies tend to be at least partially composed on the basis of seat guarantees.

There are also two Italian parties, where the appropriate identification of the top leadership bodies is problematic. The Giunta Esecutiva Centrale (executive committee) of the Christian Democrats (DC) is a small body of no more than seven members which 'co-ordinates the activities of the head of the party central office'. Since it is in charge of running the party day to day – in conjunction with the Segretario Politico (general secretary) – it has been coded as executive committee. From 1984 onwards, the newly created Ufficio Politico was explicitly given executive tasks. Although the Giunta Esecutiva Centrale continued to exist, the Ufficio Politico was thereafter coded as executive committee (cf. Lill and Wegener 1991: 94–7).

The Italian Social Movement (MSI) is a similar case. For a long time, the MSI had a dual structure at the top, that is, above the national executive. From 1966 onwards, the Segretaria Politica Nazionale existed alongside the Esecutivo Nazionale. Both bodies functioned to 'assist the Segretario Nazionale' (the party chairperson). However, the Segretaria Politica Nazionale was not coded until 1981, because it had no clearly defined additional powers. The Esecutivo Nazionale, on the other hand, had a wider range of functions including the control of the party press, the control of lower-level party organisations and federations and the control of electoral lists (from 1966 onwards). In 1982, the Esecutivo Nazionale was abolished and explicitly replaced by the Segretaria Politica Nazionale, which corroborates our judgement that the Segretaria Politica Nazionale was a rather subordinate body before 1982.

Distinguishing rule-making bodies is the second task in our search for an equivalent characterisation of political parties. The operational definition of a party congress stipulates that in order to qualify as a congress, a party body must fulfil two conditions: it must be the highest rule-making body and it must be the

Table 7.2 Party organisation of the Austrian People's Party (ÖVP)

Name of party body		Bundesparteileitung	Bundesparteivorstand	Erweiterter Bundesparteivorstand	Bundesparteivorstand[a]	Bundesparteipräsidium[b]	Bundesparteileitung
Period of time		–1988	–1988	1980–88	1989	1989	1989
Type	**Attributes**						
Executive committee	Smallest leadership body (15–20)	No (34–50)	Yes (17–24)	No (24)	No (34)	Yes (17–24)	No (34–50)
	No seat guarantees	No	No	No	No	No	No
	Day-to-day management	No	Yes	No	No	Yes	No
National executive	Larger than smallest leadership body (around 50)	Yes	No	Yes	Yes	No	Yes
	Seat guarantees (optional)	Yes	Yes	Yes	Yes	Yes	Yes
	Strategic leadership	Yes	No	No	Yes	No	No
Classification		National executive	Executive committee	Excluded from analysis	National executive	Executive committee	Excluded from analysis

Notes:
[a] Former Erweiterter Bundesparteivorstand.
[b] Former Bundesparteivorstand.

ultimate sovereign in selecting the top leadership. The example of the Belgian
Volksunie (see Table 7.3) shows, however, that in cases where one condition
cannot be met unambiguously, the second criterion assumes a critical role.[8] Until
the end of 1987, the Partijraad had the power to define the party line and decide
all important matters not discussed by the Congres. This would suggest the
supremacy of the Congres. However, given that the Congres had no explicit
decision-making power and lacked the power to select leadership, the Partijraad
was categorised as the ultimate law-making body – that is, the party congress. The
distribution of power changed in 1988, when the Congres was explicitly designated the 'highest organ of the party'. At the same time, the party statutes
declared that the Partijraad was, 'after the party congress, the highest organ of
the party'. Nevertheless, the case of the VU remained something of an anomaly,
because the national executive continued to be elected by the Partijraad.

The example of the traditional Dutch Christian parties illustrates that it can be
deceptive to rely too readily on the name of party bodies. A close look at the
Partijcongres (party congress) and the Partijraad (party council) of the Catholic
People's Party (KVP) shows that the latter had de jure the powers which normally
rest with a party congress (see Table 7.3). Again, as in the case of the Volksunie,
only one of the essential criteria can be used for the classification, because no
details on the selection of the top leadership are available. The Christian Historical Union (CHU) had two assemblies: the Unieraad (party council) and the
Algemene Vergadering (party congress). Until 1971, the categorisation of both
party assemblies suited their labels, despite the fact that the party council elected
the party chairperson. But in 1972, the two bodies effectively swapped their
position in the party's internal power structure (see Table 7.3). The party council
was given the 'general conduct of the party' and the right to elect the entire
national executive. Similarly, in the Anti-Revolutionary Party (ARP), the Partijraad took over the powers of the former party congress (Deputatenvergadering),
when the latter was abolished in 1971 (see Table 7.3).

The case of the Danish Conservative People's Party (KF) exemplifies how our
operational typology can be applied to a party organisation which, at first sight,
appears to have created parallel assemblies at the national level (see Table 7.3).
The Landsrådsmødet (national conference) and the Repræsentantskabet
(national council) both meet once a year and both have the task to 'discuss the
policy of the parliamentary group'. Whereas the national conference is identified
as party congress because it is the 'highest authority in party policy', the party
council is only the 'highest authority in organisational matters'. In addition, the
Landsrådsmødet elects the party chairperson.

Finally, we turn to the distinction between leadership bodies and rule-making
bodies. The national leadership bodies of the Irish Fine Gael show the overriding
importance of the relative positions of party bodies when other criteria of the
operational typology fail. Between 1963 and 1969, the national council was the
highest formally elected party body (see Table 7.4). It was obviously too large to
permit efficient executive leadership, which suggests that much real leadership
rested with a virtually unregulated 'standing committee' and informal inner

Table 7.3 Party congress or party council?

			Type		Party council		Party congress			
Country	Period of time	Name of party body	Attributes		Higher frequency of meetings	Inferior rule-making body	Lower frequency of meetings	Highest rule-making body	Selects the top leadership[a]	Classification
Belgium		*Volksunie*								
	1960–65	Congres			No (1/year)	Unclear	No	Unclear	No	Party council
	1960–65	Partijraad			No (1/year)	Unclear	No	Unclear	Yes	Party congress
	1966–87	Congres			No (1/year)	Unclear	Yes	Unclear	No	Party council
	1966–87	Partijraad			Yes (12/year)	Unclear	No	Unclear	Yes	Party congress
	1988–89	Congres			No (0.5/year)	No	Yes	Yes	No	Party congress
	1988–89	Partijraad			Yes (12/year)	Yes	No	No	Yes	Party council
Denmark		*KF*								
	1971–89	Repræsentantskabet			No (1/year)	Yes	No (1/year)	Yes	No	Party council
	1971–89	Landsrådsmodet			No (1/year)	No	No (1/year)	No	Yes	Party congress
Netherlands		*KVP*								
	1960–66	Partijcongres			No (0.5/year)	Yes	Yes	No	n.a.	Party council
	1960–79	Patijraad			Yes (1/year)	No	No	Yes	n.a.	Party congress
Netherlands		*ARP*								
	1960–70	Deputatenvergadering			(Not fixed) (2/year)	No	Only one assembly	Yes	Yes	Party congress
	1960–70	Partijkonvent			Only one assembly	Yes		No	No	Party council
	1971–79	Partijraad			Only one assembly	Only one assembly	Only one assembly	Yes	Yes	Party congress

continued

Table 7.3 continued

Country	Period of time	Name of party body		Party council		Party congress			Classification
			Type	Attributes					
				Higher frequency of meetings	Inferior rule-making body	Lower frequency of meetings	Highest rule-making body	Selects the top leadership[a]	
Netherlands		*CHU*							
	1960–71	Algemene Vergadering		Unclear (1/year)	No	Unclear	Yes	Yes[b]	Party congress
	1960–71	Unieraad		Unclear (No rule)	Yes	Unclear	No	Yes[c]	Party congress
	1972–79	Algemene Vergadering		No (1/year)	Yes	Yes	No	No	Party council
	1972–79	Unieraad		Yes (2/year)	No	No	Yes	Yes	Party congress

Notes:
[a] This is a necessary attribute unless the top leadership is selected through membership ballots.
[b] Elects additional members in national executive. The remaining members are delegated from party district executives.
[c] Elects party chairman.

Table 7.4 National executive or party council?

Country	Period of time	Name of party body	Attributes	Party council			National executive			Classification
			Type	Lower frequency of meetings	Larger body	No executive power	Higher frequency of meetings	Smaller or smallest body	Executive power	
Ireland		*Fine Gael*								
	1963–69	National council		(4/year)	No	No		Yes (95–103)	Yes	National executive
	1970–89	National council		Yes (2/year)	Yes (43–85)	Yes	No	No	No	Party council
	1970–89	National executive		No	No (33–45)[a]	No	Yes	Yes	Yes	National executive
Italy		*PCI*								
	1960–89	Comitato Centrale		Yes (6/year)	Yes (128–357)	Yes	No	No	No	Party council
	1960–89	Direzione		No	No	No	Yes	Yes	Yes	National executive

Note:
[a] The membership of national council and national executive was significantly reduced at the same time; the national executive was consistently the smaller party body.

circles. Nevertheless, the national council may be categorised as national executive, because any political organisation needs a formal peak and it effectively
served as one during these years. It should be added that internal party life in
those years was still strongly constituency centred, which means that there was
comparatively little need for central organisational action (Farrell 1994: 224). As
late as 1970, a new, smaller party body was created, which was given the executive
powers of the national council.

The Italian case provides another example. The Comitato Centrale (central
committee) of the PCI had 128 members in 1960 and 357 in 1990 (Bardi and
Morlino 1994: 263). Although it met every two months and was stipulated by
statute to 'direct' the party between congresses, it was too large for any real
executive function. It was, therefore, categorised as party council (see Table 7.4).
In addition, there was a smaller body above the Comitato Centrale. The real
executive power rested with the national executive (Direzione), which led the
party between meetings of the Comitato Centrale.

The previous discussion has dealt with the problem of categorising party bodies
of eleven parties. In most cases, this involved only two of the parties' bodies for a
portion of the time series. Given that a total of seventy-seven parties are included
in the analysis (most of which have at least three relevant party bodies), the vast
majority of party bodies can be assigned unambiguously to one of the categories
as they are described above. If we treat each party body in each year as one unit of
observation, we have a total of 5,442 cases. Only 469 (8.6 per cent) had to
undergo the rigorous classification procedure documented above. In each case
a satisfactory decision upon the adequate categorisation could be reached.[9]

These results corroborate the theoretical argument suggested in this chapter.
Functional requirements do indeed induce equivalent core power structures.
Notwithstanding the persisting influence of specific historical traditions and systemic moulding, all parties have developed a similar pyramid of power. To be
sure, the variation in detail is enormous. For instance, parties may or may not
admit ex officio members to their centres of power; they may permit the co-
determination of collateral organisations or stick to the principle of territorial
representation; or they may vary the size of their principal leadership bodies
considerably, and so on. But as is the case for parliamentary democracies, the core
functions of rule-making and executive decision-making can be clearly located. All
parties have a highest rule-making body; that is, a party congress or, occasionally,
a general assembly. They also all have an executive body, which leads the party
organisationally and politically.

The impression of uniformity changes, however, when we focus on the existence
of 'secondary' party arenas, that is, the party council and the executive committee.
They are, from a functional perspective, not indispensable for a viable political
organisation. Throughout the period covered by this study, forty-four parties have
had a second, smaller executive body, and an additional four parties have had an
executive committee for some of the time. In addition, thirty-nine parties have
had a secondary rule-making body (the party council), and eight parties have had
a party council for part of the time. In this case, the above-mentioned nation-

specific influences are clearly identifiable. As regards the existence of an executive committee, six of the eleven countries are homogeneous, which means that either all or none of the parties have such a party body (Finland, Germany, Ireland, Norway, Sweden, and Great Britain). Dominant patterns are also clearly identifiable in the remaining countries except in Italy.

Patterns of national organisational cultures are somewhat less pronounced in the case of the party council. Only three countries are completely homogeneous on this count (Finland, Germany, Great Britain), but a pattern prevails in all cases except Austria, Ireland, and Sweden. This observation of large, country-specific differences can be validated statistically by calculating the coefficient of association between the existence of such party bodies and the variable 'nation'. The results show clearly that party structures are remarkably similar within national party systems. For both party bodies, there is a very strong association with nation.[10] In a nutshell, the core power structures of Western European parties are very similar, because their organisations must all meet similar functional requirements. Beyond the essential tasks of rule-making and executive leadership, however, substantial variation exists which seems related to specific national conditions.

The development of linkage patterns in Western European parties

Now that we have established that Western European parties have comparable formal power structures, we can compare the linkages of these parties with collateral organisations for specific party arenas. As mentioned in the introduction, data for this analysis have been generated through coding the party statutes in the data handbook edited by Katz and Mair (1992a). The coding scheme was designed to capture substantive differences between the following two principal forms of organisational access. Collateral organisations may be *represented* in party bodies (that is, the party itself decides who is admitted to its bodies), or collateral organisations may have the right to send *delegates* (that is, the organisation is fully sovereign when selecting delegates). A specific selection procedure may exist, or certain organisational office holders may have an ex officio right to participate in meetings of particular party bodies. Arguably, the latter kind of linkage represents a stronger tie, because its maintenance presupposes basic agreements between the organisations, whereas a party may continue to select and admit representatives who are in a minority position within their own organisation. An even weaker kind of linkage exists if members of a collateral organisation are admitted only as guests to certain party bodies, with no right to vote.

In order to reflect the strengths of different kinds of organisational access, these differences were given distinct numeric weights. The right of an organisation to send guests to a given party arena was coded '1', regardless of the way the guests were selected, and the right to send representatives with full voting rights was coded '2'. Compared to delegates with full voting rights, both of these modes of organisational representation are clearly weaker. Admitting guests to party bodies does not involve true power sharing and is obviously the weakest form of linkage. Although granting access to representatives with voting rights does share power with extraneous organisations, it still gives the party discretion about who is actually allowed to participate in core decision-making processes. The unconditional admittance of delegates from collateral organisations, on the other hand, subjects the party to the political will of its collateral organisations to some degree and thus represents the strongest connection to its organisational environment. In order to reflect this substantive difference, delegates with full voting rights were coded '4'. At any time, several collateral organisations may have access to a party arena through one of these linkages. In that case, the linkage score used in the subsequent analysis is simply the sum of these scores for a given party arena or for the party as a whole. If a linkage score for a party as a whole is calculated, however, it needs to be standardised by the number of party arenas in order to make this score comparable across parties with differing numbers of party arenas.

At the beginning of this chapter, we suggested that the loosening hold of external collateral organisations on their clientele should have induced a process of growing organisational independence between them and the political parties to which they were formerly tied. This may be reflected either in an overall receding linkage score for external collateral organisations or in the relocation of such linkages to more deliberative bodies like the party council or the party congress. At the same time, parties can be expected to have sought compensation for their diminishing organisational contact with their constituencies through the expansion of their own networks of internal collateral organisations. This, in turn, should be reflected in growing linkage scores for internal collateral organisations.

When we look at the average overall linkage scores for political parties (that is, for all relevant party bodies), we see first that linkages to party-sponsored (that is, internal) collateral organisations far outweigh those to external collateral organisations (see Figure 7.1). Generally speaking, political parties in Western Europe depend primarily upon their own organisational efforts when trying to stabilise their electorates, and they can rely only moderately on external assistance. Furthermore, the different trends for linkages to external and internal collateral organisations corroborate our theoretical expectations. On average, external collateral organisations have become less relevant for political parties in Western Europe, while internal interest organisations have increased at roughly the same rate. The overall picture, then, is one of declining linkage to external interests offset by the increasing representation of internal interest organisations.

A closer look at the party congress and the national executive – the common core structure of all Western European parties – yields a more differentiated result. The downward trend for external collateral organisations is even more pronounced for their formal access rights to the centre of executive decision-making power, the national executive (see Figure 7.2). At the same time, however, the representation of internal interests has remained virtually unchanged. This means that, over time, the principal leadership bodies of Western European political parties have become organisationally more remote from relevant

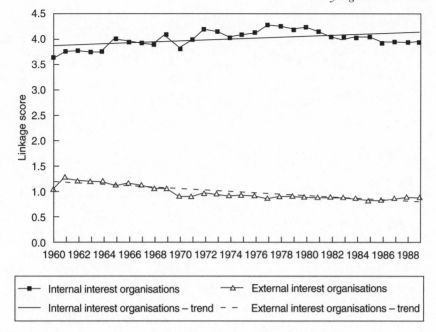

Figure 7.1 Overall linkage to different types of collateral organisations

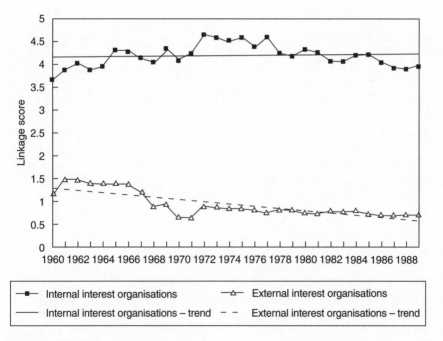

Figure 7.2 Linkage to national executives

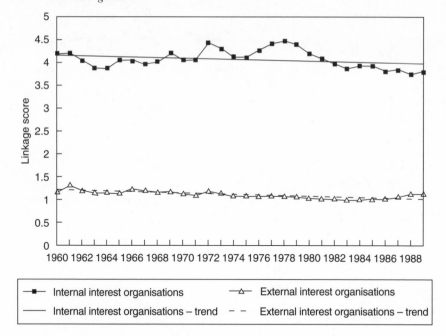

Figure 7.3 Linkage to party congresses

segments of their electorates. Contrary to the potential organisational strategy suggested above, there was not simply a shift of external interest representation to the party congress, which is, arguably, less relevant for the organised formal exchange between political parties and collateral organisations. Figure 7.3 depicts the linkage scores for the party congress. Over time, average linkage scores for both types of collateral organisations have declined moderately. Significantly, however, none of these trends is particularly pronounced. In the light of truly dramatic changes in Western European societies over the same period, this is certainly the most remarkable result of this analysis. Admittedly, this picture has been painted with a very broad brush. Further, more refined analyses are needed to decide whether these results are generally true for Western European political parties or whether more pronounced changes among specific groups of parties have been offset by changes in the opposite direction among other groups – or even by the emergence of new parties.

Conclusion

This chapter began by identifying a general problem of comparative research on party organisations. Although certain party arenas may have similar names or may look alike, comparative investigations are on safe ground only if they use unambiguous, generally applicable criteria to identify party arenas which are functionally equivalent within the internal power structure. To be sure, many relevant empirical questions on party organisations have been investigated without spending much time on these aspects. The literature on party organisational types (Weber 1980: 837–51; Duverger 1964; Kirchheimer 1965; Katz and Mair 1993) tends to focus on general characteristics of party organisations like the properties of their basic units or the nature of their roles as intermediaries between state and society. Similarly, the literature on party strength or decline tends to avoid identifying equivalent party bodies by concentrating on indicators which measure a party's overall organisational strength (for instance, party finance, party membership, or professionalisation) (see, for example, Webb 1995). Both perspectives, however – particularly the latter – could benefit by more precisely locating organisational resources. This need, in turn, presupposes a rigorous classification of party arenas. Furthermore, if we wish to get really inside party organisations and compare, for example, their distribution of internal power or their linkage patterns to collateral organisations, we must first be able to identify equivalent party bodies. The approach presented in this chapter accomplishes two things: (1) it yields relevant empirical results which show that Western European parties have indeed developed equivalent core power structures, and (2) it represents a suitable tool for comparative and longitudinal research on a wide range of questions related to the internal functioning of political parties.

Notes

1 I am indebted to Rüdiger Schmitt-Beck and Jan W. van Deth for helpful comments on this chapter.
2 The following countries were included: Austria, Belgium, Denmark, Finland, Germany, Ireland, Italy, the Netherlands, Norway, Sweden, the United Kingdom, and the United States.
3 The Belgian parties which split into linguistically defined sister parties are counted separately. No data are available for the Belgian PSC.
4 Individual party organisations after each relevant rule change are treated as units of analysis in this process.
5 Parties without a party council normally assign these powers to their national congress.
6 All data are taken from Katz and Mair (1992).
7 Both party bodies have a peculiar position in the overall party structure, because they are not fully independent. Together with the Parteivorstand, the Parteikontrolle forms the Parteivertretung, which is also inferior to the national executive (Parteivorstand).
8 The frequency of meetings is a complementary criterion.
9 Obviously, far fewer actual decisions needed to be made, because party bodies remained unchanged for several years after each relevant rule change (see Tables 7.1–7.4).
10 Cramer's V is 0.70 for the party council and 0.82 for the executive committee.

8 Party positions

Gábor Tóka[1]

Introduction

Scholarly literature on political parties and party systems often refers to policy distances[2] between parties. This is most obvious in the vast literature on the spatial theory of voting, but polarisation between the parties has also been suggested to influence many things, including the stability and/or quality of democracy (Sartori 1976; Mainwaring and Scully 1995), the occurrence of minority governments (Dodd 1976; Strom 1990), cabinet endurance (King *et al.* 1990), and electoral turnout (Crepaz 1990). Whatever indicators of polarisation these studies used, they seem to have understood them as a measure of policy distances summed across one or more policy dimensions. They seem to have agreed that the degree of distance is one of the most important traits of a party system. Similarly, individual parties are routinely called 'centrist' or 'extremist', and such positions are considered among their most salient traits.

However, the same distance between the policies of two parties may mean different things depending on the clarity of party positions. Inter-party relations, the accountability of representatives, voters' behaviour, and even regime stability may be differently affected if: (1) all significant parties are clearly close to each other on relevant issues, or (2) all significant parties have obscure, fuzzy positions. For instance, some studies suggest that the sheer clarity of party positions may increase electoral support for parties over and above the level explained by their relative proximity to the voters on the various issues (Bartels 1986; Iversen 1994; Rabinowitz and Macdonald 1989; Reynolds 1974). Clearly, then, the relative obscurity of party positions is relevant for party competition.

The more obscure the issue positions of parties and candidates, the more likely they should appeal to voters via routes other than policy proposals. Since charismatic leaders rarely abound, clientelistic linkages are the most obvious alternative. But the absence of distinctive, predictable and consequential policy differences between the parties may undermine the accountability of political leaders or let the exchange of personal favours become the dominant bond between parties and their voters. As Kitschelt (1995a) has argued, political cynicism is likely to grow in the electorate in either case, and the quality of democracy cannot be very high. In addition, the more obscure party positions are, the less analysts gain by applying

'Western' theoretical frameworks which emphasise the role of cleavages, issues, and policy distances in party competition.

Furthermore, the clarity of party positions is more easily and unambiguously linked to themes in normative democratic theory than polarisation. It is simply not obvious whether relatively great policy distances between the parties are good or bad for the quality of democracy. The responsible party government ideal requires that competing parties have distinctive, unambiguous, and binding policy commitments. In the absence of policy differences between the parties, governments cannot be held accountable for their policies. But the requirements of responsible party government may well conflict with the ideal of responsive government (cf. Pennock 1979: 283–6, 293–303). In a purely Downsian world, Tweedledee and Tweedledum may converge around a single position – either as a consequence or an anticipation of electoral pressure – and thus create responsive party government. Here, the dearth of policy differences between the competitors would actually help to ensure that popular preferences (whatever that means) determine public policies.[3] However, the clarity – as opposed to the differentiation – of party positions at any one point in time is part of both responsible and responsive party government ideals. In both cases, parties offer identifiable products. Therefore, the clarity – not the differentiation – of party positions is the decisive sign of programmatic party competition.

The competing pledges of convergent parties can hardly be distinguished from each other. This is the phenomenon that Stokes (1963) called a 'valence' issue. Suppose that the parties in question are as firmly committed to a certain position on an issue as anyone can be, and thus have identifiable positions. Even so, they may create confusion about party positions – in responses to survey questions about party positions, for instance – if they compete on that issue by intensely questioning the true position, credibility, and commitment of their opponents, rather than by outmanoeuvring them by changing their own position. In this case, perceptions of party positions may vary widely depending on the partisanship of the observer, yet the parties do compete with each other in terms of offering identifiable collective goods. Party positions are clear, even if not uncontested.

The predictability of party positions is not just a potentially important factor, it is likely to vary considerably across countries. As Kitschelt (1994 and 1995a) has argued at length, the emergence of programmatic parties – that is, parties which appeal to voters mostly by promising to deliver collective goods if elected – is not automatically guaranteed after transitions to democracy. In the medium term, clientelistic parties, social movements, and parties built around charismatic leaders may be more easily developed and maintained. Since programmatic parties can provide superior solutions to the organisational needs of a voluntary political organisation (by providing for an enduring organisation, building on selective incentives, and extracting support from unpaid members and voters by offering collective goods), it is no surprise that the literature on 'old' Western party systems often overlooks variations in the degree to which programmatic differences regulate the dynamics of inter-party relations. Once we consider emerging and/or non-Western democracies, however, variations in the clarity of party positions –

and, even more fundamentally, in the sheer institutionalisation of political parties (see Mainwaring and Scully 1995) – become more readily visible. Regarding the four countries analysed in this chapter, Kitschelt (1994; 1995a and 1995b) predicted that because of differences in: (1) education and affluence of the population; (2) traditions of democratic party competition; (3) emphasis on personalistic factors in electoral competition by the institutional framework (for instance, Poland has a semi-presidential regime with open-list PR while the three others have parliamentary systems with little or no opportunity for within-party electoral choices); and (4) the influence of the mode of transition (for instance, revolution in Czechoslovakia, negotiated transition in Poland and Hungary, and incumbent-controlled in Bulgaria) on programmatic differentiation between the former communist parties and their challengers, the Czech Republic and Bulgaria would, respectively, have significantly clearer and significantly more obscure positions than Poland or Hungary.[4]

The identifiability of party positions is primarily a characteristic of the relative position of a set of parties on an individual issue. The meaningful question is not whether a single party has a 'clear' position in some absolute sense. Rather, the degree of predictability is always relative to the range of positions people believe may be taken by one or another actor within the party system. The next section of this chapter proposes a measure of the clarity of party positions on this level, that is, on individual issues. This measure enables us to make cross-national comparisons on the same issue and cross-issue comparisons within the same country.

Next, we confront the more difficult question of how to construct a cross-nationally valid measure of the overall degree of programmatic crystallisation in a national party system. Given the obvious cross-national differences in the political agenda, we need a country-specific weighting of the issue domains.

Finally, we consider how the validity of these measures can be checked. We offer a partial empirical test and discuss the results together with the general relationship between the clarity of party positions and their popular perception.

Identifying party positions on individual issues

Data

As Laver and Hunt (1992: 31) have eloquently argued, the single best method of collecting comprehensive and comparable cross-national data on policy distances between parties is to conduct an expert survey. This seems all the more advisable since policy distances between parties affect human behaviour via perceptions. While Laver and Hunt (and several less outspoken defenders of the methodology who preceded them) interviewed small national samples of political scientists,[5] this chapter relies on judgements provided by more partisan actors: mid-level party activists. The two crucial advantages to this solution are that: (1) larger samples can be obtained even in small countries, and (2) the analyst need not speculate about how 'objective' policy distances translate into the actors' perceptions.

The data base was created by a project directed by Herbert Kitschelt, and co-directed in Bulgaria, the Czech Republic, Poland, and Hungary by Dobrinka Kostova, Zdenka Mansfeldova, Radoslaw Markowski, and the author, respectively. In each country, we conducted face-to-face structured interviews with 100 to 135 mid-level party activists (that is, municipal and regional party executives, mayors, committee chairs of city councils, etc.) stratified by party[6] and region[7] in spring 1994. In the computation of most of the indices reported below, the respondents are weighted to adjust the data for the slightly unequal representation of the parties in the sample.[8] The assumption is that in this way we obtain the message that the voters would receive from the parties if all significant parties had equal access to all channels of elite-mass communication. While this assumption obviously does not hold, it yields a rule no worse than any alternative, and it is at least unambiguous – which would not be the case if we tried weighting the data by the size of the parties (that is, by their share of votes or seats in the most recent election). Table 8.1 lists the parties covered by the perception data and roughly indicates their political orientation.

The respondents were asked to tell how important some ten potentially controversial issues were for their party and to locate all parties on a twenty-point scale of the issues, plus some abstract ideological scales (for instance, clerical versus secular). All of the questions defined explicitly two opposite policy or ideological positions as points 1 and 20 of the scale. For example, the first question stated:

> Some politicians think that social policy cannot protect citizens from all risks, but they also have to rely on themselves. For instance, all costs of medical treatment should be paid either directly by everybody from his or her own pocket, or by joining voluntary health insurance schemes individually.
>
> In contrast, other politicians think that the social policy of the state must protect citizens from every sort of social risk. For instance, all medical expenses should be financed from the social security fund.

Table 8.1 Objects of evaluations in four countries

Orientation	Bulgaria	Czech R.	Hungary	Poland
Post-communist	BSP	LB	MSZP	SLD
Agrarian	BANU	LSU	FKGP	PSL
Social democrat	BSDP	CSSD		UP
Christian		CSL	KDNP	ZChN
Liberal I		ODA	SZDSZ	UD
Liberal II		SD	FIDESZ	KLD
Nationalist		SPR-RSC	MIÉP	KPN
Ethnic	DPS	CMSS		
Conservative I	SDS	ODS	MDF	BBWR
Conservative II		KDS		PC
Other				NSZZ'S'

Thus, every respondent had to locate every party on the respective scales which had its own parliamentary party or which seemed to have (according to public opinion polls) a reasonable chance of gaining parliamentary representation in the next election. The basic unit of observation was the combination of respondents and rated parties. Thus, in the present analysis, we have 500 cases in the Bulgarian data; that is, 100 respondents rating five different parties, and so on.[9]

Table 8.2 summarises briefly the content of the various scales (the full text of the items is shown by Kitschelt *et al.*, 1998).[10] On VAR51, respondents evaluated the parties in terms of sympathy–antipathy. This variable does not define an issue domain, but is, rather, a measure of partisanship. But precisely because it is a measure of partisanship, it generates certain patterns in the answers as a real 'valence issue' would have – had any been present in the questionnaire. Therefore, data on the results of the sympathy scales are presented with those of the issue and ideological scales in order to show which of the latter tend to behave – under certain conditions – as valence issues.

The present analysis uses the mean rating of the parties. This means that we ignore the difference between a respondent who located a certain party on point 10 of a scale, and another who located the same party on points 8, 10, and 12 of the same scale. The mean$_{ijk}$ matrix provided directly by respondents i about the mean location of parties j on scale k was replaced with the xmean$_{ijk}$ matrix (see the definitions below). In substantive terms this means that we analyse the positions of the parties *vis-à-vis* each other rather than the verbally defined endpoints of the scales.[11] In our first issue question, for instance, one alternative mentioned covering 'all medical expenses' by the social security. Perhaps some Hungarian respondents believed that this hinted at also covering ordinary dental treatment, while others might have recalled the widely publicised treatment of a famous TV personality in a private clinic in Mexico covered by private donations. Such differences in the interpretative framework ought not to have prevented the respondents from indicating essentially the same policy distance between parties, but we are clearly better off if we eliminate this 'noise' from the data on perceived party positions.

To sum up:

- mean$_{ijk}$ is the mean placement of party j on issue k by respondent i on a twenty-point scale; and
- xmean$_{ijk}$ is the mean placement of party j on issue k by respondent i relative to his or her anchor point$_{ik}$; where
- anchor point$_{ik}$ is the average location of all rated parties on issue k by respondent i.

In other words, xmean$_{ijk}$ is the deviation of party j's mean position on issue k in the judgement of respondent i from the average of the mean position on issue k of all parties that respondent i rated on that issue.

Table 8.2 A guideline to the content and endpoints of the scales used

Point 1	'Issue' scales	Point 20
	VAR30: social security	
Citizens pay		Compulsory insurance
	VAR31: desirable size publ. sector	
Privatise all companies		Substantial public sector
	VAR32: speed vs justice of privatisation	
Justice		Speed and efficiency
	VAR33: inflation vs unemployment	
Fight inflation		Fight unemployment
	VAR34: foreign investment	
Welcome		Dependence
	VAR35: income taxation	
More progressive		More equal
	VAR36: immigration (not asked in Bulgaria)	
Restrictive		Permissive
	VAR37: women at work	
Subsidise kindergartens		Women stay home
	VAR38: abortion (not asked in Bulgaria)	
Extreme pro-life		Extreme pro-choice
	VAR39: churches and schools	
Churches should influence		Should not
	VAR40: urban–rural	
Neutral or pro-urban		Pro-agrarian
	VAR41: authority–autonomy in education	
Authority		Autonomy
	VAR42: environment protection	
Industry first		Environment
	VAR43: censorship of magazines	
Against		In favour
	VAR44: former communists	
Discriminate		Equal rights
	VAR45: national issue I	
Bulgaria: pro-Turkish		Anti-Turkish
Hungary: for basic treaties		Against basic treaties
	VAR52: national issue II	
Bulgaria: pro-Turkish		Anti-Turkish
Czech Republic: centralist		Favours regional autonomy
	VAR53: effectiveness of decentralisation	
Czech Republic: centralist		Favours regional autonomy
	Abstract scales	
	VAR46: state intervention–free market	
State		Free market
	VAR47: individual–tradition	
Freedom		Tradition
	VAR48: national–pan-European	
Nation		Europe
	VAR49: clerical–secular	
Clerical		Secular
	VAR 50: Left–Right	
Left		Right
	VAR51: sympathy	
Unsympathetic		Sympathetic

Programmatic crystallisation, asymmetry of judgements, and random noise

Kitschelt (1994) measured the 'diffuseness' of party positions on a given issue by the standard deviation of the placements of party j given by the respondents. While this proposition has considerable merit, it also has two problems. The smaller one is what was indicated above in the discussion of valence issues: some of the variation in the placement of a party on an issue reflects merely the diversity of partisan viewpoints in the jury. It does not reflect a genuine lack of an identifiable party position. This problem is easily handled by a simple adjustment. The standard deviation of the xmean$_{ik}$ ratings of each party j can be computed separately for each partisan group of jurors, and then averaged (with an appropriate weighting of the groups). This adjusted version of Kitschelt's measure of 'diffuseness' can be seen as a perfectly valid measure of the clarity of party positions for comparing parties on a given issue.

There remains, however, a fundamental problem with all measures based on standard deviation. Their value is dependent on the definition of the endpoints of the scales. Had, for instance, point 20 of our income tax scale meant a poll tax (instead of a less progressive tax than the existing one), the same respondents might (indeed should) have placed the same parties in a narrower range. Then, the standard deviation of the judgements on party j's position would have been smaller. Obviously, sensible researchers never define the endpoints of their issue scales arbitrarily. Rather, they try to design scales that do not prevent respondents from expressing large differences between the parties on the issues. Hence, the endpoints must denote positions at least as extreme as those taken by any significant political force in the country. At the same time, they must allow for minute distinctions among non-extreme parties and avoid the appearance of treating the question frivolously. But this is exactly the heart of the matter: issue scales are (and must be) constructed to reflect political reality. Therefore, they take for granted some, indeed most, of what researchers should explain. To put it in another way, *a unit distance (or variance) on an identically phrased scale is not cross-nationally comparable for it is not obvious why the range of conceivable positions on an issue would be identical across countries.*

Needless to say, distances and variances are not comparable across issue domains either – as long as we cannot define an explicit exchange rate between a unit difference on issue A (income taxation) and issue B (abortion rights or NATO-membership). Therefore, I introduce relative measures of the clarity of party positions, which I call random noise and image crystallisation. These are percentage-based measures. Their minimum value (0) indicates the total absence of the respective trait in the relevant data, and their maximum value (100) suggests that the trait totally determines the responses and leaves the respondents no room to deviate from a given pattern.

Technically, the xmean$_{ij}$ variance on every issue k (that is, the total variation in the responses concerning all of the parties' positions on each of the issues) is decomposed into three parts. Three percentage figures are obtained, each showing

Table 8.3 Deconstructing the variance of judgements about party positions and the mean salience of the issues (percentages and means)

Variable no.	Content domain	NOISE	CRYST	ASYMM	Issue salience
(a) Bulgaria					
30	Social security	65	24	11	4.8
31	Size public sector	49	45	6	4.8
32	Privatisation	87	9	4	4.8
33	Inflation–unemployment	59	37	3	4.8
34	Foreign investments	55	40	6	4.3
35	Income taxation	85	5	10	4.7
36	Immigration (not asked)				
37	Women at work	83	5	12	3.9
38	Abortion (not asked)				
39	Churches, schools	56	25	19	4.3
40	Urban–rural	45	51	5	4.5
41	Authority–autonomy	67	27	6	4.6
42	Environment	66	25	9	4.5
43	Censorship	76	11	13	4.4
44	Former communists	35	57	8	4.4
45	Minority rights	38	60	2	3.8
46	State–free market	49	48	3	
47	Individualism–tradition	66	23	11	
48	National–European	72	19	10	
49	Clerical–secular	65	27	8	
50	Left–right	39	59	3	
51	Sympathy	28	17	55	
52	Relations with Turkey	40	58	2	4.2
(b) Czech Republic					
30	Social security	32	64	4	4.3
31	Size public sector	27	69	4	3.9
32	Privatisation	34	63	3	4.2
33	Inflation–unemployment	25	71	4	4.2
34	Foreign investments	24	73	3	3.9
35	Income taxation	35	60	5	4.0
36	Immigration	62	27	11	3.5
37	Women at work	42	51	7	3.7
38	Abortion	27	69	5	3.3
39	Churches, schools	22	75	3	3.1
40	Urban–rural	30	65	5	4.3
41	Authority–autonomy	70	17	12	3.8
42	Environment	69	14	17	4.4
43	Censorship	64	26	10	3.9
44	Former communists	38	53	9	3.8
45	(Not asked)				
46	State–free market	29	65	6	
47	Individualism–tradition	58	32	11	
48	National–European	47	46	7	
49	Clerical–secular	25	71	4	

continued

Table 8.3 continued

Variable					
no.	Content domain	NOISE	CRYST	ASYMM	Issue salience
50	Left–right	24	73	3	
51	Sympathy	33	17	50	
52	Decentralisation I	57	18	25	4.2
53	Decentralisation II	53	18	29	
(c) Hungary					
30	Social security	59	26	15	4.5
31	Size public sector	62	31	7	4.8
32	Privatisation	56	36	8	4.6
33	Inflation–unemployment	69	24	7	4.7
34	Foreign investments	41	46	13	4.3
35	Income taxation	79	16	5	4.1
36	Immigration	49	45	5	3.7
37	Women at work	43	52	5	4.2
38	Abortion	23	72	5	4.1
39	Churches, schools	16	81	3	4.1
40	Urban–rural	50	42	9	4.6
41	Authority–autonomy	22	74	4	4.1
42	Environment	69	7	24	4.3
43	Censorship	34	62	4	4.0
44	Former communists	27	69	4	3.5
45	Foreign policy	28	68	4	4.3
46	State–free market	38	40	22	
47	Individualism–tradition	24	75	2	
48	National–European	28	65	7	
49	Clerical–secular	15	82	3	
50	Left–right	16	82	2	
51	Sympathy	21	6	72	
(d) Poland					
30	Social security	40	54	6	4.4
31	Size public sector	39	53	8	4.5
32	Privatisation	45	49	6	4.6
33	Inflation–unemployment	37	58	5	4.6
34	Foreign investments	36	58	6	3.9
35	Income taxation	45	47	8	4.4
36	Immigration	54	39	8	3.0
37	Women at work	59	34	7	3.7
38	Abortion	25	72	3	3.7
39	Churches, schools	20	77	3	3.7
40	Urban–rural	35	60	5	3.8
41	Authority–autonomy	39	55	7	4.0
42	Environment	75	9	16	4.1
43	Censorship	39	55	6	3.5
44	Former communists	19	78	3	3.4
45	(Not asked)				
46	State–free market	38	56	6	

Table 8.3 continued

Variable No.	Content domain	NOISE	CRYST	ASYMM	Issue salience
47	Individualism–tradition	32	63	5	
48	National–European	30	66	4	
49	Clerical–secular	24	73	4	
50	Left–right	32	62	6	
51	Sympathy	29	5	66	

Notes:
NOISE: random noise, percentage of variance unexplained by VAR4, VAR22 and the VAR4*VAR22 interaction term. CRYST: Image crystallisation, percentage of variance explained by VAR22. ASYMM: Systematic asymmetries of judgements, percentage of variance explained by the VAR4* VAR22 interaction term. Issue salience: the mean of the responses to the question 'How important is this topic for your party?' (5 = very important, 1 = not really important). The question was not asked about VAR46 to VAR51. In calculating the above figures, the data are weighted as described in Note 8.

the relative amount of variance due to one or another component and all three totalling 100. Table 8.3 shows the numerical values for each scale in each country. The same table also shows the average salience rating of the issue by the respondents (that is, 'how important' the issue is for their party).

The first component is *image crystallisation*. Judges agree that on the given scale, party A is a certain distance and direction from party B, and they respond to the issue question accordingly. Irrespective of the extent of polarisation and whether or not polarisation can have a standardised measure, image crystallisation will be high whenever a strong consensus on individual party stances on the issue tends to be the only source of variation in the responses about party positions. Conversely, even if the polarisation of parties on issue k is very great, the respondents may disagree on whether the true distance between two parties is 4 or 7 units. If this is so, the variance of xmean$_{ij}$ explained by the identity of the rated party (VAR22) will be less than 100 per cent of the total.

But predictable party positions do not imply a perfect consensus of perceptions. If programmatic party competition is strong, then the members of different parties are unlikely to agree on the precise size of the policy distance between their parties. Some parties are likely to feel electorally insecure on some issues (for instance, pro-market parties on welfare state issues when they sense a statist electoral majority). In this case, a sophisticated respondent is apt to understate or overstate the between-party differences on the issue, depending on whether or not her (or his) party is on the electorally advantageous side. The crucial question is whether the judges share an understanding of which party should understate and which should overstate the between-party differences.[12] To the extent they do, programmatic party competition may be well developed even though the variation of responses concerning each party j's position is seemingly high. This is precisely the case with the sympathy scale in our data. The judges apparently agree that being sympathetic is better than being unsympathetic, but they disagree on which party is more sympathetic. Yet high systematic asymmetry does not necessarily signal the clarity of party positions. In fact, the opposite is more likely. Depending on whether consensus or disagreement on values exists within the parties, the variance due to systematic asymmetries of judgements may be either the main source of variation in the answers or a negligible source compared to the vast amount of random noise likely to be generated by the internal division within each party on the issue.[13]

In technical terms, the *systematic asymmetry of judgements* will be measured here as the impact of an interaction term (party membership of the judge (VAR4) by identity of the rated party (VAR22)) on the total variance of the $xmean_{ijk}$ values. This, in other words, is the amount of variance explained by which party is judged by which party's members. Not all asymmetric judgements are part of this phenomenon. Most importantly, when different types of asymmetric judgements by members of party A cancel each other out in terms of the mean placement of party B, I will count that as random noise.

The term 'random noise' refers to the tendency that members of party j attribute different positions to party g (where j and g may denote the same party). The greater portion of the total variance in the $xmean_{ijk}$ values is due to this tendency, the more obscure party positions are. The amount of random noise is easily measured as the variance explained by none of the previous two factors. In the absence of announced party positions, the preferences of party members and their judgements about their own party's position are likely to vary considerably. Members of a Christian party may wonder whether Christian humanism or the dogma of original sin would dictate their party's platform on using the stick or the carrot in the classroom or in rearing children. Some liberals may consider the stick the symbol of inviolable parental rights, while radical socialists may treat advocates of the carrot as representatives of middle-class cultural imperialism, and so on.

Random noise measures the inverse of 'image crystallisation'. Not surprisingly, the correlation of the two measures across the issues is negative and extremely strong (see Table 8.4). Where they differ is in the assumptions they make about voters. If, in judging party positions on issues, voters can discount for the conflicting signals (systematic asymmetries) they receive from the various sources, then the first is the better measure of programmatic party competition. If they cannot, then 'image crystallisation' has the greater validity. In practice, little difference exists between the results obtained with the two measures.

To sum up, the measures are derived from a variance analysis of the $xmean_{ij}$ values on each scale k. This analysis shows how much of the variance in the party placements are explained by the identity of the rated party (image crystallisation), by which party is rated by the members of which party (systematic asymmetries of judgements), and by how much of the variance remains unexplained by these factors (random noise).

Results

Let us evaluate briefly the results on an issue-by-issue basis. Overall, the data seem to have some face validity. Hungarian parties have a well-established reputation for fuzzy stances on economic issues and stark disagreement on unambiguously non-economic issues related to different concepts of nationhood, morality, religion in society, and retroactive justice. In contrast, Czech parties differentiate sharply on economic issues but less sharply on a number of non-economic issues than either their Polish or Hungarian counterparts (cf. Tóka 1997). These common-places seem to be nicely echoed in the results obtained with the above proposed indicators.

Random noise is the most important indicator of the clarity in the responses about party positions. It seems to have the lowest variation across issues in Poland, where it is quite low on virtually any issue question. The extremes are apparently high confusion on party positions towards environment versus industry and unusually low confusion on the religious issues (VAR38 and VAR39) and on the treatment of former communists (VAR44). In the Czech Republic, religious issues elicit as little (and quasi-economic issues [VAR36 on immigration, VAR37 on kindergartens, and VAR40 on urban–rural conflicts] about as much) random noise as in Poland. On other non-economic issues (VAR41, VAR43, and VAR44), the Czech parties appear to have vastly less (and on the economic issues (VAR30 to VAR35) somewhat more) crystallised profiles than do the Polish parties.

On VAR42 (environment) we find somewhat less random noise in the Bulgarian than in the Czech and Polish answers, and on the appropriate treatment of ex-communists (VAR44) there may be somewhat more clarity concerning Bulgarian than Czech party positions. Otherwise, however, Bulgaria is a world apart. The random noise of the Bulgarian answers is high, not only in a cross-national perspective, but also in absolute terms. On the average issue question, three-fifths of the total variance in the Bulgarian answers is 'random noise'. Even fellow party members disagree on where the five parties stand *vis-à-vis* each other. Significantly, this picture emerges even though several parties and issues were eliminated from the Bulgarian questionnaire following the respondents' inability to make sense of them during the pilot study.

In terms of the amount of the random noise surrounding party positions, Hungary sits in between Poland and the Czech Republic on the one hand, and Bulgaria on the other. By and large Hungary may be closer to the former, even though four issues (the 'economic' VAR31 and VAR33, the 'quasi-economic' urban–rural conflict, and environment) generate slightly less random noise in Bulgaria than in Hungary. On economic issues, the Hungarian respondents see much fuzzier parties than the Czechs and the Poles, but – on the bulk of the economic items, including the abstract ideological VAR46 – not quite as fuzzy parties as the Bulgarians. On non-economic issues, Hungarian party images appear the best crystallised of all. The only exceptions to this rule are environment and – on a more significant scale – urban–rural conflict.

On the amount of systematic asymmetries in judgements, overall cross-national differences seem negligible, though Poland may have somewhat less than the other three countries. As a result, the average difference between Poland and the Czech Republic in terms of 'image crystallisation' is almost as big as the average difference between the Czech Republic and Hungary.

To conclude that Poland has the clearest party positions, however, would be premature. While there is no evidence that our fourteen to sixteen issue scales represent all relevant issues in each of the four countries,[14] the ranking of Poland, the Czech Republic, and Hungary is at least partly a question of the weighting of economic and non-economic issues. If we believe that the former should be given more weight, then the Czech Republic would probably obey Kitschelt's hypothesis (1994) and end up with apparently less average random noise than either Poland or Hungary. However, if the opposite is true, then even Hungary may end up 'ahead' of the others. What can we do to measure programmatic clarity on the national rather than single-issue level?

Country-specific weight of individual issues

One obvious way to deal with national differences is to weight issues and issue domains by their salience in the countries in question (or, indeed, by their salience for individual parties).[15] Table 8.3 reveals that economic issues are clearly more salient than anything else in all four countries except in the Czech Republic, where environment tops the list. Hungarian politicians, in contrast, find religious issues (VAR38 and VAR39) much more salient than do the Czechs. If this is so, is it not possible that the Czech Republic actually has the more obscure party positions overall, especially given the greater crystallisation of party positions on non-economic issues in Hungary?

Table 8.4 provides a tentative answer. In all four countries, a weak positive

Table 8.4 Bivariate Pearson correlations between 'random noise', 'image crystallisation', 'systematic asymmetries', and 'issue salience'

	NOISE	CRYST	ASYMM
(a) Bulgaria (N = 14)			
CRYST	−0.97		
ASYMM	0.36	−0.56	
SALIENCE	0.29	−0.25	−0.05
(b) Czech Republic (N = 16)			
CRYST	−0.99		
ASYMM	0.77	−0.87	
SALIENCE	0.16	−0.19	0.24
(c) Hungary (N = 16)			
CRYST	−0.98		
ASYMM	0.51	−0.68	
SALIENCE	0.49	−0.50	0.34
(d) Poland (N = 15)			
CRYST	−1.00		
ASYMM	0.90	−0.93	
SALIENCE	0.12	−0.14	0.19

Note: VAR46 to VAR51 and VAR53 were excluded from the computation of the correlations.

correlation exists between random noise and salience. And in all of the countries but Bulgaria, a weak positive correlation exists between salience and the systematic asymmetry of judgements[16] (though the correlation is probably strongest in Hungary).[17] Therefore, if we weight the issues by their salience, we will probably obtain the same, even bigger, difference between Hungary and the Czech Republic. This is already suggested by Table 8.3: namely, that party positions are clearer in the Czech Republic than in Hungary.

More often than not, however, a brief look at the noise-salience correlations does not answer the question, and an explicit weighting is probably called for. Yet if we derive the weight of individual issues from a survey question on issue salience, we encounter fundamental problems. If we multiply the value of 'random noise' for each issue by its weight and sum the products, then we implicitly give a higher weight to the issue domains represented with more items in the question-naire. However, some highly salient dimensions may be so nicely captured by just one item (think of VAR45 in Bulgaria, about the language rights of the Turkish minority) or linked to so few issues that the number of items devoted to a dimension in our sample of issues has nothing to do with its importance. Reducing the number of dimensions by factor analysis or multi-dimensional scaling cannot resolve this problem. The issue dimension(s) represented by just one item in the questionnaire will most likely be lost in the process. Conversely, if several issues of different salience load highly on a factor, then estimating the salience of the dimension becomes anything but uncontroversial.

Factor analysis relies on the notion of internal or construct validity. Items uncorrelated to all other items in the study are made automatically suspect and probably invalid by this method. Thus, when there is no guarantee that every relevant dimension is represented by more than one measurement in a study and there is no proportionality in the representation of underlying dimensions among the indicators, we must instead maximise the external validity of the resulting composite measures. This can be done if: (1) we find a presumed correlate of the variable under construction, and (2) the theory linking this criterion to the variable-to-be is not related to the theory we are about to test once the measures are validated. Unfortunately, this is not the case with these variables. We have no firm theoretical expectations of what variables would correlate with the overall clarity of party positions. Or, inasmuch as we have, we would prefer to test these theories instead of relying on them to calibrate the other side of the equation.

Thus, we must take a further step. Let us assume that the weight of an issue dimension in defining the overall clarity of party positions is identical to its relative weight for the actors' calculus of political utility. Consequently the more impact an issue dimension has on electoral decisions or on politicians' coalition preferences, the more weight we should assign it in measuring the identifiability of party positions in a given country.

In the context of the present chapter, we need a measure of the utility of the evaluated political parties for the respondents (this is readily provided by their sympathy ratings of the parties), and we need to regress it on the distance between the respondents' ideal points on each issue from the perceived position of the party in question on the same issue. Unfortunately, our survey has no question on the respondents' own issue preferences. In place of it, I substitute the position they attribute to their own party. The downside of this choice is that it makes the distance between the respondents' 'own' position and their own party's issue positions, by definition, zero. Therefore, I have excluded from the regression analyses the observations referring to a respondent's evaluation of the party he or she belongs to.

In order to be sure that each party has an appropriate representation in the jury, I replace the missing xmean$_{ijk}$ values with estimates,[18] and I design a weighting procedure which insures that: (1) each party is equally represented in the weighted national sample, and (2) the weighted number of cases in the analysis[19] is identical to the actual number of respondents in the survey. This step is necessary since the approximate significance level of the regression slopes is of interest in finding the weights of the various issue dimensions.

Various experiments with the data suggest that the estimated ranking of the four countries by the overall clarity of party positions may differ radically depending on how we tackle the strong multicollinearity between the newly created variables measuring the distance between the ideal point of the respondents 'and their perceptions' of party *j*'s issue position on the various topics. Below, is described the alternative I consider technically most sound. In this solution the multicollinearity between the party-respondent distances is cured by replacing the ten-odd issue scales (15 in Bulgaria and Poland, 16 in Hungary, and 17 in the Czech Republic) with their unrotated principal components. The distances between the perceived party positions and the respondents' own ideal points (that is, the position they attribute to their own party) are calculated for each of the 15 to 17 principal components, and the sympathy ratings of the parties are regressed on the components in each country separately. In every country, three to four coefficients seem statistically significant.[20]

The regression coefficients are taken to indicate the importance of the given dimensions for politicians' sympathy ratings in the given country. Note that they have a common metric since all principal components have a unit standard deviation. The random noise, image crystallisation and systemic asymmetry components of the respective three to four principal components are computed according to the procedure described in the first section above. Then they are weighted by the respective regression coefficients (divided by a constant).[21] Because the metric regression coefficients refer to the same metric as the principal components (which all have a standardised unit variance), the final estimates of random noise etc. on the national level can be directly computed by multiplying the weights with the percentage of variance in the respective principal components stemming from random noise, image crystallisation and systematic asymmetries in the respondents' judgements.

Table 8.5. presents the results of these computations. Poland and the Czech Republic seem to have equally clear party positions. The only difference between them is that systematic asymmetries are more pronounced, and straight image crystallisation probably less pronounced, in the Czech Republic than in Poland. In

Table 8.5 Overall levels of 'image crystallisation', 'systematic asymmetries', and 'random noise'

	DPC1	DPC2	DPC3	DPC10	Total
(a) Bulgaria					
Weight:	0.23	0.19	0.31	0.27	
CRYST	64.93	50.30	25.65	4.01	33.35
ASYMM	5.41	4.81	27.25	4.61	11.78
NOISE	29.66	44.89	47.09	91.38	54.87
(b) Czech Republic					
Weight:	0.57	0.15	0.28		
CRYST	83.82	32.63	44.41		64.95
ASYMM	2.83	26.57	10.23		8.54
NOISE	13.34	40.86	45.36		26.52
(c) Hungary					
Weight:	0.50	0.13	0.18	0.19	
CRYST	81.17	38.62	18.00	25.27	53.66
ASYMM	3.34	15.26	30.27	5.72	10.20
NOISE	15.49	46.13	51.73	69.13	36.16
(d) Poland					
Weight:	0.36	0.44	0.20		
CRYST	77.64	72.04	41.47		68.10
ASYMM	2.75	6.65	8.50		5.60
NOISE	19.56	21.36	50.03		26.31

Notes: The last column (heading: *Total*) shows the final estimates of the overall amount of image crystallisation, systematic asymmetries, and random noise on the national level.

DPC1, DPC2, etc. refer to the distance between the respondents' own ideal point (measured by the position they attribute to their own party) and the position they attribute to each party *j* on the first, second, etc. unrotated principal components of the $xmean_{ijk}$ ratings (with missing values on the latter substituted by estimates as explained in the notes).

The *weights* of DPC1, DPC2, etc. derive from a regression analysis as explained in the second section of the main text.

CRYST, ASYMM and NOISE are the percentage values of image crystallisation, systematic asymmetries and random noise on the first, second, etc. unrotated principal components of the $xmean_{ijk}$ ratings (with missing values on the latter substituted by estimates as explained in the notes).

other words, the former has slightly more centripetal competition on (partially) valence issues, while the latter has slightly more cross-party consensus regarding the divergence of party positions. Hungary, and particularly Bulgaria, have even more valence competition than the Czech Republic. Since image crystallisation is considerably weaker in Hungary and even weaker in Bulgaria than in the Czech Republic and Poland, Bulgaria and Hungary owe a considerably larger part of their little programmatic party competition to predictable and systematic patterns in how competing parties question each other's issue positions.

Obviously, then, the starting hypothesis about the ranking of the four countries is partly rejected for Poland and partly supported for the other three countries. The unexpected clarity of party positions in post-communist Poland may be because Poland had more electoral contests and a greater turnover of parties in government than the other East European countries at the time of our survey (Kitschelt 1995b).

Validating the measures

A common problem in studies of unexplored territory is the absence of previous measurements to validate the newly introduced instruments. With his measures of the clarity of party positions, Kitschelt (1994 and 1995b) obtained very similar results in the survey analysed in this chapter as in his four-country pilot survey of national level party office-holders in early 1993. While this strongly favours the cross-national comparability of the survey data at hand, it has no bearing on the question of whether Kitschelt's measures (not to mention ours) truly capture the clarity of party positions.

Perhaps the most promising way to validate our measures is by analysing announcements and comments by partisan sources on policy issues. However, cross-national coding of the clarity and differentiation of party positions from manifestos in any other way than counting the sentences or words devoted to topics appears to be prohibitively labour-intensive and probably impossible (cf. Budge *et al.* 1987). Such a coding was carried out for many post-1990 East European party manifestos by Klingemann and his associates, but these data reveal only whether or not individual manifestos tend to combine issue concerns like their competitors. Even if we follow Converse (1964) and interpret this as an expression of ideological constraint (deeming, for instance, a party which simultaneously stresses law and order, religious education, and generous welfare provisions as less ideological than one which mixes the first two with free enterprise and private initiative), it is better treated as a different phenomenon than the clarity of party positions. The clarity of party positions may well be influenced by the degree of 'ideological constraint' in party appeals, but they are not identical characteristics.

In the absence of valid comparable measures, we can examine only whether the measures in question show the expected relationships with some other variables. In the present case, the most straightforward proposition seems to be that the clarity of party positions must influence the degree to which the general public recognises policy differences between the parties on the issue. Obviously, no deterministic relationship can be expected here.[22] Furthermore, it is not clear whether we should expect a very clear replication of the elite level systematic asymmetries of judgements about party positions on the mass level.

Be that as it may, strong doubts about the validity of the measures will appear if the clarity of party positions turns out to be totally unrelated to the degree to which voters are capable of distinguishing between party positions. Thus, I will attempt to compute the same measures of the clarity of perceived party positions on the same issues in mass survey data as were computed from the elite data. Then I will compute the correlations between the two sets of estimates across issues and countries.

Unfortunately, comparable, relevant mass survey data are available only for the

Czech Republic, Hungary, and Poland – and even that data covers somewhat different issues and uses a different question format than the elite survey. Nevertheless, in April 1994 Hungarian and November 1994 Czech and Polish surveys (CEU 1994a and 1994b), responses are available from national samples about which (up to three) parties are most, and which are least, 'likely to pursue' certain goals, including five that seem to tap nearly the same issue dimensions as VAR31, VAR33, VAR46, VAR39, VAR45 and VAR47 in the elite survey. (On the phrasing of the questions, see Table 8.4.)

From these materials, we created a new data base parallel to the elite data. Here, too, the unit of observation was the combination of respondent i and party j. The same parties were considered as those rated by the elite respondents, except that the Polish UD and KLD (which merged between the time of the elite and the mass survey) were replaced with UW, and the mass responses about the Czech Socialist Party and their Agrarian ally were considered equivalent to the elite responses about their coalition, the LSU. Initially, each party j mentioned by respondent i as likely to pursue the goal in question was coded +1; the party 'least likely' to do that was coded -1; and all others were coded 0. Then, exactly as in the elite level analysis, the anchor point of each respondent i was computed for each issue k, and subtracted from his or her rating of each party j on that issue. The variance due to systematic anchor point differences across the respondents was thus fixed to zero. Finally, the same variance analyses were carried out for each issue as on the elite level, with the rating of parties j by respondents i as the dependent variable, and the identity of the rated party and the party preference of respondent i as the two independent variables. Only those respondents were included in the analysis who said that in an election next weekend they would vote for one of the parties covered by the sample of the elite survey. Table 8.6 shows the percentages of the random noise, systematic asymmetries, and image crystallisation components of both the mass and elite answers. Table 8.7 displays the pairwise correlations between the elite and the mass level findings.

Overall, the results conform to expectations. True, some cross-country variations are hard to explain. For instance, the correlation between the elite and the mass level random noise is 0.98 in the Czech Republic and 0.89 in Poland and is practically non-existent (and is, in fact, negative) in Hungary. Yet the main point is that for both image crystallisation and random noise, the expected positive, sizeable, but only moderately strong correlations obtained in the pooled three-country sample (N = 15; that is, five issue domains in each of three countries) and the results for the individual countries (N = 5 for each) are by and large consistent with this general pattern. The prevalence of asymmetric judgements in elite and mass level responses are also consistently correlated, though apparently less strongly than the measures of image crystallisation on the two levels. As noted above, this is not unexpected.

Deviations between the elite and mass level findings seem to be twofold. First, however clear party positions are on nationalism-related issues in the elite survey, confusion ensues in the mass responses on the question of which parties are most and least likely to seek a strengthening of national consciousness. It may well be

Table 8.6 'Random noise', 'image crystallisation', and 'systematic asymmetries' at the elite and mass level on five issue domains (percentages)

Issue domain:	NOISE		CRYST		ASYMM	
	Elite	Mass	Elite	Mass	Elite	Mass
(a) *Czech Republic*						
Privatisation	27	39	69	57	4	3
Market economy	29	45	65	43	6	11
Church influence	22	41	75	57	3	2
Former communists	38	55	53	40	9	5
Nationalism	58	87	32	2	11	11
(b) *Hungary*						
Privatisation	62	88	31	9	7	3
Market economy	38	83	40	5	22	11
Church influence	16	64	81	35	3	2
Former communists	27	83	69	14	4	4
Nationalism	24	91	75	5	2	4
(c) *Poland*						
Privatisation	39	86	53	8	8	6
Market economy	38	87	56	5	6	8
Church influence	20	56	77	42	3	2
Former communists	19	61	78	34	3	5
Nationalism	32	86	63	5	5	9

Notes: NOISE: random noise, percentage of variance unexplained by the party of the respondent, the identity of the rated party, and the interaction of the two independent variables. CRYST: image crystallisation, percentage of variance explained by the identity of the rated party. ASYMM: systematic asymmetries of judgements, percentage of variance explained by the interaction of the party of the respondent and the identity of the rated party. The phrasing of the issue alternatives in the mass (M) and elite (E) surveys were as follows (on the question format see the main text):

Privatisation, (E): 'According to some politicians the privatisation of the state owned companies and the selection of the new owners should be directed by the goals of economic efficiency and fast privatisation. According to other politicians, the aspects of social and political justice must also be taken into account even if this leads to a slow down of the privatisation process.' (M): 'Speed up the privatisation of state-owned companies' [pro or con].

Market economy, (E): 'Please place each party on a scale where supporters of state intervention into the economy are on the one end, and supporters of free market economy on the other.' (M): 'Help the development of private enterprises and a free market economy in . . . [country]' [pro or con].

Churches, (E): 'According to some politicians religion has to provide the moral guidelines for post-communist . . . [country]. Therefore, it is mandatory for the state to help promoting religious faith [*belief*], and the churches must have a significant say in the content of public education. According to other politicians religion belongs to the private sphere and it is not the responsibility of the state to help promote religious faith. Thus, churches should not exercise a significant influence on the curricula of state run schools.' (M): 'Increase the influence of religion and the Church(es)' [pro or con].

Former communists, (E): 'According to some politicians the former upper and intermediate level leaders of the . . . [ruling party of communist period], because of their past sins, must be excluded from political life and from the privatisation of state property by legal, administrative and political means. According to other politicians former communists must be guaranteed the same opportunities to exercise political and economic rights as anybody else. They think that any law, administrative or political rule that aims at excluding former communists from economic or political life is unjustifiable.' (M): 'Removing former communist party members from positions of influence' [pro or con].

Nationalism, (E): 'Please place each party on a scale where supporters of the values of liberal individualism are on one end, and supporters of traditional . . . [Polish, Czech, Hungarian] culture and national solidarity are located on the other end.' (M): 'Strengthen national feelings' [pro or con].

Table 8.7 Bivariate Pearson correlations between the 'random noise', 'image crystallisation', and 'systematic asymmetries' components of elite and mass responses across five issues and three countries

	NOISEE	NOISEM	CRYSTE	CRYSTM	ASYMME
(a) Czech Republic (N = 5 issue domains)					
NOISEM	0.98				
CRYSTE	−1.00	−0.97			
CRYSTM	−0.98	−0.99	0.97		
ASYMME	0.94	0.90	−0.96	−0.91	
ASYMMM	0.64	0.63	−0.65	−0.75	0.67
(b) Hungary (N = 5 issue domains)					
NOISEM	−0.12				
CRYSTE	−0.94	0.07			
CRYSTM	−0.54	−0.76	0.58		
ASYMME	0.29	0.14	−0.59	−0.41	
ASYMMM	0.99	−0.16	−0.97	−0.52	0.39
(c) Poland (N = 5 issue domains)					
NOISEM	0.89				
CRYSTE	−1.00	−0.90			
CRYSTM	−0.94	−0.98	0.94		
ASYMME	0.97	0.95	−0.98	−0.95	
ASYMMM	0.79	0.59	−0.77	−0.75	0.64
(d) Pooled three country sample of issues (N = 15)					
NOISEM	0.36				
CRYSTE	−0.97	−0.37			
CRYSTM	−0.55	−0.96	0.56		
ASYMME	0.47	0.28	−0.68	−0.37	
ASYMMM	0.82	0.34	−0.80	−0.57	0.40

Notes: NOISEE: Random noise component (%) of the elite responses. NOISEM: Random noise component (%) of the mass responses. CRYSTE: Image crystallisation component (%) of the elite responses. CRYSTM: Image crystallisation component (%) of the mass responses. ASYMME: Systematic asymmetries component (%) of the elite responses. ASYMMM: Systematic asymmetries component (%) of the mass responses.

that this question – a pale attempt at having an identical item on nationalism in three countries where ethnic heterogeneity is nearly nil – is too abstract and fails to capture the same issue dimension as its elite level match.

Second, even in the case of a similar clarity on the elite level, any issue – particularly any economic issue – is likely to generate more noise and less meaningful pattern in the Polish and Hungarian than in the Czech mass responses. This seems to fit nicely Carmines and Stimson's argument about why the same clarity of party positions may not be able to produce as much issue voting on hard as on easy issues, particularly in relatively less sophisticated parts of the electorate. Three of the major Czech parties (CSL, CSSD, KSCM) are historical parties whose ideological orientation has changed relatively little since the First Republic (1918–39). In contrast, in Poland and Hungary only the agrarian parties (the PSL and FKGP, respectively) have a historical pedigree, and even they changed their relative ideological location considerably in the party space compared to the 1940s. Partly because of this, the main issue dimensions and their hierarchy in contemporary party politics seem to show a much more pronounced continuity with the previous democratic regime in the Czech Republic than in Poland or Hungary. Thus, socio-economic and cultural left–right issues may be much 'easier' for Czech voters. Furthermore, given the much greater endurance of the previous democratic regime, the higher levels of affluence, the smaller size of the rural population, and the slightly higher educational levels in the Czech Republic, Czech voters may also be more politically sophisticated than voters in Poland or Hungary.

These are, of course, exactly the kind of arguments which anticipate the postulate above: the clarity of party positions on the elite level has no one-to-one relationship with the crystallisation of party images on the mass level. Yet, the expected positive correlation does obtain in the data, despite substantial differences between the phrasing of items in the mass and the elite surveys.

Conclusion

The measures proposed here seem promising for a cross-national comparison of the clarity of party positions. Their development has been cumbersome, but most complications (for instance, the weighting of the elite data and the argument about the incomparability of policy distances across issues and countries) have been triggered by the very demands of comparative inquiry: namely, by its call for an explicit discussion of problems too often dealt with intuitively. Hopefully, this chapter has managed to show that tackling uneasy technical questions may be beneficial for both concept and theory formation.

First, we have argued that policy differences between competing parties affect mass and elite behaviour not only by their size. It is worth recalling that classic discussions of party and electoral behaviour (for instance, Lipset and Rokkan 1967) have stressed the importance of the relative salience and the negotiability of issues (with conflicts involving world views and ethnic or religious identities less negotiable than those involving material interests). Following the theoretical arguments and revising the measurement proposals of Kitschelt (1994 and 1995b), this chapter has focused on yet another factor: the clarity of party positions. This trait is conceptually distinct from either the size, the salience, or the negotiability of inter-party policy differences. Only with these four measures together can one hope to capture the impact of policies on inter-party competition, conflict, and co-operation, and the clarity of the party positions may have important effects of its own. Apart from Kitschelt's theory, some empirical studies of electoral behaviour have been cited to indicate the factors that may be directly affected by the latter.

Second, we have developed a procedure to arrive at a cross-nationally valid indicator of the clarity of party positions.

Third, we have used recent data from four East and Central European countries to demonstrate that the clarity of party positions can vary widely across countries and issue domains. Given how similar these four polities would seem to be from a worldwide perspective, it is striking how the sample shows almost as much variation on the variable of interest as is theoretically possible.

Finally, we have used mass survey data to validate the measurement instrument. By and large, we have observed the theoretically predicted correlations between the clarity of party positions and their most immediate mass level consequence.

Two more general methodological propositions seem to arise from the cumbersome journey reported above. Measuring policy distances across different issues but within the same country raises similar problems of comparability to those encountered in cross-national research. A promising way of treating those problems in the absence of a metric properly standardised across contexts (that is, issues or nations) is to define the values of the variable in question relative to a theoretical maximum and minimum. This is precisely the case when one measures X as the percentage of variance on Y explained by Z. What the development of such an instrument requires (indeed, prompts) is above all theoretical reflection on what we really want to measure. In the absence of either a satisfactory standardised metric or an identifiable theoretical maximum and minimum on a variable, valid comparisons are hampered across both issues and nations. However, the reason for such failures is probably less the nature of the phenomenon than the insufficient definition of the concept used in the analysis. This, it has been suggested, is probably the case with polarisation, at least as long as it is a concept distinct from the negotiability, salience, and clarity of policy differences.

A second general proposition concerns the aggregation of information across issues in such a way as to reflect the context-dependent nature of (national) issue agendas. We have proposed that the notion of criterion-related validity might help in assigning country-specific weights to – partly or entirely – country-specific issue dimensions in the calculus of the overall clarity of party positions in a country. While numerous problems must be overcome, the key methodological point is simple: the greater the role of an issue dimension in a country, the greater the importance of the clarity of party positions on that issue for the overall clarity of party positions in that country. The road to measuring identical phenomena in different countries leads through an explicit recognition of cross-country differences in the measurement process.

Notes

1 This chapter has grown out of a study of programmatic party competition in four East Central European countries directed by Herbert Kitschelt (Duke University, Durham, North Carolina), and in response to some of his ingenious proposals (see Kitschelt 1994). The comments and encouragement received at various stages of my work on this topic from him, Zsolt Enyedi (Central European University, Budapest), Radoslaw Markowski (Institute of Political Studies, Warsaw), George Rabinowitz (University of North Carolina at Chapel Hill), and the participants in the 'identity and equivalence' workshops convened by Jan W. van Deth at the University of Mannheim are gratefully acknowledged. The remaining errors are, of course, mine. The present chapter has been written largely

while I was a guest researcher at the Mannheim Centre for European Social Research at the University of Mannheim.

2 That is, a spatially represented difference in what government actions and legislation they favour.

3 The decisive factor in guaranteeing this outcome is free competition, just as for the ideal of responsible government.

4 The prediction about the precise ranking of Poland and Hungary is less clear, but the latter is probably more likely to lead the former on the third and fourth factor. It is less clear which of the two nations has weaker traditions of free party competition, and the two socio-economic variables (affluence and educational level) rank them differently.

5 In a few smaller countries, Laver and Hunt's sample also included newspaper editors and party, union, and employers' federation chairs (Laver and Hunt 1992: 35–6).

6 The interviewees were recruited in approximately equal numbers from each party investigated in the given country. Major deviations from this rule occurred in the case of extremist parties: in the Czech Republic SPR-RSC members declined to participate in the survey, and no attempt was made to interview MIÉP members in Hungary. (At three out of four sampling points, there was no trace of their local organisation.) In the Czech Republic, ODS, KDS, and CMSS members are under-represented in the sample.

7 The fieldwork was completed before the first round of the May 1994 Hungarian elections. Each country had the following sampling points: the capital city, a relatively agricultural area, a major provincial industrial centre, and a fourth area/city with idiosyncratic electoral returns (as different from the election results at the three other sampling points as possible).

8 In fact, two different weighting procedures are employed depending on the number of issue scales considered simultaneously. In this section, every computation involves just one scale at a time. The weighting procedure ensures an equal representation of judges from each party on the issue in question. First, the number of respondents from party x who gave a valid answer about the position of party j on issue k is calculated. This number is denoted by n_{xjk} (where x and j may mean the same party). To guarantee the equal representation of each party j in the jury on all divisions, a weight of $20/n_{xjk}$ (where 20 is an arbitrarily selected constant) is assigned to each respondent i from party x who gave a valid answer about the position of party j on issue k. In this section missing values are deleted from the analysis listwise.

9 This fact has clear implications for the use of significance tests – which would be of dubious value anyway given that: (1) the sample is stratified, and (2) the data are weighted (see above).

10 Fewer parties and fewer items were covered in Bulgaria than elsewhere. The reason for this is that the pilot study revealed only confusion about some issues and about the position of some parties. Therefore these items and parties were eliminated from the final questionnaire. Whether or not this was a mistake, it certainly made it easier to reject the key hypothesis of the project that Bulgaria had fuzzier parties than the other three countries.

11 The reason for this is simple and purely technical. Suppose we had just four respondents, all from the same party, and they were asked to rate just two parties on a left–right scale, where 1 means the leftmost, and 20 the rightmost position. Assume that two of them placed party A on point 8 and party B on point 12, and the other two placed party A on point 6 and party B on point 10. Obviously, there is uncertainty in the sample about whether party B is centrist or centre-right, but such implicit differences in the precise meaning of the mid-point of a twenty-point scale can only be expected.

12 Of course, it is of interest too whether or not this shared understanding of public

opinion is correct. But the present analysis avoids this question which poses measurement problems as difficult as the ones tackled here.

13 Suppose that there can be just two positions on the issue and everybody tends to claim his or her favoured position for his or her party. If each party is divided by the same 6 : 4 ratio on the issue, then the collective judgement of the sample: (1) will not see much difference between the individual parties; but (2) systematic asymmetries will be substantial (on average, members of each party *j* will see their own party closer than the other parties to the majority view); yet (3) systematic asymmetries will only explain a smaller part of the total variance in the responses, as the bulk of it will be explained by within-party disagreements about where each party *j* stands on the issue.

14 Indeed, I am genuinely puzzled about what would comprise good criteria of such representativeness.

15 I do not discuss here the serious problems of conveying the notion of salience in interviews. It suffices to note that our interviewers reported that respondents were puzzled about the meaning of the question on issue importance. Furthermore, the problem at hand seems analogous to introspective assessments of our own motives – the results of which are proverbially suspect. For instance, while it is hard to believe that all issues in the questionnaire (including those on which parties have hardly any identifiable position) would be at least moderately salient for each party, our respondents almost never declared any of the issues 'not really important' for their party. Partly because of this, it is unclear whether an average rating of 4 represents twice as high, or just 25 per cent higher, salience than an average rating of 3.

16 The consistency of this pattern suggests that as issue salience increases, party positions become blurred and inter-party disputes about true party positions and their credibility become more intense.

17 Note that the dubious representativeness of our – or any other – issue sample prohibits the use of significance tests, which would be of limited value anyway given the small number of cases in this analysis.

18 Each missing xmean$_{ijk}$ value was replaced with the average placement of party *j* on issue *k* by the fellow party members of respondent *i*. Since the originally calculated anchor point of respondent *i*, and the deviation of the other parties from this point, obviously depend on which party or parties were not evaluated by a respondent, all xmean$_{ijk}$ ratings provided by the respondent had to be adjusted after the replacement of missing values. Namely, for each respondent who evaluated some but not all party *j* on issue *k*, the (sum of the) value(s) substituted for the missing ratings of party (parties) *j* on issue *k* was divided by the number of parties evaluated on the given issue, and the result subtracted from their own xmean$_{ijk}$ of these parties.

19 The unit of analysis is the combination of respondent *i* and the evaluated party *j*, except that the evaluations given by the respondents about their own parties are excluded from the regression analyses.

20 First, all the 15 to 17 independent variables were entered into the equation. The theoretical expectation (that they have either negative or statistically insignificant effect on the sympathy ratings) was borne out in all four countries. Next, the regressions were re-run with all independent variables with a T-value below an absolute value of one eliminated from the equation. Finally, from the remaining set, the independent variables (the effect of which failed to reach the 0.10 significance level) were eliminated one by one. Since the sample is far from random, this procedure is open to criticism – but no unproblematic alternative seems to have been available.

21 To assure that the weights add up to one in each country, the raw regression coefficients were divided by their sum.

22 A previous study showed, for instance, that in 1980 the American electorate failed to realise widely publicised, firm and clear differences between Jimmy Carter's and Ronald Reagan's views on abortion rights (Granberg and Holmberg 1988: 41). Carmines and Stimson (1980) have speculated that at least three issue-specific factors

may influence the extent that voters (and the less sophisticated voters in particular) can grasp policy differences between candidates and parties. The factors are whether the issue: (1) has already fuelled partisan divisions for a long time; (2) is framed as a disagreement about goals rather than about means, ('technical details'); and (3) is easily related to the group identities of the voters (as in racial issues, for instance).

9 Institutional regimes

André Kaiser

New institutionalism and democratic political systems

In the wake of the recent revival of institutionalist approaches in comparative politics (Lane 1997: 99), empirical democratic theory has rediscovered the institutional regimes of political systems. To talk of institutional regimes is to emphasise the fact that political systems are based on interrelated institutional and organisational features that systematically structure the way political actors make decisions. Institutional regimes is not something found in the real world but is an analytical concept about the causes of conflict or co-operation between political actors.[1]

This new institutionalism must be distinguished from what may be called classical institutionalism (Kaiser 1997a) as well as from political-sociological or behaviourist approaches. In contrast to the latter, which employ quantitative methods to cope with large numbers of cases (and by and large disregard the importance of institutional variables), new institutionalism self-confidently uses qualitative methods for research designs with a small number of cases (Collier 1991). It proceeds from the assumption that institutions such as the electoral system, the cameral structure of parliament, executive–legislative relations, inter-governmental relations between central government and regional governments, independent central banks, or the powers of a constitutional court generate incentives for political action and therefore structure political choice.

In contrast, classical institutionalism usually conceptualises types of political systems on the basis of one distinguishing institutional variable held to be all-important. Examples include parliamentary and presidential types of government as two different ways to arrange executive–legislative relations; federal and unitary political systems according to the number of governmental levels with autonomous powers; and two-party versus multi-party systems. Which of these institutional devices is causally the most relevant? A comparison of the United States, Britain, and Germany is illustrative. Which two countries are most similar (Tsebelis 1995: 291)? The United States and Britain are characterised by two-party systems unlike Germany; Germany and the United States are federal systems unlike Britain; and Britain and Germany belong to the parliamentary type of government unlike the United States.

Unlike classical institutionalism, new institutionalism starts from the observation that democratic political systems contain a myriad of institutional constellations that cannot easily be reduced to only two basic types. This has led to the proposal of new frameworks that help overcome the problem of under-specification immanent in the classical types of democracy. Such frameworks also allow us to match the complexity of institutional arrangements in real democratic political systems in such a way that causal relationships can be more satisfactorily modelled (Kaiser 1997a).

This field of research has been dominated so far by Lijphart's two polar types of democracy whose institutionalised decision-making procedures either assist or constrain majority rule: 'majoritarian' and 'consensus democracy' (Lijphart 1984). Lijphart's well-known institutional devices are eight in number (see Table 9.1): the type of cabinet formed; the relationship between the executive and the legislature; the existence and legislative impact of a second chamber; the type of party system; the number of social cleavages dimensions; the type of electoral system; the extent of centralisation or federalisation of legislative authority; and the existence of a rigid constitution and judicial review. According to Lijphart, 'the initial conjecture was that, because the eight majoritarian characteristics are derived from the same principle and hence are logically connected, they would also occur together in the real world, and that, likewise, the eight consensual traits would be found together' (Lijphart 1990: 72).

In his factor analysis results, however, Lijphart found that democratic political systems cluster along two dimensions: an executives–parties dimension and a federal–unitary dimension. The main reason for this is that federalism is a crucial variable because it is generally accompanied by bicameralism, a codified constitution and judicial review. All in all, we get a two-dimensional matrix where the

Table 9.1 Construction of institutional regimes

Institution	Lijphart	Huber et al.	Colomer	Schmidt
Cabinet type	x	—	—	—
Executive–legislative relations	x	x	—	—
Bicameralism	x	x	x	x
Electoral system	x	x	—	—
Party system	x	—	x	—
Number of cleavage dimensions	x	—	—	—
Federalism	x	x	x	x
Reinforced majority rule for constitutional amendment	x	—	—	x
Referendum	(x)	x	—	x
Directly elected president	—	—	x	—
Supranational integration	—	—	—	x
Independent central bank	—	—	—	x

Note: x = covered by index; — = not covered by index. Lijphart tests the correlation between direct democracy and his two types of democracy but concludes that there is neither an empirical nor a logical connection (Lijphart 1984: 206). See, however, Jung (1996).

polar cases are represented by: (1) Britain and New Zealand as virtually perfect examples of majoritarian democracy (prior to the electoral reform of 1993: Kaiser 1998a); (2) Australia and Canada as examples of majoritarian-federal democracy; (3) Finland as a prime example of consensus-unitary democracy; and (4) Switzerland as an excellent example of consensus democracy. Similar proposals for operationalising institutional regimes by constructing indices of institutional assistance or constraint of majority rule have been presented by Huber *et al.* (1993: 728), Colomer (1996: 13), and Schmidt (1997: 554). Table 9.1 lists the indices used in these concepts.

These new institutionalist concepts are increasingly used in research on three different dimensions in empirical democratic theory: (1) policy dimension (What is the impact of a given set of political institutions on policy performance?); (2) politics dimension (What are the structural implications of political institutions for political action?); and (3) polity dimension (How can we explain the existence of astonishingly divergent sets of political institutions in democratic political systems?). No doubt these concepts are very valuable frameworks for comparative research on established democracies and on newly democratising countries. However, what they all have in common is that they are based on arbitrary sets of identical indicators; that is, on more or less extensive catalogues of institutional devices which themselves derive from concrete political systems.

As can be gathered from Table 9.1, no consensus exists on the core attributes of an institutional regime. Only bicameralism and federalism are included in all four concepts – a surprising fact in itself. Federal countries are clearly in a minority regarding democratic political systems.[2] In Lijphart's case, Britain serves as role model for a system with extremely wide and undispersed political decision-making powers for a parliamentary majority actor. This list is then systematically contrasted with its logical opposite: a system that exhibits as many power-sharing mechanisms as possible. The idea is that in this way the degree of majoritarianism or consensus decision-making can be measured.

Colomer's list is based on the institutional variation in Western Europe, with a strong emphasis on the difference between parliamentary and the so-called semi-presidential[3] democracies. Schmidt's concept is also very European in character in that it stresses the importance of supranational integration as well as central bank independence, a factor held to be highly relevant for policy performance. Huber *et al.* seem to base their concept on the perceived differences between the Anglo-American and the continental European types of democracy.

The problem with this typological method is that it is implicitly based on the assumption: (1) that each and every additional institution affects the regime independently of the other institutions, and (2) that this effect will in all cases strengthen its overall consensual character. Therefore, the second section of this chapter deals with various problems stemming from using identical sets of institutions. The third section of the chapter introduces a conceptual framework that explicitly aims at equivalence. It climbs the ladder of abstraction until it arrives at a level of generality extensive enough for as many political systems as possible but where it does not 'suffer unnecessary losses in precision and empirical testability'

(Sartori 1970: 1041). This concept is based on the idea that institutions establish strategic contexts for political actors that may serve as 'veto points' in decision-making processes.

I distinguish between four types of institutional veto points according to their regime effects: a strengthening of consensual decision-making; the delegation of political authority to functionally or territorially defined actors; the transfer of decision-making power to experts; and the inclusion of minorities in legislative processes. The properties of the concept are defined in a way that allows a mid-level balance of its extension and intension between universality and contextuality. The variable meanings of institutions are reduced to their effect in decision-making processes.

The fourth section of the chapter employs this concept of 'institutional veto points' to show that Lijphart's opposition of majoritarian to consensus democracies misses a central point. In his *Theory of Democracy Revisited*, Sartori rightly argues that Lijphart's concept 'is in danger of overstating his case. The contrast is empirically overdrawn . . . in that no real-world democracy abides by *absolute* majority rule . . . The majority rule in question is always, if a democracy is to survive as such, a *limited* majority rule' (1987: 239; emphasis original). Majoritarian democracy will only be acceptable in the longer run if equivalents develop for what in consensus democracies are constitutionally embedded procedures that include all relevant political actors in deciding the rules of the political game. Seen in this light, the question is in which way does consensus-building in majoritarian democracies work? This line of reasoning will be illustrated by focusing on the prototypical majoritarian, and therefore counter-intuitive, case of Britain. We shall see that in majoritarian democracies the lack of formal checks of majority rule is compensated for by informal procedures of delegation and negotiation which are overlooked if we employ the current concepts of analysing institutional regimes.

The problem of identical indicators

Current concepts of institutional regimes are based on what may be termed the additivity assumption. Each institution added to a political system independently affects the regime and strengthens its consensual character. This is at least true for the indices constructed by Colomer, Huber *et al.*, and Schmidt. Lijphart distinguishes between two dimensions and thus acknowledges that simple one-dimensional additivity does not work. In his case, however, as well as in the other concepts, further methodological problems arise insofar as their context-boundedness is overlooked or at least underestimated. We arrive at a list of four fundamental methodological problems discussed separately below. The first two derive from the problem of additivity, the latter two from the conceptual problems of indices constructed from concrete political systems instead of analytical approaches.

Similar institutions may have dissimilar effects in different regimes. If that is the case, it is impossible to construct a simple one-dimensional index of institutional regimes. The impossibility is illustrated by looking at the difficulties we face when applying Lijphart's concept to presidential systems like those in the United States. Although we know that presidential systems are prone to extensive bargaining between the separate institutions of president and legislature – with the legislature being in fact two chambers involved in bicameral negotiations themselves – Lijphart's index points to a strongly majoritarian character of the executive–parties dimension of the United States' political system. Four out of five institutional devices (the number of social cleavages dimensions, the type of cabinet formed, the party system and the electoral system) are more or less majoritarian while only the relationship between the executive and the legislative branches points to the opposite. But this last institution is crucial to the overall logic of the political system. Executive–legislative relations in presidential systems are shaped by the fact that both the president and the legislature are separately elected for fixed terms of office. Both institutional actors can therefore claim legitimacy independently from one another. The incentive effect of this arrangement on political actors is best termed 'double majoritarianism'. It leads to strong pressures for negotiations in the political process.

A similar problem confronts us when we analyse the impact of federalism in different countries. Contrary to Lijphart's assumptions, federalism does not necessarily strengthen consensual decision-making. While German-style systems of co-operative federalism actually restrain majority rule because state governments are directly involved in decision-making on the federal level, the system of dual federalism in Australia (Nelson 1998) is compatible with majoritarian institutions at both levels of government. In Canada the same constellation has caused political scientists to talk about 'federal–provincial diplomacy' (Simeon 1972), as if the two levels of government meet like foreign nations in conferences.

In both cases – executive–legislative relations in presidential systems and dual federalism especially in Anglo-American democracies – an institutional constellation exists which can have variable effects according to circumstances. This structure of 'double majoritarianism' can lead to benign neglect between the actors involved, to non-decisions, to conflict bargaining, or to consensual decision-making. It differs completely from executive structures that imply broad consensus-building between all the actors involved: for instance, the German power-sharing constellation of federal and state governments that has produced an informal 'Grand Coalition State' (Schmidt 1996: 95), or the Swiss national executive which since 1959 is proportionally composed of representatives of the four most important political parties according to the so-called 'magic formula' of $2:2:2:1$.

In a parallel way, the same effect on the overall institutional regime may be caused by different, yet functionally equivalent, institutions. To illustrate this I use a telling example from Colomer's study of institutional regimes in Western Europe.[4] He proceeds from a similar but somewhat reduced concept as regards the number of institutional devices to that of Lijphart for measuring the degree of majoritarianism. His index consists of the type of party system, the cameral structure of parliament, the existence of a directly elected head of state and the degree of regional autonomy. Given these defining attributes, Colomer (1996: 13) arrives at a seemingly perplexing result: Sweden gets the same score as Britain and belongs to the group of the most majoritarian systems in Europe. This is in stark contrast to what we normally associate with the famous 'Scandinavian model' and what we find in the comparative literature (Elder *et al.* 1988). How can this paradox be explained? Lane and Ersson argue that 'Nordic politics does not fit conventional democracy models such as the Anglo-Saxon Westminster model or the Continental consensus model' (1996: 254). Sweden, especially after the constitutional reforms of 1975, combines a constitutional framework of the Westminster style with an elaborate system of corporatist interest inter-mediation and policy formulation as well as minority governments. 'Its core is a blend of adversarial and compromise politics, where party competition is nested together with political and social co-operation' (Lane and Ersson 1996: 255). Therefore decision-making resembles that of consensus-type democracies although Sweden's basic constitutional structures are clearly different. Corporatism is functionally equivalent to other consensual political institutions in that it introduces a strong element of power sharing into the policy process (Lane and Ersson 1997: 18). The same holds true for the extensive use of minority governments in Scandinavian countries. Only if we define the underlying concepts analytically rather than develop them on the basis of a model political system can we avoid the fallacy of overlooking equivalent indicators.

The Swedish case also nicely illustrates the problems that derive from deciding what to include in a conceptual framework for comparative research. We have just seen that including or excluding interest group inter-mediation and representation in decision-making may completely change the result. This is also the case with many more institutional devices that can be added to the original Lijphartian list of institutional characteristics of majoritarian and consensus government in stable democracies. They include the type and the degree of independence of the central bank, the number of quasi-autonomous non-governmental agencies, and the number of consultative bodies in policy-making. Tellingly, the four indices by Lijphart, Huber *et al.*, Colomer, and Schmidt presented in Table 9.1 correspond to only a small part.

Table 9.2 rank orders the twenty-three democratic political systems on the four indices (as amended and corrected by Schmidt 1995: 244 and 1997: 554). In Table 9.3, these are correlated for the four indices of institutional regimes.

As expected Lijphart I, Huber *et al.*, Colomer, and Schmidt correlate not at all, while Lijphart II, Huber *et al.*, Colomer, and Schmidt, correlate only moderately. This confirms what I pointed out earlier. The Huber *et al.*, Colomer, and Schmidt indices are much more sensitive to what Lijphart terms the federal–unitary dimension than to his executive–parties dimension. And it underlines the fact that simple additive constructions tell only half the story. This, however, is a puzzling finding, given the attention that factors like the electoral system, executive–legislative relations, or the party system format normally receive in comparative politics about the way political systems work. Huge differences exist between the ranking of some countries, most obviously the United States. As indicated

Table 9.2 Scales of institutional regimes

Country	Lijphart I Score	Rank order	Lijphart II Score	Rank order	Huber et al. Score	Rank order	Colomer Score	Rank order	Schmidt Score	Rank order
Australia	0.95	19	−0.99	6	4	4	4	5	3	5.5
Austria	0.84	17	−0.37	7	1	13	3	9.5	2	11
Belgium	−0.74	6	0.19	12	1	13	3	9.5	3	5.5
Canada	1.55	23	−1.22	4	4	4	5	3	3	5.5
Denmark	−0.89	5	0.49	16	0	20	2	15	2	11
Finland	−1.65	2	0.46	15	1	13	3	9.5	0	22
France	0.11	13	0.36	14	2	7.5	3	9.5	1	17.5
Germany	0.11	13	−1.79	1	4	4	4	5	5	2
Great Britain	1.30	21	1.40	22	2	7.5	1	19.5	1	17.5
Greece	0.90	18	0.64	18	2	7.5	0	22.5	1	17.5
Iceland	−0.38	8	0.81	21	0	20	2	15	1	17.5
Ireland	0.73	16	0.76	19	0	20	2	15	2	11
Italy	−1.18	4	0.01	11	1	13	4	5	3	5.5
Japan	−0.01	11	−1.11	5	2	7.5	3	9.5	2	11
Luxembourg	0.30	15	0.79	20	0	20	1	19.5	2	11
Netherlands	−1.58	3	0.33	13	1	13	2	15	1	17.5
New Zealand	1.36	22	2.16	23	0	20	0	22.5	0	22
Norway	−0.30	9	−0.08	9	1	13	1	19.5	2	11
Portugal	−0.50	7	0.61	17	0	20	2	15	1	17.5
Spain	0.11	13	−0.23	8	1	13	3	9.5	2	11
Sweden	−0.14	10	−0.06	10	0	20	1	19.5	0	22
Switzerland	−1.88	1	−1.53	3	6	2	6	1.5	5	2
USA	0.97	20	−1.62	2	7	1	6	1.5	5	2

Note: Lijphart I is the executives–parties dimension; Lijphart II the federal–unitary dimension. The data are taken from Schmidt (1997: 554) for the Huber *et al.*, Colomer, and Schmidt indices, from Schmidt (1995: 244) for the Lijphart I and II scales. The data are not completely comparable because the time periods covered are slightly different. Lijphart I: high values with a negative sign indicate strong consensual traits; high values with a positive sign indicate strong majoritarian traits. Lijphart II: high values with a negative sign indicate strong federalism; high values with a positive sign indicate a strong unitary structure. Huber *et al.*, Colomer, Schmidt: low scores indicate strong majoritarian traits; high scores indicate strong consensual traits.

Table 9.3 Correlations between indices of institutional regimes

	Huber et al.	Colomer	Schmidt
Lijphart I	−0.24	0.12	−0.04
Lijphart II	0.69	0.78	0.71
Huber *et al.*		0.66	0.57
Colomer			0.75

Note: Entries are Spearman's rank order correlation coefficients. Lijphart I and Lijphart II have not been correlated because they have not been designed to reflect similarities in any way.

above, Lijphart's measure of the executive–legislative dimension strongly over-stresses this political system's majoritarian character. Yet leaving his distinction between two dimensions aside for a moment and focusing only on the scales of Lijphart II, Huber *et al.*, Colomer, and Schmidt, the rankings differ considerably for Denmark, Finland, France, Great Britain, Greece, Italy, Luxembourg, Norway, and Sweden. There are clearly too many problematic cases in a sample of just twenty-three countries.

Obviously, one could argue that the catalogue of relevant institutions should be restricted to fundamental constitutional structures. Yet if we are interested, as Colomer has put it (1996: 9), in the question of 'how many . . . actors can be considered necessary to agree in order to make a policy decision', we should start from an analytical approach based on a broad understanding of the political process rather than on a narrow, conventional constitutional framework. If not, we fall back into a formal-legal understanding of the political process, a perspective that was rightly criticised by political-sociological approaches in comparative politics some decades ago (Macridis 1955: 7–22).

The last problem I want to point out derives from the fact that the underlying concept of consensus in the original proposal by Lijphart is ill-defined. The term 'consensus democracy' has obvious normative implications, and I fully agree with Sartori that, 'If we say "consensus democracy" we already have in our hand of cards the winning trump. Can anybody ever hold that a non-consented democracy is as good as a consented one' (Sartori 1994a: 70)? Furthermore, majoritarian and consensus democracy seem to be defined on two different levels. While majoritarian democracy is named for the basic decision-making rule it employs, consensus democracy is named for an intended outcome of the political process. This is not just a semantic problem. Lijphart underestimates the fact that a minimum of consensus is vital to both types of political systems. Majoritarian democracy requires consensus on the constitutional framework as well as on the actual rules of the political game. These are the preconditions 'of the acceptability and practicability of the majority rule itself' (Johnson 1986: 152).[5] Consensus in this context means 'agreement to differ'. Lijphart's concept, on the other hand, is based on procedures which aim at consensus on substantive issues. Unanimity, however, will be the exception rather than the rule simply because decision-making costs would otherwise get prohibitively high. Thus, consensus of this second type generally implies reinforced majority (that is, super majority) rule.

Evidently there are two quite different meanings of consensus involved: input consensus versus output consensus. Whereas consensus democracies stress the output side, majoritarian democracies emphasise the input side. That means we should expect institutional requisites for consensus building in both types of democracy – although at different stages of the political process. There is a clear limit for political action in majoritarian democracies. If a majority actor wants to change the basic rules of the political game or to carry through major policy shifts, he is well advised to obtain a certain level of consensus. In contrast to consensus democracies, where rules are rigidly institutionalised and force political actors to reach compromises (or, alternatively, to leave issues undecided), a majority actor in governments of the Westminster type can determine with whom he wants to consent. Consensus building here is necessarily more *ad hoc* and is based on conventions of political behaviour.

As a result, the concept of consensus does not clearly distinguish between the types of democracy. I therefore prefer to replace 'consensus democracy' with the more neutral term 'negotiation democracy' to indicate institutional regimes with many devices that induce political actors to seek compromises. The term 'consensus' should be reserved for procedures or structures explicitly aimed at broad agreement. Where negotiation democracies are characterised by formally fixed negotiation procedures, majoritarian democracies rely on majority actors that from time to time are willing to compromise. This distinction has the additional advantage of indicating more exactly the prevailing mode of decision-making. This does not mean, of course, that no real differences exist between majoritarian democracy and its opposite. However, it strongly reminds us to look explicitly for negotiating devices in both types of democracy.

Equivalence in the analysis of institutional regimes

How do we arrive at a conceptual map of institutional regimes that renders equivalence possible? The first rule of thumb is not to start from a concrete political system – such as the famous Westminster model of democracy – but from a systematic analysis of all imaginable institutional restrictions of bare majority rule. The second rule is to classify these devices not according to some inherent 'essence' but according to their role in decision-making. Federalism, for instance, does not mean the same thing in different institutional constellations. Third, we must choose from this map the institutional devices that might be relevant for specific research designs. There is simply not one institutional regime covering a whole political system but differing regimes in different policy arenas.[6]

The following proposal starts from the proposition that democratic political systems contain institutional veto points which shape the strategies of political actors (Kaiser 1997a: 434–40). As polar types, democracies with a minimum of veto points are majoritarian, and democracies with a maximum of veto points are negotiation democracies. The more veto points a political system has, the more difficult it is to change policies. Veto points are neither physical entities nor mere metaphor. They are structural incentives providing windows of influence for political actors. Most important, they function as 'points of strategic uncertainty where decisions may be overturned' (Immergut 1992: 27–8). Institutions in this sense may be basic constitutional structures, but also formal or conventional rules of behaviour, standing orders, or organisations with decision-making power.

Contrary to the one-dimensional (or in Lijphart's approach, two-dimensional) concepts discussed before, I distinguish between four different types of veto points according to their functions and effects in different arenas of policy-making.

1   *Consociational veto points* are explicitly intended to foster consensual decision-making. Examples are proportional electoral systems which encourage the

formation of coalition governments; conventions of proportional representation in cabinet; and dual executives, where the head of state and the prime minister share political power.

2   *Delegatory veto points* are those which spatially or functionally compartmentalise political authority. Examples include regional autonomies and supranational integration, hived-off quasi-governmental agencies with relatively autonomous powers, tripartite bodies for corporatist interest inter-mediation, and other conventional procedures of consultation with sectional groups that aim at compromises based on shared information.

3   *Expert veto points* are non-democratic modes of decision-making in institutions which are relatively isolated from elective or appointive political power and have no direct responsibility towards a constituency. Examples include judicial review, independent central banks, or arbitration boards in industrial relations.

4   *Legislatory veto points* are those like the constitutional protection of minority rights, reinforced majority rule in constitutional amendment formulas and other policy areas, bicameralism, obligatory referendums, but in a temporal perspective also alternation of parties in government.

These veto points are obviously open to changes to varying degrees. While legislatory veto points are normally an intrinsic feature of the overall constitutional structure, expert veto points, conventions on consultation prior to decision making or the delegation of decision-making power to quasi-governmental agencies can be removed or modified much more easily. Therefore we must distinguish between veto points according to how easily majority actors may change them. *Hard veto points* are constitutionally fixed and can be changed only by a broad consensus of political actors. *Soft veto points* are much easier to change; it is up to the respective majority to change them or not. In a static research design (that is, at a given point of time), we need not worry about different degrees of changeability, but in a dynamic perspective the distinction is much more relevant.

It is clear from this conceptual map that the list of institutional devices influencing the ease and speed of policy changes is: (1) much longer than the list used to date, and (2) made up of different types of veto points defined by their function in institutional regimes. Consensus is only one of those points. Legislatory veto points aim mainly at blocking majority rule decisions and at enforcing negotiations. Delegatory and expert veto points aim at transferring policies into arenas that are to a certain extent shielded from electioneering. This classification makes simple one-dimensional rankings between cases difficult. It reminds us to look for the scores on four different dimensions and for possible interrelationships between different types of veto points. A political system may score low on one dimension but high on another.

Furthermore, it is important to keep in mind that it is not institutions per se but political actors looking for windows of opportunity that interest us when we analyse institutional regimes comparatively. Take the case of a parliamentary opposition party interested in changing a governmental bill. Depending on the institutional constellation, very different options may be open to the opposition: for instance, the use of a second chamber in federal systems; an appeal to the constitutional court to review the bill; or standing orders in the parliamentary committee system or in plenary sessions that delay decision-making until the government is willing to concede points to save valuable parliamentary time. Democratic political systems differ widely as to the number of veto points they provide. The lower the number, the more majoritarian the institutional regime. However, veto points in a policy arena also vary among different institutional constellations as well as between policy arenas in one political system. We may even find policy arenas where most democratic political systems show astonishingly similar practices, notwithstanding the fact that they are very dissimilar in their overall structure. A prime example is foreign policy-making, where executive dominance is characteristic of both majoritarian and negotiation democracies.[7] Hence, it does not make much sense to use an all-encompassing list in each and every research design. The institutional regimes of democratic political systems on economic policy-making differ from those on constitutional reform. So do the concepts we must use in both. In the latter case, we are interested in the number of legislatory and consociational veto points that political systems exhibit. In the former, we may be more interested in the number of delegatory and expert veto points.

Consensus-building in majoritarian democracies: the case of Britain

It is a mistake with possibly far-reaching consequences to assume that majoritarian democracies do not exhibit consensual traits. Their form of consensus merely differs from what we find in negotiation democracies. *Only an explicit equivalence perspective can lead us to identify those mechanisms.* It is not so much a consensus on policy outputs which characterises this type of political system but on the constitutional framework and on the rules of the game. This implies more than a relatively homogeneous political culture with no fundamental conflicts, in contrast to plural societies with linguistic, ethnic, regional, or cultural cleavages, as Lijphart puts it (1984: 3–4, 220). A constitutional and procedural consensus must be renewed constantly if relevant political actors are to accept this formal distribution of political power. Hence, we should expect ad hoc negotiations in cases where policy-making touches issues of national interest or where constitutional reform (that is, the rules of the game themselves) is on the agenda. The logic is that majority actors will calculate the costs and benefits of negotiating with their political opponents and conclude that consenting is preferable to pushing their decision-making powers to the limits. Majority actors who take more than a purely self-interested, short-term perspective are aware of the fact that only in this way can they expect their opponents to do the same if these get into government. To use the language of game theory: political actors in majoritarian democracies know that they are not playing a one-shot game. Therefore, they uphold a convention of mutual fairness which, if ignored, casts doubts upon the legitimacy of the institutional regime with possibly far-reaching consequences.[8]

We have now gathered the conceptual tools for an empirical analysis of consensus-building devices in majoritarian democracies. Which equivalents can we find for constitutionally embedded negotiation procedures in the so-called consensus democracies? Do majority actors always behave as we expect them to do? What happens if they do not? This is not the place for a comprehensive analysis of an extensive sample.[9] I therefore confine myself to the case of Britain, the prototype of majoritarianism in Lijphart's concept.

Following the rules developed in the previous section, I distinguish between Britain's institutional regimes in ordinary policy-making and constitutional reform debates and discuss four different dimensions of institutional veto points: consociational executive structures; delegation of political authority to quasi-governmental agencies, tripartite bodies and consultative structures; transfer of decision-making power to experts; and legislatory power-sharing. In this way contextual information can be introduced that generates additional insights. It is especially important to look for compensating interrelationships between the dimensions.

Ordinary policy-making

Day-to-day policy-making in Britain is clearly characterised by majoritarianism and adversary politics. One-party governments with a majority of seats in the House of Commons are able to decide what they want. Virtually no formal institutional veto points, at least in the executive structure, can be used to force them to compromise. Yet we should not ignore Britain's strong delegation of political authority. Policy-making is traditionally characterised by extensive consultation with interest groups as well as by expertise from Royal Commissions and Committees of Inquiry. Furthermore, many policy arenas such as regional development or environmental protection are dominated by quasi-governmental agencies. Policy networks basically function by a 'logic of negotiation' (Richardson 1993: 94). Majority governments are free to decide which procedures and which level they adhere to, but they are expected to consult widely the relevant interests. Contrary to the neo-liberal rhetoric of Conservative governments in recent years, empirical research shows that continuity rather than disruption typifies the dominant mode of government–interest groups relations (Baggott 1995; Kaiser 1998b).

Compromise politics is further strengthened by the parliamentary select committee system implemented in 1979, which is still finding its place in the political process. Both opposition and government members of the committees have learned very quickly that their influence on government decisions depends on the extent to which they are able to unify against ministers and civil servants. This means that a rudimentary mode of negotiation has been established alongside the majority principle in parliament. In an extensive survey of MP attitudes about this new institution, Jogerst suggests 'that these committees were established as a means of countering executive domination, that at times this domination has been challenged, that further challenges to party government and executive domination will continue, and that governments will accept committee recommendations when changing, introducing, or abolishing national policies' (1993: 201). The select committee system remains, of course, far different from what we find in systems with a 'working' legislature such as the US Congress. It is, however, a first step in that direction because it is an incentive for the professionalisation and specialisation of MPs who strive to use their expertise in policy-making.

By definition, we find few traces of legislatory veto points in majoritarian democracies. Yet we should hesitate before deciding that nothing like the power-sharing structures of negotiation democracies exists. The House of Lords, Britain's second chamber, may be a pre-democratic (and in many ways anachronistic) institution in that its members are not elected but are made peers by succession or are nominated life peers. This does not mean, however, that the Lords is entirely without influence on the policy process. It has formal powers to block legislation by a delaying veto and has done so in recent decades against both Labour and Conservative governments on a number of major bills. Since parliamentary time is scarce in modern governance, the Lords can at times extract major concessions by simply slowing down the decision-making process (Kaiser 1997b: 90–100).

'National interest' and policy-making

British politics has always used a different mode of decision-making under exceptional circumstances. In threatening times, such as the two world wars and the world economic crisis of the 1930s, coalition governments have been formed and party government has been put temporarily to rest (Searle 1995).[10] The famous British post-war consensus on the establishment of a welfare state and a mixed economy had its origins in the reconstruction programme for peace-time – a programme developed by the war coalition government of Conservative Prime Minister Winston Churchill and his Labour deputy Clement Attlee (Addison 1975). This quasi-consensus on major policies lasted at least until the late 1960s, when British politics began to polarise between the major parties who feared economic decline.

The neo-liberal project of Thatcherism can be understood as a deliberate attempt to destroy the post-war consensus and as a drastic shift in many policy areas. After nearly two decades, British neo-liberalism became characterised on the one hand by compromise techniques in day-to-day policy-making and on the other by conflict on 'high politics' issues. This does not mean that no policy consensus has appeared in recent years on the latter level. On issues of national interest, informal consultation between the Prime Minister and the Leader of the Opposition remains an unwritten rule. This can be seen, for instance, in the policies towards Northern Ireland. Irrespective of which party happens to be in government, both major parties have long stayed in close contact about what to do.[11]

Constitutional reform

The first and foremost precondition of the legitimacy of majoritarian democracy is a regular pattern of change in government or at least a reasonable chance for that change.[12] Only then can the political opposition be expected to accept the rules of the game. A long period of one-party rule undermines the logic behind the system. In such situations, the most fundamental veto point is temporal power sharing – paradoxical as it may seem at first sight. If we analyse the relationship between acceptance of the constitutional framework and patterns of alternation in government, Britain reveals that this is indeed the case. Participation in government was evenly split between the Conservative and the Labour Party from 1945 to 1979. Since then – until 1997 – the Conservatives dominated politics in a way that British political scientists seriously wondered if alternation would be possible at all in the future (Margetts and Smyth 1994). It is exactly in this period that discussion of constitutional reform emerged – from a relatively unimportant issue proposed by third parties (the natural losers of the majoritarian political game) to one of the most relevant issues on the agenda.

This not only had to do with the long absence of political alternation. The Thatcherite project of the 'free economy and the strong state' (Gamble 1988) was only feasible by way of an institutional regime that equipped government with formally unlimited political power. This points to a more general problem underlying the maintenance of consensus in this type of democracy. 'It has become much harder to isolate consensus on political methods from . . . the effects of conflicts provoked by particular policy changes and the impact on entrenched interests and expectations of objective circumstances, for instance changes in the world economy, new technological developments etc.' (Johnson 1986: 163). The Labour Government of 1997 has proposed a long list of reforms that might transform Britain's constitutional structure fundamentally. Among the most momentous reforms are a Scottish Parliament, a Welsh Assembly, a referendum on electoral reform, and reform of the second chamber. Having profited immensely from the current rules of the game (by winning 65 per cent of the seats in the House of Commons with just 44 per cent of the votes), it remains to be seen if Labour will implement a major shift towards negotiation democracy with several institutionally fixed veto points.

The current constitutional-reform agenda leads directly to another aspect of majoritarian democracies. How can constitutional reform achieve more consensual political structures if it relies on majoritarianism? 'Major constitutional change in Britain during this century has, so far as possible, usually been preceded by agreement between the Government and the Opposition – or at least by an attempt to reach such agreement' (Brazier 1991: 2). Typical procedures have been Speaker's conferences if technical aspects of electoral reform were debated, or conferences of party leaders if more substantial changes were sought.[13] Here, as in ordinary policy-making, a tradition of voluntary consultation in small, non-public committees[14] functions as an equivalent to more formal institutional veto points. The experience of the last two decades has led opposition parties to negotiate on common proposals for far-reaching structural changes. This started in Scotland where Labour, the Liberal Democrats, several interest groups, and the Scottish church met in a Scottish Constitutional Convention that proposed a proportionally elected Scottish Parliament with a considerable range of powers. Now that Labour has regained power in Westminster this common opposition platform is the starting point for its devolution programme. Other constitutional reform plans were also substantially agreed upon by a joint consultative committee of Labour and Liberal Democrats in the months before the general election of 1997 (Labour Party and Liberal Democrats 1997).

The discussion of the British case emphasises the fact that, if the rules of the game are to be truly acceptable, the absence of formalised consociational and legislatory veto points in majoritarian systems must be compensated for by a range of consensus-building and consensus-maintaining conventions of consultation, delegation and negotiation. If not, the constitutional framework itself becomes the object of political debate as happened in the 1980s. Mulgan's view of New Zealand, the second prototype of majoritarianism in Lijphart's study, remains true. When 'governments are relatively unconstrained by constitutional checks and balances informal, political processes . . . take on correspondingly greater significance' (Mulgan 1992: 518). This comes as no surprise to a specialist in British politics, but in a comparative perspective it shows how important it is to define institutional regimes broadly and to search for functional equivalences between their dimensions.

Conclusion

Typological concepts still dominate qualitative research designs in comparative politics. This procedure is based mainly on Max Weber's notion of constructing ideal types – a notion worth quoting at length:

> An ideal type is formed by the one-sided *accentuation* of one or more points of view and by the synthesis of a great many diffuse, discrete, more or less present and occasionally absent *concrete individual* phenomena, which are arranged according to those one-sidedly emphasized viewpoints into a unified *analytical* construct (*Gedankenbild*). In its conceptual purity, this mental construct (*Gedankenbild*) cannot be found empirically anywhere in reality . . . Research faces the task of determining in each individual case, the extent to which this ideal-construct approximates to or diverges from reality.
>
> (Weber 1949: 90; emphasis original)

The central problem of ideal-typical constructions is how to develop indicators that meet the requirements of equivalence and noncontextuality. Weber clearly notices this problem and therefore stresses the necessity of travelling to sufficiently abstract terms. 'Unified analytical constructs' must be developed for comparative research, he says. But how?

I have shown in this chapter that new institutionalist concepts for comparing institutional regimes have considerable difficulty in achieving this level of general-ity. The main reason is that they start from concrete political systems instead of developing an analytical framework. Alternatively, one can start from an analysis that takes into account all institutional veto points imaginable, and one can ask explicitly which devices may be functionally equivalent for what brings about power-sharing in traditional constitutional frameworks. In order to do this I have followed Sartori's advice and taken a few steps up the 'ladder of abstraction' (1970: 1040).

In substantive terms, I have shown that much more variance exists than is currently indicated between political systems and between the institutional regimes of a political system. Why is this so? Because from an analytical perspec-tive, numerous sub-constitutional norms, formal and informal rules, and organi-sations appear as possible institutional veto points in the political process. Does that mean that the original concept has become meaningless and that we have fallen into a trap of 'pseudo equivalence' that blurs the real differences between political systems (Niedermayer 1997: 74)? It has been my intention to show that Lijphart's original concept overdraws the differences between majoritarian and consensus systems because it starts from problematic meanings of both terms. It does not sufficiently take into account that under conditions of democracy, major-ity rule is more than a technical decision-making procedure. It is based on norms of mutual fairness. It also has a temporal dimension as the importance of alter-nation in majoritarian democracies illustrates. Consensus has more facets than to imply only an intended outcome on specific issues.

My analysis of the British case has tried to show that focusing on functional equivalence reveals many mechanisms which can easily be overlooked in a simple, one-dimensional or two-dimensional concept of basic constitutional devices. How-ever, that does not necessarily inflate the number of attributes contained in the concept. This problem can be overcome by concentrating on the functional effects of institutional devices. If a fundamental consensus is to survive over time, political systems with few consociational and legislatory veto points must compensate by establishing consultative procedures. Hence, democratic systems differ clearly not only to the degree that political actors are included in or excluded from decision-making but also in the way that they ensure integration through negotiations. I do not deny that. To the contrary, I argue that careful classification of institutional veto points and the likelihood and speed of their changeability may help us unravel the wide variance of practices and their effects in a comparative perspective.

Notes

1 Colomer (1996: 2) seems to be the first to have used the term 'institutional regime' in the context of political systems, although without any precise definition of its meaning. The term as it is employed here is, of course, borrowed from the rich literature on interna-tional regime analysis. Stephen Krasner defines international regimes as 'sets of implicit or explicit principles, norms, rules and decision-making procedures around which actors' expectations converge' (Krasner 1983: 2). A similar use can be found in Esping-Ander-sen's study of modern welfare states (1990: 2).

2 Lane lists 11 of 35 'firm democracies' as federal states; 23 employ a bicameral legislature; 12 are unicameral (1996: 201, 205).

3 For a critique of proposals to construct a third mixed or hybrid type alongside parliamentary and presidential government, see Kaiser (1997a).

4 See also Table 9.2 for the Swedish score. The Huber *et al.* and Schmidt indices actually indicate higher majoritarianism for Sweden than for Britain.

5 It is, of course, tempting to interpret the institutional variation between Lijphart's types of democracy in terms of modernisation theory as Johnson seems to have in mind in his study of the development of the majority principle in British constitutional history: 'It was in general precisely where consensus existed that it usually proved possible to make the transition to regular application of the majority principle. It was some degree of consensus which made possible the division into majority and minority, and encouraged the toleration of minorities as the essential counterpart of the majority principle' (1986: 152).

6 This last rule is especially important to bear in mind if new institutionalist and policy network approaches in comparative research are to be successfully integrated, but that is beyond the scope of this chapter.

7 This approach is also open to including transnational or international private/public veto points, which become more and more important in modern governance. I thank Ray Goldstein and the other participants of a seminar at Victoria University of Wellington, New Zealand, for pointing this out to me.

8 This is, of course, different in cases where a majority can be assured of staying in power in the foreseeable future, as for instance in Northern Ireland. The resulting problems of legitimacy of majoritarianism in such situations is only proof of the above reasoning.

9 This is the perspective I start from in a study on institutional reform in Australia, Britain, Canada, and New Zealand currently under way.

10 But only then. At times there have been minority governments, most recently in 1974, 1976–79, and for some time in the last two years of the Major Government. These have always been informally backed by third parties in the House of Commons. It is characteristic indeed that even where majoritarian government is numerically impossible, British political parties decline from forming real coalitions.

11 Northern Ireland is an interesting case in itself in that there have been several proposals for formal power-sharing arrangements by successive British governments in order to overcome the strong divisions between the Catholic and Protestant communities.

12 Lijphart does not deny that fact (1984: 22). However, the consequences for his concept of institutional regimes are largely ignored.

13 For a historical treatment, see Fair (1980).

14 Sartori argues that the 'committee-type *modus decidendi*' is *per se* prone to consensual decison-making (1987: 239).

10 Of readers, viewers, and cat-dogs

Rüdiger Schmitt-Beck[1]

Introduction

When citizens make political choices, a wide variety of considerations are important in their decision-making. They include factors like issue concerns, retrospective and prospective judgements about the parties' performance, and evaluations of the candidates running for office. It is far from easy for voters to arrive at such assessments. As 'outsiders' of the institutions and processes of political decision-making (Carmines and Kuklinski 1990: 244), ordinary citizens lack the experience to make judgements on the basis of first-hand knowledge. Rather, their political experience is essentially a mediated one. As a consequence, if citizens are so highly dependent on mediating institutions in order to form political beliefs and opinions, and to make decisions, these institutions enjoy considerable influence over such orientations (Ball-Rokeach 1985).

The most important mediating institution in contemporary democracies are the mass media. Newspapers, news magazines, television, and radio expose the electorate continuously to large amounts of political information. What they tell us about the 'world outside' becomes the foundation of the 'pictures in our heads' (Lippmann 1922: 3–32) – the beliefs and opinions, for example, upon which we act by choosing a candidate or party in an election.

But the mass media are not neutral mirrors of political realities. Their role is not exhausted by transmitting news of distant events into our homes and by giving 'objective' accounts of those events. Rather, by selecting (and highlighting) certain topics or events and by neglecting others, and by arranging and integrating the topics and events into narratives, the news media transform the reality of political processes into a specific 'media reality' (Nimmo and Combs 1990). This reality can be seen as a construction, derived from professional rules of 'news making' (Gamson 1988; Schulz 1989). Through the news media, a small number of communicators controls which version of political reality the majority of citizens perceive. These communicators encompass not only the media professionals, whose role it is to inform the mass public, but political actors like governments, parties, interest organisations, and social movements. They orchestrate their actions in such a way as to secure for themselves and their world views the utmost presence on the media agenda (Blumler 1990). All these various communicators are engaged in a continuous 'struggle for the agenda' (Asp 1983). Together they occupy a key role in forming public opinion, because they define and delimit the political world as it is experienced by the audience (Kleinnijenhuis and Rietberg 1995). This makes the analysis of news media influences on the minds and actions of citizens necessary and worthwhile.

A problem detected

Comparative media research: an underdeveloped area

During the past four decades, sizeable efforts have been undertaken to demonstrate how mass communication shapes the beliefs, opinions, attitudes, values, and behaviour of audiences.[2] Interest in and the productivity of political communication research differ widely among countries. Most of the work has been done in the United States, but British, German, and Canadian studies have contributed important findings. However, in most other Western democracies political communication has tended to be ignored by the social sciences (Semetko 1996a). As a consequence, there is a massive bias to political communication research, and what we know about the political consequences of mass communication is connected to a small number of national contexts. 'Thus, although many theoretical propositions about the social and political functions of the mass media are couched in universal terms, the evidence adduced in support of them is almost always culture-specific' (Gurevitch and Blumler 1990: 308). It remains an open question whether and to what extent these results can be generalised to other political systems.

A remedy for this shortcoming is, of course, cross-national comparative research. However, in this respect media research is a latecomer. Only in recent years have mass communication scholars begun to promote this strategy as a pathway for research (Blumler and Gurevitch 1975; McLeod and Blumler 1987; Gurevitch and Blumler 1990; Blumler *et al.* 1992; Kleinsteuber 1993; Semetko 1996b; Kaase *et al.* 1997: 5–6). Yet comparative knowledge in the field of political mass communication is still very limited. Most studies are macro-analytic both with regard to levels of analysis and observation. Partly descriptive, partly explanatory in aspiration, they have provided valuable insights into the differences and similarities between national media systems, or between specific types of media in various countries.[3] But very few comparative studies have treated the news media as independent variables and tried to disentangle in micro-analytic terms how mediated political communication influences individual receivers.

Most of the existing comparative surveys of the interaction of the media and their audiences were conducted in the context of a larger project on campaign communication at the occasion of the European Parliamentary Elections of 1979 and 1989. This project was preceded by a similarly focused analysis of the 1974 national election campaigns in Belgium, France, and Great Britain. Located in the theoretical tradition of the so-called 'uses and gratifications' approach (cf. Severin and Tankard 1997: 329–42), the perspective of these studies is audience-centred.

Consequently, the studies are rich in descriptive results regarding the exposure of European electorates to various sources of political information, factors that boosted or inhibited attention to these sources, and audience evaluations of them (Blumler *et al.* 1978a and 1978b; Blumler and Fox 1980; Thoveron 1983; Cayrol 1983, 1991; Scherer 1995). However, few contributions to this research sought to analyse political influences of the media on their audiences. Most concentrated on the question of to what degree the media contributed to gains in their audience's political knowledge and cognitive involvement (Thoveron and Sauerberg 1983; Schönbach 1983b; Schulz and Blumler 1994). Apart from the large-scale research effort of the European Election Studies, other studies also have mostly been interested in how the media raise citizens' political knowledge. All of these studies include American voters. Miller and Asp (1985) compare them to Swedish voters, Robinson and Levy (1986: 87–105) to British voters, Semetko and Borquez (1991) to French voters. In their study, Dimock and Popkin (1997) discuss comparative results from seven nations (United States, Canada, Britain, France, Germany, Italy, Spain).

Typical of these studies is that they make little analytic use of what macro-analytic comparative research has uncovered regarding the significant differences between national media systems. Rather, they rely on global, identical measures of individual media exposure. Surfacing empirical indications of cross-national differences in the meaning of these indicators are at most discussed *ex post facto* by mere ad hoc reasoning. No attempts are made to acknowledge such differences in the political meaning of specific media already in the stage of conceptualisation, prior to the operationalisation of measurement instruments and to data collection. Implicitly or explicitly, such studies depart from the working hypothesis that (seemingly) identical media have similar effects in all settings. They thus neglect that 'the way elections are presented in the news, the range and quality of information available to electors via the news media, and the effects of the media on political elites and the public may vary considerably from country to country' (Semetko 1996a: 254).

Media and media need not mean the same

A common strategy of analysing the media's effects on audiences is the search for covariations between the intensity of the recipients' exposure to the media and the attitudinal or behavioural orientations presumably influenced by them. The rationale behind this approach is that if the media are able to shape beliefs, opinions, attitudes, or behaviour, there should be systematic differences on these orientations between individuals who pay the media regular attention, individuals who pay it less attention, and individuals who pay it no attention at all. The following survey question is typical of comparative inquiries into media effects which seek to determine the extent of individual media exposure:

About how often do you
(a) watch the news on television?

(b) read the news in daily papers?
— Every day, several times a week, once or twice a week, less often, never.

This question is taken from the questionnaire of a Eurobarometer survey. Since 1980, it has been regularly included in such surveys conducted every six months on behalf of the European Commission in all member nations of the European Community and respectively the European Union.

Several macro-analytic comparative studies of national media systems suggest that television and newspapers in one country may differ considerably from those in another country. To complicate matters further, even within one country such media may mean divergent things. Gurevitch and Blumler (1990: 317) remind us that 'perhaps the most common danger in designing comparative research is that of conceptual parochialism' which has to do with the apparent face-validity of the simple distinction between television and the press. Another facet of parochialism may lie in the origin of most of the theoretical inspiration for media effects research from a country with a television monoculture and a press landscape of less diversity than that of many other countries (the United States). While claiming to speak about 'newspapers' and 'television' as such, American scholars, in fact, only refer to American newspapers and American television – a television system that is almost unique in the world.

In the following section we seek to determine the equivalence of the concepts 'television' and 'newspapers' across a number of West European countries. Euro-barometer data[4] are used to perform an analysis of the two concepts' external consistency (cf. van Deth, this volume). As criteria we relate the intensity of viewing television news programmes and of reading newspapers to various indicators of citizens' individual political awareness. We start, however, by taking a look at the importance of television news and newspapers in terms of their societal reach in each of the countries under study.

Media usage in Western Europe

Figure 10.1 shows the percentages of voters in West European countries who claim to read a newspaper every weekday, claim to watch the news on television every weekday, claim never to read a newspaper, and claim never to watch the news. Obviously there is much more variation regarding the press than television.[5] In all of Western Europe, television is a ubiquitous medium, and in some countries usage of the press is just as common. In other countries, however, reading a daily paper is close to a minority phenomenon. Daily news watching is especially common in Italy (83 per cent) and relatively rare in Portugal (58 per cent). In all other countries, between 65 and 75 per cent of the electorate follow the news every day of the week. Correspondingly, only a tiny fraction of the electorate never watches television news.

The daily press is very important in Northern Europe (Norway, Denmark, Luxembourg, Netherlands, Germany East and West). Indeed, it is almost as important as television. In Ireland and the United Kingdom, dailies are somewhat

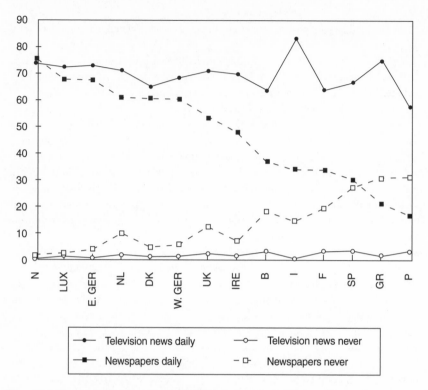

Figure 10.1 Usage of television news and daily newspapers in Western Europe (percentages of the electorates; Eurobarometer data)

less important. Finally, in Belgium as well as in all Southern European countries, including France, the press receives little attention. In these countries, the percentage of daily readers does not exceed one-third of the electorate. It is thus only about half as high as the rate of daily news watching in these countries. In some Southern European countries, most notably Portugal and Greece, more citizens claim never to read a newspaper than to read one on a daily basis. Belated socio-economic modernisation has contributed to the historic weakness of the press in these countries (cf. Deutsch 1961; de Macedo 1983: 56–60). In more recent times, the competition of television, but also rather mundane problems such as inefficient distribution systems, have prevented the emergence of a mass readership. For instance, in Mediterranean countries, newspapers are rarely subscribed to. Instead, they usually must be purchased, copy by copy, at news-stands.

Obviously, while television is similarly – and highly – important in all Western European countries, the importance of the daily press as a source of current political information differs widely. But is television in one country the same as television in another country? And what about the press? Does reading newspapers in Norway mean the same as reading newspapers in the United Kingdom or in Greece? If we focus on the media's function as transmission belts of political information, we might expect the habits of media usage to be connected to a citizen's political awareness: 'the extent to which individuals have encountered and comprehended media reports of political events, issues, and personages' (Zaller 1990: 126).

We will seek to determine the degree to which the media in various countries are equivalent as providers of political information by studying how strongly the frequency with which they are used is linked to three aspects of political awareness of individual voters:

1 interest in politics as an indicator of eagerness to be informed;
2 knowledge of political facts as an indicator of being informed;
3 levels of formal education as an indicator of the ability to process and integrate information, especially political information.

If the media are equivalent as conveyors of political information, the relationships between awareness and media usage found in the various countries should be: (1) of similar strength, and (2) related to each other in a similar fashion. Based on the results of American studies, we would expect all measures of political awareness to be more strongly correlated with reading newspapers than with watching television (cf. Weaver and Buddenbaum 1980; Schönbach 1983a: 28–35; Robinson and Levy 1986: 57–105). And indeed, on the aggregate level this expectation is clearly confirmed. All variables are correlated positively to usage of both media and each variable is more strongly correlated with the frequency of reading newspapers than with watching television news.

Can we find similar patterns when switching to individual-level analysis? For each country, Figure 10.2 shows how television usage and newspaper usage are connected to the indicators of political awareness. Obviously, expectations of uniformity of relationships across European countries are disconfirmed. Both the reading of daily newspapers and the viewing of television news are linked very differently to political awareness. To be sure, most relationships are positive, indicating that higher levels of media usage are accompanied by higher levels of political awareness. But there are numerous exceptions.

As a rule, political awareness is particularly strongly linked to reading newspapers in Southern European countries where the press is not widely read. Obviously, in these countries the audience of the print media is highly concentrated among the rather narrow strata of society that are both highly motivated and highly capable of monitoring the events of national politics – the level of 'activists' in the terminology of Neuman (1986: 170–2). In Spain and Portugal, all awareness indicators are closely linked to reading the papers. In Greece, the Netherlands, and Italy, some of the correlations are very strong. The same applies to West Germany and Denmark regarding political interest and to Luxembourg regarding objective political knowledge. Surprisingly, in some countries – most notably Luxembourg, East Germany, the United Kingdom, and France – the frequency of reading a daily paper is slightly negatively tied to education, indicating

(a) Political interest

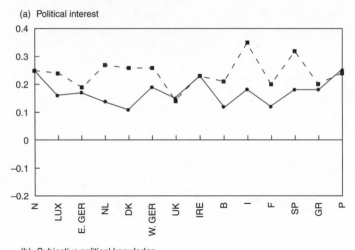

(b) Subjective political knowledge

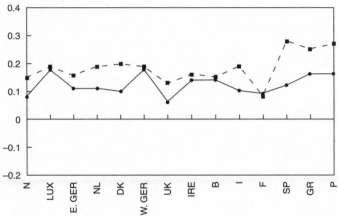

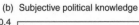

(c) Objective political knowledge

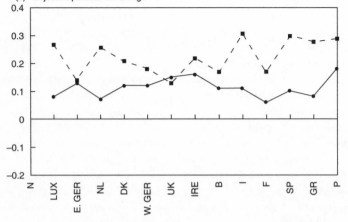

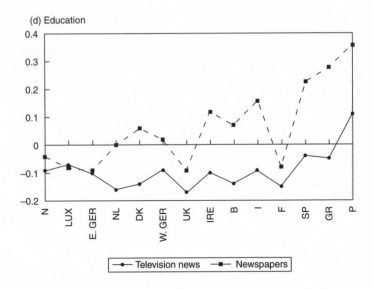

Figure 10.2 Correlations between media usage and political awareness (Tau$_b$; Eurobarometer data)

that the regular audience of the daily press is composed of people with lower levels of education.

Like the extent of viewership, cross-country differences are also smaller in correlations between the frequency of following television news and political awareness. Only Portugal stands out as a context where news watching is relatively closely – and positively – tied to political interest, objective knowledge, and education. In all other countries, it is the lesser educated rather than the well educated that are more inclined to watch the news on TV. The expectation of a stronger linkage for the press versus television exists in most, but not in all, countries. For each indicator of political awareness, nearly identical correlations between the press and TV appear in Norway, the United Kingdom, Ireland, and East Germany. In contrast, the two media most clearly differ in Spain, Italy, Greece, and the Netherlands.

In sum, cross-national differences of the relationships between newspaper reading, television watching, and political awareness are considerable. Furthermore, although most countries display, as expected, a greater political awareness with newspapers than with television, there are significant exceptions. In some countries the relationship is neutral. And for some measures, the relationship is even somewhat stronger for television than for the press. In a similar fashion, a study of seven Western democracies, including the United States and Canada, shows substantial variance in the degrees to which television and newspaper usage are linked to levels of objective political knowledge (Dimock and Popkin 1997; see also Miller and Asp 1985; Robinson and Levy 1986: 87–105).

As conveyors of political information, therefore, the newspapers and television news programmes of Western democracies seem to differ considerably. These results create serious doubts about both the cross-national equivalence of the standard measures of media exposure (like those used in the Eurobarometer surveys) and the generalisability of results derived from national studies using the same kind of measures.[6] If one wants to compare the influence of the mass media on the political beliefs, opinions, and behaviour of individual citizens, measures that distinguish between only television and newspapers can be misleading. Although they are identical in terms of question wording, they may be, in Sartori's (1970: 1035) terms, 'pseudo-equivalent'. It may be that 'the [technical, RSB] medium is not the entire message' (Dimock and Popkin 1997: 223). For many research problems in the field of micro-analytic political communication research, the broad categories of television news and daily newspapers may be yet another example of Sartori's 'cat-dog': classes which lump objects together that for theoretical reasons should be kept apart.[7] Lumping them together may hide meaningful differences with regard to the explanatory problem at hand.

A solution proposed

Descending the 'ladder of abstraction'

Sartori's (1970: 1040–5) notion of a 'ladder of abstraction' may help us proceed from this point. It refers to 'an orderly way – indeed, a method – of relating universals to particulars'; its basic principle consists in organising 'our categories along a ladder of abstraction whose basic rule of transformation (i.e. upward aggregation and downward specification) is that the connotation (intension) and denotation (extension) of concepts are inversely related. Thus, in order to make a concept more general, we must reduce the characteristics or properties. Conversely, in order to make a concept more specific (contextually adequate), we must increase its properties or characteristics' (Sartori 1991: 254). The crucial criterion for determining the appropriate level of abstraction is which properties we deem important on theoretical grounds, given our research problem. Figure 10.3 shows how such a ladder of abstraction might look in the context of research interested in political influences of the mass media on individual citizens.[8]

The most general level of abstraction in the ladder is connected to the general notion of 'mass communication', a type of social communication defined by a number of distinctive properties (cf. McQuail 1987: 31–2; Hunziker 1988: 5–10; Schulz 1994: 140–4; Severin and Tankard 1997: 4):

- it takes place in public: i.e. participation is open to every citizen;
- it is directed towards large, heterogeneous, and anonymous audiences;
- it is basically a one-directional form of communication, since the recipients of the transmitted messages have only very limited opportunities to respond and send feedback;

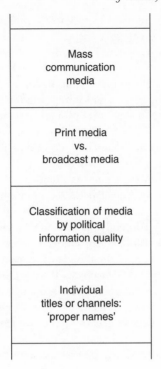

Figure 10.3 A mass media related ladder of abstraction

- it is an indirect form of communication, mediated by technical means for multiplying and distributing messages;
- it is impersonal in the sense that the relationship between the sender and receiver of a message is physically and socially distant. It is also impersonal insofar as communicators act not as individual personalities but as occupants of professional roles within complex formal organisations. Their messages do not originate from a desire for personal expression but from the application of professional rules of organised message production.

The term 'mass communication media' refers to the technical and organisational aspects of the institutions producing and sending mass communication messages.

To be sure, these concepts of 'mass communication' and 'mass communication media' are not the most general concepts imaginable. If we broaden our research question, we can easily extend the ladder of abstraction upwards, in the direction of higher generality. By introducing the notion of 'social communication', for instance, we can climb up a step, for this concept includes not only mass communication but also interpersonal communication (Schulz 1994: 141). Such a personal exchange of messages may take place either face-to-face or mediated by some technical device – from old-fashioned letters over telecommunication facilities to computer networks. This level of conceptualisation may well become more relevant in the future, as new media technologies blur the distinction between broadcasting and 'narrow casting' and lead to a partial merging of the two types of social communication (Neuman 1991). Beyond that level, a further step of abstraction is conceivable, referring to the general notion of 'societal information flows'. The level of 'social communication' is characterised by the intentional exchanging of meaningful messages. In contrast, the level of general 'societal information flows' includes all transfers of information, intended or unintended (Schement 1993; Schulz 1994: 148–53). For example, watching the expression on the face of a friend looking at a campaign poster may tell me as much about her political preferences as would her words.

Yet, in our present discussion we are not aiming at greater abstraction but at greater specificity. Rightfully, Semetko (1996a: 255) characterises the notion of 'the mass media' as a 'catch-all term' that masks important differences between various types of media. Accordingly, there is not much research at this level of abstraction.[9] However, descending the ladder of abstraction in a theoretically controlled way presupposes conceptual thinking, in order to gain clarity about the potentially relevant properties of our object. If we are interested in the influences exerted by mass communication on the beliefs, opinions, or behaviour of citizens, we need a clear theoretical understanding of how such effects come about. Merten (1994: 311–13) maintains that, in general, three bundles of factors must be taken into account in order to understand and detect media effects: (1) the content that is transmitted by the media; (2) the recipients' 'internal context' (that is, their personal preconditions regarding previous experiences, knowledge, attitudes, and values); and (3) the recipients' 'external context' (that is, the situational and social context in which the transfer and reception of content take place, including features of the communication media themselves).

An important facet of the latter domain is the notion of 'media formats'. It can serve as a conceptual tool to descend the ladder of abstraction. This concept takes into account that not all media are the same as channels for transmitting information. Analogous to grammar in language, media formats are defined as 'the rules and logic that transform and mold information (content) into the recognisable shape and form of the specific medium. Formats are formulas that serve as strategies for presenting categorical subject matter to an audience' (Altheide and Snow 1988: 199). In terms of political communication, they can be seen as distinctive strategies or styles for processing and presenting the news, that is, for transforming political events into messages. Different media are typically characterised by distinct formats. With regard to possible media effects this may be of significance, because a format 'functions as a logic that guides and defines more general experience'. In so far as 'form "informs" content', media formats are one of the factors that contribute to the complicated process of generating media effects (Altheide and Snow 1991: 18). They constitute the logic that guides and defines the ways various media present the same topics. Thus the same subjects dealt with by different media may reach the audience in substantially different forms.

The format-related distinction that has traditionally dominated research, is of course the one between print media, such as newspapers and news magazines, and broadcast media, such as television and radio. The key difference between these two types of mass communication concerns the technical facilities for distributing messages. The possibility for the technical multiplication of texts was made feasible through the invention of the printing press in the sixteenth century. Newspapers, of which the first examples date from the early seventeenth century, are thus the oldest mass medium. The principal carrier of messages within the medium is written text, with visuals like photos, cartoons or charts playing a limited, supplementary role. Historically, the broadcast media are much younger. The discovery of electromagnetic waves in 1888 laid the scientific foundation for the technology. The first radio stations went on the air in the 1920s, and the first regular television broadcasts began after the Second World War. The legal definition given in German media laws catches the electronic media's key distinction: they distribute audio-visual messages to the public by means of electric waves, either wireless or via a technical transmission medium, such as cable. Whereas literacy is the core requirement for the audience of the press, radio or television broadcasts require appropriate reception equipment.

Most past research has concentrated on television and newspapers. For a number of reasons, both media are credited with a very divergent capacity to influence their audience. Television is often said to be a unique medium whose appearance deeply changed the nature of political communication in Western democracies (Neuman 1986: 142). As Noelle-Neumann puts it: 'Nothing is like it was before' (1994: 546). In general, television is considered better suited to influence people's opinions and attitudes, whereas print – as already touched upon earlier – is considered superior in its capacity to exert cognitive effects, that is, to shape beliefs (Weaver and Buddenbaum 1980).

However, as the analyses presented above have strongly suggested, by conceptualising our theory and designing our measurement instruments at the general level of television versus print, we may be missing an important point. Perhaps property dimensions of mass media exist which are of consequence regarding their influence on public opinion but which lie beyond the simple distinction between television and the press. Everyone acquainted with the media systems of various countries may have an intuitive sense of this. A number of macro-analytic comparative studies of news content confirm such impressions. For instance, news on the BBC differs significantly from news presented by the German entertainment channel RTL. At national elections in the 1980s, the BBC and ITV carried far more campaign-related information than all three US networks together (Semetko 1996a: 257). Spain's *El País* has obviously a very different style of covering politics than Germany's *Bild-Zeitung*, while the *Frankfurter Allgemeine Zeitung* differs sharply from the British *Sun*. But such reasoning leads us where we do not want to end up in substantive and analytical comparative research: to the level of individual newspaper titles and individual television channels. To be sure, much single-country research is done exactly on this level. Yet, the fundamental problem of such studies is that their findings are unclear in general terms. Although the results of such studies are often phrased in terms of 'television effects' or of 'newspaper effects', they at best demonstrate the influences of particular titles or channels, and not of newspapers or television news as such.

In aiming at titles and channels we have descended too far on the ladder of abstraction and are in danger of entering the realm of idiographic instead of nomothetic research. We are studying historical and social entities in the form of specific newspapers and television channels without accounting for what their specificity consists in, if phrased in the language of general concepts. Instead we should recall what Przeworski and Teune (1970: 26–30) see as the essence of comparative research: to replace proper names – in our case the names of newspapers or television channels – by variables. To some degree specific newspapers and television channels are probably indeed historic and social 'personalities'. They all have developed styles of political reporting that are to some degree unique. Moreover, they operate in highly competitive markets where distinctiveness is a prerequisite to survival and success.

However, one can conceive of several meaningful categories for classifying newspapers and television broadcasts beyond the level of proper names but below the global distinction between print and audio-visual media. One is the media's political leaning. Media can differ with regard to the extent of bias or neutrality in political coverage and with regard to the parties or ideologies favoured. Another aspect concerns the prevalence of factual versus opinion-oriented reporting (though this distinction concerns rather the difference between daily news media and news magazines and television magazines). Here we will focus on a third dimension: an aspect of media formats characterised as 'information quality'. Both television channels and newspapers can differ considerably from each other with respect to the amount, depth, and complexity of the political information they offer their audiences. These variations can be characterised as differences in information quality. As a taxonomic device this dimension is specific enough to avoid overlooking 'differences that make a difference' (Luhmann) and general enough to facilitate genuine comparative research beyond specific newspapers and broadcasters.

Classifying media by information quality

This approach to comparative media research helps avoid the fallacy of the wrong level of abstraction, which – as we have seen – seems attached to the use of identical indicators as already discussed. To solve our measurement problem we use non-identical but equivalent indicators. Data were collected in the context of the 'Comparative National Elections Project (CNEP)' – a joint endeavour of a multinational research group conducted during the early 1990s at the occasion of national elections in various Western democracies. The data analysed here were collected in West and East Germany (1990), Spain (1993), and the United States (1992).[10] Unfortunately we do not have surveys from the same set of countries as the Eurobarometer analyses presented above, but for those countries[11] included in both databases we can use more refined results to qualify the conclusions based on the general indicators.

Instead of using simple indicators like those discussed above, data collection in the CNEP surveys started essentially at the level of 'proper names'. By means of open-ended questions the media respondents actually used were registered as specifically as possible. The possibility of parallel use of several newspapers and of several television programmes was taken into account. It was then asked how often all media were used. This procedure yielded a long list of newspaper titles and television channels for each country, plus information about the extent and intensity of usage. The media were then classified by information quality (see Table 10.1).

As mentioned above, 'information quality' refers to the amount of information the media convey and the degree of 'intellectuality' in their style of presentation. The first aspect concerns the number and range of topics covered, the second the depth and complexity with which each topic is treated (cf. Kleinnijenhuis 1991). The fact that the media differ with respect to these aspects can be seen as the result of processes of market segmentation, reflecting differentiations of audience demands. As uses-and-gratifications research has shown, media can fulfil broadly diverse needs for their audiences (Severin and Tankard 1997: 329–42). Gathering political information is only one of these and not necessarily the most important. Competing or complementing needs include entertainment and diversion, emotional or aesthetic experiences, or value reinforcement. Even the surveillance need itself, in which political information is usually subsumed, includes not only matters of national politics, but may also encompass political and non-political local affairs.

To sort newspaper titles and television channels by their information quality presupposes an idea about which levels of information quality are distinctive properties of which titles or channels. Whether or not these classifications are valid can then be tested empirically. This will be done in the next subsection. To classify the media in our four countries, we apply a conceptual scheme that distinguishes three types of daily newspapers and two types of television stations. In the case of television, the scheme is based on the theory that public broadcasters are typically characterised by higher levels of information quality than private broadcasters. In the case of the press, the scheme is different; its assumption of three levels of information quality is based on the conventional wisdom of many descriptive studies of the media systems of the countries being investigated.

In British media studies it is common to distinguish three types of daily newspapers: 'qualities', 'middle market' dailies, and 'mass market' or 'popular' dailies (Huggins and Turner 1997: 399). Similar distinctions are also used in other countries as, for instance, Germany (Pürer and Raabe 1994: 162–76). In such studies it is common to characterise certain titles as belonging to the 'quality press' – a notion that, without explicitly referring to the concept, obviously suggests high information quality. As an additional formal criterion, such titles typically enjoy nationwide distribution. In general, features like comprehensiveness of coverage, background reports, in-depth news articles, lack of 'sensationalism', and analytical stories are typical of the quality press. Such papers are often produced by journalists of high professional reputation – known in Germany as the 'noble quills'

Table 10.1 Information quality and societal reach of media

Information quality	Newspapers total (%):	West Germany 73[a]	East Germany 90	Spain 45	USA 84
Very high	National quality press	*Die Welt* *Frankfurter Allgemeine Zeitung* *Süddeutsche Zeitung* *Frankfurter Rundschau* *Die Tageszeitung*	*(Die Welt* *Frankfurter Allgemeine Zeitung* *Süddeutsche Zeitung* *Frankfurter Rundschau* *Die Tageszeitung)*[b]	*ABC* *Ya* *Vanguardia* *Diario 16* *El Mundo* *El País*	*New York Times* *Washington Post* *Los Angeles Times* *Wall Street Journal*
		11%	1%	21%	14%
High	Local/ regional press	About 120 editions (with about 1,300 local sub-editions)	About 35 editions (with about 300 local sub-editions)	About 140 editions	About 1,650 editions; also: *USA Today* (national distribution)
		54%	86%	32%	77%
Low	Tabloid press	*Bild-Zeitung* *Abendzeitung* *BZ* *Express* *Hamburger Morgenpost* *tz*	*Bild-Zeitung* *(Abendzeitung* *BZ* *Express* *Hamburger Morgenpost* *tz)*	Does not exist	(Few local titles)
		28%	43%	–	–
	Television news total (%):	95	97	86	97
High	Public television	ARD ZDF	ARD ZDF DFF	TVE	(PBS)
		93%	97%	62%	(–)
Low	Private television	RTLplus SAT1 (Other, less important channels not included in survey)	(In 1990 already beginning to become a relevant market segment, but not included in survey)	Antena 3 Tele 5 Canal +	NBC CBS ABC CNN Local news
		38%	(–)	50%	97%

Source: CNEP Study.

Notes:
[a] Proportions of respondents using medium at least occassionally.
[b] Entries in brackets refer to media that cannot be analysed separately, due to insufficient data.

(*Edelfedern*). They cater to the information needs of the national elite and often occupy an opinion-leader role within national media systems (Merrill and Fisher 1980: 3–23). As can be seen from Table 10.1, the audience of the quality dailies varies considerably between countries. An interesting case is Spain. While general newspaper readership is considerably less frequent than in both Germany and the United States, the proportion of citizens reading a quality title is actually higher. In East Germany, no generic quality press has developed. The West German titles are in principle available, but barely receive any attention.

All four of our countries are characterised by a decentralised structure of the daily press. Their markets are dominated by a broad variety of newspapers of local or regional distribution. In terms of information quality this local and regional press can be seen as a middle stratum. Regarding national politics, these dailies typically cover fewer topics than the quality press, and their reporting does not achieve the same analytic breadth and depth. To a large degree they rely on wire services. This is partly due to their lack of resources and partly to their different role in the media system. These papers emphasise local and regional information that the national press does not deliver.

Titles that are assigned to the 'popular' or tabloid press make up the third segment of the daily press. This is a category for which low information quality is considered typical. Such titles are distributed either nationally or regionally. German media studies often point out that popular titles can be obtained only from street vendors (so-called *Straßenverkaufszeitungen*), while the rest of the daily press is distributed via subscriptions. However, such a formal criterion cannot be generalised since there are countries, Spain among them, where subscription is very uncommon for any paper. In terms of content, the tabloid press typically does not separate facts and opinion to the same degree as do the national quality press and the local and regional press. The tabloids' mode of presentation is emotional, sensationalistic, and simplistic. Personalisation is an important stylistic device, and high emphasis is placed on visual appearance. Articles are typically very short and written in easy-to-understand, everyday language. The thematic spectrum of tabloids is more varied than that of the serious press and includes sex, crime, and sports as well as politics.[12] Tabloids thus cater more to entertainment than to information needs (Bruck and Stocker 1996: 9–33).[13] Of the countries in our sample, only Germany has a significant daily tabloid press. In contrast to both the quality press and the local and regional press, West German tabloids, especially the *Bild-Zeitung*, have attracted a sizeable readership in both West and East Germany. In 1991, however, an attempt to launch a similar product in Spain, entitled *Claro*, ended in economic failure. In the United States, only some local titles, like the *New York Post*, can be considered tabloids in the European sense. However, observers have begun to criticise a trend towards a general 'tabloidisation' of the American daily press (Hume 1996).[14]

Regarding television, the distinction between public and private broadcasters can be expected to have important implications for the quality of political information. Commercial television stations are much more dependent on audience markets than are public television stations. For them, the dominant motive behind programming decisions is mass attractiveness and so it directs the amount and type of news offered to the audience. In contrast, public stations are often kept free of market pressures by means of public subsidies or audience fees. At the same time, public stations are to varying degrees dependent on political actors like governments or political parties, while commercial stations are free of such pressures. Public stations thus typically deliver political information more suited to the communication needs of political elites (Pfetsch 1991: 43–7). Content analyses from Germany suggest that, although there are signs of convergence in programming policies, viewers of public television not only get more information, but the information is more comprehensive. In contrast, private stations offer fewer news shows, and the programmes are shorter, more simplistic, and less strongly dominated by topics of 'hard' politics. They place greater emphasis on 'human interest' themes. In addition, whereas public television tends to cultivate a quasi-official style of news presentation, private stations rely on easy-to-digest 'infotainment' (Pfetsch 1991 and 1996; Krüger 1992).

Since the 1980s, both Germany and Spain have moved from 'pure public' to 'dual' broadcasting systems, characterised by the co-existence of public and commercial channels. In Spain, more dramatically than in Germany, private television quickly became a popular alternative for daily news. In order to fully understand the East German situation, one must know that the German CNEP survey was conducted during the transitional period shortly after German uni-fication in autumn 1990. At that time, two different types of public television were available to East Germans: the West German channels ARD and ZDF and the former state television of socialist East Germany DFF. Before being finally dis-banded by the end of 1991, DFF was run according to the principles of public broadcasting, under supervision of a newly installed West German director (cf. Hoffmann-Riem 1991). About 77 per cent of East German voters claimed to watch the news of this station, while 85 per cent watched West German public news programmes. West German private channels had also already found a sizeable audience in East Germany but were not included in the East German survey. As is well known, the United States offers the prototype of a purely commercial television system (Comstock 1991: 3–13), dominated by the three networks NBC, CBS, and ABC, and, in recent years, by the cable news channel CNN. The audience share attracted by public television (PBS) is negligible, so it has not been included in the CNEP survey. In recent years, local news has risen in importance. Of the American sample, 87 per cent watch at least on occasion the national news of the networks and CNN. Local news is seen by 95 per cent.

Testing the classification's validity

Similar to our analyses of the Eurobarometer data above, this section presents the results of a test of external consistency of the media categories outlined in Table 10.1. It will be supplemented by a test of internal consistency of the more fine-grained classes of media. We expect to find systematic patterns. If the media have been categorised correctly in terms of information quality, linkages to political awareness should be stronger for media of higher information quality. This pattern should become visible for each country and for both newspapers and television. In addition, usage of newspapers and of television channels of similar information quality should be positively linked. This expectation assumes that citizens have generalised habits of media use: i.e. that they pay attention to both print and audio-visual media of either similarly low or similarly high information quality. Our measures of media usage distinguish three groups of people: those who do not use the medium, those who use it occasionally, and those who use it regularly.[15] Again we refer to political interest, political knowledge, and education as indicators of the individual citizen's political awareness.

Tables 10.2 and 10.3 display the results of two types of analyses. First, analogous to the analyses performed with the Eurobarometer data, they show the bivariate relationships between using the various types of media and our three

Table 10.2 Predictive power of political interest and education for various types of media usage (unstandardised effect coefficients; estimated by multiple logistic regressions)

	Zero-order correlations *(Tau_b)*		Causal analyses			
			Total usage		Regular usage	
	Political interest	Education	Political interest	Education	Political interest	Education
West Germany (N_min = 1,307)						
Quality press	0.25	0.31	2.82[a]	4.62[a]	2.44[a]	4.09[a]
Local and regional press	0.15	−0.01	1.61[a]	1.28^{-1}	1.57[a]	1.47^{-1}[a]
Tabloid press	−0.07	−0.21	1.04^{-1}	4.35^{-1}[a]	1.04	7.69^{-1}[a]
Public television	0.21	−0.01	1.81[a]	2.44^{-1}[a]	2.46[a]	1.67^{-1}[a]
Private television	0.00	−0.06	1.00	1.31^{-1}[b]	1.45[a]	2.27^{-1}[a]
East Germany (N_min = 636)						
Local and regional press	0.22	0.08	2.15[a]	1.93	1.94[a]	1.02
Tabloid press	0.04	−0.05	1.19	1.45^{-1}	1.48	2.22^{-1}
Public television (West)	0.09	0.07	1.05^{-1}	2.10	1.28[b]	1.36
Public television (East)	0.19	0.10	1.73[a]	1.34	1.54[a]	1.28
Spain (N_min = 1,310)						
Quality press	0.26	0.30	2.22[a]	3.76[a]	2.09[a]	3.63[a]
Local and regional press	0.15	0.18	1.49[a]	2.11[a]	1.71[a]	1.85[a]
Public television	0.06	−0.04	1.20	1.10^{-1}	1.37[a]	1.54^{-1}[a]
Private television	0.12	0.12	1.36[a]	1.78[a]	1.48[a]	1.34[b]
USA (N_min = 1,276)						
Quality press	0.14	0.23	1.72[a]	5.98[a]	2.49[a]	6.07[a]
Local and regional press	0.12	−0.00	1.36[a]	1.34^{-1}[b]	1.58[a]	1.05^{-1}
Private television (nat. news)	0.17	−0.05	2.15[a]	1.24^{-1}	1.71[a]	1.65^{-1}[a]
Private television (local news)	0.20	−0.05	1.37	2.38^{-1}[a]	2.14[a]	1.46^{-1}[a]

Source: CNEP study.

Notes:
[a] $p < 0.01$.
[b] $p < 0.05$.

Table 10.3 Predictive power of various types of media usage for political knowledge (unstandardised effect coefficients, controlled for political interest and education; estimated by multiple logistic regressions)

	Zero-order correlations	Causal analyses	
	(Tau-B)	Total usage	Regular usage
West Germany (N_{min} = 1,307)			
Quality press	0.17	2.13[a]	3.84[a]
Local and regional press	0.01	1.12	1.09
Tabloid press	−0.02	1.05^{-1}	1.42^{-1}
Public television	0.13	1.32	1.45[a]
Private television	−0.02	1.36^{-1} [a]	1.92^{-1} [a]
East Germany (N_{min} = 636)			
Local and regional press	0.07	1.13^{-1}	1.21^{-1}
Tabloid press	0.06	1.07	1.79
Public television (West)	0.07	1.63[b]	1.34
Public television (East)	−0.01	1.35^{-1}	1.58^{-1} [a]
Spain (N_{min} = 1,310)			
Quality press	0.21	1.79[a]	2.22[a]
Local and regional press	0.19	1.94[a]	1.68[a]
Public television	0.00	1.11	1.11^{-1}
Private television	0.09	1.10	1.13^{-1}
USA (N_{min} = 1,276)			
Quality press	0.16	1.67[a]	1.71
Local and regional press	0.02	1.08^{-1}	1.07^{-1}
Private television (nat. news)	−0.07	1.04	1.30^{-1}
Private television (local news)	0.02	1.26^{-1}	1.19^{-1}

Source: CNEP study.

Notes:
[a] $p < 0.01$.
[b] $p < 0.05$.

measures of political awareness. In addition, they contain the results of more sophisticated multivariate causal analyses. Each of these analyses was performed with regard to two significant distinctions in the intensity of media usage: first, the contrast between citizens who use a certain type of media at least occasionally and those who never use it (total usage); and, second, the contrast between those who use a certain type of media regularly and those who use it less often or not at all (regular usage). These analyses assume that political interest and education are antecedents of media usage and that gain in political knowledge is its result. Therefore, in Table 10.2 media usage is predicted simultaneously by political interest and education. According to McQuail (1992: 197), the 'ultimate criterion of information quality is the potential for audiences to learn about reality'. In Table 10.3, political knowledge is thus predicted by media usage, controlling for political interest and education, in order to isolate the media's genuine influence.

The dependent variable of political knowledge is dichotomised at the mean. The analyses thus show to what degree media usage predicts whether an individual's level of political knowledge is above or below average. Entries on the table are unstandardised effect coefficients estimated by logistic regression. An effect coefficient can be interpreted as the (multiplicative) factor by which the odds of, for instance, Prob(Reading a quality newspaper) and Prob(Not reading a quality newspaper) changes if the value of the respective independent variable is increased by one unit. Hence, an effect coefficient of size unity indicates that the independent variable has no effect on the dependent variable.

On the whole, the results of this test of external consistency confirm our classification. However, this applies more to the press than to television. In the latter, interesting anomalies materialise that partly call for a revision of our categories. In all countries reading a quality paper has a stronger positive linkage to political interest and an even stronger linkage to education than reading a local or regional daily. And in both West and East Germany reading a local or regional newspaper is more strongly connected to political interest than reading a tabloid. In fact, whereas political interest is virtually uncorrelated to reading a tabloid, education has a strong inverse effect. It is the lesser educated who are more prone to look at a tabloid, especially on a regular basis. Remarkably, in all countries except Spain, the local and regional press also seems to be somewhat more attractive for citizens with lower levels of education. Regardless of country, the quality press reveals a substantial independent capacity to raise its readers' political knowledge. Only in Spain do we also observe significant, though weaker, contributions of the local and regional press to political knowledge.

Regarding television, results are more mixed. As concerns the influence of political interest, the expected pattern – a stronger positive connection for public television – is only clearly visible in West Germany. With respect to education, all coefficients are negative. Independent of political interest, higher education implies a tendency to avoid any contact with the news on private television, and even more strongly on public television. However, regarding regular viewing, the negative influence of higher education is greater for private than for public television. Regular viewers of public news programmes are also significantly better informed about politics. In contrast, as the frequency of watching the news on private television increases, viewers' average level of political knowledge actually decreases.

In terms of supply structure on the television market, the Spanish case seems closest to that of West Germany. However, what we observe is a surprising reversal of relationships. It is the private channels, not the public ones, that are more closely linked to political interest. In addition, whereas viewing TVE is more prevalent among the less educated, the news offered by private channels appears more attractive for the higher educated, both in terms of total and regular viewing. This surprisingly twisted pattern may be explained as a result of TVE's style of news presentation that some claim to be no less oriented to infotainment than that of the private stations. That both types of broadcasters appear to be equally inefficient with regard to gains in voters' political knowledge seems proof of that contention. As a result, in Spain only the print media contribute to voters' political understanding. TVE's programming policy can be attributed to the fact that it receives very limited public subsidies, so that it is not much less dependent on advertising revenues than commercial channels. Another relevant feature may be TVE's notorious pro-government bias (Bustamante 1989) to which, besides the press, only the private channels can serve as a counterweight. This makes them attractive for citizens who value more pluralistic news. Thus, our classification seems flawed by the uniqueness of TVE among international public television broadcasters. At the same time, it becomes manifest that private broadcasters under specific conditions can fulfil functions that are normally typical of public stations.

Since our key distinction between public and private television does not apply to the difference between network and local news in the United States, it does not come as a surprise that we find no large differences between these two types of information programmes. Usage of both is connected positively to political interest, and negatively to education and – insignificantly – political knowledge. As predicted, American commercial television's news programmes thus seem to be rather inefficient means for raising their audience's level of political knowledge. In contrast, both PBS and specialised cable channels like C-SPAN seem to have a significant capacity to inform their audience, as is – well in line with the argument presented here – suggested by a study by Robinson and Levy (1996). In East Germany, the historical circumstances of the unification year 1990 may be reflected in our results. Again, with regard to our key distinction, there is no difference between the two types of broadcasters being investigated – both are of the public variety. None the less, a pattern appears. Politically interested citizens have a stronger tendency to watch DFF than to watch ARD or ZDF. However, the West German channels are clearly more effective in raising their audience's political knowledge. This may be due to the fact that our knowledge index focuses primarily on the traditional political landscape of West Germany. Hence, it seems that West German news is a better bridge to political knowledge than was East German news.

The test of our measures' external consistency can be supplemented by a test of their internal consistency via countrywise principal components analyses. It is expected that usage habits of media of similar information quality will be grouped together on the same factors. At the outset, it must be mentioned that zero-order correlations are generally fairly low: Pearson's r rarely exceeds 0.30. None the less principal components analyses partly reveal structures that fit into our assumptions (Table 10.4). In West Germany the pattern of interrelationships lends additional support to our classification. Watching the news on private channels goes hand in hand with reading tabloids. The second factor is a pure print factor, defined by the polarity between the local and regional press and the national quality press. It reflects choice tendencies, given the fact that few people read more than one paper at a time. The third factor mirrors, so to speak, the typical 'modal recipient's' usage pattern: to watch public news programmes and to read a local or regional daily. The analysis also provides further evidence that in Spain private channels are equivalent to public channels in other countries. We find a

Table 10.4 Patterns of mass media usage (factor loadings; results of principal components analysis with oblimin rotation)

	Factor 1		Factor 2		Factor 3
West Germany (N = 1,312)					
Quality press	−0.18		−0.81		0.27
Local and regional press	−0.20		0.68		0.40
Tabloid press	0.76		0.01		−0.04
Public television	0.11		−0.05		0.91
Private television	0.70		0.01		0.13
Eigenvalues	1.23		1.17		0.99
% of variance explained	24.5		23.4		19.8
Correlations of factors		0.02		0.05	
			−0.10		
East Germany (N = 668)					
Local and regional press	0.78		0.07		
Tabloid press	0.08		0.73		
Public television (West)	−0.08		0.72		
Public television (East)	0.77		−0.07		
Eigenvalues	1.22		1.06		
% of variance explained	30.6		26.5		
Correlation of factors		−0.02			
Spain (N = 1,304)					
Quality press	0.66		0.09		
Local and regional press	0.28		0.57		
Public television	−0.21		0.86		
Private television	0.81		−0.12		
Eigenvalues	1.25		1.06		
% of variance explained	31.2		26.5		
Correlation of factors		0.11			
USA (N = 1,270)					
Quality press	0.16		0.81		
Local and regional press	0.18		−0.72		
Private television (nat. news)	0.80		−0.00		
Private television (local news)	0.80		−0.00		
Eigenvalues	1.40		1.12		
% of variance explained	35.0		28.1		
Correlation of factors		−0.09			

Source: CNEP study.

two-factor solution: (1) combining reading of national quality dailies and watching private news programmes, and (2) combining reading local or regional papers and watching TVE (again, the 'modal recipient' pattern).

For the United States, the analysis extracts a single television factor, with positive loadings for both network news and local news (see also Patterson 1980: 64), and, once again, a print choice factor, defined by the polarity of the local and regional press versus the national quality press. This pattern neatly mirrors the less varied supply structure of the American media system. Only the

East German results carry no clear message in terms of information quality. For East Germany we also find a two-factor solution: (1) combining the local and regional press with DFF, and (2) combining the tabloid press and ARD and ZDF. This pattern becomes meaningful only with a closer look. The first factor is defined by generic East German media (where the local and regional press consists mostly of privatised East German titles formerly owned by the Socialist Party or one of its affiliate organisations), while the second factor is defined by West German media: the two West German public channels and the tabloid press.

With minor exceptions, our typology is largely validated. If we consider the relative importance of the various types of media in terms of societal reach in each of the countries (Table 10.1), these patterns of relationships help us to understand the differences that the Eurobarometer analyses of West Germany, East Germany, and Spain show (Figure 10.2). To recapitulate: for all indicators of political awareness, bivariate correlations with usage of newspapers were strongest in Spain, weaker in West Germany, and still weaker in East Germany. This pattern clearly mirrors the differing average levels of information quality in the national press systems. In Spain the quality press is of higher importance than in Germany, whereas the tabloid press is missing entirely. In East Germany the situation is quite the reverse: tabloids are more important than in West Germany, and the quality press is nearly irrelevant.

Concerning television, correlations between countries differ less. On most measures, linkages are strongest in West Germany, followed by Spain and East Germany. This suggests that public television's information quality is higher in Germany than in Spain. That East Germany partly displays lower correlations than West Germany (Eurobarometer data of 1994) is due to the fact that, in the years following German unification, East Germans shifted their viewing habits to a considerably larger extent from public to private channels than did West Germans (Spielhagen 1995). Thus, the divergences between countries with regard to the relationships between political awareness and general newspaper and television usage can be explained as an expression of the different structures of national press and television systems with regard to the information quality of the various media.

Conclusion

When looked at in various national settings, neither newspapers and newspapers nor television and television necessarily mean the same thing. Drawing on Sartori's imagery, the two concepts may be characterised as 'cat-dogs'. They are mixed bags of objects with considerable differences on property dimensions that seem meaningful with regard to the research question at hand.

Our results indicate that these global categories do not totally miss their point in the country from which most media research originates. Television in the United States is characterised by a near-monoculture, and the press does not display the same degree of diversity as in many European countries. However, in the European countries studied above, both television and the press deviate widely from this prototype. Differences are considerable not only between countries but also, even more importantly, within countries. Such peculiarities may seem acceptable if we are satisfied with the observation that media effects differ from country to country because of cross-national differences in the structure of national media systems. However, if we are interested in a more fine-grained, micro-level comparative inquiry of what creates media effects and what types of media create specific effects, this way of conceptualising the independent variable seems inadequate. The analyses presented above suggest that distinguishing newspaper titles and television channels by their information quality can help us come closer to truly comparable, relevant categories. These categories can no longer be operationalised by means of identical indicators, and so measurement gets much more cumbersome. Yet, what one gains are classifications for which the crucial assumption of cross-national equivalence rests on firmer grounds.

'Studying the role and influence of the news media in elections is difficult enough in one society. To expand this to many countries requires much time, effort, and funding' (Semetko 1996a: 278). This chapter has helped explain the special effort connected to the problem of operationalisation, and, above all, conceptualisation in comparative research on political communication effects. The media of mass communication can be conceived of as highly complex bundles of technical, economical, social, cultural, and political property dimensions. It is the task of conceptualisation to develop ideas about which properties are relevant to specific research questions. Only by avoiding the fallacies of face-validity through careful theory-based conceptualisation can they be discovered.

Notes

1 The author is indebted to Russell Dalton and Katrin Voltmer for helpful comments on a draft version of this paper.

2 For recent reviews, see e.g. Ansolabehere *et al.* (1993: 129–205); Severin and Tankard (1997: 247–342).

3 More or less clearly guided by common categorical frameworks, descriptive studies present overviews of the structures of media systems or segments of them in a number of selected nations (e.g. Ostergaard 1992; Hans-Bredow-Institut 1996). Explanatory macro-analyses mostly focus on the mass media as a dependent variable. They are interested either in structures of media systems or in the political content they deliver to their audiences. A well-known example of the former is the classic study by Siebert *et al.* (1963) that shows how fundamental differences in dominant political philosophies determine the legal bases and economic structures of media systems all over the world. Browne (1989) asks how political factors help to explain differences and similarities of basic structures and developmental trajectories of broadcasting systems in countries as diverse as France, Japan, and the Soviet Union. Voltmer (1998) focuses on the content that press and broadcasting systems offer to their audiences. She shows how legal regulations and informal rules of conduct determine the plurality of content to which audiences in the OECD countries get access. Dalton *et al.* (1996) compare newspapers and television channels of various Western democracies in terms of partisanship. Semetko *et al.* (1991) compare how British and American newspapers and television channels report on national elections. They demonstrate that the greater political dependence of public media leads to a stronger influence of political parties on their

thematic agenda. In contrast, commercial media have a greater 'discretionary power'. They are less easily influenced by political actors, and tend to make their own agenda. Studies comparing television news across countries show us that the way politics is presented in the news is influenced by the legal, institutional, economic, and political-cultural constraints under which broadcasters in various countries operate (Rositi 1977; Hallin and Mancini 1984; Ernst 1987; Faul 1989; Gurevitch 1989; Gerstlé *et al.* 1991; Schütte 1994; Semetko 1996b). Political television spot ads from various Western democracies have been compared by Holtz-Bacha *et al.* (1994) as well as by Kaid (1991).

4 All analyses are based on Eurobarometer 42.0 of November 1994 because this data set is relatively recent and contains more indicators of political awareness than other Eurobarometer data sets. The data were kindly provided by ZEUS, University of Mannheim.

5 Hasebrink (1992: D38) presents similar results, based on commercial ratings research.

6 As, for instance, analyses based on the American NES data, e.g. Bartels (1993).

7 Here is the story of the cat-dog as recounted by Sartori: 'When a researcher sets out on a world-wide safari to study the mysterious cat-dog – an animal hypothesised to emit the sound "bow wow" – he finds that some cat-dogs do not actually make the sound. Perhaps the cat-dog emits another sound like "meow meow". Again, some do and some don't. What this means is "simply that the cat-dog *does not exist*"' (1991: 247; emphasis original).

8 For a similar hierarchical conceptualisation see Voltmer (1998).

9 An example is Converse's classic study on 'Information Flow and the Stability of Partisan Attitudes' (1966), where media exposure is measured by counting the number of different media used by a voter.

10 Principal investigators of the German CNEP project are Max Kaase, Hans-Dieter Klingemann, Manfred Küchler, and Franz Urban Pappi. It is directed by Rüdiger Schmitt-Beck. Also involved are Rolf Hackenbroch, Rainer Mathes, Barbara Pfetsch, Peter Schrott, Katrin Voltmer, and Bernhard Weßels. The Spanish project is directed by Richard Gunther, José Ramón Montero, Francisco Llera, and Francesc Pallarès. The American project is directed by Paul Allen Beck, Russell J. Dalton, and Robert Huckfeldt. The author wishes to thank the Spanish and American colleagues for allowing him to use their data for the analyses presented in this chapter.

11 The distinct political heritage of the former German Democratic Republic makes it necessary to study it separately. In order to avoid complications of terminology, we use the term 'four countries', although East Germany is not a country any more.

12 For comparisons of content structures of the various types of newspapers, see Wilke (1994: 90–3) for Germany, and Negrine (1996: 55) for Britain.

13 As an illustration it is worth mentioning that many readers of the German *Bild-Zeitung* seem not to regard it as a genuine newspaper. In the German CNEP study many respondents answered 'none' when asked if they read a daily newspaper, but answered affirmatively when asked whether they read the *Bild-Zeitung*.

14 While daily tabloids are only marginally important in the United States (and thus cannot be analysed separately here), there is a widely read weekly tabloid press. However, these notorious 'supermarket tabloids' (e.g. *National Enquirer*) fill their pages mostly with celebrity gossip and 'paparazzi' photos plus a bizarre mix of stories about monsters and aliens, while only scarcely paying attention to political matters.

15 Regular usage is operationally defined as habitual reception on six or seven days per week.

References

Aarts, K. (1995) Intermediate Organizations and Interest Representation, in H.-D. Klingemann and D. Fuchs (eds), *Citizens and the State*. Oxford: Oxford University Press, pp. 227–57.

Abramson, P. R. and R. Inglehart (1995) *Value Change in Global Perspective*. Ann Arbor: University of Michigan Press.

Addison, P. (1975) *The Road to 1945. British Politics and the Second World War*. London: Cape.

Adorno, T. W., E. Fraenkel-Brunswick, D. J. Levinson, and R. N. Sanford (1950) *The Authoritarian Personality*. New York: Harper.

Allerbeck, K. R. (1977) Analysis and Inference in Cross-national Survey Research, in A. Szalai, R. Petrella, S. Rokkan, and E. K. Scheuch (eds), *Cross-national Comparative Survey Research. Theory and Practice*. Oxford: Pergamon Press, pp. 373–402.

Allport, G. W. (1958) *The Nature of Prejudice*. New York: Doubleday.

Almond, G. A. and S. Verba (1963) *The Civic Culture. Political Attitudes and Democracy in Five Nations*. Princeton: Princeton University Press.

Altheide, D. L. and R. P. Snow (1988) Toward a Theory of Mediation, in J. A. Anderson (ed.), *Communication Yearbook* (Vol.11). Newbury Park: Sage, pp. 194–223.

Altheide, D. L. and R. P. Snow (1991) *Media Worlds in the Postjournalism Era*. New York: de Gruyter, Inc.

Alwin, D. F., M. Braun, J. Harkness, and J. Scott (1994) Measurement in Multi-national Surveys, in I. Borg and P. P. Mohler (eds), *Trends and Perspectives in Empirical Social Research*. Berlin: de Gruyter, pp. 26–39.

Alwin, D. F., M. Braun, and J. Scott (1992) The Separation of Work and the Family. Attitudes Toward Women's Labour Force Participation in Germany, Great Britain, and the United States. *European Sociological Review*, 8(1), pp. 13–37.

Alwin, D. F., J. Scott, and M. Braun (1996) Sex-Role Attitude Change in the United States: National Trends and Cross-national Comparisons, unpublished manuscript.

Amenta, E. and J. D. Poulsen (1994) Where to Begin. A Survey of Five Approaches to Selecting Independent Variables for Qualitative Comparative Analysis. *Sociological Methods & Research*, 23(1), pp. 22–53.

Anderson, C. J. and C. A. Guillory (1997) Political Institutions and Satisfaction with Democracy: A Cross-national Analysis of Consensus and Majoritarian Systems. *American Political Science Review*, 91(1), pp. 66–81.

Anheier, H. K. and W. Seibel (1990) The Third Sector in Comparative Perspective: Four Propositions, in H. K. Anheier and W. Seibel (eds), *The Third Sector: Comparative Studies of Nonprofit Organizations*. Berlin: de Gruyter, pp. 379–87.

Ansolabehere, S., R. Behr, and S. Iyengar (1993) *The Media Game. American Politics in the Television Age.* New York: Macmillan.

Asp, K. (1983) The Struggle for the Agenda. Party Agenda, Media Agenda and Voters' Agenda in the 1979 Swedish Election Campaign, in W. Schulz and K. Schönbach (eds), *Massenmedien und Wahlen. Mass Media and Elections: International Research Perspectives.* München: Ölschläger, pp. 301–20.

Babchuk, N. and A. Booth (1969) Voluntary Association Membership. *American Sociological Review,* 34(1), pp. 31–45.

Bachman, J. G. and P. M. O'Malley (1984) Yes-saying, Nay-saying, and Going to Extremes: Black–White Differences in Response Styles. *Public Opinion Quarterly,* 48(2), pp. 491–509.

Baggott, R. (1995) From Confrontation to Consultation? Pressure Group Relations from Thatcher to Major. *Parliamentary Affairs,* 48(3), pp. 484–502.

Ball-Rokeach, S. J. (1985) The Origins of Individual Media-System Dependency. A Sociological Framework. *Communication Research,* 12(4), pp. 485–510.

Bardi, L. S. and L. Morlino (1994) Italy: Tracing the Roots of the Great Transformation, in R. S. Katz and P. Mair (eds), *How Parties Organize. Change and Adaptation in Party Organizations in Western Democracies.* London: Sage, pp. 242–77.

Barnes, S. H., M. Kaase, K. R. Allerbeck, B. G. Farah, F. Heunks, R. Inglehart, M. Kent Jennings, H.-D. Klingemann, A. Marsh, and L. Rosenmayer (1979) *Political Action. Mass Participation in Five Western Democracies.* Beverly Hills: Sage.

Bartels, L. M. (1986) Issue Voting under Uncertainty: An Empirical Test. *American Journal of Political Science,* 30, pp. 709–28.

Bartels, L. M. (1993) Messages Received: The Political Impact of Media Exposure. *American Political Science Review,* 87(2), pp. 267–85.

Bartolini, S. and P. Mair (1990) *Identity, Competition and Electoral Availability. The Stabilization of European Electorates, 1885–1985.* Cambridge: Cambridge University Press.

Baumann, Z. (1991) Moderne und Ambivalenz: Das Ende der Eindeutigkeit, in U. Bielefeld (ed.), *Das Eigene und das Fremde – Neuer Rassismus in der Alten Welt?* Hamburg: Junius, pp. 23–49.

Baumgartner, F. R. and J. L. Walker (1988) Survey Research and Membership in Voluntary Associations. *American Journal of Political Science,* 32(4), pp. 908–27.

Baumgartner, F. R. and J. L. Walker (1990) Response to Smith's 'Trends in Voluntary Group Membership: Comments on Baumgartner und Walker': Measurement Validity and the Continuity of Results in Survey Results. *American Journal of Political Science,* 34(3), pp. 662–70.

Beck, U. (1986) *Risikogesellschaft. Auf dem Weg in eine andere Moderne.* Frankfurt a. M.: Suhrkamp.

Becker, J. W. and R. Vink (1994) *Secularisatie in Nederland 1966–1991: de verandering van opvattingen en enkele gedragingen.* Rijswijk: Sociaal en Cultureel Planbureau.

Bendix, R. (1963) Concepts and Generalizations in Comparative Sociological Studies, *American Sociological Review,* 28(4), pp. 532–9.

Benninghaus, H. (1989) *Deskriptive Statistik.* Stuttgart: Teubner.

Berger, P. (1977) *Facing up to Modernity.* New York: Basic Books.

Berry, D. (1969) Party Membership and Social Participation. *Political Studies,* 17(2), pp. 196–207.

Berthouzoz, R. (1991) Religion und Glaube, in A. Melich (ed.), *Die Werte der Schweizer.* Bern: Lang, pp. 167–231.

Bielefeldt, H. (1994) Toleranz und Menschenrechte, in A. Wierlacher (ed.), *Jahrbuch Deutsch als Fremdsprache.* München: Iudicium, pp. 177–84.

Blumler, J. G. (1990) Elections, the Media and the Modern Publicity Process, in M. Ferguson (ed.), *Public Communication. The New Imperatives*. London: Sage, pp. 101–13.

Blumler, J. G. and A. D. Fox (1980) The Involvement of Voters in the European Elections of 1979: Its Extent and Sources. *European Journal of Political Research*, 8(4), pp. 359–85.

Blumler, J. G. and M. Gurevitch (1975) Towards a Comparative Framework for Political Communication Research, in S. H. Chaffee (ed.), *Political Communication. Issues and Strategies for Research*. Beverly Hills: Sage, pp. 165–93.

Blumler, J. G., A. Ewbank, R. Cayrol, C. Geerts, and G. Thoveron (1978a) A Three-Nation Analysis of Voters' Attitudes to Election Communication. *European Journal of Political Research*, 6(2), pp. 127–56.

Blumler, J. G., G. Thoveron, R. Cayrol, C. Geerts, and A. Ewbank (1978b) *La télévision – fait-elle l'élection? Une analyse comparative: France, Grande-Bretagne, Belgique*. Paris: Presses de la Fondation Nationale des Sciences Politiques.

Blumler, J. G., J. M. McLeod, and K. E. Rosengren (eds) (1992) *Comparatively Speaking: Communication and Culture Across Space and Time*. Newbury Park: Sage.

Bollen, K. A., B. Entwisle, and A. S. Alderson (1993) Macrocomparative Research Methods. *Annual Review of Sociology*, 19, pp. 321–51.

Borg, I. and P. Groenen (1997) *Modern Multidimensional Scaling. Theory and Application*. New York: Springer.

Borg, I. and S. Shye (1995) *Facet Theory: Form and Content*. Newbury Park: Sage.

Bortz, J. (1989) *Statistik für Sozialwissenschaftler*. Berlin: Springer.

Braun, M. (1993) Potential Problems of Functional Equivalence in ISSP 1988 (Family and Changing Gender Roles), paper presented at the ISSP Scientific Meeting.

Braun, M. (1994) The International Social Survey Program (ISSP), in P. Flora, F. Kraus, H.-H. Noll, and F. Rothenbacher (eds), *Social Statistics and Social Reporting in and for Europe*. Bonn: Informationszentrum Sozialwissenschaften, pp. 305–11.

Braun, M. (1997) Methodological Experiments on Gender-Role Attitudes, unpublished manuscript.

Braun, M., D. F. Alwin, and J. Scott (1994) Wandel in den Einstellungen zur Rolle der Frau in Deutschland und den Vereinigten Staaten, in M. Braun and P. P. Mohler (eds), *Blickpunkt Gesellschaft, 3. Einstellungen und Verhalten der Bundesbürger*. Opladen: Westdeutscher Verlag, pp. 151–73.

Braun, M. and P. P. Mohler (1991) Die allgemeine Bevölkerungsumfrage der Sozialwissenschaften (ALLBUS): Rückblick und Ausblick in die neunziger Jahre. *ZUMA-Nachrichten*, 29, pp. 7–28.

Braun, M. and J. Scott (1998) Multidimensional Scaling and Equivalence – Or: Is 'Having a Job' the Same as 'Working', in J. Harkness (ed.), *Cross-cultural Survey Equivalence*. Mannheim: Zentrum für Umfragen, Methoden und Analysen. ZUMA-Nachrichten Special No. 3.

Braun, M., J. Scott, and D. F. Alwin (1994) Economic Necessity or Self-Actualization? Attitudes towards Women's Labour-Force Participation in East and West Germany. *European Sociological Review*, 10(1), pp. 29–47.

Brazier, R. (1991) *Constitutional Reform. Re-shaping the British Political System*. Oxford: Clarendon Press.

Browne, D. R. (1989) *Comparing Broadcast Systems. The Experiences of Six Industrialized Nations*. Ames: Iowa State University Press.

Bruck, P. A. and G. Stocker (1996) *Die ganz normale Vielfältigkeit des Lesens. Zur Rezeption von Boulevardzeitungen*. Münster: Lit.

Budge, I., D. Robertson, and D. Hearl (eds) (1987) *Ideology, Strategy and Party Change. Spatial*

Analyses of Post-War Election Programmes in 19 Democracies. Cambridge: Cambridge University Press.

Bustamante, E. (1989) TV and Public Service in Spain: A Difficult Encounter. *Media Culture and Society*, 11(1), pp. 67–87.

Carmines, E. G. and J. H. Kuklinski (1990) Incentives, Opportunities, and the Logic of Public Opinion in American Political Representation, in J. A. Ferejohn, and J. H. Kuklinski (eds), *Information and Democratic Processes*. Urbana: University of Illinois Press, pp. 240–68.

Carmines, E. G. and J. A. Stimson (1980) The Two Faces of Issue Voting. *American Political Science Review*, 74(1), pp. 78–91.

Cattell, R. B. (1966) *Handbook of Multivariate Experimental Psychology*. Chicago: Rand McNally.

Cayrol, R. (1983) Media Use and Campaign Evaluations: Social and Political Stratification of the European Electorate, in J. G. Blumler (ed.), *Communicating to Voters. Television in the First European Parliamentary Elections*. London: Sage, pp. 163–80.

Cayrol, R. (1991) European Elections and the Pre-electoral Period: Media Use and Campaign Evaluations. *European Journal of Political Research*, 19(1), pp. 17–29.

CEU (Central European University) (1994a) The Development of Party Systems and Electoral Alignments in East Central Europe. The April 1994 Survey in Hungary. Machine Readable Data File. Budapest: Department of Political Science: Central European University.

CEU (Central European University) (1994b) The Development of Party Systems and Electoral Alignments in East Central Europe. The Fall 1994 Surveys in Poland and the Czech Republic. Machine Readable Data Files. Budapest: Department of Political Science: Central European University.

Cherlin, A. and P. Barnhouse Walters (1981) Trends in United States Men's and Women's Sex-Role Attitudes: 1972 to 1978. *American Sociological Review*, 46(4), pp. 453–60.

Clausen, A. R. (1967) Measurement Identity in the Longitudinal Analysis of Legislative Voting. *American Political Science Review*, 61, pp. 1,020–35.

Coleman, J. S. (1988) Social Capital in the Creation of Human Capital. *American Journal of Sociology*, 94 (supplement), pp. 95–119.

Collier, D. (1991) The Comparative Method: Two Decades of Change, in D. A. Rustow and K. P. Erickson (eds), *Comparative Political Dynamics: Global Research Perspectives*. New York: Harper Collins, pp. 7–31.

Colomer, J. M. (1996) Introduction, in J. M. Colomer (ed.), *Political Institutions in Europe*. London: Routledge, pp. 1–17.

Comstock, G. (1991) *Television in America*. Newbury Park: Sage.

Converse, P. E. (1964) The Nature of Belief Systems in Mass Publics, in D. E. Apter (ed.), *Ideology and Discontent*. New York: The Free Press, pp. 206–61.

Converse, P. E. (1966) Information Flow and the Stability of Partisan Attitudes, in A. Campbell, P. E. Converse, W. E. Miller, and D. E. Stokes (eds), *Elections and the Political Order*. New York: Wiley, pp. 136–57.

Crepaz, M. M. L. (1990) The Impact of Party Polarization and Postmaterialism on Voter Turnout: A Comparative Study of 16 Industrial Democracies. *European Journal of Political Research*, 18(2), pp. 183–205.

Crutchfield, R. S. and D. A. Gordon (1947) Variations in Respondents' Interpretations of an Opinion-Poll Question. *International Journal of Opinion and Attitude Research*, 1, pp. 1–12.

Curtis, J. E., E. G. Grabb, and D. E. Baer (1992) Voluntary Association Membership in Fifteen Countries: A Comparative Analysis, *American Sociological Review*, 57(2), pp. 139–52.

Cutler, S. J. (1973) Voluntary Association Membership and the Theory of Mass Society, in

E. O. Laumann (ed.), *Bonds of Pluralism: The Form and Substance of Urban Social Networks*. New York: Wiley, pp. 133–59.

Dalton, R. J. (1984) Cognitive Mobilization and Partisan Dealignment in Advanced Industrial Democracies. *Journal of Politics*, 46(1), pp. 264–84.

Dalton, R. J. (1994) *The Green Rainbow. Environmental Groups in Western Europe.* New Haven: Yale University Press.

Dalton, R. J., S. C. Flanagan, and P. A. Beck (eds) (1984) *Electoral Change in Advanced Industrial Democracies: Realignment or Dealignment?* Princeton: Princeton University Press.

Dalton, R. J. and M. Kuechler (eds) (1990) *Challenging the Political Order. New Social and Political Movements in Western Democracies.* New York: Oxford University Press.

Dalton, R. J., H. Semetko, and K. Voltmer (1996) Media Content and the Intermediation Process: Cross-national Comparisons. Paper prepared for presentation at the Conference of the Comparative National Elections Project, Madrid.

Davis, J. A. and R. Jowell (1989) Measuring National Differences: An Introduction to the International Social Survey Program (ISSP), in R. Jowell, S. Witherspoon, and L. Brook (eds), *British Social Attitudes: Special International Report.* Aldershot: Gower, pp. 1–13.

Davis, J. A. and T. W. Smith (1996) *General Social Surveys, 1972–1996.* Chicago: National Opinion Research Center.

de Macedo, B. J. (1983) Newspapers and Democracy in Portugal: The Role of Market Structure, in K. Maxwell (ed.), *The Press and the Rebirth of Iberian Democracy.* Westport: Greenwood Press, pp. 55–89.

de Meur, G. and D. Berg-Schlosser (1994) Comparing Political Systems: Establishing Similarities and Dissimilarities. *European Journal of Political Research*, 26(2), pp. 193–219.

De Wit, H. and J. Billiet (1995) The MTMM Design: Back to the Founding Fathers, in W. E. Saris and Á. Münnich (eds), *The Multitrait-Multimethod Approach to Evaluate Measurement Instruments,* Budapest: Eötvös University Press (pp. 39–60).

DeFelice, E. G. (1980) Comparison Misconceived. Common Nonsense in Comparative Politics. *Comparative Politics*, 13(1), pp. 119–25.

Deutsch, K. W. (1961) Social Mobilization and Political Development. *American Political Science Review*, 55, pp. 493–514.

Deutscher, I. (1968) Asking Questions Cross-culturally: Some Problems of Linguistic Comparability, in H. S. Becker, B. Geer, D. Riesman, and R. S. Weiss (eds), *Institutions and the Person.* Chicago: Aldine Publishing Company, pp. 318–41.

Dimock, M. A. and S. L. Popkin (1997) Political Knowledge in Comparative Perspective, in S. Iyengar and R. Reeves (eds), *Do the Media Govern? Politicians, Voters and Reporters in America.* Thousand Oaks: Sage, pp. 217–24.

Dobbelaere, K. (1984) Secularization Theories and Sociological Paradigms: Convergences and Divergences. *Social Compass*, 31(2–3), pp. 119–219.

Dobbelaere, K. (1995a) Religion in Europe and North America, in R. de Moor (ed.), *Values in Western Society.* Tilburg: Tilburg University Press, pp. 1–29.

Dobbelaere, K. (1995b) The Surviving Dominant Catholic Church in Belgium: A Consequence of its Popular Religious Practices, in W. C. Roof, J. W. Carroll, and D. A. Roozen (eds), *The Post-War Generation and Establishment Religion: Cross-cultural Perspectives.* Boulder: Westview, pp. 171–90.

Dobbelaere, K. and W. Jagodzinski (1995) Religious Cognitions and Beliefs, in J. W. van Deth and E. Scarbrough (eds), *The Impact of Values.* Oxford: Oxford University Press, pp. 197–217.

Dodd, L. C. (1976) *Coalitions in Parliamentary Government.* Princeton: Princeton University Press.

Duchesne, S. and P. Frognier (1995) Is There European Identity?, in O. Niedermayer and R. Sinnot (eds), *Public Opinion and Internationalized Governance*. Oxford: Oxford University Press, pp. 193–226.

Durkheim, E. (1981[1985]) *Les règles de la méthode sociologique*. Paris: Presses Universitaires de France.

Duverger, M. (1964) *Political Parties. Their Organization and Activity in the Modern State*. London: Methuen (3rd edn).

Ehrlich, H. J., J. W. Rinehart, and J. C. Howell (1962) The Study of Role Conflict: Explorations in Methodology. *Sociometry*, 25, pp. 85–97.

Eisinga, R. (1995) World Views in Support of Traditional Christian Religion, in L. van Vucht Tijssen, J. Berting, and F. Lechner (eds), *The Search for Fundamentals. The Process of Modernisation and the Quest for Meaning*. London: Kluwer Academic, pp. 83–93.

Eisinga, R. and A. Felling (1990) Church Membership in the Netherlands, 1960–1987. A Methodological Note. *Journal for the Scientific Study of Religion*, 29(1), pp. 108–12.

Eisinga, R., J. Lammers, and J. Peters (1990) Localism and Religiosity in the Netherlands. *Journal for the Scientific Study of Religion*, 29(4), pp. 496–504.

Elder, N., A. H. Thomas, and D. Arter (1988) *The Consensual Democracies? The Government and Politics of the Scandinavian States* (rev. edn). Oxford: Blackwell.

Ernst, J. (1987) Democratic versus Autocratic Communications: A Comparison of American News and the German Nachricht. *Communications*, 13(3), pp. 47–54.

Esping-Andersen, G. (1990) *The Three Worlds of Welfare Capitalism*. Oxford: Polity Press.

Esser, H. (1996) *Soziologie. Allgemeine Grundlagen*. Frankfurt a. M.: Campus.

Etzioni, A. (1993) *The Spirit of Community*. New York: Crown Publishers.

Etzioni, A. (1997) *The New Golden Rule. Community and Morality in a Democratic Society*. New York: Basic Books.

Eulau, H. (1977) Multilevel Methods in Comparative Politics. *American Behavioral Scientist*, 21(1), pp. 39–62.

Evans, S. M. and H. C. Boyte (1992) *Free Spaces*. Chicago: University of Chicago Press.

Fair, J. D. (1980) *British Interparty Conferences: A Study of the Procedure of Conciliation in British Politics, 1867–1921*. Oxford: Clarendon Press.

Farrell, D. M. (1994) Ireland: Centralization, Professionalization, and Competitive Pressures, in R. S. Katz and P. Mair (eds), *How Parties Organize. Change and Adaptation in Party Organizations in Western Democracies*. London: Sage, pp. 216–41.

Faul, E. (1989) Frankreich und die Bundesrepublik Deutschland im Fernsehen. Bilder und Gegenbilder, in M. Kaase and W. Schulz (eds), *Massenkommunikation. Theorien, Methoden, Befunde*. Opladen: Westdeutscher Verlag, pp. 150–64.

Feagin, J. R., A. M. Orum, and G. Sjoberg (eds) (1991) *A Case for the Case Study*. Chapel Hill and London: University of North Carolina Press.

Feldkircher, M. (1997) Geteiltes Volk – geteilte Werte? Eine Erziehungszielanalyse in West- und Ostdeutschland, in W. Müller (ed.), *Soziale Ungleichheit. Neue Befunde zu Strukturen, Bewußtsein und Politik*. Opladen: Leske + Budrich, pp. 205–33.

Felling, A., J. Peters, and O. Schreuder (1987) *Religion im Vergleich: Bundesrepublik Deutschland und Niederlande*. Frankfurt a. M.: Lang.

Ferree, M. M. (1974) A Woman for President? Changing Responses: 1958–1972. *Public Opinion Quarterly*, 38(3), pp. 390–9.

Fetscher, I. (1990) *Toleranz. Von der Unentbehrlichkeit einer kleinen Tugend für die Demokratie. Historische Rückblicke und aktuelle Probleme*. Stuttgart: Radius-Verlag.

Fix, E. (1995) Die Genese der 'Bewegungspartei' als neuer Parteityp im politischen System Italiens, in B. Nedelmann (ed.), *Politische Institutionen im Wandel*. Sonderheft 35 der Kölner

Zeitschrift für Soziologie und Sozialpsychologie. Opladen: Westdeutscher Verlag, pp. 188–214.

Frenzel, I. (1974) Das Dilemma einer Idee. Ein historischer Rückblick, in U. Schultz (ed.), *Toleranz. Die Krise der demokratischen Tugend und sechzehn Vorschläge zu ihrer Überwindung.* Reinbek b. Hamburg: Rowohlt, pp. 7–21.

Fritzsche, K. P. (1995) Toleranz im Umbruch. Über die Schwierigkeiten, tolerant zu sein, *Aus Politik und Zeitgeschichte. Beilage zur Wochenzeitung Das Parlament*, B(43), pp. 9–17.

Fukuyama, F. (1995) *Trust: The Social Virtues and the Creation of Prosperity.* New York: The Free Press.

Furlong, P. F. (1988) Authority, Change, and Conflict in Italian Catholicism, in T. M. Gannon (ed.), *World Catholicism in Transition.* New York: Macmillan, pp. 116–32.

Gabriel, O. W. (1998) Fragen an einen europäischen Vergleich, in R. Köcher and J. Schild (eds), *Wertewandel in Deutschland und Frankreich. Nationale Unterschiede und europäische Gemeinsamkeiten.* Opladen: Leske + Budrich, pp. 29–51.

Gamble, A. (1988) *The Free Economy and the Strong State. The Politics of Thatcherism.* London: Macmillan.

Gamson, W. A. (1988) The 1987 Distinguished Lecture: A Constructionist Approach to Mass Media and Public Opinion. *Symbolic Interaction*, 11(2), pp. 161–74.

Gaskin, K. and J. D. Smith (1995) *A New Civic Europe? A Study of the Extent and the Role of Volunteering.* London: Volunteer Centre UK.

Gerstlé, J., D. K. Davis, and O. Duhamel (1991) Television News and the Construction of Political Reality in France and the United States, in L. L. Kaid, J. Gerstlé, and K. R. Sanders (eds), *Mediated Politics in Two Cultures: Presidential Campaigning in the United States and France.* New York: Praeger, pp. 119–44.

Glover, J. (1996) Epistemological Considerations in Secondary Analysis, in L. Hantrais and S. Mangen (eds), *Cross-national Research Methods in the Social Sciences.* London and New York: Pinter, pp. 28–37.

Granberg, D. and S. Holmberg (1988) *The Political System Matters. Social Psychology and Voting Behavior in Sweden and the United States.* Cambridge: Cambridge University Press.

Gurevitch, M. (1989) Comparative Research on Television News. Problems and Challenges. *American Behavioral Scientist*, 33(2), pp. 221–29.

Gurevitch, M. and J. G. Blumler (1990) Comparative Research: The Extending Frontier, in D. L. Swanson and D. Nimmo (eds), *New Directions in Political Communication. A Resource Book.* Newbury Park: Sage, pp. 305–25.

Haller, M. and E. Janes (1996) Soziale Determinanten von Kirchlichkeit und Religiosität in Österreich, in M. Haller, K. Holm, K. H. Müller, W. Schulz, and E. Cyba (eds), *Österreich im Wandel. Werte, Lebensformen und Lebensqualität 1986 bis 1993.* Wien: Verlag für Geschichte und Politik; München: Oldenbourg, pp. 243–74.

Hallin, D. C. and P. Mancini (1984) Speaking of the President. Political Structure and Representational Form in U.S. and Italian Television News. *Theory and Society*, 13(6), pp. 829–50.

Halman, L. and R. de Moor (1993) Comparative Research on Values, in P. Ester, L. Halman, and R. de Moor (eds), *The Individualizing Society. Value Change in Europe and North America.* Tilburg: Tilburg University Press, pp. 21–36.

Hans-Bredow-Institut (ed.) (1996) *Internationales Jahrbuch für Rundfunk und Fernsehen 1996/97.* Baden-Baden: Nomos.

Harding, S., D. Phillips, and M. P. Fogarty (1986) *Contrasting Values in Western Europe. Unity, Diversity and Change.* Houndmills: Macmillan.

Hartmann, J. (1995) *Vergleichende Politikwissenschaft. Ein Lehrbuch.* Frankfurt a. M.: Campus.

Hasebrink, U. (1992) Medienangebot und Mediennutzung in Europa – ein Überblick, in Hans-Bredow-Institut (ed.), *Internationales Jahrbuch für Rundfunk und Fernsehen 1992/93*. Baden-Baden: Nomos, pp. D28–D43.

Helmreich, R. L., J. T. Spence, and R. H. Gibson (1982) Sex-Role Attitudes,1972–1980. *Personality and Social Psychology Bulletin*, 8(4), pp. 656–63.

Helms, L. (1995) Parteiensysteme als Systemstruktur. Zur methodisch-analytischen Konzeption der funktional vergleichenden Parteiensystemanalyse. *Zeitschrift für Parlamentsfragen*, 4, pp. 642–57.

Herzog, D. (1997) Die Führungsgremien der Parteien: Funktionswandel und Strukturentwicklungen, in O. W. Gabriel, O. Niedermayer, and R. Stöss (eds), *Parteiendemokratie in Deutschland*. Bonn: Bundeszentrale für politische Bildung, pp. 301–22.

Hillmann, K.-H. (1986) *Wertwandel. Zur Frage soziokultureller Voraussetzungen alternativer Lebensformen*. Darmstadt: Wissenschaftliche Buchgesellschaft.

Hoepflinger, F. (1987) *Wandel der Familienbildung in Westeuropa*. Frankfurt a. M.: Campus.

Hoffmann-Riem, W. (1991) The Road to Media Unification: Press and Broadcasting Law Reform in the GDR. *European Journal of Communication*, 6(4), pp. 523–43.

Hofstadter, D. R. (1985) Analogies and Roles in Human and Machine Thinking, in D. R. Hofstadter (ed.), *Metamagical Themas: Questing for the Essence of Mind and Pattern*. New York: Basic Books, pp. 547–603.

Höllinger, F. (1991) Frauenerwerbstätigkeit und Wandel der Geschlechtsrollen im internationalen Vergleich. *Kölner Zeitschrift für Soziologie und Sozialpsychologie*, 43(4), pp. 753–71.

Holtz-Bacha, C., L. L. Kaid, and A. Johnston (1994) Political Television Advertising in Western Democracies: A Comparison of Campaign Broadcasts in the United States, Germany, and France. *Political Communication*, 11, pp. 67–80.

Honderich, T. (1995) *The Oxford Companion to Philosophy*. Oxford: Oxford University Press.

Huber, E., C. C. Ragin, and J. D. Stephens (1993) Social Democracy, Christian Democracy, Constitutional Structure, and the Welfare State. *American Journal of Sociology*, 99(3), pp. 711–49.

Huggins, R. and J. Turner (1997) The Politics of Influence and Control, in B. Axford, G. K. Browning, R. Huggins, B. Rosamond, and J. Turner (eds), *Politics. An Introduction*. London: Routledge, pp. 369–407.

Hume, D. (1969 [1739]) *A Treatise of Human Nature*, in E. C. Mossner (ed. with an intro.). Harmondsworth: Penguin.

Hume, E. (1996) The New Paradigm for News, in K. Hall Jamieson (ed.), *The Media and Politics* (Annals of the American Academy of Political and Social Science 546). Thousand Oaks: Sage, pp. 141–53.

Hunyady, Y. and Á. Münnich (1995) A Modified True Score MTMM Model for Analysing Stereotype Effects of Characterizations of Nations, in W. E. Saris and Á. Münnich (eds), *The Multitrait-Multimethod Approach to Evaluate Measurement Instruments*. Budapest: Eötvös University Press, pp. 173–84.

Hunziker, P. (1988) *Medien, Kommunikation und Gesellschaft. Einführung in die Soziologie der Massenkommunikation*. Darmstadt: Wissenschaftliche Buchgesellschaft.

Hyman, H. H. and C. R. Wright (1971) Trends in Voluntary Association Memberships of American Adults: Replication based on Secondary Analysis of National Samples Surveys. *American Sociological Review*, 36(2), pp. 191–206.

Immergut, E. M. (1992) *Health Politics: Interests and Institutions in Western Europe*. Cambridge: Cambridge University Press.

Inglehart, R. (1977) *The Silent Revolution: Changing Values and Political Styles Among Western Publics*. Princeton: Princeton University Press.

Inglehart, R. (1990) *Culture Shift in Advanced Industrial Society.* Princeton: Princeton University Press.

Inglehart, R. (1995) Public Support for Environmental Protection: The Impact of Objective Problems and Subjective Values in 43 Societies, *Political Science & Politics*, 28(1), pp. 57–71.

Inglehart, R. (1997) *Modernization and Postmodernization. Cultural, Economic, and Political Change in 43 Societies.* Princeton: Princeton University Press.

Inglehart, R. and P. Abramson (1992) Value Change in Advanced Industrial Society: Problems in Conceptualization and Measurement. Paper presented at the annual meeting of the Western Political Science Association, San Fransisco.

Inglehart, R. and M. Carballo (1997) Does Latin America Exist? (and Is There a Confusion Culture?) A Global Analysis of Cross-cultural Differences, *Political Science & Politics*, 30(1), pp. 34–46.

Iversen, T. (1994) The Logics of Electoral Politics: Spatial, Directional, and Mobilizational Effects, *Comparative Political Studies*, 27(2), pp. 155–89.

Jackman, R. W. (1985) Cross-national Statistical Research and the Study of Comparative Politics, *American Journal of Political Science*, 29(1), pp. 161–82.

Jagodzinski, W. and K. Dobbelaere (1995) Secularization and Church Religiosity, in J. W. van Deth and E. Scarbrough (eds), *The Impact of Values*. Oxford: Oxford University Press, pp. 76–119.

Jennings, M. Kent, J. W. van Deth, S. H. Barnes, D. Fuchs, F. J. Heunks, R. Inglehart, M. Kaase, H.-D. Klingemann, and J. J. A. Thomassen (1990) *Continuities in Political Action: A Longitudinal Study of Political Orientations in Three Western Democracies*. Berlin: de Gruyter.

Jogerst, M. (1993) *Reform in the House of Commons. The Select Committee System*. Lexington: University of Kentucky.

Johnson, N. (1986) The Majority Principle and Consensus in the British Constitutional Tradition, in H. Hattenhauer and W. Kaltefleiter (eds), *Mehrheitsprinzip, Konsens und Verfassung*. Heidelberg: Müller, pp. 151–67.

Jung, S. (1996) Lijpharts Demokratietypen und die direkte Demokratie. *Zeitschrift für Politikwissenschaft*, 6(3), pp. 623–45.

Kaase, M. (1982) Partizipatorische Revolution – Ende der Parteien?, in J. Raschke (ed.), *Bürger und Parteien: Ansichten und Analysen einer schwierigen Beziehung*. Opladen: Westdeutscher Verlag, pp. 173–89.

Kaase, M., F. Neidhardt, and B. Pfetsch (1997) Politik und Ökonomie der Massenkommunikation: Forschungsdesiderate unter veränderten Strukturbedingungen des Mediensystems. *Publizistik*, 42(1), pp. 3–15.

Kaid, L. L. (1991) The Effects of Television Broadcasts on Perceptions of Presidential Candidates in the United States and France, in L. L. Kaid, J. Gerstlé, and K. R. Sanders (eds), *Mediated Politics in Two Cultures. Presidential Campaigning in the United States and France*. New York: Praeger, pp. 247–60.

Kaiser, A. (1997a) Types of Democracy: From Classical to New Institutionalism. *Journal of Theoretical Politics*, 9(4), pp. 419–44.

Kaiser, A. (1997b) House of Lords and Monarchy: British Majoritarian Democracy and the Current Reform Debate on its Pre-democratic Institutions, in U. Jordan and W. Kaiser (eds), *Political Reform in Britain, 1886–1996: Themes, Ideas, Policies*. Bochum: Brockmeyer, pp. 81–109.

Kaiser, A. (1998a) Pfadabhängigkeit und Lernen: Zur Dynamik der neuseeländischen Institutionenreformen, in A. Kaiser (ed.), *Regieren in Westminster-Demokratien*. Baden-Baden: Nomos (forthcoming).

Kaiser, A. (1998b) Verbände und Politik, in H. Kastendiek, K. Rohe, and A. Volle (eds), *Großbritannien. Geschichte – Politik – Wirtschaft – Gesellschaft* (second edn). Frankfurt a. M.: Campus, pp. 230–44.

Kalleberg, A. L. (1966–1967) The Logic of Comparison. A Methodological Note on the Comparative Study of Political Systems. *World Politics*, 19, pp. 69–82.

Katz, R. S. and P. Mair (1993) The Evolution of Party Organization in Europe: The Three Faces of Party Organization, in W. Crolly (ed.), *Parties in an Age of Change*. Special Issue of the *American Review of Politics*, 14, pp. 593–617.

Katz, R. S. and P. Mair (1995) Changing Models of Party Organization and Party Democracy: The Emergence of the Cartel Party. *Party Politics*, 1(1), pp. 5–28.

Katz, R. S. and P. Mair (eds) (1992a) *Party Organizations. A Data Handbook on Party Organizations in Western Democracies, 1960–90*. London: Sage.

Katz, R. S. and P. Mair (1992b) Introduction: The Cross-National Study of Party Organizations, in R. S. Katz and P. Mair (eds), *Organizations. A Data Handbook on Party Organizations in Western Democracies, 1960–90*. London: Sage, pp. 1–20.

Katz, R. S. and P. Mair (eds) (1994) *How Parties Organize. Change and Adaptation in Party Organizations in Western Democracies*. London: Sage.

Kelley, J. and N. D. de Graaf (1997) National Context, Parental Socialization, and Religious Belief: Results from 15 Nations. *American Sociological Review*, 62(4), pp. 639–59.

Kim, J.-O. and C. W. Mueller (1978) *Factor Analysis. Statistical Methods and Practical Issues*. London: Sage.

King, G., J. Alt, N. E. Burns, and M. Laver (1990) A Unified Model of Cabinet Dissolution in Parliamentary Democracies. *American Journal of Political Science*, 34(3), pp. 846–71.

King, G., R. O. Keohane, and S. Verba (1994) *Designing Social Enquiry. Scientific Inference in Qualitative Research*. Princeton: Princeton University Press.

Kinsey, A. C., W. P. Pommeroy, and C. E. Martin (1948) *Sexual Behavior in the Human Male*. Philadelphia: Saunders.

Kirchheimer, O. (1965) Der Wandel des westeuropäischen Parteisystems. *Politische Vierteljahresschrift*, 6(1), pp. 20–41.

Kitschelt, H. P. (1994) Party Systems in East Central Europe: Consolidation or Fluidity. Paper prepared for presentation at the 1994 Annual Meeting of the American Political Science Association.

Kitschelt, H. P. (1995a) The Formation of Party Cleavages in Post-communist Democracies: Theoretical Propositions. *Party Politics*, 1(4), pp. 447–72.

Kitschelt, H. P. (1995b) Patterns of Competition in East Central European Party Systems. Paper prepared for presentation at the 1995 Annual Meeting of the American Political Science Association.

Kitschelt, H. P., Z. Mansfeldova, R. Markowski, and G. A. Tóka (forthcoming) *Postcommunist Party Systems: Competition, Representation, and Inter-Party Cooperation*. Cambridge: Cambridge University Press.

Kleinnijenhuis, J. (1991) Newspaper Complexity and the Knowledge Gap. *European Journal of Communication*, 6, pp. 499–522.

Kleinnijenhuis, J. and E. M. Rietberg (1995) Parties, Media, the Public and the Economy: Patterns of Societal Agenda-Setting. *European Journal of Political Research*, 28(1), pp. 95–118.

Kleinsteuber, H. J. (1993) Mediensysteme in vergleichender Perspektive. Zur Anwendung komparativer Ansätze in der Medienwissenschaft – Probleme und Beispiele. *Rundfunk und Fernsehen*, 41(3), pp. 317–38.

Kohn, M. L. (1989) Cross-national Research as an Analytic Strategy, in M. L. Kohn (ed.), *Cross-national Research in Sociology*. Newbury Park: Sage, pp. 77–101.

Kornhauser, W. (1959) *The Politics of Mass Society*. London: Routledge.

Krasner, S. D. (1983) Structural Causes and Regime Consequences: Regimes as Intervening Variables, in S. D. Krasner (ed.), *International Regimes*. Ithaca: Cornell University Press, pp. 1–21.

Krüger, U. M. (1992) *Programmprofile im dualen Fernsehsystem 1985–1990. Eine Studie der ARD-ZDF-Medienkommission*. Baden-Baden: Nomos.

Kuechler, M. (1991) The Dynamics of Mass Political Support in Western Europe: Methodological Problems and Preliminary Findings, in K. Reif and R. Inglehart (eds), *Eurobarometer: The Dynamics of European Public Opinion*. Houndmills: Macmillan, pp. 275–93.

Kuhnle, S. and P. Selle (1992) Government and Voluntary Organizations: A Relational Perspective, in S. Kuhnle and P. Selle (eds), *Government and Voluntary Organizations. A Relational Perspective*. Aldershot: Avebury, pp. 1–33.

Labour Party and Liberal Democrats (1997) (Report of the Joint Consultative Committee on Constitutional Reform – Press Release). London.

Laeyendecker, L. (1989) Secularisatie: een systematische verkenning, in A. Houtepen (ed.), *Secularisatie: noodlot of opdracht: perspectieven voor zending en oecumene in de context van de secularisatie*. Leiden: Interuniversitair Instituut voor Missiologie en Oecumenica, pp. 5–54.

Lane, J.-E. (1996) *Constitutions and Political Theory*. Manchester: Manchester University Press.

Lane, J.-E. and S. O. Ersson (1996) The Nordic Countries. Contention, Compromise and Corporatism, in J. M. Colomer (ed.), *Political Institutions in Europe*. London: Routledge, pp. 254–81.

Lane, J.-E. and S. O. Ersson (1997) The Institutions of Konkordanz and Corporatism: How Closely Are They Connected?, *Swiss Political Science Review*, 3(1), pp. 5–29.

Lane, R. E. (1997) *The Art of Comparative Politics*. Boston: Allyn and Bacon.

LaPalombara, J. (1970) Parsimony and Empiricism in Comparative Politics: An Antischolastic View, in R. T. Holt and J. E. Turner (eds), *The Methodology of Comparative Research*. New York: The Free Press, pp. 123–49.

Laver, M. and W. B. Hunt (1992) *Policy and Party Competition*. New York: Routledge.

Lawson, K. (1980) Political Parties and Linkage, in K. Lawson (ed.), *Political Parties and Linkage. A Comparative Perspective*. New Haven: Yale University Press, pp. 3–24.

LeVine, R. A. and D. R. Price-Williams (1974) Children's Kinship Concepts: Cognitive Development and Early Experience Among the Hausa. *Ethnology*, 13, pp. 25–44.

Lijphart, A. (1977) *Democracy in Plural Societies: A Comparative Exploration*. New Haven: Yale University Press.

Lijphart, A. (1984) *Democracies. Patterns of Majoritarian and Consensus Government in Twenty-One Countries*. New Haven: Yale University Press.

Lijphart, A. (1990) Democratic Political Systems, in A. Bebler and J. Seroka (eds), *Contemporary Political Systems. Classifications and Typologies*. Boulder: Lynne Rienner, pp. 71–87.

Lijphart, A. (1996) The Framework Document on Northern Ireland and the Theory of Power-Sharing. *Government and Opposition*, 31(3), pp. 267–74.

Lill, R. and S. Wegener (1991) Die Democrazia Christiana Italiens (DC) und die Südtiroler Volkspartei (SVP), in H.-J. Veen (ed.), *Christlich-demokratische und konservative Parteien in Westeuropa 3. Italien, Griechenland*. Paderborn: Schöningh, pp. 17–203.

Lippmann, W. (1922) *Public Opinion*. New York: Macmillan.

Lipset, S. M. and S. Rokkan (eds) (1967) *Party Systems and Voter Alignments: Cross-national Perspectives*. New York: The Free Press.

Loewenberg, G. (1972) Comparative Legislative Research, in S. C. Patterson and J. C. Wahlke (eds), *Comparative Legislative Behavior: Frontiers of Research*. New York: Wiley, pp. 3–21.

Lowe, E. J. (1989) What Is a Criterion of Identity? *The Philosophical Quarterly*, 39(154), pp. 1–21.

Luhmann, N. (1970) *Soziologische Aufklärung. Aufsätze zur Theorie sozialer Systeme*. Opladen: Westdeutscher Verlag.

Luhmann, N. (1977) *Funktion der Religion*. Frankfurt a. M.: Suhrkamp.

Lupri, E. (1983) *The Changing Position of Women in Family and Society: A Cross-national Comparison*. Leiden: Brill.

Maccoby, E. E. and N. Maccoby (1954) The Interview: A Tool of Social Science, in L. Gardner (ed.), *Handbook of Political Science*. Cambridge: Addison-Wesley, pp. 449–87.

Macridis, R. C. (1955) *The Study of Comparative Government*. New York: Random House.

Mainwaring, S. and T. R. Scully (1995) Introduction: Party Systems in Latin America, in S. Mainwaring and T. R. Scully (eds), *Building Democratic Institutions. Party Systems in Latin America*. Stanford: Stanford University Press, pp. 1–34.

Mair, P. (1996) Comparative Politics: An Overview, in R. E. Goodin and H.-D. Klingemann (eds), *A New Handbook of Political Science*. Oxford: Oxford University Press, pp. 309–35.

Margetts, H. and G. Smyth (eds) (1994) *Turning Japanese? Britain with a Permanent Party of Government*. London: Lawrence and Wishart.

Marsh, R. M. (1967) *Comparative Sociology. A Codification of Cross-societal Analysis*. New York: Harcourt, Brace & World, Inc.

Mason, K. O. and L. L. Bumpass (1975) U.S. Women's Sex-Role Ideology, 1970. *American Journal of Sociology*, 80(5), pp. 1212–19.

Mason, K. O., J. L. Czajka, and S. Arber (1976) Change in U.S. Women's Sex-Role Attitudes, 1964–1974. *American Sociological Review*, 41(4), pp. 573–96.

Mason, K. O. and Y.-H. Lu (1988) Attitudes Toward Women's Familial Roles: Changes in the United States, 1977–1985. *Gender & Society*, 2(1), pp. 39–57.

Mayntz, R. and R. Ziegler (1977) Soziologie der Organisation, in R. König (ed.), *Handbuch der empirischen Sozialforschung* (second edn), Vol. 9. Stuttgart: Ferdinand Enke Verlag, pp. 1–141.

McClosky, H. and A. Brill (1983) *Dimensions of Tolerance. What Americans Believe about Civil Liberties*. New York: Russel Sage Foundation.

McLeod, J. M. and J. G. Blumler (1987) The Macrosocial Level of Communication Science, in C. R. Berger and S. H. Chaffee (eds), *Handbook of Communication Science*. Newbury Park: Sage, pp. 271–322.

McQuail, D. (1987) *Mass Communication Theory. An Introduction* (second edn). Beverly Hills: Sage.

McQuail, D. (1992) *Media Performance. Mass Communication and the Public Interest*. London: Sage.

Merrill, J. C. and H. A. Fisher (1980) *The World's Great Dailies: Profiles of Fifty Newspapers*. New York: Hastings House.

Merten, K. (1994) Wirkungen von Kommunikation, in K. Merten, S. J. Schmidt, and S. Weischenberg (eds), *Die Wirklichkeit der Medien. Eine Einführung in die Kommunikationswissenschaft*. Opladen: Westdeutscher Verlag, pp. 291–328.

Meulemann, H. (1993) Säkularisierung und Werte. Eine systematische Übersicht über Ergebnisse aus Bevölkerungsumfragen in westeuropäischen Gesellschaften, in B. Schäfers (ed.), *Lebensverhältnisse und soziale Konflikte im neuen Europa. Verhandlungen des 26. Deutschen Soziologentages in Düsseldorf 1992*. Frankfurt a. M.: Campus, pp. 627–35.

Middendorp, C. P. (1991) *Ideology in Dutch Politics: The Democratic System Reconsidered, 1970–1985*. Assen: van Gorcum.

Milbrath, L. W. and M. L. Goel (1977) *Political Participation*. Chicago: Rand McNally.

Miller, A. H. and K. Asp (1985) Learning about Politics from the Media. A Comparative Study of Sweden and the United States, in S. Kraus and R. M. Perloff (eds), *Mass Media and Political Thought. An Information-Processing Approach*. Beverly Hills: Sage, pp. 241–66.

Mitscherlich, A. (1974) Zwischen konstruktiver und verstiegener Ideologie, in U. Schultz (ed.), *Toleranz. Die Krise der demokratischen Tugend und sechzehn Vorschläge zu ihrer Überwindung*. Reinbek b. Hamburg: Rowohlt, pp. 22–35.

Mokken, R. J. (1971) *A Theory and Method of Scale Analysis. With Applications in Political Research*. The Hague: Mouton.

Mulgan, R. (1992) The Elective Dictatorship in New Zealand, in H. Gold (ed.), *New Zealand Politics in Perspective* (third edn). Auckland: Longman, pp. 513–32.

Müller, W. C. (1992) Austria (1945–1990), in R. S. Katz and P. Mair (eds), *Party Organizations. A Data Handbook on Party Organizations in Western Democracies, 1960–90*. London: Sage, pp. 21–120.

Müller, W. C. (1996) Die Organisation der SPÖ, 1945–1995, in W. Maderthaner and W. C. Müller (eds), *Die Organisation der österreichischen Sozialdemokratie, 1889–1995*. Wien: Löcker Verlag, pp. 195–356.

Müller, W. C. (1997) Vergleichende Sozialstrukturforschung, in D. Berg-Schlosser and F. Müller-Rommel (eds), *Vergleichende Politikwissenschaft. Ein einführendes Studienhandbuch* (third edn). Opladen: Leske + Budrich, pp. 121–41.

Nas, M. (1995) Green, Greener, Greenest, in J. W. van Deth and E. Scarbrough (eds), *The Impact of Values*. Oxford: Oxford University Press, pp. 275–300.

Negrine, R. (1996) *The Communication of Politics*. London: Sage.

Nelson, H. (1998) Verfassungsanomalien in föderalen Mehrheitsdemokratien: Der australische Fall, in A. Kaiser (ed.), *Regieren in Westminster-Demokratien*. Baden-Baden: Nomos, (forthcoming).

Neuhold, L. (1988) *Wertwandel und Christentum*. Linz: Veritas.

Neuman, W. R. (1986) *The Paradox of Mass Politics. Knowledge and Opinion in the American Electorate*. Cambridge: Harvard University Press.

Neuman, W. R. (1991) *The Future of the Mass Audience*. Cambridge: Cambridge University Press.

Niedermayer, O. (1997) Vergleichende Umfrageforschung: Probleme und Perspektiven, in D. Berg-Schlosser and F. Müller-Rommel (eds), *Vergleichende Politikwissenschaft. Ein einführendes Studienhandbuch* (third edn). Opladen: Leske + Budrich, pp. 89–103.

Nießen, M. (1982) Qualitative Aspects in Cross-national Comparative Research and the Problem of Functional Equivalence, in M. Nießen and J. Peschar (eds), *International Comparative Research. Problems of Theory, Methodology and Organisation in Eastern and Western Europe*. Oxford: Pergamon Press, pp. 83–104.

Nimmo, D. and J. E. Combs (1990) *Mediated Political Realities* (second edn). New York: Longman.

Noelle-Neumann, E. (1994) Wirkung der Massenmedien auf die Meinungsbildung, in E. Noelle-Neumann, W. Schulz and J. Wilke (eds), *Publizistik. Massenkommunikation*. Frankfurt a. M.: Fischer, pp. 518–71.

O'Kane, R. H. T. (1993) The Ladder of Abstraction. The Purpose of Comparison and the Practice of Comparing African Coups d'Etat. *Journal of Theoretical Politics*, 5(2), pp. 169–93.

Obler, J., J. Steiner, and G. Dierickx (1977) *Decision-Making in Smaller Democracies: The Consociational 'Burden'*. Beverly Hills: Sage.

Oertzen, P. (1974) Die Grundlagen der Demokratie, in U. Schultz (ed.), *Toleranz. Die Krise der demokratischen Tugend und sechzehn Vorschläge zu ihrer Überwindung*. Reinbek b. Hamburg: Rowohlt, pp. 195–208.

Orum, A. M., J. R. Feagin, and G. Sjoberg (1991) The Nature of the Case Study, in I. J. R. Feagin, A. M. Orum, and G. Sjoberg (eds), *A Case for the Case Study.* Chapel Hill: University of North Carolina Press, pp. 7–26.

Osgood, C. E. (1967) On the Strategy of Cross-national Research into Subjective Culture. *Social Science Information,* 6, pp. 5–37.

Ostergaard, B. S. (1992) *The Media in Western Europe. The Euromedia Handbook.* London: Sage.

Panebianco, A. (1988) *Political Parties: Organization and Power.* Cambridge: Cambridge University Press.

Parker, R. N. (1983) Measuring Social Participation. *American Sociological Review,* 48(4), pp. 864–73.

Patterson, S. C. and J. C. Wahlke (1972) Trends and Prospects in Legislative Behavior Research, in S. C. Patterson and J. C. Wahlke (eds), *Comparative Legislative Behavior: Frontiers of Research.* New York: Wiley, pp. 289–303.

Patterson, T. E. (1980) *The Mass Media Election. How Americans Choose their President.* New York: Praeger.

Pedersen, M. N. (1983) Changing Patterns of Electoral Volatility in European Party Systems, 1948–1977: Explorations in Explanation, in H. Daalder and P. Mair (eds), *Western European Party Systems: Continuity and Change.* London: Sage, pp. 29–66.

Pennock, J. R. (1979) *Democratic Political Theory.* Princeton: Princeton University Press.

Peters, B. G. (1996) Theory and Methodology, in H. A. G. M. Bekke, J. L. Perry, and A. J. Toonen (eds), *Civil Service Systems in Comparative Perspective.* Bloomington: Indiana University Press, pp. 13–41.

Peters, J., A. Felling, and P. Scheepers (1993) Individualisierung und Säkularisierung in den Niederlanden in den achtziger Jahren, in B. Schäfers (ed.), *Lebensverhältnisse und soziale Konflikte im neuen Europa. Verhandlungen des 26. deutschen Soziologentages in Düsseldorf 1992.* Frankfurt a. M.: Campus, pp. 636–45.

Pfetsch, B. (1991) *Politische Folgen der Dualisierung des Rundfunksystems in der Bundesrepublik Deutschland. Konzepte und Analysen zum Fernsehangebot und zum Publikumsverhalten.* Baden-Baden: Nomos.

Pfetsch, B. (1996) Convergence Through Privatization? Changing Media Environments and Televised Politics in Germany. *European Journal of Communication,* 11, pp. 427–51.

Poguntke, T. (1994) Parties in a Legalistic Culture: The Case of Germany, in R. S. Katz and P. Mair (eds), *How Parties Organize. Change and Adaptation in Party Organizations in Western Democracies.* London: Sage, pp. 185–215.

Price-Williams, D. R. (1985) Cultural Psychology, in L. Gardner and E. Aronson (eds), *Handbook of Social Psychology. Volume II: Special Fields and Applications.* New York: Random House, pp. 993–1,042.

Przeworski, A. and H. Teune (1966) Equivalence in Cross-national Research. *Public Opinion Quarterly,* 30(4), pp. 551–68.

Przeworski, A. and H. Teune (1970) *The Logic of Comparative Social Inquiry.* New York: Wiley.

Przeworski, A., M. Alvarez, J. A. Cheibub, and F. Limongi (1996) What Makes Democracy Endure? *Journal of Democracy,* 7(1), pp. 39–55.

Pürer, H. and J. Raabe (1994) *Medien in Deutschland. Band 1: Presse.* München: Ölschläger.

Putnam, R. D. (1993) *Making Democracy Work.* Princeton: Princeton University Press.

Putnam, R. D. (1995a) Bowling Alone: America's Declining Social Capital. *Journal of Democracy,* 6(1), pp. 65–78.

Putnam, R. D. (1995b) Tuning In, Tuning Out: The Strange Disappearance of Social Capital in America. *Political Science and Politics,* 28(4), pp. 664–83.

Rabinowitz, G. and S. E. Macdonald (1989) A Directional Theory of Issue Voting. *American Political Science Review*, 83(1), pp. 93–121.

Ragin, C. C. (1987) *The Comparative Method. Moving Beyond Qualitative and Quantitative Strategies*. Berkeley: University of California Press.

Ragin, C. C. (1989) New Directions in Comparative Research, in M. L. Kohn (ed.), *Cross-national Research in Sociology*. Newbury Park: Sage, pp. 57–76.

Ragin, C. C. and D. Zaret (1983) Theory and Method in Comparative Research: Two Strategies. *Social Forces*, 61(3), pp. 731–55.

Reynolds, H. T. (1974) Rationality and Attitudes towards Political Parties and Candidates. *Journal of Politics*, 37(3), pp. 983–1,005.

Richardson, J. J. (1993) Interest Group Behaviour in Britain: Continuity and Change, in J. J. Richardson (ed.), *Pressure Groups*. Oxford: Oxford University Press, pp. 86–99.

Robinson, J. P. and M. R. Levy (1986) *The Main Source. Learning from Television News*. Beverly Hills: Sage.

Robinson, J. P. and M. R. Levy (1996) News Media Use and the Informed Public: A 1990s Update. *Journal of Communication*, 46(2), pp. 129–35.

Rokkan, S. (1969) Cross-national Survey Research: Historical, Analytical and Substantive Contexts, in S. Rokkan, S. Verba, J. Viet, and E. Almasy (eds), *Comparative Survey Analysis*. The Hague: Mouton, pp. 5–55.

Rokeach, M. (1973) *The Nature of Human Values*. New York: The Free Press.

Roller, E. and B. Wessels (1996) *Contexts of Political Protest in Western Democracies: Political Organization and Modernity*. Berlin: WZB.

Rose, R. (1991) Comparing Forms of Comparative Analysis. *Political Studies*, 39, pp. 446–62.

Rositi, F. (1977) L'information télévisée: Découpage et recomposition de l'image de la société – Une recherche sur les journaux télévisés de quatre chaînes européennes. *Etudes De Radio-Télévision*, 24, pp. 123–48.

Rossi, P. H. and S. L. Nock (1982) *Measuring Social Judgements: The Factorial Survey Approach*. Beverly Hills: Sage.

Rothstein, B. (1996) Political Institutions: An Overview, in R. E. Goodin and H.-D. Klingemann (eds), *A New Handbook of Political Science*. Oxford: Oxford University Press, pp. 133–66.

Rucht, D. (1993) Parteien, Verbände und Bewegungen als Systeme politischer Interessenvermittlung, in O. Niedermayer and R. Stöss (eds), *Stand und Perspektiven der Parteienforschung in der Bundesrepublik Deutschland*. Opladen: Westdeutscher Verlag, pp. 251–75.

Saris, W. E. (1997) Comparability across Mode and Country, in W. E. Saris and M. Kaase (eds), *Eurobarometer. Measurement Instruments for Opinions in Europe*. Mannheim: Zentrum für Umfragen, Methoden und Analysen (ZUMA), pp. 125–39.

Saris, W. E. (1995) Designs and Models for Quality Assessment of Survey Measures, in W. E. Saris and Á. Münnich (eds), *The Multitrait-Multimethod Approach to Evaluate Measurement Instruments*. Budapest: Eötvös University Press, pp. 9–37.

Saris, W. E. and Á. Münnich (eds) (1995a) *The Multitrait-Multimethod Approach to Evaluate Measurement Instruments*. Budapest: Eötvös University Press.

Saris, W. E. and A. Scherpenzeel (1995b) Correction for Measurement Error in Life Satisfaction Research, in W. E. Saris and Á. Münnich (eds), *The Multitrait-Multimethod Approach to Evaluate Measurement Instruments*. Budapest: Eötvös University Press, pp. 243–67.

Sartori, G. (1970) Concept Misformation in Comparative Politics. *American Political Science Review*, 64(4), pp. 1033–53.

Sartori, G. (1976) *Parties and Party Systems. A Framework for Analysis*. Cambridge: Cambridge University Press.

Sartori, G. (1987) *The Theory of Democracy Revisited. Part I: The Contemporary Debate.* Chatham: Chatham House.

Sartori, G. (1991) Comparing and Miscomparing. *Journal of Theoretical Politics,* 3(3), pp. 243–57.

Sartori, G. (1994a) *Comparative Constitutional Engineering: An Inquiry into Structures, Incentives and Outcomes.* London: Macmillan.

Sartori, G. (1994b) Compare Why and How. Comparing, Miscomparing and the Comparative Method, in M. Dogan and A. Kazancigil (eds), *Comparing Nations. Concepts, Strategies, Substance.* Oxford: Blackwell, pp. 14–34.

Schement, J. R. (1993) Communication and Information, in J. R. Schement and B. D. Ruben (eds), *Between Communication and Information.* London: Transaction, pp. 3–33.

Scherer, H. (1995) Kommunikationskanäle in der Europawahl 1989. Eine international vergleichende Studie, in L. Erbring (ed.), *Kommunikationsraum Europa.* Konstanz: Ölschläger, pp. 203–21.

Scheuch, E. K. (1989) Theoretical Implications of Comparative Survey Research: Why the Wheel of Cross-cultural Methodology Keeps on Being Reinvented. *International Sociology,* 4(2), pp. 147–67.

Scheuch, E. K. (1990) The Development of Comparative Research: Towards Causal Explanations, in E. Øyen (ed.), *Comparative Methodology. Theory and Practice in International Research.* London: Sage, pp. 19–37.

Schmid, J. (1995) Expertenbefragung und Informationsgespräch in der Parteienforschung: Wie föderalistisch ist die CDU?, in U. v. Alemann (ed.), *Politikwissenschaftliche Methoden: Grundriß für Studium und Forschung.* Opladen: Westdeutscher Verlag, pp. 293–326.

Schmidt, M. G. (1995) *Demokratietheorien. Eine Einführung.* Opladen: Leske + Budrich.

Schmidt, M. G. (1996) Germany. The Grand Coalition State, in J. M. Colomer (ed.), *Political Institutions in Europe.* London: Routledge, pp. 62–98.

Schmidt, M. G. (1997) Parteien und Staatstätigkeit, in O. W. Gabriel, O. Niedermayer, and R. Stöss (eds), *Parteiendemokratie in Deutschland.* Opladen: Westdeutscher Verlag, pp. 537–58.

Schmidtchen, G. (1986) Die Relativität der Meßinstrumente zur Bestimmung des Wertwandels, in F. Gehrmann (ed.), *Arbeitsmoral und Technikfeindlichkeit. Über demoskopische Fehlschlüsse.* Frankfurt a. M.: Campus, pp. 145–54.

Schmitt, K. (1985) Religiöse Bestimmungsfaktoren des Wahlverhaltens: Entkonfessionalisierung mit Verspätung?, in D. Oberndoerfer, H. Rattinger and K. Schmitt (eds), *Wirtschaftlicher Wandel, religiöser Wandel und Wertewandel. Folgen für das politische Verhalten in der Bundesrepublik Deutschland.* Berlin: Duncker & Humblot, pp. 291–329.

Schönbach, K. (1983a) *Das unterschätzte Medium. Politische Wirkungen von Presse und Fernsehen im Vergleich.* München: Saur.

Schönbach, K. (1983b) What and How Voters Learned, in J. G. Blumler (ed.), *Communicating to Voters. Television in the First European Parliamentary Elections.* London: Sage, pp. 299–318.

Schulz, W. (1989) Massenmedien und Realität. Die 'ptolemäische' und die 'kopernikanische' Auffassung, in M. Kaase and W. Schulz (eds), *Massenkommunikation. Theorien, Methoden, Befunde.* Opladen: Westdeutscher Verlag, pp. 135–49.

Schulz, W. (1994) Kommunikationsprozeß, in E. Noelle-Neumann, W. Schulz, and J. Wilke (eds), *Publizistik. Massenkommunikation.* Frankfurt a. M.: Fischer, pp. 140–71.

Schulz, W. and J. G. Blumler (1994) Die Bedeutung der Kampagnen für das Europa-Engagement der Bürger. Eine Mehr-Ebenen-Analyse, in O. Niedermayer and H. Schmitt (eds), *Wahlen und die Europäische Einigung.* Opladen: Westdeutscher Verlag, pp. 199–223.

Schütte, G. (1994) *Informationsspezialisten der Mediengesellschaft. Die Produktion und Präsentation von*

Fernsehnachrichtensendungen in den USA, der Bundesrepublik Deutschland und der DDR. Wiesbaden: DUV.

Scott, J. C. (1957) Membership and Participation in Voluntary Associations. *American Sociological Review,* 22(3), pp. 315–26.

Searle, G. R. (1995) *Country Before Party. Coalition and the Idea of 'National Government' in Modern Britain, 1885–1987.* London: Longman.

Semetko, H. A. (1996a) The Media, in L. LeDuc, R. G. Niemi, and P. Norris (eds), *Comparing Democracies. Elections and Voting in Global Persepective.* Thousand Oaks: Sage, pp. 254–79.

Semetko, H. A. (1996b) Political Balance on Television. Campaigns in the United States, Britain, and Germany. *The Harvard International Journal of Press/Politics,* 1(1), pp. 51–71.

Semetko, H. A., J. G. Blumler, M. Gurevitch, and D. H. Weaver (1991) *The Formation of Campaign Agendas: A Comparative Analysis of Party and Media Roles in Recent American and British Elections.* Hillsdale: Erlbaum.

Semetko, H. A. and J. Borquez (1991) Audiences for Election Communication in France and the United States: Media Use and Candidate Evaluations, in L. L. Kaid, J. Gerstlé, and K. R. Sanders (eds), *Mediated Politics in Two Cultures. Presidential Campaigning in the United States and France.* New York: Praeger, pp. 223–45.

Severin, W. J. and J. W. Tankard (1997) *Communication Theories. Origins, Methods and Uses in the Mass Media* (fourth edn). New York: Longman.

Siebert, F. S., T. Peterson, and W. Schramm (1963) *Four Theories of the Press. The Authoritarian, Libertarian, Social Responsibility and Soviet Communist Concepts of What the Press Should Be and Do.* Urbana: University of Illinois Press.

Sigelman, L. (1976) In Search of Comparative Administration. *Public Administration Review,* 6, pp. 621–25.

Simeon, R. (1972) *Federal–Provincial Diplomacy: The Making of Recent Policy in Canada.* Toronto: University of Toronto Press.

Sjoberg, G., N. Williams, T. R. Vaughan, and A. F. Sjoberg (1991) The Case Study Approach in Social Research: Basic Methodological Issues, in J. R. Feagin, A. M. Orum, and G. Sjoberg (eds), *A Case for the Case Study.* Chapel Hill: University of North Carolina Press, pp. 27–79.

Smelser, N. J. (1973) The Methodology of Comparative Analysis, in D. P. Warwick and S. Osherson (eds), *Comparative Research Methods.* Englewood Cliffs: Prentice-Hall, pp. 42–86.

Smith, J. D. (1993) Volunteering in Europe: Opportunities and Challenges for the 90s, in J. D. Smith (ed.), *Voluntary Action Research.* London: Volunteer Centre, pp. 5–9.

Smith, T. W. (1990) Trends in Voluntary Group Membership: Comments on Baumgartner and Walker. *American Journal of Political Science,* 34(3), pp. 646–61.

Sontheimer, K. (1974) Das Allgemeine und das Akademische, in U. Schultz (ed.), *Toleranz. Die Krise der demokratischen Tugend und sechzehn Vorschläge zu ihrer Überwindung.* Reinbek b. Hamburg: Rowohlt, pp. 50–65.

Spielhagen, E. (1995) Ergebnisse der Ost-Studie der ARD/ZDF-Medienkommission. *Media Perspektiven,* 8, pp. 362–92.

Stark, R. and W. S. Bainbridge (1987) *A Theory of Religion.* New York: Lang.

Steininger, R. (1975) *Polarisierung und Integration. Eine vergleichende Untersuchung der strukturellen Versäulung der Gesellschaft in den Niederlanden und in Österreich.* Meisenheim a. G.: Anton Hain.

Stevens, J. (1992) *Applied Multivariate Statistics for the Social Sciences.* Hillsdale: Erlbaum.

Stokes, D. E. (1963) Spatial Models of Party Competition. *American Political Science Review,* 57(2), pp. 368–77.

Streeck, W. (1987) Vielfalt und Interdependenz. Überlegungen zur Rolle von intermediären

Organisationen in sich ändernden Umwelten. *Kölner Zeitschrift für Soziologie und Sozialpsychologie*, 39(3), pp. 471–95.

Strom, K. (1990) *Minority Government and Majority Rule. Studies in Rationality and Social Change.* Cambridge: Cambridge University Press.

Swanson, G. E. (1960) *The Birth of the Gods: The Origin of Primitive Beliefs.* Ann Arbor: University of Michigan Press.

Tajfel, H. and J. C. Turner (1986) The Social Identity Theory of Group Behavior, in S. Worchel and W. G. Austin (eds), *Psychology of Intergroup Relations* (second edn). Chicago: Nelson-Hall, pp. 7–24.

Teune, H. (1990) Comparing Countries: Lessons Learned, in E. Øyen (ed.), *Comparative Methodology. Theory and Practice in International Social Research.* London: Sage, pp. 38–62.

Thoma, M. and M. Braun (1997) Attitudes towards Family and Society in Germany: A 3-mode Experimental Study. Unpublished technical report.

Thomas, A. (1994) Ist Toleranz ein Kulturstandard?, in A. Wierlacher (ed.), *Jahrbuch Deutsch als Fremdsprache.* München: Iudicium, pp. 153–75.

Thornton, A. (1989) Changing Attitudes toward Family Issues in the United States. *Journal of Marriage and the Family*, 51(4), pp. 873–93.

Thornton, A., D. F. Alwin, and D. Camburn (1983) Causes and Consequences of Sex-Role Attitudes and Attitude Change. *American Sociological Review*, 48(2), pp. 211–27.

Thornton, A. and D. S. Freedman (1979) Changes in Sex Role Attitudes of Women, 1962–1977: Evidence from a Panel Study. *American Sociological Review*, 44(5), pp. 832–42.

Thoveron, G. (1983) How Europeans Received the Campaign: Similarities and Differences of National Response, in J. G. Blumler (ed.), *Communicating to Voters. Television in the First European Parliamentary Elections.* London: Sage, pp. 142–62.

Thoveron, G. and S. Sauerberg (1983) Did Voters Get the Message?, in J. G. Blumler (ed.), *Communicating to Voters. Television in the First European Parliamentary Elections.* London: Sage, pp. 284–98.

Tóka, G. (1997) Political Parties and Democratic Consolidation in East Central Europe. Studies in Public Policy, No. 279. Glasgow: Centre for the Study of Public Policy, University of Strathclyde.

Treiman, D. J. (1975) Problems of Concept and Measurement in the Comparative Study of Occupational Mobility. *Social Science Research*, 4, pp. 183–230.

Treiman, D. J. and K. Terrell (1975) Status Attainment in the United States and Great Britain. *American Journal of Sociology*, 81, pp. 568–83.

Tsebelis, G. (1995) Decision Making in Political Systems: Veto Players in Presidentialism, Parliamentarism, Multicameralism and Multipartyism. *British Journal of Political Science*, 25(3), pp. 289–325.

Tucker, L. R. (1971) Relations of Factor Score Estimates to Their Use. *Psychometrika*, 36, pp. 427–36.

UNESCO (1994) *Tolerance: The Threshold of Peace. A Teaching/Learning Guide for Education for Peace, Human Rights and Democracy.* Paris: UNESCO ED94/WS/8.

UNESCO (1995) *Backgrounder Year for Tolerance.* Paris: UNESCO.

van de Vijver, F. and K. Leung (1997) *Methods and Data Analysis for Cross-cultural Research.* Thousand Oaks: Sage.

van Deth, J. W. (1986) A Note on Measuring Political Participation in Comparative Research. *Quality and Quantity*, 120, pp. 261–72.

van Deth, J. W. (1990) Interest in Politics, in M. K. Jennings, J. W. van Deth *et al.*, *Continuities in Political Action. A Longitudinal Study of Political Orientations in Three Western Democracies.* Berlin: de Gruyter, pp. 275–312.

van Deth, J. W. (1996) Social and Political Involvement: An Overview and Reassessment of Empirical Findings. Paper presented at the ECPR-Joint Sessions of Workshops, Oslo.

van Deth, J. W. (ed.) (1997) *Private Groups and Public Life: Social Participation and Political Involvement in Representative Democracies*. London: Routledge.

van Deth, J. W. and M. Leijenaar (1994) *Maatschappelijke participatie in een middelgrote stad*. Den Haag: SCP/VUGA.

van Deth, J. W. and E. Scarbrough (1995a) The Concept of Values, in J. W. van Deth and E. Scarbrough (eds), *The Impact of Values*. Oxford: Oxford University Press, pp. 21–47.

van Deth, J. W. and E. Scarbrough (eds) (1995b) *The Impact of Values*. Oxford: Oxford University Press.

van Meurs, A. and W. E. Saris (1995) Memory Effects in MTMM Studies, in W. E. Saris and Á. Münnich (eds), *The Multitrait-Multimethod Approach to Evaluate Measurement Instruments*. Budapest: Eötvös University Press, pp. 89–102.

Verba, S. (1967–68) Some Dilemmas in Comparative Research. *World Politics*, 20, pp. 111–27.

Verba, S. (1969) The Uses of Survey Research in the Study of Comparative Politics: Issues and Strategies, in S. Rokkan, S. Verba, J. Viet, and E. Almasy (eds), *Comparative Survey Analysis*. The Hague: Mouton, pp. 56–105.

Verba, S., K. L. Schlozmann, and H. Brady (1995) *Voice and Equality: Civic Voluntarism in American Politics*. Cambridge: Harvard University Press.

Voltmer, K. (1998) The Structures of Diversity in Press and Broadcasting Systems, in H.-D. Klingemann (ed.), *Political Structure and Political Performance: Macro-Analyses of the OECD Countries, 1945–90*. Oxford: Oxford University Press (forthcoming).

Weaver, D. H. (1980) Audience Need for Orientation and Media Effects. *Communication Research*, 7(3), pp. 361–76.

Weaver, D. H. and J. M. Buddenbaum (1980) Newspapers and Television. A Review of Research on Uses and Effects, in C. G. Wilhoit and H. De Bock (eds), *Mass Communication Review Yearbook* (Vol. 1). Beverly Hills: Sage, pp. 371–80.

Webb, P. D. (1995) Are British Parties in Decline? *Party Politics*, 1(3), pp. 299–322.

Weber, M. (1949) *The Methodology of the Social Sciences*, in E. A. Shils and H. A. Finch (eds and trans.). New York: The Free Press.

Weber, M. (1980) *Wirtschaft und Gesellschaft. Grundriß der verstehenden Soziologie* (fifth edn). Tübingen: Mohr.

Wessels, B. (1991) Vielfalt oder strukturierte Komplexität? Zur Institutionalisierung politischer Spannungslinien im Verbände- und Parteiensystem der Bundesrepublik. *Kölner Zeitschrift für Soziologie und Sozialpsychologie*, 43(3), pp. 454–75.

Wessels, B. (1996) Organizing Capacity of Societies and Modernity. Paper presented at the ECPR–Jointsessions of Workshops, Oslo.

Wessels, B. (1997) Organizing Capacity of Societies and Modernity, in J. W. van Deth (ed.), *Private Groups and Public Life: Social Participation and Political Involvement in Representative Democracies*. London: Routledge, pp. 198–219.

Westle, B. (1996) *Kollektive Identität im vereinigten Deutschland – Nation und Demokratie in der Wahrnehmung der Deutschen*. Mannheim: Habilitationsschrift.

Westle, B. (1997) Das 'Neue Deutschland' in Europa: Kollektive Identität und Haltungen gegenüber Fremden. *Wissenschaft und Frieden*, 15(2), pp. 51–4.

Wierlacher, A. (1994) Was ist Toleranz? Zur Rehabilitation eines umstrittenen Begriffs, in A. Wierlacher (ed.), *Jahrbuch Deutsch als Fremdsprache*. München: Iudicium, pp. 115–37.

Wilke, J. (1994) Lokal, Regional, National, International – zu Angebot und Nutzung der

Tageszeitung, in M. Jäckel and P. Winterhoff-Spurk (eds), *Politik und Medien. Analysen zur Entwicklung der politischen Kommunikation*. Berlin: Vistas, pp. 89–101.

Williams, C. F. J. (1989) *What Is Identity?* Oxford: Clarendon Press.

Wittgenstein, L. (1963[1921]) *Tractatus Logico-philosophicus. Logisch-philosophische Abhandlung*. Frankfurt a. M.: Suhrkamp.

Zaller, J. (1990) Political Awareness, Elite Opinion Leadership, and the Mass Survey Response. *Social Cognition*, 8(1), pp. 125–53.

Zapotoczky, K. (1986) Vermittlung von Lebenssinn durch Religion, in H. Bogensberger, T. M. Gannon, and K. Zapotoczky (eds), *Religion und sozialer Wandel*. Linz: Veritas, pp. 55–74.

Zentralarchiv für Empirische Sozialforschung (1991) *ISSP 1988 – Family and Changing Sex Roles I. Codebook ZA-No.1700*. Cologne: ZA.

Zentralarchiv für Empirische Sozialforschung (1997) *ISSP 1994 – Family and Changing Gender Roles II. Codebook ZA-No.2620*. Cologne: ZA.

Zulehner, P. M., H. Denz, M. Beham, and C. Friesl (1991) *Vom Untertan zum Freiheitskünstler. Eine Kulturdiagnose anhand der Untersuchungen 'Religion im Leben der Österreicher 1970 bis 1990' – 'Europäische Wertestudie-Österreichteil 1990'*. Freiburg: Herder.

Name index

Note: page numbers in **bold** indicate chapters

Subject index

Note: Page numbers for major topics (chapters) are in **bold**

abstraction: 'descending ladder of' 230–4; increasing level of 6–7, 9, 10–11
adversary politics 216; *see also* Britain
age: and gender-role attitudes 129–32; and postmaterialism 73–80; and voluntary associations 147–51
ALLBUS (Germany) 111–12, 115, 133
ambiguity *see* equivalence; language
analogy, reasoning by 6
Anglo-Saxon countries: gender roles 111–12, 114–15, 120, 121, 124, 127–33; institutional regimes 205, 207–12, 217, 219, 221; voluntary associations 135–8, 140–2, 145–6, 149–51, 154; *see also* Australia; Britain; Canada; Ireland; New Zealand; Northern Ireland; United States
arbitration 161
Argentina 10; political values 68, 79, 80–1
ARP (Anti-Revolutionary Party, Netherlands) 170, 171
Asia: gender roles 72, 74, 78, 79–80, 83, 85, 112, 130; political values 62, 68–83, 85; *see also* East Asia; Russia
associations *see* voluntary associations
Australia: gender roles 112, 121, 128; institutional regimes 207, 209, 211, 221; political values 62
Austria 59; gender roles 112, 120, 121, 127–30; institutional regimes 211; party organisations 166–8, 169, 175, 179; political values 62, 79, 81; religion *see* religious orientations; voluntary associations 138, 154
Austrian People's Party 168–9
auxiliary information 7

Bangladesh 112, 130
banks (central), independent, 205, 206, 207, 210
Belarus: equivalence 10; political values 69, 79, 81; tolerance 25, 28, 33, 35, 37, 44–5, 47, 49–53, 55
Belgium: equivalence 11; institutional regimes 211; media 223, 226, 228–9; party organisations 165, 170, 171, 179; political values 67, 79, 81; religion *see* religious orientations; tolerance 24, 28, 31–2, 34, 39–42, 44–5, 47, 49–53, 56–7; voluntary associations 137–8, 140, 141–3, 145–6, 149–50
bicameralism 206, 207, 209, 217, 218, 221
'Big Mac' standard/currency 4–5, 18
birth cohorts *see* age
Brazil: political values 62, 68, 79, 80, 81
Britain: gender roles 111–12, 114, 115, 121, 128, 133; institutional regimes 205, 207, 208, 210, 211–12, 221 (*see also* consensus-building); media 223, 224, 225–6, 227–9, 233, 235, 245; party organisations 175, 179; political values 67, 79, 81; tolerance 24, 28, 32, 34, 39–42, 43–5, 47, 49–53, 56–7; voluntary associations 137–8, 141–2, 145–6, 149–50; *see also* Northern Ireland
Bulgaria: gender roles 112, 128; political values 69, 81; tolerance 25, 28, 33, 35, 36, 37, 43–5, 47, 49–54, 55; voluntary associations 138; *see also* party positions

Canada: gender roles 112, 121, 126, 128; institutional regimes 207, 209, 211, 221; media 223, 224; political values